**SPEAKING TRUTH TO CANADIANS
ABOUT THEIR PUBLIC SERVICE**

# SPEAKING TRUTH TO CANADIANS

ABOUT
THEIR PUBLIC
SERVICE

DONALD J. SAVOIE

McGill-Queen's University Press
Montreal & Kingston • London • Chicago

© McGill-Queen's University Press 2024

ISBN 978-0-2280-2138-4 (cloth)
ISBN 978-0-2280-2190-2 (ePDF)
ISBN 978-0-2280-2191-9 (ePUB)

Legal deposit third quarter 2024
Bibliothèque nationale du Québec

Printed in Canada on acid-free paper that is 100% ancient forest free (100% post-consumer recycled), processed chlorine free

This book has been published with the help of a grant from the Donald J. Savoie Institute.

We acknowledge the support of the Canada Council for the Arts.
Nous remercions le Conseil des arts du Canada de son soutien.

McGill-Queen's University Press in Montreal is on land which long served as a site of meeting and exchange amongst Indigenous Peoples, including the Haudenosaunee and Anishinabeg nations. In Kingston it is situated on the territory of the Haudenosaunee and Anishinaabek. We acknowledge and thank the diverse Indigenous Peoples whose footsteps have marked these territories on which peoples of the world now gather.

---

Library and Archives Canada Cataloguing in Publication

Title: Speaking truth to Canadians about their public service / Donald J. Savoie.
Names: Savoie, Donald J., 1947– author.
Description: Includes bibliographical references and index.
Identifiers: Canadiana (print) 20240296621 | Canadiana (ebook) 20240296702 | ISBN 9780228021384 (cloth) | ISBN 9780228021919 (ePUB) | ISBN 9780228021902 (ePDF)
Subjects: LCSH: Public administration—Canada. | LCSH: Civil service—Canada. | LCSH: Policy sciences—Canada. | LCSH: Government accountability—Canada.
Classification: LCC JL75.S28 2024 | DDC 351.71—dc23

---

This book was typeset in 10.5/13 Sabon.

Dedicated to J.E. "Ted" Hodgetts

# CONTENTS

Preface ix

Introduction 3
1  The Setting and the Machinery 20
2  Inward Looking 44
3  Poets and Plumbers 64
4  The Unwritten Code 83
5  Bolts of Lightning 105
6  Try Grabbing Smoke 130
7  Ministers: The Buck Does Not Stop There 149
8  Deputy Ministers: On the Inside Looking Everywhere 171
9  Own What You Do 190
10 What Do Canadians Want the Federal Public Service to Be? 209
11 Attitudes, Values, and Behaviours 229
12 What Now? 248

Notes 261
Index 305

# PREFACE

I decided to write this book because the public sector is in urgent need of fresh thinking. It is being challenged like never before, even in countries like Canada, where governments have long enjoyed broad public support. I continue to believe that government can play a positive role in society. I have only to look to the experiences of my fellow Acadians for evidence – in fifty short years, Acadians made the transition from a backward, poverty-stricken people lacking in education to a vibrant, dynamic people scoring successes in all sectors, including the business world, the public sector, the arts, and sports. Governments played a pivotal role in that transition.

I write as a friend of the public sector, not as an antagonist. My purpose is to support the public sector, not tear it down. I do not see government as a threat to freedom, as Milton Friedman did. I do believe, however, that governments, notably the federal government, have either overreached their capacity to define new policies and deliver programs or are not able to manage operations efficiently. I hold that this explains, in large measure, why Canadians are losing trust in the public sector. The question Canadians should be asking is: Can the public sector be fixed? I believe that this is one of the most important questions confronting Canadians. This book is my contribution to the debate.

I decided on *Speaking Truth to Canadians about Their Public Service* as the title of the book because it captures my core message. Aaron Wildavsky borrowed the phrase *speaking truth to power* from the Bible to coin the title for his widely acclaimed 1979 book, *Speaking Truth to Power: The Art and Craft of Policy Analysis*.[1] Wildavsky's book title struck a lasting chord with students, public servants, journalists, and politicians. The phrase has since become little more than a slogan, but it also implies that establishing "truth" in policy making or government operations is possible. Anyone who has served in government, either as a politician or as a career official, knows that truth in government is, at best, a moving target or that there are often several versions of the truth. Still, I decided to embrace the term. It has always been employed to send a message to politicians, suggesting that they need to hear the "truth" on policy or administration, as defined by career officials. The time has come to speak to Canadians about the state of the federal public service. I believe that the federal public service has lost its standing. For the reasons outlined in this book, if change is to take place, Canadians will need to take a strong interest in government operations and become the voices for change.

My original title was *Speaking Truth to Public Servants*. A former federal public servant read the manuscript and urged me to change the title. His point – federal public servants "know well the content of the manuscript and the well-informed public servants are all too well aware of the challenges confronting their institution and the weaknesses in the government's program delivery capacity. They live the problem every day." I did not see much merit in *Speaking Truth to Politicians* because the prime minister and senior ministers do not have the incentives and interest to fully address the problem. The necessary change in the way government decides and operates will require a substantial wrench of the wheel because there are always strong forces in the federal government that would want to stay the course. Unless Canadians demand change, the status quo will prevail. Politicians respond to the wishes of voters – hence the title.

Senior public servants have been unwilling or unable to ask fundamental questions, at least publicly, about their role, the role of the public service, how public servants should relate to the political class, and whether government bureaucracies require more or less financial and human resources than what they currently have for what they deliver. They have not come forward with measures to reform their own institution, except for various vision exercises that always fail to live up to expectations. The waves of recent reform measures have, for the most part, been driven from outside the government bureaucracy. Do career officials always believe that it is best to leave well enough alone, however lacking it may be? What motivates public servants? I seek to answer these and other questions. That is why, in this book, I focus on public servants rather than on politicians.

My hope is that this book will help Canadians and public servants gain fresh insights into the workings of the federal public service. I believe that there is a direct link between efficiency in government operations and trust in government. I also believe that the machinery of government requires either ambitious and far-reaching reforms or that politicians and public servants need to reinvigorate the requirements of the founding institutions of our system of government. In my numerous discussions in recent years with politicians, partisan political advisors, and senior public servants about the challenges confronting the public sector, all see problems with government operations, none more so than public servants themselves, especially those who have recently retired.

As a life-long student of government, I have published extensively on the workings of our national political and administrative institutions and have occasionally served in senior positions with the federal government. Since my late teen years, I have also always been associated with universities as a student or faculty member, often writing about machinery of government issues. In addition, I have accepted several temporary assignments with the federal government: in a line department, which delivers programs and services to Canadians, and in two central agencies – the Treasury Board and the Privy Council Office (Federal-Provincial Relations). For one year, I was the acting head of the Canadian Centre for Management Development, a federal government agency that has since been renamed the Canada School of Public Service. I served as a consultant-advisor on public policy issues on numerous occasions at the federal, provincial, and international levels. I was also director of research for the Commission of Inquiry into the Sponsorship Program and Advertising Activities (the Gomery Inquiry) in the Government of Canada.

As my career comes to a close, I decided to draw on my experience in government and my publications to explore the challenges confronting the federal public service. The reader will note that I turn to my previous publications and to my work in government to support my observations. The reader will also note that in drawing on my work experience in Ottawa and when reporting on the views of my former work associates, I paint a picture of a male-dominated federal government. Until recently, the federal government was male-dominated, particularly at the most senior levels in the public service. I recall that well into the 1980s and 1990s few women occupied senior executive positions in the federal government. Things have changed for the better, particularly since the early 2000s, and took a decisive turn when Jocelyne Bourgon, a friend and one of the most competent federal public servants I have ever worked with, became clerk of the Privy Council and secretary to the cabinet in 1994. She cleared the way and things have improved sharply for women since then.

I want to underline the point, once more, that my purpose is to strengthen the public service, not to denigrate it. I point to its shortcomings only in the hope that they will be addressed. I hold that public servants themselves need to deal with many of the shortcomings in the public service for it to regain or strengthen its standing with Canadians. I also hold that the most promising avenue to gain insights into the work of the federal public service is to explore what motivates public servants and how the government's accountability requirements work. The time has come to stop blaming only politicians for many of the problems in government operations.

A conversation I had with John Bragg, a remarkable entrepreneur with a deep appreciation of the public good and a keen interest in management, encouraged me to write this book. He said: "Good managers need to own what they say, own what they do and own their mistakes." He explained that, unless managers come to terms with these requirements, they will always be lacking as managers, and further, that no one will be able to properly assess their performance. Given his business successes, Bragg is well suited to see how good managers are made and I readily see the merit of his point. His comment prompted the question – how can this apply in government? If it does not, then the many efforts we have seen, over the past forty years, to import private sector management measures to government operations, have missed the mark. I decided to pursue the matter in this book, convinced that the findings will help improve policy making, in particular government operations, and shed new light on Ottawa's accountability requirements.

But management and efficiency in government operations only tell part of the story and for many senior public servants, not the most important one. Sir Robin Butler, a former senior British civil servant who has occasionally helped me with my research, once summed up his evaluation of the British civil service, an assessment that applies equally well to the Canadian public service. He explained: "There was nothing else to do in the 1950s, 60s, and 70s, if you were an economist then you wanted to work in government. We ended up with far more talented people in the Treasury than we could possibly find interesting things for all of them to do. Times have changed. Now we feel a great deal of hostility toward the civil service. You have the feeling that ministers look at economists in the civil service and think – if you are really smart, why don't you go work with McKinsey or the banks?"[2] I am also convinced that the Canadian public service has far more talented people than it can possibly find interesting work for. Though many still join the federal public service to work on policy, policy work no longer looks like it did fifty years ago, at least for public servants. We need to understand what has changed in government operations and why management in government remains the poor cousin to working on policy. This, among other things, has made it extremely difficult to improve efficiency in government operations.

I decided to dedicate this book to J.E. "Ted" Hodgetts, widely known as the father of Canadian public administration, for good reason. He published a number of seminal books and articles in public administration and held the pen for the Glassco Commission on Government Organization. He was my role model and I have very fond memories of every discussion I had with him. He helped me in several important ways with the publication of my first book, *Federal-Provincial Collaboration: The Canada-New Brunswick General Agreement*. I also turned to him for advice on several occasions when I served as editor of the Institute of Public Administration of Canada (IPAC) Series in Public Management and Governance. When Justice John Gomery asked me to serve as director of research for the Commission of Inquiry into the Sponsorship Program and Advertising Activities, I asked Ted Hodgetts to serve as an advisor to the commission. It proved to be a very wise decision.

I owe a debt to two anonymous reviewers of the McGill-Queen's University Press for their foresight and perceptive and constructive criticism of an earlier draft of this study. Two former federal public servants read the manuscript: Ralph Heintzman, who has published extensively in the public administration field, and Richard Saillant. Both made important suggestions to improve the study.

Over the course of my career, I have benefited from numerous conversations I had with former prime ministers, leaders of the opposition, a number of current and former cabinet ministers, current and former members of Parliament, current and former deputy ministers, including clerks of the Privy Council and other federal public servants at various levels in central agencies and line departments. These conversations have proven invaluable to understanding how the federal government operates and makes decisions. I make this point not only to report on what shaped my thinking on public administration but also to encourage students of public administration to meet with government officials to gain a full understanding of their field of study.

Once again, I owe a special thank you to Linda for putting up with my insatiable appetite for work. She always supports my work with good cheer, despite my desire to sacrifice evenings and weekends to my writing. Ginette Benoit and Céline Basque, as before, were there helping me to bring the manuscript into its final form. As always, I am responsible, answerable, and accountable for all errors and deficiencies.

DONALD J. SAVOIE
Canada Research Chair (Tier 1)
in Public Administration and Governance
Université de Moncton

**SPEAKING TRUTH TO CANADIANS
ABOUT THEIR PUBLIC SERVICE**

# INTRODUCTION

Canadians, Americans, the British, the French, and Australians no longer trust government to the extent that they once did. French president Emmanuel Macron talks about a crisis in liberal democracies and points to a lack of efficiency in government as an important component of the crisis.[1] Public opinion surveys in Organisation for Economic Co-operation and Development (OECD) countries reveal that only four out of ten people now trust their national governments. The OECD explains why trust in government is key to good government: "Trust is the foundation upon which the legitimacy of democratic institutions rests."[2]

In Canada, trust in government is on a downward slide. A recent public opinion survey reveals that trust in government among Canadians was at 34 per cent in 2022, down from 37 per cent in 2021 and 45 per cent in 2018.[3] A Léger public opinion survey reported in February 2023 that "67 per cent of Canadians" believe that "Canada is broken." The two Léger pollsters argued that "the notion of brokenness raises the question of how the relationship between citizens and those elected can be repaired. Perhaps the question – is Canada broken? – should be replaced by – is Canada able to act on citizens' concerns and show they are making an impact?"[4] A number of reasons have been suggested to explain the declining trust in government: poor institutional performance; politicians; the rise of social media; confusion between what is news and what is opinion; globalization; income inequality; democratic disengagement, as more and more citizens become convinced that their vote does not matter; and the belief that only political, bureaucratic, and economic elites have any influence.[5]

The book explores five related themes, all tied to accountability: the difficulties the Canadian public service has in planning and delivering programs and services; the effect of the concentration of power in the hands of prime ministers and their advisors on government operations; how the introduction of private sector management practices has transformed the public service; why accountability requirements in government operations have fallen into disrepair; and why federal public servants can only identify problems in government operations after they leave government. I believe that many of the points made in this book also apply to the public sector writ large. Many Canadians believe that there is a double standard at play, one for the public sector and another for all the other sectors. Globalization, for example, has meant job losses for some private sector firms as they moved their operations to low-cost jurisdictions whereas the public sector has remained immune to these developments. In short, the thinking outside government is that public servants have been sheltered from the global economy and other economic forces that have pushed private firms and their workers to be more competitive.

And yet, regardless of the generous employment benefits, there are many signs that not all is well inside the Canadian public service: it is plagued with a continuing morale problem; sick leaves have shot up by 68 per cent in the last ten years; clerks of the Privy Council have launched at least three vision exercises over the past thirty years with little to show for them; public servants have repeatedly been told to emulate the private sector, also with little success; and career officials, by their own account, no longer hold the influence they once did in shaping public policy.[6] Federal public servants are less willing to reach beyond the bureaucracy with the self-assurance and confidence in their institution that they once did.

Public opinion surveys also reveal that Canadians are not satisfied with the level of services they receive from the federal government. Some 20 per cent of Canadians report that they are "very unsatisfied" and another 26 per cent report that they are "unsatisfied" with the services the federal government provides. Only 8 per cent report that they are "very unsatisfied" with the level of services they receive from their provincial governments."[7]

Government bureaucracies have never been popular down through the ages. In a 1964 article, Anthony Downs wrote that the term bureaucrat is "universally regarded as an insult."[8] If anything, the word is even more of a pejorative today than it was sixty years ago. It conjures up images of unmotivated public servants, consistently drowning in red tape, known for their unimaginativeness, resisting change, underperforming, having little accountability for their work, and being responsible for the profligate spending of public funds.

From the media, one could conclude that career government officials have few friends outside of government. They are also increasingly being challenged inside government, even by the politicians on the government side that they are asked to serve. Since the 1980s, politicians throughout the Western world have strengthened their offices so they can act as a counterweight both to the policy advice and to the administrative work of career officials.[9] Some politicians even label government bureaucracy the "deep state," an entity that always pursues its own interests with little regard for the broader public interest or the wishes of its political leaders. They insist that it is a development that needs to be addressed, though they have been short on solutions.[10] The long-standing bargain that guided the relationship between politicians and public servants is now broken.[11]

The media and academe tend to focus on what went wrong in government and not report on success stories. I have pointed to failures in government operations, in the past and again in this book, but it is important to underline the point that public servants are not solely responsible for the failures. There have also been successes, with public servants playing an important part. Understanding the reasons for the failures can help to identify ways to strengthen the capacity of the federal public service to provide policy advice and improve the delivery of programs and services.

It is also important to note that government bureaucrats have rarely enjoyed broad public support over the years. By 1850, some British political observers were taking dead aim at government bureaucracy, arguing that it was paving "the way to waste and inefficiency ... its very nature unaccountable and it would stifle individual responsibility and initiative."[12] This and other developments led the British government to launch a fundamental review of the work of the civil service. The Northcote-Trevelyan Report, published in 1854, has had a profound and lasting effect on the British civil service, leading to a comprehensive overhaul of the British civil service, and later on both the Canadian and the American civil services. The report reads: "Admission into the Civil Service is indeed eagerly sought after, but it is for the unambitious, and the indolent or incapable that it is chiefly desired ... and those whom indolence of temperament or physical infirmities unfit for active exertions, are placed in the Civil Service."[13] Canada followed with the Murray Report and the United States with the *Pendleton Act*.[14] The objective in all three cases was to move to a permanent, non-partisan, and merit-based civil service.

The reports and reform measures did have a positive effect. At one point, government career officials were held in high esteem, at least in Anglo-American democracies, and they had a golden age of sorts between the early 1940s and the mid-1960s. I recognize the tendency to look at the past through rose-coloured glasses when explaining our present discontent. It has always been so. In the sixteenth century, Niccolò Machiavelli wrote that "men always praise (but not always reasonably) the ancient times and find fault with the present."[15] Still, by the end of the Second World War, the public's belief in the ability of government to get things done was high in the United States, Britain, Australia, New Zealand, and Canada. Not only had the Allies won the war, but governments had planned the war effort and run the economy very well. Unemployment was down to nearly zero and yet prices had been held down, at least when goods were available. It became clear that in moments of crisis and when moved by an overriding goal, governments were able to lead their countries and accomplish great things. Politicians and most citizens trusted career officials to define proper policy prescriptions and deliver programs efficiently. The relationship between politicians and career officials was healthy and productive, as published memoirs of politicians from that era reveal.[16]

When concerns turned to the post-war economy, many feared that the end of the war would trigger a recession, if not another depression. Career officials once again responded, with plans to deal with a severe economic downturn. Keynesian economics was the answer and Franklin D. Roosevelt's New Deal program was showing the way. Career government officials also enjoyed the support of citizens far more than they do today. In the 1960s, an American president, Lyndon B. Johnson, decided to promote a "Great Society" and a Canadian prime minister, Pierre Trudeau, promoted a "Just Society." Both saw government paving the way.

Trust in government and in the public service was high then. In the United States, for example, in 1964, 77 per cent of respondents said that they trusted the federal government to do the right thing nearly always or most of the time. By 2015, however, only 19 per cent of respondents said that they could trust the federal government to do what is right "most of the time." Trust in government in the United States has essentially remained at the 2015 level.[17] Canada does better than the United States under the "trust in government" factor but trails a number of other countries, including, among others, Denmark, Germany, and Portugal.[18]

Some observers argue that the public service is one reason for the decline in trust Canadians have toward public institutions.[19] The Task Force on Values and Ethics in the Public Service, chaired by John Tait, a widely respected former deputy minister with the federal government, concluded that "the future of the public service will be determined in large measure by the level of trust it will be able to sustain in its mission as an important public institution. This will be even more true as public servants come to hold their accountabilities in more public ways."[20] Ralph Heintzman, who also had a direct hand in shaping the task force report, added: "The bottom line for the public sector is not a financial bottom line. Its bottom line is trust. The trust of public sector employees, the trust of elected leaders, and the trust of the people of Canada."[21] Writing several years later, Heintzman sees the federal public service losing still more ground on the trust factor.[22]

I have also had numerous informal discussions in recent years with senior federal public servants, retired public servants, politicians, and political staffers. Virtually all acknowledged that government, notably the public service, has serious challenges. Their consensus was that something was not right with government. They recognize that Canadians are losing trust in their public institutions and that the status quo is no longer sustainable. But I did not see any consensus on what should be done. I did, however, see the blame game on full display – politicians blamed public servants, public servants blamed politicians and their partisan advisors and all three blamed the media, in particular social media. They point the finger at someone else, not at their own institution.

In the summer of 2022, it took up to five months in some cases for Canadians to obtain a passport and a majority of Canadians labelled delays at airports a "national embarrassment."[23] The government pointed to COVID-19 as the reason, but many observers disagreed. They argued that the government had had plenty of time to plan for the surge in passport applications in the immediate post-COVID period. To be sure, the Ottawa bureaucracy has policy units in central agencies and in all the line departments with mandates to look ahead and provide advice on how to deal with issues flowing from the COVID period. One can only conclude that they were not able to do so or, if they did, that the program units responsible ignored the advice. Observers also pointed out that, though the level of passport applications in the spring and summer of 2022 was not much higher than it had been before COVID, Ottawa had hired an additional 600 staff to help process the applications. They maintained that it was executives and managers' inability to bring back officials working from home that was an important part of the problem.[24]

I see no consensus on why government was falling short of expectations in delivering services. Retired federal public servants insist that the federal public service is too big and too bureaucratic, and no longer up to the task, whereas current senior public servants point the finger at ministerial offices, making the case that there are far too many political staffers generating far too much unproductive work for public servants. They also make the case that the growing number of oversight bodies and the work of central agencies have made government operations overly cautious, slow, and bureaucratic, involving several layers of decision making, forcing them to be always on the lookout to avoid risks. Political staffers, meanwhile, point the finger back at "the bureaucrats" for always slowing things down and their unwillingness to question the status quo or to look at doing things differently. Former and current federal politicians, for the most part, continue to be critical of the federal public service, though they often have positive things to say about individual public servants.

I have published extensively on government operations, both from a Canadian and a comparative perspective. I often turned to these sources while developing the arguments in this book. Two of my earlier books, *Whatever Happened to the Music Teacher: How Government Decides and Why* and *What Is Government Good At? A Canadian Answer* developed some of the arguments in this book. I was also able to draw on interviews with practitioners whom I consulted, over the years, for these two and other books. In addition, between 15 May and 1 December 2022, I held discussions with six current and former federal politicians, three ministerial political staffers, fifteen current and former senior federal public servants, and five private sector executives. I made no effort to produce a representative sample and I did not have a set of prepared questions. I knew all of them and it was more of an extended conversation than a formal interview.

I also had an experience that spoke to at least part of the problem in government operations. In the fall of 2021, I was asked if I would be willing to serve as a member of the Independent Advisory Board for Senate Appointments for New Brunswick. I agreed and was told that the appointments would be made by early 2022. After much waiting, the Privy Council Office (PCO) finally informed me in August 2022 that the appointment had gone through. I was informed that the prime minister had to sign off on the appointment, which explained the delay. Why would the prime minister need to sign off on a fairly inconsequential appointment? Surely, I thought, the responsibility could be delegated.

In August 2022, during my discussion with an assistant deputy minister in a line department in Ottawa, he insisted that the problem with federal government operations lies with the ever-growing ministerial offices and the constant requests for briefing material. I said that pointing the finger at ministerial staffers or central agencies or elsewhere, does not help to come up with a solution. How, I asked, can we fix government? His response, which I also heard from other senior federal government public servants, was: "We need to cut back the size of ministerial offices and central agencies, as a start." What comes after "as a start" is the important question but he had little to offer. I had discussions with central agency officials and they had a different take, at least when it came to solutions. One made the point that Canadians and their governments do not stay focused on any problem long enough to see it through to a solution. He blamed the media for this state of affairs.

I believe that the challenges confronting the federal government extend beyond the size of ministerial offices in Ottawa or the media. National governments, particularly those the size of Canada's, face a conundrum. They are too small or do not have anywhere near the degree of influence to deal with large issues such as climate change and a globalized economy but are too big or too complex to deliver programs and services effectively and efficiently. As a result, we are seeing a growing disconnect between governance and public administration, between politicians and career public servants, at least when it comes to national governments.

The golden age for national governments and their bureaucracies, to the extent that it existed, is no more. One can thus easily appreciate why government career officials would want to look inward to protect their institutions. All too often, politicians, even on the government side, no longer support their public servants. A former minister responsible for the British civil service said this in 1985, in light of Margaret Thatcher's reforms: "There will be real tasks with real measurable chances for condemnation or praise or even monetary rewards ... you now get young civil servants in their thirties who are going out into the jungle of bureaucracy and coming back with booty in the form of significant savings and significantly better ways of doing things; and they get noticed, they get noticed younger. They are not involved simply in pushing paper about until they reach the upper levels of Whitehall in the way they were."[25] Forty years later, there is little evidence that young or older public servants are coming back with booty in the form of significant savings either in Britain or Canada. Ministers in the former Boris Johnson government, including Johnson himself, were highly critical of the civil service, suggesting that the civil service had either reverted to its old ways or that career officials gave the appearance of change while standing still as they went about trying to reform government operations. In Canada, politicians on both the political right and left have become critical of career government officials, at times publicly.[26]

The easy working relationship that once existed between political leaders and senior career officials is on shaky ground. Politicians and their partisan advisors today often talk about public servants employing well-crafted strategies to thwart their efforts to overhaul policies or launch new measures. These include deliberately underperforming, leaking information to the media, outright refusing to implement policies or decisions, and withholding information. The list goes on.[27] One of Canada's leading political observers recently wrote about public servants turning to "defensive resistance" and the need to rebuild respect "between politicians and public servants."[28] Another leading journalist wrote that "the service-delivery problems the Liberal government is experiencing has more to do with cynicism within the bureaucracy than bungling."[29] But it is a two-way street. Public servants often point their finger at politicians as the culprits for their deteriorating relationship and politicians point their finger right back at public servants. Paul Tellier, former clerk of the Privy

Council and cabinet secretary, writes about the growing lack of trust between politicians and senior level officials in the public service. He adds that the PMO, which now calls all the shots, is "destroying" the Canadian public service.[30]

The changing relationship between the prime minister, the PMO, ministers, and senior career officials has wide implications for how the machinery of government operates.[31] This has already been well documented.[32] The literature, however, has not paid sufficient attention to the effect the changes have had on accountability requirements in government. I hold that failing accountability is at the core of what is wrong with government. Our Westminster-inspired parliamentary system still sees accountability as straightforward: public servants are accountable to ministers, ministers are accountable to Parliament, and members of Parliament are accountable to their constituents. In turn, accountability requires both giving an account and being held to account.[33] I argue that the chain of accountability has broken down. This study seeks to understand where and why.

To the likely surprise of many practitioners, accountability is a relatively recent addition to the public administration vocabulary. J.E. Hodgetts writes that the term "accountability ... had not previously been applied to our system of government, until it found its way into the title of the Lambert Commission (1979)."[34] The Glassco Commission, which had a profound effect on federal government operations, was not even asked to consider Parliament in its work.[35] I argue that accountability only became an issue after the federal government added more and more responsibilities and grew substantially. In response to these two developments, Ottawa jettisoned its rigid system of centrally prescribed administrative and financial rules and controls in favour of numerous reporting requirements. In the process, it added to the federal government's institutional complexities, making Ottawa's accountability requirements more opaque.

The book's central argument is that every time the federal government introduces new accountability and transparency requirements, accountability becomes more impenetrable. This not only makes government thicker and less accessible, it also motivates policy and decision makers to design strategies to sidestep or manage newly introduced requirements, thus lessening their effect or, preferably, making them ineffective. Managing the blame game and dealing with accountability requirements have dominated the agenda of both senior politicians and public servants in Ottawa all too often. What happens on the front lines or where programs and services are delivered to Canadians takes a back seat.

This book argues that there are two public services in the federal government – one is a machine-like organization where outputs and outcomes can often be observed, while the other houses policy, evaluation, communications, and liaison units, for which neither outputs nor outcomes can be easily observed or measured. Machine-like organizations can still operate, to some degree, in relative isolation from other organizations.[36] They are more self-contained and can focus on the task at hand – for example, a superintendent in one of Canada's national parks or a warden running a correctional facility has a clear purpose and does not need to spend much time looking at mission statements or at the work of other departments and central agencies or other governments, notably provincial governments. But even there, things are changing, and program implementation is increasingly becoming the product of many hands.

Public servants working in a central agency, in a policy-oriented department, or in a policy unit know that they and their units can never constitute the full story. They have to look up to the political agenda of prime ministers and their ministers, to other departments, and in many cases, to other governments. Canada's climate change strategy, for example, involves at least fourteen departments and agencies, a complex series of 250 programs, provincial governments, and the territories as well as the international community. Prime ministers and senior leaders of the federal public service are looking to promote public servants who understand policy making, have a broad outlook, and recognize that government initiatives are now the product of many hands and many departments. The two organizations – machine and coping – have their own distinct cultures and traditions. The question that we need to answer is – should federal government accountability requirements between the two organizations be different?

## THE QUESTIONS

I seek to answer a number of questions dealing with accountability in government. I argue that the lack of effective accountability requirements explains in large measure why Canadians are losing trust in the public sector. One former senior federal government official told me that accountability is the "hole in the doughnut," the missing part in government operations and in the machinery of government. I argue that whenever one looks at reforming operations in the public sector, the most important part should be accountability, and that governments missed the mark in reforming the public service when politicians looked for solutions outside their own institutions, making government operations thicker, costlier, less efficient, and less accountable.

Only prime ministers have the mandate and the power to overhaul accountability requirements and make them stick. However, it is not in the interest of prime ministers to strengthen accountability in their government. In addition, they always have too many things on their plate to give the issue the priority it requires for it to have any chance of success. The rarest commodity in Ottawa is that of securing time with the prime minister. Prime ministers have an incredibly busy agenda. Dealing with accountability requirements can never compete with other pressing issues on the prime minister's agenda, the number of individuals asking for a meeting, the latest political crisis, appointments that have to be made, or the political issue of the day that dominates the media. For prime ministers, accountability is a no-win issue that always takes a back seat to the need to deal with the constant demands on their time or the pressing issues that require their attention.

They will very likely underline the need to strengthen accountability when in opposition, and in election campaigns, but things look very different in the prime minister's chair. Once in power, they see no need and certainly no advantage in introducing more demanding accountability requirements on their government. Those on the government side, and this includes career officials, for the most part, view accountability as a "gotcha" game to be carefully managed, certainly not to be expanded. Senior permanent officials also have a crowded agenda and little interest in promoting accountability reform measures. They know that reforming accountability holds little benefit for them, their central agencies, or their departments. History has taught us that the status quo always benefits someone and that that someone will resist change – accountability in government is a case in point.

One former senior government of Canada official recently called for a Northcote-Trevelyan-type review of the state of the Canadian public service. He insists that "the actual machinery of government has ceased to function – it don't work." He goes on to make the case that a "reworking of the public service is long overdue" and that "Canada has far too many challenges in the coming decades to rely on an apparatus that's proven itself time and again to be obsolete."[37] His call continues to fall on deaf ears, declining trust in government notwithstanding. If the machinery of government "don't work," we need to know why before we can begin to fix it. I note that career officials are quick to call for reform measures once in retirement, but much less so while serving in government. If a theme has emerged in conversations with past and present federal public servants in recent years, it is this: current public servants are on the defensive about the state of the federal public service, pointing to several reasons why things do not work as well as they should, while former public servants readily acknowledge that the federal public service is now lacking in several areas and they are willing to point the finger at the public service itself for at least some of the problems.

There are sure signs that all is not well with government operations, and not just in Canada. In early 2022, the *Economist* magazine reported on the health of liberal democracies in the Western world and its verdict was anything but positive.[38] Protesters in the truck convoy in Ottawa in February 2022 were making the case that government had to be deconstructed. Some may dismiss such protest movements as fringe groups with little public support and that it's best to ignore them. I argue that they should not be so easily dismissed. There is something wrong with government operations if populist leaders can exploit them for political purposes and gain public support. A leading member of Canada's Conservative party, Pierre Poilièvre, publicly supported the protesters in the truck convoy, notwithstanding the fact that they had broken laws in downtown Ottawa.[39] He was later elected Conservative Party leader and became leader of the opposition; in our system of government, the prime minister in waiting. It will also be recalled that the People's Party gained 5 per cent of the popular vote in the 2022 general election in which only 62.5 per cent of registered electors voted.[40] On the truck convoy, Lawrence Martin wrote: "One of the world's leading democracies has stood by hapless and helpless as the protesters brought the core of its capital to a standstill."[41]

Nik Nanos, one of Canada's best-known pollsters, declared in October 2022 that Canada has "joined the club of angry, polarized countries." When Canadians were asked to describe the federal government, not from a partisan perspective either as Liberal or Conservative, but rather about the work of the government in general, the top two answers were "pessimism" and "anger." Nanos adds: "This polarization ... leads to gridlock, division and an overall decay in the confidence of our democratic institutions."[42] It is much too easy to simply point the finger at politicians as the reason and leave it at that.

Several questions come to mind: What ails government? What ails the Canadian public service? What should Canadians expect from the federal public service? Why have past efforts at reforming the federal public service failed to live up to expectations? Why have prime ministers and ministers decided to substantially expand their offices? I argue that answers to these and other questions lie in the government's accountability structure and a dated machinery of government. This despite several ambitious and costly reform measures that have been introduced over the past fifty years to make government more effective, more efficient, and more accountable. I maintain that the reforms have had the opposite effect – they have made government less effective, less efficient, and less accountable. If accountability requirements are lacking, it follows that government operations will not perform as well as they should. If government accountability cannot be fixed, then government operations cannot be improved and reform measures will continue to fail or only play at the margins.

## LOOKING TO THE PRIVATE SECTOR FOR SOLUTIONS: THE WRONG PLACE TO LOOK

Margaret Thatcher came to office determined to "fix" government bureaucracy. Senior career officials had carefully reviewed her party's electoral platform and had prepared policy options for her to consider. They did not see any need to overhaul government operations or to offer advice on how to improve management in government departments. Thatcher, however, had a very different perspective and never let up on her attempts to fix government operations. If senior officials had no solution to offer, she knew where to look for solutions: she turned to private sector executives for advice, inviting some to serve in government.[43] In doing so, however, she left accountability requirements in government largely intact. With hindsight, we now see that this considerably weakened her reform measures.

Canada followed her lead. In the 1984 election campaign, Brian Mulroney made overhauling government bureaucracy a priority. He pledged to give pink slips and running shoes to bureaucrats, suggesting that accountability was in need of repair. Like Thatcher, he said that his government would instill a bias for action in the public service and do away with fuddy-duddy bureaucrats. And, again like Thatcher, Mulroney looked to best management practices in the private sector to inspire change in the federal public service, also asking some private sector executives to serve in government. At Thatcher's urging, the two leaders often compared notes on how to fix government operations.[44]

The Mulroney government established several task forces and invited private sector executives to serve on them, together with career officials, with a mandate to reduce government spending and fix government operations. The efforts were not successful by any measure.[45] Unlike Thatcher, Mulroney lost interest in reforming the bureaucracy after only a few years in power, turning his attention to other more pressing issues, notably national unity, international relations, negotiating a free trade agreement with the United States, and putting in place measures designed to ensure that his government would be re-elected. Mulroney also left the government's accountability requirements intact.

No matter, the belief became widespread in Western countries that the private sector had and still has superior management practices and that they could successfully be imported to government. It takes only a moment's reflection to appreciate that this approach requires changes to the government's accountability structure. This was not done, and again it explains in large measure why efforts to reform management in government have failed. It also explains why accountability instruments and processes in government have become ineffective.

I want to deal with the blame game early. As already noted, I argue that politicians alone are not solely to blame for the growing distrust between Canadians and their federal government. Career officials must also accept blame. I maintain that the federal government costs more to operate while delivering less than in years past, that it is overstaffed, and that its operations are poorly managed and costly. It seems that no one is accountable for this state of affairs. There was a time when the federal public service could point, with satisfaction, to its parsimonious culture. Not any more.[46] Canadians have every right to ask Ottawa if it could not accomplish much more than it does given its $400-billion-plus annual budget. They could also remind public servants that the responsibility for managing government programs and operations lies largely with them, not with politicians.[47] Canadians also have every right to ask Ottawa what they are receiving in return for the $55 billion in the federal government's wage bill (2022) and the $17.5 billion in outsourced consultant contracts (2023–24).[48] Waves of reform measures since the early 1980s have all avoided dealing with the hole in the doughnut. They have failed to consider how ministerial responsibility works, failed to review how ministers and career officials interact, failed to deal with the changing relationship between central agencies and line departments and agencies, failed to deal with the vested interest that government bureaucracies have in their own economic well-being and growth; and failed to see that the public and private sectors differ in important ways.

Though this book is about Canada's federal government and its public service, the reader will note that, although this is not a comparative study, I often look to the experiences of other countries, notably Anglo-American countries. I continue to believe that we can gain a better understanding of government operations of one country by comparing them with the experiences of other countries. How Britain, for example, went about reforming its civil service can shed light on the Canadian experience.

### OUTLINE OF THE STUDY

The machinery of government has become a specialized field in its own right. The federal government is home to a wide variety of organizations: some are designed to generate policy advice, others to deliver programs and services, others to regulate activities inside and outside government, and still others to generate appointments to government bodies and the judiciary. How the machinery of government is organized is important because it will influence how government decides and also how government operates.

All institutions, public or private, tend to be inward looking, particularly when it comes to protecting their interests. I argue that the federal public service has become more and more inward looking in recent years. This, at the same time as new transparency requirements continue to be introduced. We need to explore why and how and also assess the effect on the government's accountability requirements.

The federal public service has taken on a different form. By adding both management levels and many policy specialists, a fault line has emerged, dividing those working on policy from those on the front lines delivering programs and services. In this sense, there are now two federal public services operating in the ambit of one institution. We need to review how the two operate and if accountability requirements between the two are different.

The expenditure budget acts as the government's nervous system. It sends out clear signals to ministers, to departments and agencies, to all public servants, and to Canadians about what is important. It lays out who wins and who loses. Two students of government argue that "budgeting is the most important annual ritual of government – the World Series of Government, or perhaps the Grey Cup of Government within the Canadian context."[49] The push to spend more comes from many forces. But there are also days of reckoning when governments have to reduce spending. We need to understand the role of both politicians and public servants in shaping the budget process.

The public service in Canada and abroad has, since the early 1980s, been subjected to unrelenting bureaucracy bashing. Journalists often take aim at federal public servants managing government programs. Politicians, even on the government side, argue that public servants are always able to produce reasons against new initiatives and change. This prompted Aaron Wildavsky to write: "The most senior bureaucracy now is only for the brave."[50] Bureaucracy bashing has led the federal public service to close ranks and to adopt an unwritten code of see no waste and talk no waste. The work of public sector unions has also served to solidify the code.

Though accountability may be the hole in the doughnut, the federal government has generated or sponsored a number of documents in recent years that essentially make the case that all is well. They argue that if there are problems with accountability requirements, all that is needed is to update the vocabulary.[51] Accountability can mean responsibility or answerability; it all depends on the circumstances and who is asking. But this hardly clarifies matters. The most senior federal government public servants do not agree on what the new vocabulary means. One can only imagine the struggles ministers and members of Parliament have in making sense of it all. When it comes to accountability, the Lambert Commission explained: "Under our system, Parliament must be the beginning and end of the governmental process." We now need to understand the impact of the changes to Parliament's role in the face of changes in the accountability vocabulary and government operations.[52]

We also need to review the work of ministers and deputy ministers. Accountability requirements may not have changed much in recent years but how ministers and deputy ministers go about their work has. Boundaries separating departments and central agencies have faded in recent years and both ministers and deputy ministers have had to adjust. This, in turn, affects government operations and accountability.

I argue that the federal public service has been knocked off its moorings. It is no longer certain what it stands for, and what it is good at. Federal public servants now admit that they are afraid to speak truth to politicians.[53] They also see that they are losing ground in their capacity to deliver government programs and services.[54] Canadians, their politicians, and public servants need to answer the question: What do we want the federal public service to be?

Changing the accountability vocabulary, if not the accountability requirements, the need to promote a "whole of government" approach to policy making, and the changing relationship between politicians and public servants are all having a profound effect on the behaviour of public servants. In the next chapters, we assess how these and other developments are shaping the behaviour and attitudes of public servants in generating policy advice and delivering programs and services.

# 1

# THE SETTING AND THE MACHINERY

The federal government's machinery of government is complex and now consists of an elaborate network of agencies, departments, and Crown corporations. By one count, this network incorporates 130 departments, agencies, and other organizations, and by another, 300-plus, covering the whole waterfront of government activities. They can be broken down into four groups: central agencies, which provide policy advice and promote coordination; line departments, which deliver services; regulatory agencies, which ensure that government regulations are respected; and Crown corporations, which perform activities that often compete with private sector firms. In short, the machinery is a hodgepodge of organizations pursuing a wide variety of mandates.[1] Parliament has to make sense of it all, since a minister is answerable to Parliament for every action a servant of the Crown takes.

Not only have many public policy issues become highly complex (how best, for example, to deal with such challenges as climate change or relations with Indigenous peoples), the machinery of government itself has also become very complex. How can a sense of purpose and coherence be brought to this vast network of departments and agencies? The machinery had great success in managing the war effort in the 1940s by establishing a series of Crown corporations.[2] But we have since overloaded the machinery with new responsibilities, new agencies, new units, and new processes, all of which contribute to making the federal government thicker, less coherent, less accountable, and more expensive.

All decisions, large and small, on machinery of government questions belong to the prime minister, on the advice of the PCO. Other than to the prime minister, the PCO reports to no one and jealously guards this responsibility, no doubt in part because the prime minister prefers it that way, but also because it clearly delineates its turf. The PCO has no competition and deals with no oversight agency other than Parliament when it comes to machinery of government matters. But even Parliament has had very little influence in shaping Ottawa's machinery of government over the years.

The PCO insists that it is simply not possible to delegate machinery of government issues to individual ministers or even to involve cabinet in the decision-making process because ministers and their departments would invariably fight to protect or expand their departments' responsibilities, resulting in continuing turf wars. Prime Minister Justin Trudeau circulated a document to his ministers shortly after coming to power in 2015 that made it clear who was the boss, at least when it comes to the machinery of government. The document reads: "The Prime Minister determines the broad organization and structure of the government in order to meet its objectives. The Prime Minister is responsible for allocating ministers' portfolios, establishing their mandates, clarifying the relationships among them and identifying the priorities for their portfolios through mandate letters."[3] The same thinking holds in Britain and in the other Westminster-inspired parliamentary systems.

## ONCE THE MACHINERY WAS SMALL AND ACCOUNTABILITY WAS CLEAR

There was a time when things were simple in government, the machinery of government was easily understood by everyone in government and Parliament, and there was no need for a specialized unit in the PCO to look after it. When Alexander Mackenzie was prime minister in 1873, for example, he functioned without a secretary, answering all correspondence himself. In 1909, the newly created Department of External Affairs was entirely housed above a barber shop in Ottawa.[4] Assigning responsibilities to line departments was straightforward: there were thirteen departments with clear mandates in 1867 and few talked about the need to bring a "whole of government approach" or to break down departmental silos.[5] They were meant to be silos by design, looking after, say, agriculture or marine and fisheries. In 1867, there were fewer than ten federal public servants for every member of Parliament. Today, there are about 1,000, not including all federal government organizations, such as Crown corporations.[6] And when it came to accountability, the Westminster parliamentary system's best days occurred when information was simple, straightforward, and highly accessible.[7]

Prime ministers and ministers, before the Second World War and the arrival of the welfare state, could easily find out everything they wanted to know and, if they so desired, could easily control the details of both policy and government operations. Between Confederation and the Second World War, prime ministers or cabinet ministers had to defend, before Parliament, such things as the hiring or firing of an engineer, a clerk, or a secretary.[8] Accountability was straightforward – members of Parliament only had to look to the prime minister or ministers for answers to their questions, even those who dealt with purely administrative matters.

Until the 1960s, growth in the federal government was carefully monitored and largely accommodated through the traditional line department structure and Crown corporations. Central agencies were small and line ministers and their departments took the lead on issues, large or small. This was the case even when the machinery of government grew to help Ottawa plan the war effort between 1939 and 1945. The prime minister turned to strong ministers, such as C.D. Howe, and their departments, and to Crown corporations, to get the job done. The machinery of government did contract in the post–Second World War period, but that was short-lived, and the federal government began to expand shortly after the war to develop and implement the welfare state. Line departments again took the lead in defining new policies and new measures and in looking after their implementation.

The election of the Pierre Trudeau government in 1968 would change things. In 1968, Ottawa had money to spend. Nation- and province-building came into fashion, with governments leading the way, and the federal government was able to carve out a large role for itself through its spending power, even in areas of provincial jurisdictions.[9] By the 1970s, some provincial governments could no longer point to a single field of jurisdiction in which the federal government was not involved, in one form or another, through various cost-sharing arrangements. Accountability requirements were not adjusted; for the most part, they were simply ignored in developing the various federal-provincial agreements.[10]

As is well known, Trudeau *père* is the architect of the modern Prime Minister's Office (PMO). He felt that the Pearson government, in which he served as the minister of justice, lacked a proper central planning capacity resulting in the Pearson years being marked by confusion and chaos. Trudeau maintained that Pearson's ministers and their departments were free to roam wherever they wanted, at times even working at cross purposes and resolved that things would be different in his government. As he explained, "One of the reasons why I wanted this job, when I was told that it might be there, is because I felt it very important to have a strong central government, build up the executive, build up the Prime Minister's Office."[11]

Trudeau set out to bring greater policy coherence to the federal government by substantially strengthening the centre of government. He expanded the size of the PMO and identified specific functions and tasks for it to perform. Tom Kent, principal secretary to Prime Minister Pearson, describes the PMO before Trudeau: "The PMO was then utterly different from what it became in the Trudeau era and has since remained. There was no bevy of deputies and assistants and principal this-and-that, with crowds of support staff."[12] No prime minister since Trudeau *père* has ever sought to turn back the clock and cut back the size of the office or to limit its functions to what they had been before.

Pierre Trudeau's reforms also gave rise to a new breed of federal public servants – policy analysts, policy coordinators, program evaluators – not only in central agencies but also across government in line departments and agencies. If central agencies were to add a coterie of policy analysts, then line departments felt that they had to respond by adding policy analysts to their staff, to answer requests for information but also to try to counterbalance the growing influence of the central agencies. This, in turn, had implications for human resources, particularly at the senior levels. There was a time when the road to the top for public servants was to manage programs and acquire an intimate knowledge of their department, its policies, and operations. Today, the road to the top lies through central agencies, not line departments, and through policy work, not managing operations. Much more is said about this later.[13]

An enlarged PMO has greatly expanded the machinery of government. It has led central agencies, notably the PCO, to substantially expand their capacity to provide a window on the policies and operations of line departments and to respond to demands for information and advice from prime ministers and their advisors and assistants. The PCO also required a capacity to serve newly established cabinet committees, designed to coordinate the policies of line departments and to review their proposals. Again, this in turn led line departments to add policy and liaison units, not only to deal with the constant demand for information from central agencies, but also to defend their turf.

When Justin Trudeau came to power in 2015, he sent a document to his ministers titled *Open and Accountable Government*, outlining in considerable detail all aspects of the federal government's machinery of government. The document informs ministers that they "have powers, duties and functions vested by statute, and the Prime Minister may assign a broad range of additional responsibilities." It essentially restates how the machinery of government should work, how government is to be held to account before Parliament, how ministers and public servants need to relate to one another, and that ministers are responsible for being accountable before Parliament. However, the document is quick to add: "As head of government, the Prime Minister has a responsibility for the effective operation of the whole of government and often has to answer in the House for the operation of all departments and agencies."[14] It is now widely accepted that the balance of power has shifted toward the prime minister and the PMO and central agencies and away from cabinet, ministers, and their departments in shaping policy, making key decisions, managing political controversies, and dealing with Parliament and the media.

Journalists and Ottawa observers have recently been writing about "kids in short pants" in the PMO actually running the government. The Samara Centre for Democracy published a document in 2018 that also made this case. The Centre consulted fifty-four politicians in Ottawa, representing the major political parties, writing: "There is a culture of governance whereby the advisors all assume more power than they should. And not only with respect to the other ministers ... unelected people are basically given the authority by the Prime Minister to say – go and tell so and so to do such and such."[15] The kids in short pants in the PMO view their role as: "to implement PMO directives, to identify and deal with critics inside government."[16] They roam wherever they want to roam, at times asking questions and at other times giving directions.[17] But few inside government are asking whether this development has any effect on the workings of Parliament's accountability requirements. Former public servants, however, have no such hesitation. Paul Tellier, former clerk of the Privy Council, recently observed: "The current government, with centralization of everything in the PMO, is in the process of destroying the public service... and the word destroying is not too strong." He added, "there's now distrust between politicians and public servants."[18]

## THE NEW BREED OF PUBLIC SERVANTS MEETS THE MACHINERY

The federal public service is different than it was fifty years ago in several important ways. The size of government has expanded, the relationship between central agencies and line departments has been redefined, and the relationship between politicians and public servants has broken new ground. Yet the structure of government and its accountability requirements have remained largely intact. Despite the addition of many new organizations, the growing number of public servants in virtually every federal government organization, and the changing relationship between the central agencies and line departments and their ministers, much of *Open and Accountable Government* could have been written in 1950.

*Open and Accountable Government* deals with the machinery of government and accountability requirements as if time had stood still. It reads: "Ministers are accountable to Parliament"; "The Cabinet decision-making process is key for achieving overall coherence and coordination in government policy"; "Public servants do not share in Ministers' constitutional accountability to Parliament"; "Cabinet government works through a process of compromise and consensus building, which culminates in a Cabinet decision"; "Deputy ministers are accountable for a wide range of responsibilities including policy advice, program delivery, internal departmental management and interdepartmental coordination"; "Exempt staff ... do not have a role in departmental operations and have no legal basis for exercising the delegated authority of Ministers. Nor may exempt staff give direction to departmental officials on the discharge of other responsibilities"; "Public servants are ultimately accountable to Ministers through their deputy minister and not to Parliament."[19]

The document, however, then goes on to outline significant changes that have reshaped how public servants work with ministers and how they are expected to deal with Canadians. It reports on the various requirements under the Access to Information legislation, the *Conflict of Interest Act*, and the *Lobbying Act*.[20] It also establishes deputy ministers and deputy heads of other government organizations as "accounting officers" representing their organizations and calls on them to appear before parliamentary committees to answer questions on managing departmental resources.[21] The document has little to say about how these and other developments affect the machinery of government or the work of career officials. And it makes no effort to reconcile how the machinery can accommodate the changes. For example, it has nothing to say about the effect the kids in short pants in the PMO have had on government operations. One can only assume that the government believes that these and other changes can be accommodated within long-standing accountability requirements. More is also said about this later.

## DISTINCT ORGANIZATIONS AND THE MACHINERY

According to one Government of Canada website, the Canadian government is home to 130 organizations. This includes twenty-three ministerial departments, seventeen departmental corporations, fifty departmental agencies, twelve operating agencies, and three service agencies.[22] But this does not tell the whole story – there are also forty-seven Crown corporations and several agents of Parliament. The organizations range from large (Canada Revenue Agency and its 47,426 employees) to small (the Secretariat of the National Security and Intelligence Committee of Parliamentarians and its six employees).[23] Another Government of Canada website reports that there are 207 organizations, while a former clerk of the Privy Council writes that there are "300-plus federal entities that exercise power and authorities conferred on them by Parliament, and for every single one of them, there is a minister who is answerable to Parliament."[24] The last two include all government organizations, such as the national museums, the Canadian Dairy Commission, the Canadian Judicial Council, and the list goes on.[25]

The prime minister sits on top of these organizations, albeit with some agencies enjoying a much higher degree of independence from the government than others. Parliament has an oversight role, and is expected to hold the organizations to account for their decisions and activities, again to varying degrees depending on their mandate. How then can the prime minister and cabinet ministers as well as

Parliament give direction to, depending on how one counts, the 130, 207, or 300-plus distinct organizations, accountable in some cases or answerable in others?

## DIRECTING THE MACHINERY

How can a prime minister and cabinet ministers, let alone members of Parliament, understand the finer points of Ottawa's machinery of government, how the various organizations relate to one another, and how to best determine the proper level of resources to do what they do? It is rare for a prime minister to have served in the public service before assuming power, where he or she would have gained a first-hand appreciation of how the machinery works. Only William Lyon Mackenzie King, Lester B. Pearson, and Pierre Elliott Trudeau had ever served in government as public servants before they became prime minister, with Trudeau only serving for three years as a desk officer in the Privy Council Office. Louis St Laurent, John Turner, Jean Chrétien, Kim Campbell, and Paul Martin all held senior cabinet positions before becoming prime minister. I note that Marcel Massé, who served in cabinet portfolios, including president of the Treasury Board in the Chrétien government, had also previously occupied senior positions in the federal public service, including a brief tenure as clerk of the Privy Council. It remains true, however, that cabinet ministers are very rarely drawn from the senior or junior ranks of the public service.

Politicians come into office from different backgrounds and with different work experiences. Few were students of government or had a background in managing large bureaucratic organizations. Elected members of Parliament have worked in a variety of occupational backgrounds before arriving in Parliament – some were businesspeople, lawyers, teachers, police officers, and members of the military; others were representatives of labour organizations and agricultural workers; and still others were former political staffers.[26] James T. Pow explains: "From dentistry to plumbing, midwifery to air traffic control, there are plenty of career paths for which prior specialist training is essential. Being a politician in a national legislature is not one of them."[27]

The 338 members of Parliament elected in the 2021 general election came from a variety of backgrounds or sectors. Among them, sixty lawyers, seventy-seven business people, fifty-one from the communications or public relations sector, four real estate agents, twelve from the arts community, and thirty-one from academe. Only sixteen came from the federal public sector. Thus, only those sixteen MPs appreciate how the federal government and its operations work, and how it makes decisions.[28] Few MPs have the background and experience to parse through the thousands and thousands of pages the Government of Canada regularly places on its various websites every month or submits to Parliament every year.

Members of Parliament have many responsibilities to attend to – sitting on parliamentary committees, attending caucus meetings, travelling to and from their constituencies, meeting with constituents and running two offices, one in Ottawa and one in their constituency. Scott Simms, a former MP, reports that he received invitations to forty firefighters' balls every year while many "MPs can easily find themselves attending six or more events in a single day, and still turning down others."[29] They then have to find time to perform one of their most important responsibilities – holding the government to account.

Former MP Brent Rathgeber asks – why would government MPs ever want to hold the government to account? They are, after all, on the same team. He writes: "They do not even pretend to be a check on the government. On a good day, they are cheerleaders for the government; on a bad day, they are government apologists."[30] Former Liberal MP Robert-Falcon Ouellette gained a reputation for being a maverick, known for voting against his party.[31] However, he voted for his party 91 per cent of the time. A Samara Centre for Democracy report found that the average Canadian member of Parliament voted for their party 99.6 per cent of the time.[32]

As Jonathan Malloy explains, when it comes to scrutiny and accountability, "MPs hold many responsibilities, and even the most diligent can only spend a limited time absorbing and thinking about scrutiny issues. And while scrutiny may be at the heart of our parliamentary system, it is often not very rewarding work, especially on an individual level." A 1990s survey of MPs found they ranked "scrutinizing government" as the lowest of five roles compared with "policy" and "helping constituents." There is little reason to think this has changed. Scrutinizing can sometimes be very tedious work, especially when looking for substantive long-term issues rather than explosive but minor items."[33]

David Docherty writes about amateurism at the political level in Canada – amateurism in the sense of limited political experience before being elected to Parliament and also because of the high level of involuntary turnover of MPs at election time – hence limited tenure.[34] Sheila Copps writes that: "Politics is the only job where the more experience you get, the more people want to get rid of you."[35] It follows that a high turnover of members of Parliament weakens the government's capacity to build a substantive expertise in public administration and in overseeing the government's management of public finances by the House of Commons and, it follows, by cabinet. In Canada, sectoral expertise also has to take a back seat because of the need to ensure balance in cabinet appointments by looking to linguistic, gender, and regional considerations.

There are any number of reasons why someone would go through the various steps needed to be elected to Parliament: the desire to make a difference, to defend the interests of one's community, to make it to cabinet, to learn and grow as a professional, and to address deficiencies in public policies or in the country's leadership, among others. Kelly Blidook argues that there "is strong evidence that MPs" wish to represent their constituencies' interests.[36] Again, the desire to scrutinize government activities does not rank high among the motivations. In any event, the public and voters do not reward scrutiny. As Jonathan Malloy explains: "Scrutiny can also feel unrewarding because the payoff for any one individual to start doing it is minimal. In rare cases, an individual MP has gained a high profile for doggedly pursuing an issue. But even when an MP does find something significant... opposition party leaders – take over."[37] Jody Wilson-Raybould reports on the experience as an MP: "It is ... a reality that MP disillusionment sets in for many, and often pretty quickly. The reality is not what you imagined it would be and that is a hard pill to swallow, especially when one sacrifices much and works so hard to get into politics and to actually get elected."[38]

Members of Parliament and cabinet ministers very often also have a short-term perspective, only a four-year period in the best of times, to get things done. Politicians have little to no interest or expertise to take on the responsibility of evaluating the machinery of government, how it works, or even the basic structure of government departments. They want to get things done, and take it for granted that the machinery will deliver what it is told to deliver. When problems arise or failures occur in how the machinery of government operates, they will point fingers at the "bureaucrats" and leave it at that, if only because there is not much more that they can do.[39]

The point is that the machinery is very complex. It has become a field of specialization in its own right. Members of Parliament, for the most part, do not have the knowledge or the interest to gain a full understanding of the machinery of government and how it works. And public servants prefer it that way.

## SUPPORTING PRIME MINISTERS AND CABINET

Prime ministers and cabinet ministers need help from central agencies and line departments to shape new policies and to direct the work of government departments and agencies. They need policy advice and help to allocate resources, manage internal regulations, make appointments, coordinate government policies, programs, and activities, and monitor the progress being made. This is where central agencies and policy specialists come in.

Both politicians and senior career officials value the policy function. That's where the action is. Politicians go into politics to make policy – whether for policy's sake or to advance their own careers – while the more ambitious and better-educated career officials go into government to help shape policy. The best place for career officials to shape policy is in a central agency, the "buckle" that links both the political and bureaucratic worlds. From this vantage point, they can see how all policies take shape in all sectors. It is also now much easier for them to be visible to the top policy makers and to be able to secure a senior public service position working in a central agency rather than in a line department or agency.

Central agencies are thus always in the thick of the debate when new policies are struck or revised and when difficult issues need to be managed. They are the meat in the sandwich between the political and the administrative, where they see first-hand how politicians operate and how career officials in line departments go about defining policy proposals. They have access to prime ministers and ministers, and they have to constantly deal with several issues, including to what extent policy advice should be self-generated or requested and to what extent that advice should be political or politically sensitive. Prime ministers need to rely on central agencies for advice, and central agency officials are in a strong position to influence policy decisions. They are rarely, if ever, taken to task when things go wrong. Line department officials are the ones on the front lines delivering the programs and services – if things go wrong, they are the ones who provide the answers.

However, not all is well with the buckle. Jonathan Craft and John Halligan maintain that political leaders struggle "to cope, let alone advance their agendas, given the byzantine nature of modern policy making and [the] rough-and-tumble requirements of politics in a Web-enabled era."[40] Craft and Halligan argue that politicians are establishing processes to check the influence of career officials, including those in central agencies, convinced that the problem with their difficulty in shaping new policy lies with career officials, not with them. Meanwhile, public servants, or at least some of them, have adjusted by attempting to be more responsive to the wishes of their political masters.[41] These developments have made evidence-based policy making less valued, less accessible, less welcomed by ministers, and less transparent to everyone else.

A government's budget says it all. It sends out clear signals about what is important to the government and what is not. As we will see, it is no exaggeration to suggest that prime ministers dominate new spending decisions but line departments and agencies still have the upper hand when it comes to budgeting for ongoing programs. So, though central agencies have helped prime ministers define new spending, they have fallen short in challenging line departments and their programs and operations.

Prime ministers, no matter the party, have shared and continue to share one common objective over the past forty years – reducing red tape. But measures to deregulate government operations run up against the desire of prime ministers to see departments and agencies run on their tracks. Prime ministers do not like surprises or administrative miscues, which invariably fuel the blame game. Paul Tellier told deputy ministers on numerous occasions that he and Prime Minister Mulroney "did not like surprises" and reminded them that he wants to "alert the prime minister" when a crisis is about to blow up in the media.[42] This has not been an easy circle to square – how to delegate more management authority to line departments and their managers while making sure that they avoid the kinds of administrative miscues that create political problems. What we have seen is a "start and stop" approach to reducing red tape. The government will launch ambitious "debureaucratizing" measures and stick to them until a widely reported scandal tied to administrative miscues hits the top of the news cycle. This will often lead to new centrally prescribed rules and regulations. Central agency officials are always in the thick of things when red tape needs to be reduced but also when new rules and regulations have to be defined and implemented, making the machinery of government even more opaque, even to long-serving public servants.

While the merit system, to the extent that it still works, is responsible for most of government employment, central agencies still have an important role to play in making numerous appointments to the more senior government jobs. Government patronage is often considered to be a sign of a less than perfectly developed system of governing and human resource management, but it is also important to remember that political leaders do need individuals in government who are committed to their policy goals, and even to them personally. We are seeing a greater use of political appointees in government, and, to some degree, the general politicization of the public service than was the case as recently as the early 1980s.[43] Politicians no long appear to trust their public servants to give them "frank and fearless" advice, or, perhaps more important, do not want advice that is at odds with their own preconceptions of what public policy should be. The emphasis on personal leadership is also a component of contemporary government as well as its rejection of expertise in favour of highly politicized "advice" that reinforces the ideas of political leaders. Central agency officials are at the centre of this development and line departments are, for the most part, left on the outside looking in. Central agencies, notably officials in the PMO and the PCO, have a direct hand in making 1,500 Order-in-Council appointments, of which "a few hundred come up for renewal each year."[44]

One of the principal tasks of central agencies is coordinating the policies of line departments. This has been a significant task since the inception of government itself but it has become all the more important in recent years, given the efforts to decentralize decision making in government operations. Governments have devised a number of mechanisms to coordinate policies. Many depend on the powers of central agencies to pursue government-wide policies to overcome the "silos" of individual policy domains.[45] The degree of emphasis on coordination will depend, in part, on the desire of the prime minister to achieve coordination, and on the structure and influence of the central agencies. The fact is, career officials in central agencies have a broader perspective on all the activities of government than officials in other organizations. They are also in a stronger position to persuade ministers to adopt more coordinated policy responses than other coordinating mechanisms, such as interdepartmental committees or task forces. This too has considerably strengthened the hand of central agencies inside the machinery of government.

To understand what is happening in government – and in society – and to control or direct the work of line departments and agencies within government, monitoring is required. Monitoring is also important for strengthening the capacity of central agencies and for prime ministers to exert control over other governmental organizations, such as line departments. Most of this monitoring work is done through organizations that deal with budgets and appointments or is the work of the central agencies. Some government monitoring may be highly politicized and involve a large number of partisan staff to ensure compliance.

The most important monitors in government are typically responsible to the legislature rather than the executive. In particular, auditing organizations such as the Office of the Auditor General of Canada (OAG) and the Office of the Commissioner of Official Languages monitor government spending, attempt to control the misuse of public money, and verify how well the *Official Languages Act* is respected. These organizations have also gained a substantial capacity to analyze policy. In the case of the auditor general, the OAG not only analyzes the legality of spending, it can also suggest more effective and efficient use of public money. These organizations have thus become a major source of monitoring and control in government, one that may conflict with what prime ministers desire. This is also a recent development – sixty years ago, only the Office of the Auditor General had an effect on government operations. Today, we have nine officers of Parliament that monitor the work of line departments and agencies.[46] This too has contributed to making the machinery of government thicker and more opaque.

## LIFE INSIDE LINE DEPARTMENTS

Line departments and agencies have been told, time and again over the past sixty years, that they are not up to the task of delivering government programs and services – hence the many measures to reform management that have been geared to line departments. They are also told that they are "silos," and are thus unable to address the important public policy issues of the day, which invariably cut across departmental lines. We have seen several royal commissions since the 1960s making the case that management in line departments is lacking – the Glassco, the Lambert, and the Gomery commissions – together with numerous consultant reports and ambitious reform efforts, PS 2000 among others. All were designed to improve management and modernize the federal public service. The Glassco Commission wanted to "let managers manage," and the Lambert Commission wanted to make managers manage and make them more accountable for their work, as did the Gomery Commission. Despite these efforts, few voices are suggesting that all is well in the operations of the federal government. However, plenty are making the case that things need to improve.[47]

The Office of the Auditor General (OAG) reports twice every year on the performance of the government. It focuses on line departments and their programs, not central agencies. It is very rare that the OAG reports on miscues committed by central agencies, by the PMO or ministerial offices, by the Finance Department, by the PCO, or by the other officers of Parliament, including the OAG itself. The finer points of a policy are often difficult for members of Parliament and the media to grasp, but program miscues or administrative missteps are not. The Passport Office, for example, took the blame in the summer of 2022 when long lineups of citizens were left waiting for service, but no one pointed the finger at the central agencies and their inability to see the challenges ahead.

There was a time when a public servant could go from an entry position and move up to be the deputy minister in the same department. No more. As Jacques Bourgault writes, nearly all deputy ministers "have occupied a senior executive position in the Privy Council Office (PCO) in the ten years preceding their appointment."[48] Rising stars, those believed to have the qualities to assume senior positions in the public service, are identified early and a stay in the PCO is now close to a requirement before becoming a deputy minister. Deputy ministers' loyalty, as Bourgault points out, is now as much to the centre as it is to their departments, and deputy ministers no longer stay in departments for an extended period, as was once the case.[49] More is said about this when we review the work and career patterns of deputy ministers in chapter 8.

I once asked a former clerk of the Privy Council why deputy ministers are no longer drawn from departments and why they are rotated so often, with virtually all of them spending only two to three years in the same department as deputy minister before they are transferred to another. The clerk said that a main challenge in government is to break down silos and to bring a whole of government perspective to defining policies. Deputy ministers, he added, cannot be wedded to a single department because they would invariably promote "a narrow perspective." They require a career track that exposes them to a variety of experiences and a broad knowledge of government policies because all important policy challenges now cut across departments.[50] Viewed from the perspective of a central agency, government has become a collection of silos – policy silos, budget silos, program silos, people silos, and data silos.[51] The goal of breaking down silos, however, goes against the grain, that is, against a machinery of government designed for a different era. The machinery still looks to line departments not only to take the lead in shaping policies and delivering programs, but also to make the government's accountability requirements work.

Attempts to break down silos by changing the career patterns of deputy ministers have not gone unnoticed by ministers and client groups. Eugene Whelan, a former minister of agriculture, told a Senate committee that deputy ministers of agriculture no longer know "a sow from a cow" and that he longed for the glory days of public service when the deputy minister of agriculture lived and breathed farming and stayed in the job for extended periods. He argued that those ministers would rather quit than be shuffled somewhere else. He said: "Some think that all you need now is a good education and you can run anything."[52]

Deputy ministers no longer identify with a single department in their careers. Unlike in years past, deputy ministers now range through a "multiplicity" of departments before retirement. It is a case of "have policy skills, will travel." Indeed, some can have up to five assignments as deputy minister before leaving government. The length of time a deputy minister stayed in one department between 1867 and 1917 was on average 12.2 years but fell to only 2.3 years between 1977 and 1987.[53] Things have not improved since.[54] Gordon Osbaldeston, in his study of accountability in government, was highly critical of the short stay of deputy ministers in line departments, claiming, among other things, that it made accountability more difficult.[55]

## Ministers

Accountability requirements in Ottawa's machinery of government are built around ministers and their departments. The Royal Commission on Financial Management and Accountability (the Lambert Commission) made this clear. It put this succinctly in its final report by turning to the doctrine of ministerial responsibility, which identifies clearly "who has the final responsibility for decisions taken – the minister, and provides a forum in which he is publicly accountable – Parliament."[56] The PCO tells ministers that they "are accountable to Parliament."[57] It also reminds ministers that the government's accountability requirements centre on ministers individually and collectively. Ministers are the ones who introduce legislation for departments and agencies, defend their departmental budgets before parliamentary committees, and answer all questions about their departments before Parliament and the media. The PCO spells it out clearly: "In providing good government for the people of Canada, Ministers are responsible and accountable to Parliament for the use of those powers vested in them by statute."[58]

Ministers could easily live with the above when government operations were simple enough that they could answer questions about the hiring of an engineer or a clerk in their departments. But things are no longer simple. Some program decisions are now the product of several departments and many hands. What happens when departmental officials make a decision that generates a highly charged political controversy that the minister had no knowledge of before it became public? We have seen a number of such decisions in recent years, with ministers refusing to take responsibility for them.[59] This poses a problem both for the machinery of government and for accountability requirements.

What are public servants to do? If they defend their decisions publicly, they become political actors and risk compromising the status of the public service as a professional non-partisan institution. Taking a position publicly on any issue may well see opposition parties responding by turning it into a partisan political debate. The PCO has remained silent on the issue, likely hoping that these cases will remain isolated. However, the PCO has also noted a difference between ministerial accountability and answerability. It argues that, in many cases, ministers are now only answerable for decisions taken in their departments rather than accountable.[60] The agency argues that answerability only "refers to the duty to inform and explain but does not include the potential personal consequences that are part of accountability."[61] The PCO acknowledges that some statutes assign powers directly to deputy ministers – the *Financial Administrative Act*, the *Public Service Employment Act*, and the *Official Languages Act*. But it is quick to add that "while the Minister cannot provide direction on specific activities in these areas, given the Minister's overall authority for the management and direction of the department, the Minister is responsible for ensuring that the Deputy Minister carries out his or her obligations under these Acts and may provide general direction to the Deputy Minister."[62] The PCO has nothing to offer if ministers are unable to ensure that their deputy ministers carry out their obligations under one of these Acts.

The current machinery of government has no solutions to the continuing weakening of the conventions of ministerial responsibility and the rights and responsibilities of Parliament.[63] Parliament continues to focus on line departments for answers and MPs do not hesitate to look to public servants for answers. Witness that the overwhelming majority of public servants who appear before parliamentary committees – 85 per cent – are from line departments. The fact that the locus of policy making has shifted away from line departments and long-established cabinet and cabinet committees has had little effect on how Parliament holds the government accountable. Central agencies, notably the PCO and the TBS, account for less than 1 per cent of all the organizations that appear before parliamentary committees, with arm's-length organizations accounting for the other 14 per cent.[64] When things go wrong in processing passport applications, in processing cheques, or in delivering programs, it is line departments and their ministers who have to explain the problem and report on what actions they've taken to correct it.

In a majority of instances (70 per cent), public servants appear before parliamentary committees without their ministers. No matter, public servants are expected to provide answers, even if it brings them into a partisan debate. This serves to make public servants less anonymous. Keelan Buck, who reviewed the appearance of public servants before parliamentary committees in Canada between 1995 and 2021, concludes: "The fact that the last 27 years have seen federal public servants become increasingly visible actors in the Canadian parliamentary environment lends further empirical support to the wide-reaching argument that the relationship between political and bureaucratic officials under Westminster no longer ensures or depends on the latter's quiet anonymity."[65]

## Deputy Ministers

The deputy minister occupies a pivotal position in the machinery of government. They stand at the crossroads between elected and non-elected officials and, as one former senior federal public servant writes, "They not only draw the line between the public service and political authority, they embody it."[66] The prime minister, on the advice of the clerk of the Privy Council, appoints deputy ministers. The relevant minister may or may not be consulted in the nomination process – that often depends on how the minister is viewed by the prime minister. Deputy ministers know full well that their past and future promotions were made and will be made by the prime minister on the advice of the clerk of the Privy Council. They may well have a stronger loyalty to these two individuals than to the minister "with whom they work on a daily basis" because it is in their interest. This, however, does little to "promote a single-minded dedication" to the interest of the department that they are asked to lead.[67] However, in the great majority of cases, deputy ministers make every effort to have a solid working relationship with their minister because that is also in their interest.

The PCO underlines three important responsibilities for deputy ministers: provide sound public service advice on policy development, provide effective departmental management, and fulfill the authorities assigned to them by their ministers or directly by legislation.[68] The PCO also reminds deputy ministers that they "must be mindful of their minister's collective responsibilities" when providing advice – hence, they are expected to provide policy advice to both their ministers and to the centre of government as they manage their departments.

The PCO highlights these responsibilities in its *Guidance for Deputy Ministers*.[69] The document explains that deputy ministers "are required to manage a complex set of multiple accountabilities which arise out of the various powers, authorities and responsibilities attached to the position." It adds: "The Deputy is accountable to his or her Minister in relation to both individual and collective responsibilities and, at the same time, they are also accountable to the Prime

Minister, through the Clerk of the Privy Council." Deputy ministers "also have accountabilities to the Public Service Commission and the Treasury Board for specific authorities directly delegated or assigned to them relating to financial and human resource management." Deputy ministers are delegated authority through legislation and certain powers under the *Financial Administration Act*, the *Official Languages Act*, and the *Public Service Employment Act* as well as other specific authorities, such as Customs, Immigration, or the *Income Tax Act*. If the accounting officer concept introduced as part of the Harper government's *Federal Accountability Act* in 2006 is to mean anything, then deputy ministers are also accountable, or at the very least, directly answerable, to Parliament. If deputy ministers find all these requirements difficult to fulfill, they are told to "consult the Clerk of the Privy Council."[70]

Deputy ministers are thus asked to look to the PCO, their ministers and their partisan staff, their departments, several oversight bodies, Parliament and its committees, and other departments and their clients, as they go about their work. In recent years, deputy ministers have been focusing more and more on the centre for direction.[71] This flies in the face of Luther Gulick's warning: "A man cannot serve two masters ... The rigid adherence to the principle of unity of command may have its absurdities; these are, however, unimportant in comparison with the certainty of confusion, inefficiency, and irresponsibility which arise from the violation of the principle."[72]

Deputy ministers also lead an increasingly complex departmental organization. In the fall of 2022, the deputy minister of environment and climate change, for example, had an associate deputy minister, a chief of staff, and thirteen assistant deputy ministers or directors general reporting directly to her.[73] The assistant deputy ministers cover all aspects of environment and climate change, including an assistant deputy minister responsible for "strategic policy," another for "corporate services and finance," one for resources management and human resources, another for public affairs and communications, and a director general responsible for audit and evaluation. Other departments follow the same pattern, adjusted of course for their portfolio responsibilities. Contrast this with a departmental organization in the early 1980s. In her 1981 book, *The Machinery of Government in Canada*, Audrey Doerr outlines the organization of a typical line department. At the time, a typical line department had a deputy minister, a chief of staff or special advisor, an assistant deputy minister responsible for programs and another for policy and planning, and a director general responsible for administration, finance, and human resources. That was it – there were no associate positions or several other assistant deputy ministers.[74]

Deputy ministers have numerous demands on their agenda. They will want to focus on policy, in part because most of them came up through policy work; they will want to keep their ministers out of political hot water because central agency officials are keeping a close eye on such developments; and they will want to keep an eye on Parliament, the media, and their departments' clients to monitor what is said about their departments. They operate not only in a complicated machinery of government but also in a complex and partisan political environment. One senior official explains: "We are in an era in which decision-making is so overly politicized that the role of the professional public servant has become diminished from what it should be. I think there is a broiling of political perspective about the role of the bureaucracy and the work that it does and is challenged to do, and the independence of that in my view is no longer understood or seen by a lot of political bodies, parties, and individuals for what it is truly supposed to be."[75]

There was a time when deputy ministers went to work with only a handful of judges looking over their shoulders – their ministers, the prime minister, Parliament and its committees, the auditor general, the media, and their departmental clients. In most cases, there were also only between two and four assistant deputy ministers reporting directly to them. Things are very different today. As we saw above, deputy ministers now have a multitude of judges looking over their shoulders. Those who urge governments to import private sector management practices to improve their operations should ponder this point. The chain of accountability from one sector to the other is dissimilar in every way. We return to this point below.

In the federal government, there is no straight line from the bottom to the top – responsibility zigzags on the way up and again on the way down. There are many hands in the soup, and everyone along the way has a say, from front-line workers, their managers, several other senior management levels, staffers working in policy units in Ottawa, political staffers, the minister or other central agencies, and the prime minister. The chain of accountability is even more complex because several oversight bodies must be added, as well as Parliament, its committees, the media, and many lobby groups.

What is on the front page of the *Globe and Mail* or *Le Devoir* matters to deputy ministers. While deputy ministers have to balance multiple objectives and numerous accountability requirements, they also have to contend with an inability to clearly establish indicators. One senior public servant once told me that the role of government is to promote "human dignity." I challenge anyone to establish measurable performance indicators to determine how well government is doing in promoting human dignity.

Contrast the above with a chief executive officer in the private sector. If the company is privately held, the CEO sees the owner or owners as often as they want. The CEO of a publicly held firm has a board of directors and shareholders to whom they report. The board meets every quarter or on a needs-only basis. Owners, boards of directors, and CEOs' decision-making machinery is simple and straightforward. Their performance and accountability requirements are equally straightforward, including revenues, expenses, gross profit, market share, productivity per worker, and the like. CEOs and their managers have few judges on their shoulders when they go to work. Gérard Veilleux, a former senior deputy minister with the federal government and later a senior executive with Power Corporation, summed up the difference in this fashion: "In the private sector, you pursue a few unambiguous goals and you manage privately. In the public sector, you have to accommodate many goals, at times conflicting ones, and you manage publicly."[76] In short, governments require a complex and elaborate machinery of government. The private sector does not. Rather than introduce measures to simplify the machinery of government, in recent years governments have done the opposite. They have made it bigger, adding new requirements and new layers, making accountability even more impenetrable.

## LOOKING BACK

The Westminster doctrine of ministerial accountability is on life support. Public servants no longer believe that they are protected by the doctrine and some ministers no longer want to be held responsible for things over which they have no say or control. How does the machinery of government work? The best that can be said is that – it depends. It depends on whether one works in a central agency or in a line department; it depends on the statutes that created the department or agency; it depends on the degree of autonomy from the government the agency enjoys; it depends on whether it is a policy or administrative issue; it depends on whether authority is delegated directly to public servants or not; it depends on whether one talks about accountability, responsibility, or answerability; it depends on whether the matter is relatively self-contained in a department or whether it involves numerous agents and agencies and even other governments; it depends if the media are taking interest in the issue; it depends on the personalities of ministers and their deputy ministers; and it depends on whether central agencies have an interest in the issue. The "it depends" question is tied to the work of anywhere between 130, 207, or 300-plus organizations. Parliament, with MPs' limited knowledge of government operations, and given their backgrounds and the high involuntary turnover at election time, is expected to make sense of it all and to find a way to hold these organizations accountable or, in some cases, answerable.

The machinery of government is failing on several fronts. Senior public servants themselves readily admit that it is still not possible to break down departmental silos or departmentalism. Many issues that were once dealt with by a minister and the department are now kicked upstairs to the centre for resolution. This, among other developments, has created an overload problem, leaving many issues and decisions unattended because the number of issues and decisions the "upstairs" can address has a limit. The machinery has overloaded itself with larger central agencies, more management levels in departments, expanded ministerial offices, added several new oversight bodies, a new vocabulary to describe accountability requirements, and asked deputy ministers to look in several directions – from the prime minister, the clerk of the Privy Council, their ministers and their departments – to establish loyalty and accountability. This, in turn, has substantially weakened accountability and explains, in no small measure, why Canadians are losing trust in public institutions, notably the federal government. It is unlikely that the PCO has raised these concerns with the prime minister or cabinet.

Machinery of government issues, accountability requirements, and the manner in which the government deals with Parliament cry out for a review. However, public servants know well that speaking truth to politicians has its limits. It is also not in the interest of either the prime minister or the PCO to take a fresh look at how the machinery of government operates, how accountability requirements could be updated, or how the government can provide more timely and accessible information to Parliament. If either revised anything in these areas, that would likely weaken the hand of both in developing policy, dealing with controversial issues, and in managing government operations.

# 2

# INWARD LOOKING

Canada's public service shares a number of characteristics with the British and American public services. All three are professional, hierarchical, merit-based, and non-partisan, albeit with some adjustments in the case of the United States' civil service. The Canadian public service, however, stands out from the other two in that it promotes more often from within its ranks and locates more of its members in the National Capital Region (NCR) than either the American or the British civil services. This makes it more insular and inward looking. In Canada, 41.1 per cent of federal public servants are located in the NCR, in sharp contrast to the United States, where only 16 per cent of its career officials live in Washington, DC, and Britain, where only 18.6 per cent of its public servants work in London. This is all the more puzzling given Canada's vast geography and strong regional identities.[1] It also flies in the face of management theory, which makes the case that it is best to locate organizational units close to clients and to delegate more authority to front-line managers.[2]

In the United States, a tier of political appointees at the most senior levels sits between the president and career officials and they bring an outside perspective to government. Presidents are able to fill about 4,000 positions in the executive branch, with some 1,200 requiring senate confirmation. Presidents value loyalty and a close association with their political parties when shaping and implementing policy.[3] This allows for a deep "changing of the guard," in all government departments and agencies, whenever there is a change of government.[4] Many presidential appointees tend to be younger than the career officials occupying senior or mid-level management positions. They also often come from the private sector, academe, or think tanks rather than the public service. They see it as their role to bring an outside perspective to government operations, challenge the status quo, and force career officials to defend both their policies and their operations.[5]

The British civil service, particularly since the Margaret Thatcher years, has moved away from a closed entry system into its managerial ranks, particularly in delivering programs and services.[6] The civil service has established executive agencies, which now account for the majority of public servants, opening up government to outsiders to serve in government at the operations or program level.[7] Executive agencies also enjoy a greater level of independence from their home department than do typical departmental units.[8] In addition, officials in the prime minister's office in Britain, some with limited government experience, have gained both influence and public visibility in recent years in their dealings with career officials. They too bring an outside perspective to government operations. Some are well-known and reputed to have more influence than even the more senior cabinet ministers.[9]

Canada's senior federal public service remains largely closed to outsiders, at least when compared with its American or British counterparts. Unlike the United States, Canada never added a layer of completely politically partisan officials between politicians and career officials or overhauled its machinery of government. Britain recruited from outside its civil service when it introduced the executive agency concept. Canada did make some attempts at establishing Special Operating Agencies (SOAs), highly watered-down versions of Britain's executive agencies. The SOA approach, however, fizzled out after only a few years and few in Ottawa now refer to it. There are still only a handful of SOAs operating in the federal government and no new SOAs have been established in thirty years.

A House of Commons committee concluded in 2019 that "public service positions are often not advertised externally and are, therefore, often limited to existing public service employees, which limits the federal government's ability to attract new talent."[10] The closed hiring process in the Canadian public service is evident at all levels, except for entry level jobs. If open positions are not advertised or open to competition to outside applicants, the merit principle has less weight. It also does not square with a central tenet of Canada's *Public Service Employment Act* which reads: "Persons from across the country have a reasonable opportunity to apply .... And to be considered for public service employment."[11] Ottawa-Gatineau-based public servants also stand a much better chance of making it to the more senior ranks of the federal public service because the great majority of the positions are located in the National Capital Region. We return to this point later.

In March 2022, thirty-seven deputy ministers (permanent heads of government departments and agencies) and thirty-nine associate deputy ministers were listed on the Government of Canada website. All had a public service background before they became deputy ministers, the great majority of them came up through the ranks of the federal public service, and many, at one point, held a position in the PCO.[12] This, too, has made the Canadian public service both highly Ottawa-centric and inward looking, particularly when compared with other public services in the Western Hemisphere.

This, combined with bureaucracy bashing since the 1980s, has led Canadian public servants to look inward for support, to their own institution or to the one institution where they are able to find support. Every year, the clerk of the Privy Council submits a report to the prime minister on the federal public service. Every year, the report sings the praises of the public service, pointing out, among other things, how well it managed the COVID-19 pandemic, how well it deals with harassment and discrimination in the workplace, and how hard public servants work "to support their ministers."[13] The review, however, never reports on when the public service is not up to the task in processing passport applications, on cost overruns in the IT sector, on its inability to make the Phoenix pay system work, on a strong reliance on outside consultants, and the like.

Since the early 1980s, Anglo-American public services have been accused of many things, at times contradictory things and, to be sure, Canada is no exception. Margaret Thatcher said that she disliked bureaucrats as a breed, Ronald Reagan declared on his inaugural day that he had come to Washington to "drain the swamp," and several senior Canadian politicians became openly critical of public servants.[14] Bureaucracy bashing remains in vogue to this day.[15] It explains, in part, why morale in the Canadian public service has plummeted and why federal public servants continue to circle the wagons to protect their institution. It is difficult to promote a confident, outward-looking public service when it is subjected to a never-ending stream of criticism from different sources. However, that is not to suggest that the criticism is invalid.

Some forty years after Thatcher, Reagan, and Mulroney set out to "fix" government bureaucracy, there is no sign that things have improved. The *Economist* magazine declared in early 2022 that though "the British civil service prides itself on being a Rolls-Royce institution but ... a better comparison would be a Morris Minor."[16] One can only imagine what it is like for public servants reading what the *Economist* has to say about their institution – little wonder that they would want to circle the wagons. In Canada, academics, journalists, politicians, and even former senior public servants are increasingly critical of government bureaucracies, generating "a steady stream of commentary on the bureaucracy problem," insisting that government bureaucracies have "become too big, remote, and inefficient."[17]

Public servants may find refuge in circling the wagons but that does not encourage fresh thinking on how to improve the public service's roles in advising on policy and delivering programs. It also follows that circling the wagons does not lead those on the inside to see what ails their institution. Plato's allegory of the cave applies in this case. As the story goes, one prisoner in Plato's cave was able to escape and discovered a new world, a new reality, outside the cave. At first, he does not believe that what he is seeing outside the cave is real. In time, however, he sees that it was the shadows in the cave that gave him a wrong view of things. He returns to the cave to tell the other prisoners that what he saw outside constituted the real world, not the shadows they were seeing in the cave. Those still in the cave do not believe him.[18] They are convinced that the world outside the cave would only be harmful to them and that it is best to stay inside. The cave, at least, offers them security, while the world outside does not.

It is worth repeating what I wrote ten years ago. A retired deputy minister explained to me over breakfast, in no uncertain terms, what was wrong with the Canadian public service. He said: "It is seriously, seriously overstaffed. There are far too many people running around pretending to be busy, creating mindless work for themselves and others. One should just decide one day to cut the size of the public service by half and you would see a dramatic improvement. That is the solution we need to look at, nothing else will work. We have tried everything else and nothing has ever worked."[19] I underline the point that he was a recently retired deputy minister and, strange thing about retired senior public servants, they are quick to see that the federal public service is too big soon after they leave government. They are no longer in the cave and they did not see or did not want to see the problem while they were inside government. When they go back to tell those still inside government that the public service is overstaffed, few inside see it or agree. Like those in Plato's cave, they believe that the world outside the public service would be harmful to them and that it is best not to go outside. Those outside include politicians, the media, the business community, and retired public servants. They see solutions that those on the inside do not see or do not want to see. This is a theme that I will return to.

I recall, as a young public servant in Ottawa, telling my deputy minister that I felt that there were too many people in our central agency for either the mandate or the required work. His reaction was swift. He proceeded to tell me that I was showing a disturbing level of disloyalty to the agency. He pointed out that if I truly felt this way, I should seriously think about leaving. I did leave, both the agency and the government. When I saw him several years later in Ottawa, he too was no longer in government. He was working as an executive in a large national private sector firm. He had just left a meeting at the PCO where, he reported, he had met with some fifteen to twenty public servants to go over what he described as a relatively minor issue. He commented on the waste of talent and resources in government and he made the point that things were not like this at his current workplace or in the private sector. Obviously, he had completely forgotten our conversation of several years earlier, but I had not. When I reminded him, he replied: "There is an old saying in government – in matters of public policy, you stand where you sit."[20]

He was making the case that there is no point in asking a federal government manager if their department, agency, or unit has too many employees. You will never get a straight answer. Instead, you are more likely to hear that still more staff and more resources are needed and that people in their departments and units are stretched to the limit. They see what they want to see or what they prefer to see, much like the prisoners in Plato's cave. So, how and to whom can one ask if the federal government is seriously overstaffed, if managers and their departments invariably argue the opposite? The onus, it seems, is not on managers to defend the level of resources allocated to their units, but rather on those outside, who want to argue that government is overstaffed. The problem is that, when it comes to government, those on the outside have no basis for determining the proper level of resources required to deliver the expected level of services.

I suspect that my former deputy minister felt that, why would he tell anyone that his agency could do what it was asked to do with less staff, while other deputy ministers in a similar situation would never come forward with such a message. Government provides no incentives for senior career officials to downsize their operations. In my book, *The Politics of Public Spending in Canada*, I wrote that when ten people meet for lunch, they have to decide whether they share one cheque or ask for ten separate ones. I argued that if they decide on one shared cheque, they will all choose the most expensive item. But if each were paying individually, they would choose differently.[21] My deputy minister applied the same logic to his agency. I wrote this nearly thirty-five years ago and that logic still applies in government. There are important advantages for senior career officials to look inward to their organizations as they go about their work.

In the fall of 1986, Brian Mulroney, then prime minister, asked me to consult a cross-section of Atlantic Canadians and prepare a report on the establishment of a federal government economic development agency for the region. He unveiled the Atlantic Canada Opportunities Agency (ACOA) in June 1987, a model that was later adopted for all Canadian regions. Mulroney accepted the majority of my recommendations and the report's central theme – entrepreneurship – was and remains key to Atlantic Canada's economic future. I recommended limiting the size of the agency to 100 officials, making the case that other federal government departments and the region's four provincial governments had more programs and human resources available than needed. If ACOA was to focus on entrepreneurs, it was best not to have a bureaucratic approach. Senior agency officials never accepted this recommendation and today the agency employs about 600 officials. I remain in contact with senior agency officials and no one is telling me that they have too many staff. Often they argue quite the opposite. I know the agency and its programs well and I still do not see why ACOA needs 600 full-time equivalents (FTEs) to deliver its programs.

In preparing the report, I worked directly with two senior government officials from the PCO, John (Jack) A. Manion, the associate clerk of the PCO, and Dalton Camp, a senior advisor in the PCO. Camp was appointed to a senior PCO position rather than in the

PMO, even though he was a well-known partisan supporter of the party in power. He also had, however, a distinguished career in the private sector and as a journalist-author.

Manion supported my work throughout the exercise. He volunteered advice on the machinery of government, on how the new agency should relate to other government departments and agencies, and on how it should deal with central agencies. In the past, I had helped Manion build a management development centre for the federal public service, later serving as his deputy. I had also worked with officials in the PCO and the Treasury Board Secretariat (TBS). Thus, I knew those inside the cave and how they went about their work. Manion and other senior PCO officials also understood that I knew my way around the federal government.

Camp, meanwhile, although he had strong personal ties to Atlantic Canada and took a keen interest in my work, did not know his way around government operations. In our many discussions while working on my report, he told me that he had great difficulty being heard in the Ottawa bureaucracy. Camp once said that the federal bureaucracy was "fighting him and his ideas off like antibodies": senior public servants blocked his input at every turn and the "bureaucrats always closed ranks" whenever he tried to influence how the agency should operate and what programs it should offer. It became clear that Camp had little influence inside government and in how ACOA took shape.

## PUBLIC SERVANTS DO NOT WANT OUTSIDERS INSIDE THEIR SQUARE

There is no reason for government departments to open up to outsiders and to share their concerns outside the immediate ambit of the department. There is no advantage but plenty of disadvantages in doing so. Organizational principles in government bureaucracies, going back to its early days, are built around top-down management control and processes. Government departments are silos because they were initially designed as such and their organizational hierarchies have long "underpinned a closed bureaucrat–bureaucrat relationship."[22]

Many government managers see a need to protect their units and their departments because no one else will. A culture of secrecy permeates government departments, so that, unless departments and their managers are compelled to share information with outsiders, they will not do so. Why would they? There is simply no advantage in sharing information or stepping outside the comfort zone that their departmental units offer.

Departments operate, to the extent that they can, as closed shops for several reasons, other than protecting their self-interest. For one thing, senior departmental managers argue that they always operate in a fishbowl – they deal with central agencies; several oversight bodies; Parliament; the media, always on the lookout for missteps; access to information legislation; and lobbyists and their clients. They know that success stories in government are rarely reported in the media or outside government but that missteps or administrative miscues often enjoy wide media attention. For another, they associate the pursuit of efficiency with their ability to exercise authority and make decisions quickly whenever the need arises while running a tight ship, free of outside interference. They can quote no less an authority than Max Weber to make their case: "[S]peed, unambiguity, knowledge of files, continuity, discretion, unity, strict subordination, reduction of friction and material costs – these are raised to the optimum point in the strictly bureaucratic administration."[23] I note, however, that Weber's work dates back over a century.

The departmental structure allows for political and administrative control. Hierarchy also enables departmental officials to close ranks to outsiders and allows ministers to reach down into their departments to secure answers to any question. That, at least, has been the thinking for generations. However, by the 1980s, ministers began to question their ability to provide policy direction to their departments and make it stick and they decided to do something about it. Career officials, meanwhile, still continue to try to close ranks but the task is now more difficult, at least when it comes to politicians on the government side.

## A STRONGER POLITICAL PRESENCE

Things have changed since 1986–87 when Camp tried to influence government decision making. Career officials no longer have the same capacity to fight partisan political advisors with the antibodies they once had. Partisan political advisors today have a much stronger presence and more influence in Ottawa. The thinking took hold in the 1980s, first in Britain and then later in Canada, that career officials had too much influence in shaping policies and that politicians needed a firmer grip on the policy-making levers. Politicians decided to do something about it by growing the size of their offices and adding more senior-level politically partisan officials.

Up to the early 1980s, a minister's office in Ottawa typically had a political exempt staff of three or four – an executive assistant, a legislative assistant, a departmental assistant, and perhaps a policy advisor, in addition to several administrative staff loaned to the office from the department to look after correspondence and the flow of documents to and from ministerial offices.[24] They were, and still are, labelled exempt staff because they are appointed by the minister, to serve at their pleasure, and are exempt from the staffing procedures of the Public Service Commission. Until about forty years ago, it was widely accepted throughout the federal government that deputy ministers were the unquestioned policy advisors to their ministers. I recall a senior deputy minister telling me in the mid-1980s that ministers did not need a policy advisor on their exempt staff because the department provided all the policy advice a minister required and that the deputy minister should always be viewed as the minister's senior policy advisor. But again, that was then, though the PCO still identifies the deputy minister as a minister's unquestioned policy advisor.[25]

Today, a minister has some twenty-two exempt staff members in addition to the staff loaned to their office by the department to look after documents flowing to and from ministerial offices and other administrative issues of interest to the department. In the summer of 2022, a minister in the Justin Trudeau government had a chief of staff, a deputy chief of staff, a director of operations, a director of policy, a senior policy advisor, two policy advisors, four regional affairs advisors, a director of parliamentary affairs, a senior advisor for issues management, three special assistants, and a four-member communications team headed by a director.[26] What are all these people doing, given that all government departments and agencies also have numerous policy advisors and policy analysts on staff as well as many communications specialists? Ministers and their staff answer this question by simply pointing to the need to counterbalance the advice and work of thousands of career officials. Partisan advisors do not sit idle in their offices – they will want to be relevant by being involved and have influence with their ministers and departments. They will also generate work for departmental officials, who are the ones called on to answer questions and to provide information to keep ministerial offices informed of new developments.

Former British cabinet minister Richard Crossman opened a veritable floodgate of criticism against government bureaucracies and the need for non-departmental policy advice when he published his widely read diaries. He wrote: "Whenever one relaxes one's guard the Civil Service in one's Department quietly asserts itself ... Just as the Cabinet Secretariat constantly transforms the actual proceedings of Cabinet into the form of the Cabinet minutes (i.e., it substitutes what we should have said if we had done as they wished for what we actually did say), so here in my Department the civil servants are always putting in what they think I should have said and not what I actually decided."[27] Another former British cabinet minister argued that the problem with the civil service was that it "sees itself as being above the party battle, above partisan politics, albeit with a political position of its own to defend against all comers, including incoming governments armed with their philosophy and program."[28]

By the late 1970s and early 1980s, politicians on both the political right and left in Canada had also begun to turn on the public service. One senior Progressive Conservative cabinet minister, Flora MacDonald, went on the lecture circuit to denounce senior public servants, claiming that when she served as the minister of external affairs they employed clever ruses to push their own agendas and to circumvent cabinet and ministerial direction. She itemized what she termed the officials' entrapment devices for ministers, including bogus policy options and delayed recommendations. The prime minister at the time, Joe Clark, also became critical of the public service, speaking of misguided programs "concocted by a small group of theorists" within the public service.[29]

That members of the Progressive Conservative party would be critical of the public service surprised few people, given that they had been in the opposition bench in Parliament for over fifteen years before the party won power in 1979. It was, however, a different story to find leading members of the centre-left Liberal party also doing so. The Liberal party had held office for forty-four of the fifty years between 1930 and 1980 and had enjoyed a particularly close working relationship with the public service. It surprised more than a few people in Ottawa's political and administrative circles when Allan MacEachen, a senior and long-time leading member of the Liberal party and deputy prime minister, who had established a strong working relationship with senior public servants, reported that, if Liberals had learned anything during their brief stay in opposition, it was that they would no longer rely, as much as they had, on the advice of senior public servants. Other senior Liberals also joined in and publicly criticized public servants' policy advice and capacity to manage their departments.[30]

Derek Bok summed things up when he argued that anti-civil-service views "are not held only by the uninformed; opinion polls consistently show that respect for government servants steadily dwindles as one moves up the scale of education and income. Indeed, among the more affluent and better educated, one of the few things that unites the left and the right is their common disdain for bureaucrats."[31] Bok made these observations over thirty years ago and disenchantment with career government officials has, if anything, only grown since then. Little wonder that public servants decided to circle the wagons, convinced that few outside their ranks understood their work and challenges or were willing to come to their defence. The desire to circle the wagons is, if anything, stronger today than in years past because the federal public service today feels even more threatened by outsiders, including substantially enlarged ministerial offices.

Career government officials, at least before they retire or leave government, do not see or, at least, do not wish to see flaws in their institution. One senior Canadian deputy minister, Bev Dewar, summed up the views of many career officials well when he said that politicians should heal their own institution before they try to heal the public service. He maintained that the workings of the country's political institutions were far more deeply flawed than those of the federal public service and that it was best to start there. Better to begin by fixing political institutions, starting with Parliament, how cabinet decides, political parties, voter turnout, and how ministers and their political advisors work with government departments. His perspective still resonates with many career officials.[32]

Public servants, particularly in machine-like organizations, that is, departments and agencies that deliver programs and services, see two different worlds with distinct interests – the political world and their own. A senior deputy minister insisting that politicians need to heal their own institutions before trying their hand at healing the public service speaks to this perspective. Public servants seeing the prime minister and ministers substantially enlarge their offices to check on their growing influence does not offer much promise in healing either political institutions or government operations. If anything, it encourages public servants to close ranks further and to look after only their own economic interest.

Politicians set out to deal with the influence of government bureaucracies by establishing parallel partisan bureaucracies in their own offices. The PMO and ministerial offices have all grown over the past fifty years. Large expanded ministerial offices have, however, made government bureaucracies thicker (they have had to grow larger to respond to constant demands for information from ministerial offices), slower (because they need to run many initiatives and decisions by ministerial advisors), and more costly (by expanding both ministerial offices and departments). In the process, these changes have blurred accountability further.

Parallel bureaucracies in ministerial offices have made government organizations still more defensive, more inward looking, more insular, and more cautious. Other developments have also contributed to this state of affairs, including: an increased level of bureaucracy bashing, stronger transparency requirements, public sector unions, and a blurring of the line between politics and public administration.

The behaviour of career government officials can be better understood if we give the necessary attention to the organizational culture of the federal public service. That culture is shaped by precedent, shared beliefs, values, attitudes, and self-interest. It has not been given the attention necessary to understand the behaviour of career government officials. There are many levels of culture in the federal public service, all of which influence individual and organizational behaviour.[33] For example, the organizational culture in a central agency or in the Department of Finance differs from that found in a line department such as Canadian Heritage, Fisheries and Oceans, or the regional development agencies. I maintain, however, that the federal public service does have an overall organizational culture, i.e., one that applies to the bureaucracy as a whole. It places a premium on protecting the interests of its members whenever their institutions or organizations are challenged. All organizations, public or private, will want to limit their vulnerabilities when attacked. The federal public service is certainly no exception. Government bureaucracies, however, have a number of advantages that other sectors do not have to help them protect their interests.

Three major developments have shaped the organizational culture in the federal public service: bureaucracy bashing, the changing relationship between politicians and career officials, and collective bargaining. The first two have been fully explored in the literature, the third much less so. Collective bargaining has a lot to answer for in protecting non-performers and insulating the public sector from effective outside scrutiny. Its effect on management in government far outweighs the various management reform measures that Ottawa has introduced over the past thirty years. We will return to collective bargaining later.

## POLITICIANS AND PUBLIC SECTOR MANAGEMENT

The prime minister, the PMO, senior ministers, and their political advisors have gained the upper hand in areas that matter to them politically. They have also taken control of political spin to defuse political crises. As for the rest, prime ministers and their staff, and senior cabinet ministers with influence prefer to let programs continue running smoothly, unless they create political problems or negative media attention. When it comes to the machinery of government, managing government operations, or dealing with issues that do not hold the interest of the most senior politicians and their partisan advisors, government bureaucracies will be free to manage things, always careful that they do not bring media attention to themselves or create problems for the prime minister and government. Senior politicians, even those sitting on the government side, have a limited interest but also a limited capacity to deal with government operations issues. As a result, senior public servants remain in the driver's seat on managing government operations, notably on issues that hold little political or media interest; for public servants, that's just as well because they insist that the responsibility belongs to them, not ministers.

Management in the federal government has become so opaque that few outside the federal government understand it or its shortcomings. Increasingly, it is also the case even for many inside government. No matter, there is plenty of evidence, anecdotal or otherwise, to suggest that the federal government has weak management practices and that they have not gone unnoticed outside government.[34] A public opinion survey carried out in 2016 reveals that "only six per cent" of Canadians expressed a lot of trust in senior federal public servants.[35] From time to time, the media report on management issues in the federal public service and also, on occasion, on the "growth in the public service." However, it is rare for the media to fully explore issues dealing with the size or role of the public service or how well government operations are managed. The *Globe and Mail*, for example, reported in January 2022 that the federal bureaucracy had grown by about 25 per cent over a six-year period, adding that spending on outsourced contracts had also grown by 41.8 per cent during the same period. It left it at that and other media outlets did not pick up on the article.[36]

When they come to power, politicians are given briefing books that urge them to deal with key policy issues and to pursue the priorities established by the prime minister and the party's policy commitments made during the last election campaign. The underlying message is clear: leave management to career officials. The briefing books remind politicians that administrative questions are not political questions. Public servants can point to several statutes to make the point – among others, the *Financial Administration Act*, the *Public Service Employment Act*, and the *Official Languages Act*, delegate authority away from ministers and directly to public servants.

This does not, however, prevent public servants in a Westminster parliamentary system from arguing that they are not accountable before Parliament, even for their activities under acts that delegate authority directly to them. Therein lies the problem. It begs the question – to whom are they accountable? Public servants also maintain that the public service does not have a personality distinct from the government of the day.[37] Robert Armstrong spoke for all public servants in Westminster-inspired parliamentary systems in 1985 when he wrote: "Civil servants are servants of the Crown. For all practical purposes the Crown in this context ... is represented by the Government of the day .... The Civil Service has no constitutional personality or responsibility separate from the duly elected government of the day."[38] This view has been challenged of late, and even Armstrong himself, once retired, saw the need for fresh thinking on the issue because he saw "a gradually increasing lack of trust in government."[39] His comment makes the case, once again, that public servants can have a change of mind on fundamental issues once they leave government or Plato's cave.

Senior Canadian public servants, even more so than in Britain, continue to make this case. The federal government, in its final submission to the 1995 Gomery Inquiry, felt the need to restate the point that "public servants as such have no constitutional identity independent of their ministers."[40] In 2006, the federal government adopted the British accounting officer concept, designed to strengthen the accountability of senior public servants. The concept makes the permanent secretary – the equivalent of our deputy minister – personally accountable to Parliament for the use of public funds.[41] However, Canada did not go nearly as far as Britain did in implementing the concept.

I recall senior public servants telling me that the accounting officer concept was a "train wreck in the making" when the idea was debated in Ottawa before it was introduced. They saw problems with pitting ministers against their deputy ministers before Parliament and the media. The concept has now been in place for nearly twenty years and it has yet to produce even a fender bender. Jean Chrétien committed to introducing the accounting officer concept but never followed through. Stephen Harper did introduce the concept shortly after he came to power but it is a far cry from what he envisaged while in opposition. One can assume that the PCO talked both of them out of the British model. The accounting officer concept has been debased in Canada to the point where one former senior federal public servant labelled it a "fraud," insisting that Ottawa had embraced the concept in name only. He explained that deputy ministers "still have neither the obligation nor the tools to draw a line, where needed, between political and public service accountability."[42]

Even so, Ottawa made sure that the accounting officer concept would remain "within the framework of ministerial responsibility," by once again making the point that the public service has no personality independent of the government of the day.[43] The PCO wants to make certain that public servants understand that their responsibility under the concept does not change how they deal with Parliament and its committees. It tells public servants that, when they appear before parliamentary committees, they appear "not as individuals but as representatives of someone else – the minister."[44] And in its submission to the Gomery Commission, the government made no mention of the authority that is delegated directly to public servants. Thus, the status quo, when it comes to accountability, remains intact. The PCO squares the circle by arguing that, in cases where authority is delegated by statutes to public servants, ministers become "answerable" to Parliament, rather than accountable, a distinction that weakens ministers' accountability further.

Accountability for public servants in the federal government now lacks clarity, even for public servants themselves. This serves the interest of both politicians and career officials. For example, even two former clerks of the PCO disagreed on a fundamental tenet of accountability. One of them, Jocelyne Bourgon, insisted that "where authority resides, so resides accountability." Another, Alex Himelfarb, argued the opposite, insisting that "authority can be delegated, but accountability can't."[45] Yet somehow we expect members of Parliament with a limited understanding of the ways of government, let alone Canadians, to make sense of it all when two former heads of the federal public service cannot.

Relations between politicians and public servants are still guided by a long-standing doctrine: the doctrine of ministerial responsibility, which combines the collective and individual responsibility of ministers. The doctrine has long been held to be the cornerstone that guides the relationship between parliaments, ministers, and public servants in Westminster-inspired parliamentary systems. However, in his seminal work on relations between politicians and career officials, Geoffrey Marshall argued that the doctrine is "vague and slippery" in that "collective and individual responsibility are two doctrines, not one and each divide in turn into a series of disparate topics."[46]

The notion that public servants are anonymous or that their every act is, legally speaking, the act of a minister, is still alive and well in some circles in Ottawa. And yet, what was once taken for granted no longer holds water. Consider the following: "Ministers are responsible for the misdeeds of civil servants; the minister is responsible for every stamp stuck on an envelope, when things go right ministers take the credit, when things go wrong they take the blame, if necessary, they offer their resignation, civil servants are anonymous and their personal failures are not matter of knowledge or debate."[47] Things no longer work this way and there are numerous recent examples where ministers or public servants did not respect the above convention.[48] In addition, no one has been able to square the requirements with the argument that "authority can be delegated, but accountability can't."

Both politicians and career officials now live in a world where they are able to take the blame but, at the same time, not accept blame. Career officials prefer it this way and so do politicians. Why would career officials and politicians want to make it easier to be held to account for their activities? They know that they operate in a fishbowl where everything is fair game and where, other than the prime minister, few own what they say, own what they do, and own their mistakes. Senior public servants will make every effort, as they did when Ottawa introduced the accounting officer concept, to keep looking inward to their institution and its long-established accountability requirements. This is easier to understand for machine-like organizations than it is for the coping-policy organizations, or agencies that have no programs or responsibility to deliver services. No matter, it holds an important advantage – it enables the public service to close ranks and keep looking inward.

Accountability in government is all too often about avoiding or diverting blame when things go wrong. No one knows better than politicians and career officials that this is the best possible approach to accountability – they know full well that the only interest opposition parties and the media have lies in reporting when things go off the rails, not when they go well. For senior career officials, it is best to avoid talking about either successes or failures altogether. Talking about success will make them visible outside the public service and there is simply no advantage for public servants to being visible before Parliament and the media. A senior Canadian central agency official explains: "My job here is to fall on hand grenades. Our role is to manage problems so that they do not become unmanageable political crises."[49] If failures should happen in government operations, then every effort should be made to ensure that public servants somehow do not become public actors by having to explain why the failures took place.

Everyone with a responsibility in addressing any shortcomings in the relationship between ministers and career officials has purposely avoided doing so. Although the PCO has kept the accountability requirements identified in Britain well over a century ago, Britain has moved away from them.[50] Neither the Glassco, Lambert, nor Gomery commissions, all with a mandate to look at government operations, ever fully addressed how public servants should deal with ministers and Parliament. The view still holds that the machinery of government, the workings of ministerial responsibility, and defining the relationship between bureaucrats and politicians should remain primarily the responsibility of career government officials in the PCO.[51] For senior public servants, it is best to make every effort to keep things that speak directly to their interest inside their tent.

Things are different in the private sector. Tobias Lutke, CEO of Shopify, one of Canada's leading e-commerce firms, told his staff and the media that he "got it wrong" when he expanded the firm by adding thousands of new employees. He unveiled a staff reduction of "1,000" in July 2022 and suggested that there could well be more layoffs in the coming months. Shopify explained that it would eliminate "over-specialized and duplicate roles."[52] Lutke was owning what he did and owning his mistakes. Unlike the government, Lutke owned the problem because he had the authority to deal with it and because the stock market kept a close eye on the firm's performance.

Deputy ministers in Ottawa would not write a memo to staff or to anyone saying that they "got it wrong." Why would they? For one thing, there are always many hands in the soup, a situation ripe for those who want to avoid blame: the deputy minister can always point the finger at the minister, at the PMO, at central agencies, at a lack of resources, at collective bargaining, and at the work of other governments or other departments working at cross purposes. The list goes on. I have been around government long enough to know that federal government departments have many over-specialized and duplicate roles, that something should be done about it, and that only senior public servants are in a position to deal with the problem. But career government officials have no incentive and no interest in dealing with the issue.

### INSIDE THE CAVE

All line government departments are inward looking by design. The public administration literature has focused of late on how best to deal with the "silos" problem. The challenge, in a nutshell, is government's failure to promote horizontal coordination, i.e., how best to promote coordination in an established structure of departmental silos or departments with specific mandates to deal with, say, agriculture, health or public safety.

The challenge is longstanding. It has, however, become even more visible in recent years because of the growth in the number of government programs and because modern public policy problems cut across many departments. Still, the coordination challenge goes back to bureaucracy's early days. Rome developed a bureaucracy to manage its empire and it looked to the military model to grow it, adopting a hierarchy and a chain of command from the top down.

It divided responsibility by functions, which gave rise to silos.[53] The Westminster parliament also picked up the Roman military model for its bureaucracy. English kings and queens embraced its top-down command and control concept which enabled them to exert greater authority over their government's activities. The same can be said for prime ministers, as power shifted from monarchs to Parliament and then to prime ministers.

The military command and control model places a premium on secrecy, for obvious reasons. The consequences of losing information to the enemy can be catastrophic. The same can be said for government departments. There is no advantage, but plenty of disadvantages, for departments to share their management problems with anyone outside the department. Government departments, like the military, have always been able to close ranks to protect their interest. We have seen, in recent years, the growth of "defensive values" in government operations in response to more demanding access to information legislation and other efforts to make government operations more transparent.[54] We should expect nothing less, given bureaucracy bashing; the rise of social media with limited editorial control; permanent election campaigns; the twenty-four-hour cable news channels fuelling the blame game; and politicians, even on the government side, less willing to come to the defence of career officials and accept responsibility when things go wrong.

## LOOKING BACK

Government bureaucracies, going back to their early days, have always sought to keep information about their work away from outside prying eyes. Those inside departments will always be careful not to voice criticisms toward their departments or programs, and with good reason. Outside voices are rarely there to applaud the work of government departments, so that, information, good or bad, is best kept inside government. Things, however, are different when public servants leave their departments to retire or go to the private sector. They are then far more willing to point to weak management practices, to overstaffing problems, and to the need to make government operations more transparent.[55] But it is very different for public servants still on the inside. They pay little attention to these challenges and are unwilling to open up their operations to outsiders – hence the analogy to Plato's cave.

This is true for all governments everywhere. It is an integral part of the organizational culture found in government bureaucracies. The Canadian public service is widely known for keeping things – good or bad – inside the tent, more so than other public services. Dennis Grube, in his comparative study of the British, American, Canadian, Australian, and New Zealand public services, found that Canada's federal public service is the most "reticent" at opening up to the public,[56] and the most "risk averse," and has a much stronger desire to "avoid controversy."[57] One senior Canadian public servant told Grube: "I think the faceless bureaucrat is an objective I want to aspire to."[58]

Public servants in line departments are circling the wagons at the same time as ministers are expanding their offices with partisan political staffers. This, also at a time when the media, in all their forms, continually try to pry more and more information from government departments. It follows that the departments would want to put up defensive strategies to protect their interest. These strategies, however, fly in the face of measures expressly designed to open up government departments (e.g., access to information legislation) and efforts to evaluate performance by adding many evaluation, policy, and coordination-liaison units in government departments. These were designed to shed light on management deficiencies and also to strengthen management practices by attaching a series of performance indicators to various activities. These and other efforts have done the opposite of what they sought to accomplish. They have made government departments thicker and more difficult for outsiders, including central agencies, members of Parliament, and the media, to grasp the inner workings of line departments and agencies. In short, departments today are more inward looking. It is far more difficult than in years past for those on the outside, even central agencies charged with management oversight, to assess performance or even determine the required level of resources needed to deliver programs and services. In the process, accountability requirements have been weakened.

# 3

# POETS AND PLUMBERS

When asked about the role they and their departments play in Canadian society, senior federal public servants invariably point to carefully selected activities that connect them directly to Canadians. They point to the Canadian Coast Guard, which deals with marine search and rescue, navigation and transportation issues, and other front-line activities. The Coast Guard agency employs 4,500 in various settings, including operating a Coast Guard college.[1] They also point to the Canadian Food Inspection Agency and its ability to safeguard food, animals, and plants, or to public servants managing Canada's Old Age Security program. Canadians can easily relate to the work of agencies with which they have direct contact. However, these activities hardly tell the whole story.

As we saw earlier, the government of Canada is now home to anywhere between 130, 207, or over 300 organizations, depending on what is included. The government employed 319,601 people in 2021–22, up from 300,450 a year earlier.[2] It divides employees into two groups – core public administration (245,739) and separate agencies (73,862). Separate agencies include organizations that conduct their own negotiations with employees and may have their own distinct classification system.[3] Employees in separate agencies remain federal public servants and enjoy all the same benefits as core public administration employees.

The Canada Revenue Agency (CRA) is one such separate agency. It was established in 1999 as part of New Public Management reform measures. The thinking was that the measures would improve management by removing more centrally prescribed rules and regulations, and delegating greater management authority directly to the agency and to its front-line managers. Both the CRA and central agencies would benefit from a new management approach with a greater emphasis on performance evaluation efforts. The agency has a board of management responsible for financial resources, administration services, property, and human resources. Its organizational structure, however, looks like any other government department and the agency manages the collective bargaining process like other departments.[4] There is little documented or even anecdotal evidence to suggest that management at the CRA is stronger than in a typical line department or than it was before it became an agency. Media reports reveal that the agency had to hire outside consultants to deal "with bullying and harassment" and to address the widespread belief that most of its staff members "feel that their unit is ineffective." A recent consultant report found "a toxic climate inside the agency"[5] – so much for better management performance when removing centrally prescribed rules.

The Government of Canada, through its TBS, which represents the employer, negotiates collective agreements with up to twenty-eight bargaining units that cover a wide array of functions, including aircraft operations, education and library science, foreign services, and program and administrative services.[6] Front-line managers have little say in the collective bargaining process – they are left to implement what was decided at the negotiation table.

The 320,000 federal government employees still do not tell the whole story. Ottawa often turns to outside experts to carry out a number of activities. One can consult the websites of federal government departments and agencies to see the variety of consultants or outside contracts, which range from helping in the information technology sector to ideas on how best to improve management practices and program efficiency. The Justin Trudeau Liberals pledged in the 2015 election campaign to establish greater efficiency controls in the spending of public funds and pointed to outside consultants as one area that called for more scrutiny.[7] However, since 2015, Ottawa's spending on outsourced contracts has increased by 41.8 per cent, while the size of the federal public service has also grown by about 25 per cent.[8]

## A LOT OF POETS

A question that we need to address is how many of the 320,000 federal public servants provide services directly to Canadians. We know that a number of agencies are focused exclusively on internal machinery of government issues, back-office services, and oversight functions and have very little to no direct dealings with Canadians. I am thinking, among others, of the TBS, the Public Service Commission of Canada, the PCO, the Public Servants Disclosure Protection Tribunal, and the list goes on and on. All departments and agencies also have units that have no or very few dealings directly with Canadians outside of the federal public service. Yet, again, senior government officials often stress the importance of delivering "direct services to citizens such as veterans' benefits; unemployment insurance; retraining and relocation for workers; statistical information; foreign aid; passports; consular services abroad; export promotion; tourism development; parks; fishery development; ports and small craft harbours; navigational aids; search and rescue; regional and industrial development" whenever they are asked about their work.[9]

The annual report on the federal public service tabled by the clerk of the PCO makes a point every year of emphasizing the program and service-delivery role public servants play in serving Canadians. I have yet to see a discussion about public servants in policy, program evaluation, coordination, or liaison units. Clerks also only report good news – the 2022 report, for example, makes the point that one federal government agency was able to register a 20 per cent reduction in approval times for small grants and contributions.[10] The 26th annual report states that three public servants "met beyond Iqaluit's rough sea ice and travelled by snowmobile across Frobisher Bay to the eastern entrance of Katannilik Territorial Park. This unconventional arrival earned community recognition. Their meetings in Kimmirut helped these public servants gain a much deeper understanding of, and respect for, the challenges and opportunities of this community."[11] Nothing was said about how service delivery was actually improved or if the authors of the report had consulted those on the receiving end of the services to see if they had seen any improvements. I have yet to read in any of the reports about where and when things have gone wrong in service delivery. There has, however, been no shortage of such cases.[12]

Public sector unions, when opposing cuts to the public service, also invariably refer to food inspectors, public health specialists, search and rescue workers, and the employees who deliver cheques to unemployed Canadians.[13] They never refer to the numerous policy, coordination, liaison, and performance evaluation units found in all government departments and agencies. Recent federal government decisions often went in the opposite direction of strengthening service delivery to Canadians. Regional and local offices have lost both staff and standing in relation to Ottawa-based head offices. A government survey was carried out in the 1980s to identify all jobs that had at least some responsibility for dealing with the general public, even if that "some" amounted to no more than 10 per cent of their work.[14] The survey found that only about 40 per cent of public servants dealt with the public as one of their responsibilities – again, even if it amounted to only 10 per cent of their work. The government has never updated this survey – it is easy to understand why. The percentage of public servants who deal directly with Canadians has very likely gone down in light of the trend, in recent years, to concentrate more public servants in the National Capital Region (NCR).

We have reached the point where over 60 per cent of federal public servants now work in policy advisory, coordination, oversight, and back-office functions, the bulk of them in the NCR, dealing with other federal public servants rather than delivering services to other Canadians. I know of no private sector firm that would tolerate such a ratio. If it did, depending on the nature of the business, it would not be in business for long. As a former senior federal government executive wrote, service delivery remains a "poor cousin" to policy and efforts to improve program implementation have "never lived up to their promise." He added that "it is harder for governments to be open about service delivery issues than it is for the private sector."[15] Peter Harder, a former senior deputy minister in several departments, including the TBS, referred in a media interview, to two kinds of federal public servants: poets (policy) and plumbers (those on the front line delivering programs and services). He added that the "credibility comes from the plumbing side. We have to get the basics right if we want to talk about policy issues."[16]

The more senior management levels you add in government, the more poets you will have. Some forty years ago, the TBS decided that reducing management levels would both "improve government operations and morale." It expressed concern that the executive category had grown to 2,562 members, pointing out that "if you take a whole layer out of the management pyramid, then the managers below automatically gain greater control over their operations."[17] In 1990, then prime minister Mulroney, with the full support of Paul Tellier, clerk of the Privy Council, called on all agencies and departments to launch their own reviews with the objective of "delayering" management levels.[18] Nothing came of these commitments and no one has even been held to account for the failure, either at the political or public service level. It is not even clear that anyone remembers that these commitments were ever made. Clerks of the Privy Council, who double up as secretaries to the cabinet and heads of the public service, have an opportunity every year to explain why the government keeps adding management levels in its annual reports to the prime minister on the public service. Not one of the twenty-nine reports has ever dealt with the issue.

The Chrétien-Martin program review of the mid-1990s eliminated a number of positions (45,000) and transferred federal government responsibilities to provincial governments and communities, including the management of airports and ports. Regardless, executive management positions have kept growing from that moment on. The Stephen Harper government declared its intention to eliminate management levels when it launched its 2012 program review, and hired outside consultants to give it a hand. By 2010, the executive category had grown to 6,784.[19] The outside help may well have worked, but only temporarily. By 2015, the number of executives had fallen to 6,400.[20] By 2021, however, that number had grown to about 8,000.[21] In six years, the executive category had grown by 1,600 without anyone in government explaining why. I do not think that politicians are responsible for this growth, any more than public servants are responsible for the remarkable growth in the number of partisan political staffers in ministerial offices. In government, growth fuels more growth.

## THE COST

The federal government does not provide a breakdown of organizational units or the type of work it houses in its departments and agencies. Ottawa's expenditure budget, however, does provide some answers. The federal government breaks down its spending plans under two distinct settings – statutory items and items that Parliament votes every year. For 2022–23, the expenditure budget amounted to $397.6 billion, with 52 per cent, or $207.3 billion, coming from statutory authorities and $190.3 billion coming from voted authorities.[22] Statutory expenditures have continuing authorities and are part of the main spending estimates, essentially for information purposes. Voted expenditures are approved by Parliament annually and the authorization ends at the close of the fiscal year.

Several categories made up the 2022–23 $207.3 billion in statutory spending. They included old age security ($52.2 billion), health transfers ($45.2 billion), equalization payments ($21.92 billion), servicing the debt ($18.74 billion), social transfers ($25.94 billion), guaranteed income supplement ($15.45 billion), climate action incentive payments ($7.09 billion), interest costs ($4.86 billion), territorial financing ($4.55 billion), payments to the Canada Infrastructure Bank ($4.53 billion) and other statutory items ($16.76 billion). The government did not provide its spending plan for "personnel expenditures" for fiscal year 2022–23.[23] We know that health transfers, equalization payments, servicing the debt, and other statutory payments employ a limited number of public servants, who are mostly poets. Provincial governments provide the plumbers to deliver programs, financed in part by federal health transfers and equalization payments, directly to Canadians.

The federal government's wage bill is, to a large extent, devoted to non-statutory spending, 48 per cent of the total budget.[24] Ottawa's wage bill amounted to $60 billion in fiscal year ending 2021, about one-third of non-statutory spending. This includes personnel costs for salaries, pension benefits, and overtime. The average cost per employee in fiscal year 2019 was $121,000.[25] The cost is expected to increase for 2023 and in subsequent years, given the number of collective agreements that have recently been negotiated. The data does not include Crown corporations, the uniformed employees of the RCMP, or the 93,000 plus employees at the Department of National Defence.[26]

It is possible to look at government spending by function on a per capita basis, not only for the federal government, but also in comparison with the provinces. Provincial governments hold jurisdictions that are labour-intensive, notably health care, education, and social services. In 2020, the federal government spent $2,904 per capita on general public services, $2,778 on economic affairs, and $1,328 on debt transactions. In contrast, Ontario, for example, spent $1,345 per capita on general public services, $5,400 on health care, and $2,869 on education.[27] General public services include spending on "the administration, development, and management of general public services."[28] Ottawa has never explained why the federal government spends more on general public services than provincial governments, even though the provinces hold jurisdiction over many of the more labour-intensive sectors.

In most cases, federal departments and agencies have a standard organizational structure. Their policy, administrative, financial, audit and program evaluation units are populated by poets. For example, Innovation, Science and Economic Development Canada has a strategy, results and research branch, a trade policy branch, a telecom and internet policy branch, strategic planning and corporate services branch, small business, digital transformation sector, an industry sector, a spectrum and telecommunications sector, a science and research sector, and five small regional offices. The department is headed by a deputy minister, and also includes an associate deputy minister, two senior assistant deputy ministers, a dozen assistant deputy ministers, and several associate assistant deputy ministers. They lead a management team that includes numerous directors general, directors, and managers. The department employs some 6,000 "full-time equivalents" in its core responsibilities.[29] I recall in the 1980s when a few federal government departments had only a few "associate" positions attached to senior executive positions. Today, all government departments have a growing number of them. It is safe to assume that the push to create "associate" positions came from senior public servants, not politicians.

Central agencies have a similar organizational structure but without regional offices or a program delivery capacity. The Department of Finance has a deputy minister, two associate deputy ministers, a senior assistant deputy minister, twelve assistant deputy ministers, five associate assistant deputy ministers, and a number of directors general and directors managing a staff complement of 929 full-time equivalents.[30] Senior executives enjoy higher classification and higher pay than their counterparts in line departments simply because they are with the Finance Department. The same applies for officials in the PCO. An assistant deputy minister in either department also enjoys a higher classification and more pay than an assistant deputy minister in a line department. In short, it pays more to be a poet than a plumber.

The TBS has a greater number of assistant deputy ministers than the Department of Finance and a staff complement of 2,202. The TBS has 612 staff members looking after "administrative leadership," 566 for its "employer" function, 73 for "regulating oversight," and 302 for its "spending oversight" function.[31] The government spends more on overseeing its employer role ($4.2 billion in 2022–23) than it does overseeing its spending oversight function ($3.6 billion in the same year).³² Like the Finance Department and the PCO, the TBS is staffed by poets. The TBS divides its responsibilities into four functions: spending oversight: challenging or monitoring the proposed spending plans of departments and agencies; administrative leadership: promoting stronger management performance; employer: managing compensation and labour relations; and regulatory oversight: defining and supporting the regulatory process.³³

How can one explain Ottawa allocating a staff of only 302 to look after the government expenditure budget while it allocates 416 for its employer function and another 642 for internal services? On the face of it, at least, one can only conclude that the TBS does not allocate sufficient resources to oversee the government's $400 billion budget. It is easy to conclude that a staff of 300 cannot possibly take on the spending plans of about 300 government departments and agencies. The best that the TBS can do is play at the margins as it packages the different expenditure budgets of federal government departments and agencies to present to Parliament. The TBS reviews the spending plans of departments, adjusts their budgets for inflation or for decisions to add new resources to the existing programs, and then packages the information to present it to Parliament. Government decisions to expand programs will invariably generate departmental requests to add staff because departments and agencies are incapable, or unwilling, to transfer human resources from low-priority measures to more important activities. This would require difficult decisions. Why do so unless you are forced to do it? Senior executives may well also argue that the new activities require different skills or that they would need long drawn-out discussions with public sector unions to transfer employees from one unit to another. There is always a reason to avoid dealing with the matter.

The Department of Finance has always been the senior partner in its dealings with the TBS. Under the watchful eye of the prime minister and the PMO, the minister of finance is solely responsible for putting together the government's fiscal framework. Next to the prime minister, the finance minister holds the key to deciding which proposals from line departments and agencies get the green light. The Department of Finance has only a limited interest, if any, in reviewing ongoing programs to see if resources could be reallocated to higher priority activities. This is where the TBS and its staff of 300 should come in. However, the TBS's track record in recommending programs to be terminated or scaled back remains weak. Ottawa has tried different approaches to impose stronger discipline on government spending. They have all failed to deliver spending cuts or impose stronger discipline. The fact remains that the problem is not so much about spending on new measures, but about continuing to spend on measures that are long past their best-by date.

## POETS ABOVE THE FAULT LINE, PLUMBERS BELOW

In my earlier publications, I wrote about a fault line that separates senior and policy-oriented officials (the poets) from program managers, especially front-line workers (the plumbers). Those above the fault line look up to senior politicians and to the clerk of the Privy Council and their deputy ministers for direction, while those below look both to their immediate supervisors and their clients. The federal Task Force on Public Service Values and Ethics picked up on the idea in its report: "Our dialogue with public servants revealed to us a certain divide between levels in the public service, perhaps especially where public service values are concerned. Many at the middle and lower levels of the public service no longer feel connected to the senior levels, and they are not sure whether they necessarily share the same values as those at higher levels." The report added that one "source of this fault line appears to be the confusion about accountability, and the tension between customer accountability and political accountability. Those closest to the front line of accountability feel their primary accountability to citizen/customers while those farther up may feel primary accountability to citizen voters and taxpayers, as mediated by the political process."[34] I note that the task force was staffed by federal public servants and only a handful of outside consultants.

The fault line plays havoc with accountability and the relationship between front-line managers and their staff and citizens/customers of the public service or government programs. The Tait Task Force reported in 1996 on the differences between managing up, with its emphasis on Parliament, cabinet, or the policy-making process, and managing down, with its emphasis on clients. The report explains: "Many senior public servants have made their careers because of their skills in managing up. They have been valued and promoted because they were adept at providing superiors with what they needed in a timely fashion, to serve ministers and the political process." On managing down, the Tait Report explains that after fifteen years of new public management measures, some public servants view managing down as "little more than empty words, the public service slipping easily back as through a natural reflex, into its natural mode of managing up."[35] Tait's point was that the federal government bureaucracy was better at managing up than managing down, the very situation that new public management measures were designed to correct, but failed to. His diagnosis remains the case to this day, if anything even more so.

The fault line and the need to manage the blame game have – in the words of Richard Dicerni, a long-serving senior deputy minister with the federal government – led public servants to promote "upward delegation" or to push decisions above the fault line.[36] What is urgent, what is important, at times what is not important, and what may be controversial, is pushed up to the prime minister's courtiers, or at least above the fault line to be resolved. It is important to underline the point that poets work above the fault line, whereas plumbers operate below it.

What the above suggests is that the difference between managing up and managing down in the public sector has become substantial and probably overshadows the differences between managing in production, procedural, craft, and coping organizations of the kind described by James Q. Wilson in his influential book, *Bureaucracy*.[37] Program managers and front-line workers in departments such as Correctional Service Canada; the Canada Revenue Agency; Innovation, Science and Economic Development Canada; and Employment and Social Development Canada have more in common with one another than with their own senior people, who are concerned with managing up issues, working with central agencies, attending to their ministers' priorities, falling on hand grenades, and working with their peers in central agencies and other departments. It is hardly possible to overstate the point that there are now two distinct spaces emerging within the public service. One is occupied by senior career officials – poets who manage up and are preoccupied with the prime minister's courtiers and keeping their ministers out of trouble: the horizontal policy process; and plumbers, who are preoccupied with dealing with program implementation and managing down to the front-line workers providing services to Canadians.

The above also suggests that the institutional structure matters, because it provides specific roles for political and administrative actors and between senior and front-line public servants. When you draw boundaries, you not only establish a space within which people can operate, but you also draw a visible understanding of how things work. When you remove boundaries, you remove this understanding, and without boundaries in government we end up with "a big conceptual mess."[38] When a fault line emerges between senior and front-line public servants, they become uncertain and confused about the proper role of the institution within which they operate. That also has wide implications for accountability. We return to this point in later chapters.

### OH LORD! DELIVER US FROM NEW APPROACHES

Elsewhere, I have outlined in detail the various systems for managing expenditures introduced by the federal government over the past sixty years and there is no need to review them again here.[39] Suffice to provide a broad overview of the various approaches. In the 1960s, Ottawa decided to do away with the line-item budgeting process. It was a remarkably simple system to operate: it concentrated on input cost and control; it presented the expenditure budget to cabinet and Parliament in considerable detail; it was also easily accessible, even to the non-specialist. It operated on a year-to-year basis and the budget process paid little or no attention to performance through systematic reviews. Performance was left to prime ministers and their ministers to determine, based on what they heard, their priorities, what their advisors said, and what made political sense.

Departmental spending plans simply outlined spending requirements for staff, travel expenses, office equipment, and program funding, and said little else. The line-item budget process had shortcomings, but it also held an important advantage – it was easy for Parliament, TBS, and ministers to understand who was getting what in great detail and to compare spending levels by program. It also generated easily answered questions for politicians. Front-line managers knew what they were getting and they could focus on their programs, operations, and clients. Dealing with senior officials in head offices was straightforward – just stay within your budget and the human resources you were given and then get on with the tasks at hand. There was no need to feed the beast upstairs, spend time trying to figure out how to manage demands for information coming from above the fault line or trying to conjure up performance indicators to evaluate their programs.

As noted earlier, a Royal Commission on Government Organization (commonly known as the Glassco Commission), established in 1960, called for sweeping changes in how the federal government managed operations. It called for the decentralization of management authority with its call to "let the manager manage" and a stronger, more demanding process for budgeting expenditures.[40] In the late 1960s, the Canadian government followed the lead of the United States and introduced the Planning, Programming and Budgeting System (PPBS). Government officials actually believed that they had finally found the Holy Grail of government budgeting in PPBS. The then minister of finance boldly declared that it was a major budget breakthrough.[41] The approach was considered to be such a powerful instrument that many believed it would actually remove politics from the budgeting process because it would provide such clear and rational answers that ministers would be compelled to embrace them. This was so widely believed in government circles that senior officials felt the need to reassure ministers that they would continue to make the key decisions and that politics would still weigh heavily in the decision-making process. For example, Al Johnson, former Treasury Board secretary, wrote, "PPBS must not seek to substitute science for politics in the decision-making process."[42]

The thinking was that the new approaches would favour the plumbers because the PPBS would establish, in a scientific fashion, which programs were performing well. It did not work out that way. The approach, however, did add many new positions for poets in central agencies in efforts to make the new approach work. In government, once positions are created, they very rarely disappear even when the reason or approval that created them is done away with. The approach did generate a number of new reporting requirements that plumbers had to produce, but not much else.

Within only a few years, it became apparent that the PPBS had important shortcomings. It generated countless meetings, paperwork, and numerous consultant contracts, and led to the hiring of new staff, mostly poets. Looking back, we now know that it led to "very few program terminations or dramatic shifts in expenditure patterns," though it did generate new administrative spending.[43] It became obvious that bringing quantitative analysis into the expenditure budget process was very difficult, if even possible. The poets were naive in thinking that politicians would simply step aside and let a new budgeting process dictate budget decisions. For one thing, defining specific and clear objectives for programs and activities proved difficult – impossible – in most cases. There was also often more than one objective for any given program and virtually every program impinged directly or indirectly on the goals of others. Thus, in defining its program objectives, a department often had to contend with those of another program, which could conflict. Program objectives, if they were even defined, were more often than not vague statements of little value, even as a checklist to evaluate the program's effectiveness. In turn, it became virtually impossible to develop a set of criteria to determine the success of the programs. But even if it were possible to make such an approach work, it is not clear that politicians would have stepped aside and let a budgeting process call the shots when deciding which programs should be expanded and which ones should be cut back.

The new approach to budgeting was on life support by the mid-1970s and pronounced dead by the end of the decade. Two keen observers of Canadian public administration wrote: "Anyone who did a cost-benefit analysis on the introduction of PPBS ... would be forced to conclude that it was not worth the effort."[44] The auditor general (AG) brought home the point with devastating criticism of Ottawa's budgeting process, a criticism that rattled Ottawa and led to the establishment of another royal commission, the Royal Commission on Financial Management and Accountability (the Lambert Commission). The AG wrote: "Parliament – and indeed the government – had lost or was close to losing effective control of the public purse."[45] PPBS was clearly not the answer for better budgeting.

Ottawa did not wish to return to line-item budgeting and the search was on again for a rational process to budget for expenditures that would identify low-priority programs and activities to be reduced or terminated. Central agency officials came up with a new expenditure budgeting process that, they insisted, would inform ministers about the effects of their decisions on the growth of government spending. The thinking was to push spending decisions away from line departments and their ministers, toward a more collective decision-making process, an approach labelled the Policy and Expenditure Management System (PEMS). Central agency officials believed that ministers happily made spending decisions and then pushed all the difficult decisions upstairs for someone else to resolve, namely the minister of finance. Under previous budget decision-making processes, cabinet ministers would make policy decisions and then leave it to someone else to make the required financial resources available, which made managing the expenditure budget process difficult to do.

Under PEMS, cabinet ministers, as members of cabinet committees, were forced to make both policy and spending decisions. Cabinet committees were given spending envelopes and new spending to manage. The spending envelopes were intended to square with Ottawa's overall fiscal plan. Ministers were then free to allocate resources as they saw fit but within the allocated spending envelopes. If they wanted to fund more initiatives than their envelopes allowed, then they were expected to cut spending in low-priority programs. The thinking was to place responsibility for spending and reducing expenditures directly on the shoulders of those who spend, the ministers. The size of the spending envelope was based on the programs and activities already in place, with some added funding to support new measures.

It was not long before PEMS also ran into problems. Ministers found that it was too bureaucratic and increased the influence of career officials in central agencies, i.e., the poets, at their and their departments' expense. By becoming part of the centre of government to shape the expenditure budget, ministers felt that they were being separated from their departments. Rather than turn to their departments for advice, they were being fed information and advice from central agency officials. Central agency officials, meanwhile, kept a lock on the PEMS process and carefully managed information flowing to and from cabinet committees, allowing the poets, both in central agencies and line departments, the upper hand.[46]

However, as PEMS was failing, the poets in the PMO, the PCO, and the Finance Department were gaining influence because cabinet and cabinet committees could not make the new expenditure budgeting process work. Somebody had to pick up the mantle. Ministers of large departments, on the advice of their departmental poets, could look inside their departments to see if they could reallocate resources to fund their priority projects, but ministers in smaller departments were unable to do so and felt that the process was unfair. This too made PEMS more difficult to manage.

The poets in central agencies have never stopped coming up with new approaches. In a back-to-the-future approach, the Justin Trudeau government established a "deliverology unit" in the PCO when it came to power in 2015. The unit attached a great deal of importance to establishing targets and generating the needed data to assess performance. This, ironically, is precisely what Trudeau *père* had sought to do when his government adopted PPBS. There is a striking similarity between how both PPBS and "deliverology" were designed to work, even in the wording used.[47]

Only two years after its introduction, Ottawa-based journalists were reporting that deliverology was falling far short of expectations. Adam Radwanski notes that "even some of those more enthusiastic about deliverology in principle have grown skeptical." He asked how anyone could possibly measure Trudeau's goal of "helping the middle class" and labelled the deliverology approach simply as "the Liberals' attempt to write their own report card."[48] One can also ask how anyone could possibly assess, in any meaningful fashion, Justin Trudeau's goal to promote "international engagement that makes a difference in the world."[49] Deliverology did not have an answer, any more than PPBS and PEMS did.

Deliverology itself has not even answered how anyone could tell if it was successful. Some keen observers dismissed it as simply a public relations exercise.[50] The deliverology unit kept track of the commitments made in the 2015 election, something that other units in the PCO and TBS also did for years. These older units, however, were not disbanded when the deliverology unit was established, thus making government even thicker. They just kept doing what they had been doing before deliverology was introduced. This is how government operates: it is excellent at launching new bureaucratic units but largely incapable of doing away with them, even though they have outlived their purpose. Poets have an uncanny ability to come up with new roles, responsibilities, and resources to keep their units running whenever they perceive that a need has arisen.

The deliverology unit's mandate closely resembled that of TBS. The latter is responsible for assessing the effect of programs, how they perform, and how departments manage operations.[51] When the deliverology unit was established, the TBS's mandate was not adjusted nor was its staff reduced. As is the way of government, both simply continued to operate with overlapping mandates, generating still more demands on line departments and agencies to provide data to the centre. These developments again strengthened the hand of the poets in central agencies in their ability to ensure that line departments run on their tracks. It is unlikely, however, that it will have any lasting effect on government decision making.

Richard French, a former federal public servant and politician, sums up deliverology's potential nicely: "Deliverology is simply the latest in a continuing flow of fads and fashions that invade ... the public sector with metronomic regularity ... They never revolutionize government ... because the enduring challenges ... are deeply rooted in a human nature highly resistant to fundamental change, in institutional inertia and – in a democracy – in the additional constraint of democratic constitutions rightly focussed upon legitimacy rather than efficiency."[52]

It is hardly the first time that government units in central agencies decided not to shed positions to reflect the adjustments in their workload. When the Chrétien government came to power, the prime minister decided to streamline the cabinet committee system. Both Trudeau *père* and Mulroney had an elaborate cabinet committee system that soaked up a lot of ministerial time. Chrétien decided to have only five cabinet committees, including the TBS, down from fifteen, at times, under Mulroney and Trudeau.[53] The PCO is organized to serve the prime minister, cabinet, and cabinet committees. The secretariats correspond to the mandates of the cabinet committees. When Chrétien abolished several cabinet committees in 1993, a number of PCO secretariats reinvented themselves and came up with new mandates. These included reviewing all developments falling under their broad areas of responsibility, monitoring controversial issues, and preparing briefing notes for the prime minister.

Without cabinet committees to service and support, one can only assume that the PCO's workload would have fallen dramatically, and one could have questioned whether some secretariats should have been abolished or, at least, reduced PCO staff numbers substantially. But that did not happen. Apart from the prime minister and the clerk of the Privy Council, no one was in a position to do anything about it. Prime ministers always have far too many issues on their plates to be concerned about the continuing viability of several policy secretariats. Prime ministers, unlike CEOs of private firms, are not motivated by the end game of profitability and, for them, it is best to leave well enough alone as long as it does not create political problems.

The heads of PCO secretariats could have gone to the clerk to report that they and their staff had become redundant. But why would they do that? Best to reinvent their work to remain at the centre of government and enjoy a high-profile position. There was simply no incentive and no interest for them to admit that their workload had been reduced. The clerk could have asked for answers, but there was also no advantage in doing that. Extra staff can deal with a potential political crisis, of which there is rarely a shortage. Unless the clerk is told by a program review exercise to cut into PCO operations, they will always have more important issues to address. If the high-profile Privy Council Office circles the wagons whenever change threatens its staff, then no one should be surprised if other departments and agencies do the same. Government departments and agencies may not be immortal, but most government units are.

## LOOKING BACK

Poets in central agencies are always in the thick of things. Making policy and making major decisions now belong to the prime minister, as do all major spending decisions, with the help of the finance minister and a handful of senior ministers. They do not look to a well-defined decision-making or budget-making process for guidance. That has been tried and failed. They look to deputy ministers and other poets in line departments for help. Ministers looking for new spending to support their priorities now make the case before the prime minister and their key advisors and the finance minister. Nothing else seems to matter.

It has now been over sixty years since Ottawa decided to embrace program evaluation as a central feature of its policy- and decision-making processes. It continues to invest a substantial amount of funds year after year, trying to make it work. It has not been successful. As recently as the fall of 2022, we learned that the government did not know, in the most basic of terms, the effect its spending had had on Canadians experiencing homelessness or chronic homelessness, despite devoting two major programs in two agencies to it. It is worth quoting the report from the auditor general on the matter at length to gain an appreciation of the failure of Ottawa's program evaluation efforts: "As the lead for Reaching Home, a program within the National Housing Strategy, Infrastructure Canada spent about $1.36 billion between 2019 and 2021 – about 40% of total funding committed to the program – on preventing and reducing homelessness. However, the department did not know whether chronic homelessness and homelessness had increased or decreased since 2019 as a result of this investment."[54]

For its part, the Canada Mortgage and Housing Corporation, as the lead for the National Housing Strategy, spent about $4.5 billion and committed about $9 billion but did not know who was benefiting from its initiatives. This was because the corporation did not measure the changes in housing outcomes for priority vulnerable groups, including people experiencing homelessness. The report also found that rental housing units approved under the national housing Co-Investment Fund that the corporation considered affordable were often unaffordable for low-income households, many of which belong to vulnerable groups prioritized by the strategy.

Despite being the lead for the National Housing Strategy and overseeing the majority of its funding, the Canada Mortgage and Housing Corporation took the position that it was not directly accountable for addressing chronic homelessness. Infrastructure Canada was also of the view that while it contributed to reducing chronic homelessness, it was not solely accountable for achieving the strategy's target of reducing chronic homelessness. This meant that despite being a federally established target, there was minimal federal accountability for its achievement.[55]

In short, Ottawa's program evaluation structure, including numerous public servants and outside consultants, failed at its most basic tasks. No one wanted to own the problem or own the mistakes. And no one is being held to account for the failure or for the enormous amount of public funds spent on these efforts over the past sixty years.

This example makes the point, once again, that program evaluation in the federal government and program evaluation units are kept busy turning a crank that is not attached to anything. It also makes the case that no one in government is accountable when things go wrong. The fact that federal government decisions are now the product of many hands has also complicated matters. More is said about this later. The same applies when the workload in government units drops. Their staff are somehow able to reinvent themselves. No one is there to hold the units accountable by asking questions about their mandate and workload. As one private sector executive explained: "When there is no work in our business, it is a legitimate reason to lay people off. This rule does not apply in government."[56] One could ask – who in government is accountable for this state of affairs? I doubt that anyone has an answer.

Since the 1960s, Ottawa has regularly come up with new approaches to government budgeting. They have all fallen far short of expectations. They have, however, created many new employment opportunities for poets and allowed them to expand their sphere of influence. The new approaches have not been of any benefit to the plumbers – they have lost influence and the measures have made life more difficult for them by adding a number of reporting requirements that only serve the interests of the poets.

# 4

# THE UNWRITTEN CODE

A former senior federal public servant said that there is an "unwritten code in the public service, that requires you not to be critical of the public service, your department and individual public servants, at least with outsiders."[1] Leaving aside universities, the code likely applies to most large organizations, not just the federal public service. I maintain, however, that the code has, in recent years, become even more enshrined in the federal public service. Bureaucracy bashing and several new transparency requirements have very often had the opposite effect of what was intended – they have motivated public servants to find ways to keep things close to their chest or to hold information that may hurt them or their departments inside their units.[2] Nothing new here and no one should be surprised.

Public servants do not work in open markets. They hold exclusive positions and they operate in an environment that allows them to be highly protective of their positions. All government departments have built-in mechanisms to help protect themselves against both internal and external influences or controls and also to try to expand their spheres of activity. This environment also enables them to test the possibility of extending their authority and expenditures for their units or programs at every opportunity. Someone in the system, either in the public service or at the political level, has to say no.[3] Winning in government for senior public servants is often about how many new financial resources and new staff members they have been able to secure. The performance of senior departmental executives is frequently determined, at least by their subordinates, on their ability to secure or save jobs for the organization at budget time or during a program review exercise. David Good, a former senior federal government official, summed it up well when he wrote: "Talk to any minister or deputy minister in Ottawa about how the town works and one is immediately struck by how much they view the world from the perspective of the allocation of public money and how much of their time and effort is devoted to trying to get new money for new policy initiatives."[4] The test for public servants in program spending departments is not what is affordable – that is always someone else's responsibility – but what is desirable when looking at expanding their activities or protecting their programs. Every government department and every manager can always identify desirable initiatives that they would like to see funded.

Government bureaucracies have deeply embedded processes that enable public servants to fend off difficult questions. It is virtually impossible for outsiders to evaluate the level of human and financial resources required for government departments and agencies to deliver their programs and services.[5] It is also extremely difficult, if at all possible, for outsiders, including central agencies, to get to the right information or to understand the workings of government departments to a point where they exert control over their resource levels. By outsiders, I include politicians, even those holding senior cabinet portfolios, and central agencies with the responsibility of reviewing ongoing government programs.

Recent management reform measures have made it even more difficult for outsiders to understand the level of financial and human resources that departments and agencies require to do what they do. Government departments have always been able to put up barriers to sharing knowledge to protect their resources. They operate as a monopoly, never having to be concerned about the competition. And no outside organization could possibly have the necessary resources to challenge the level of resources government departments say they need to operate. All government departments and agencies serve a clientele that supports their programs and there are always politicians at the ready to speak on behalf of the clientele. When senior departmental managers sense danger, they can alert their departmental clients or others with an interest in the department's programs to speak to the media or the political class on their behalf.

Again, nothing new here. What is new are the recently introduced private-sector-inspired approaches to management that have swept governments in Anglo-American democracies. The goal of the management reform measures was to make management in government look like private sector management. Many politicians, going back forty years, have come to government convinced that programs and operations were being poorly managed, at least when they first arrive in government. They ran election campaigns against government waste and pledged to do something about it once elected. Most senior public servants meanwhile rarely see a need to improve management practices. As they see it, they are there to help politicians pursue their policy agendas and politicians have no business poking around government operations, evoking the old bugaboo that politicians and politics have no business managing the public service and government operations.

Politicians believed – and many still do – that it is possible to introduce private sector management practices to government and that they would be no less effective than they are in the private sector. At a minimum, they would substantially improve management in government. "Empowerment" became the word underpinning new management measures that have been pursued in government over the past forty years, and again, Canada is no exception. Empowerment, if it is to be meaningful, requires a capacity to assess performance. It is fairly straightforward in the business world, with indicators such as market share, profitability, individual sales, and client retention, to establish performance and to hold managers and their staff accountable.

Government, however, can never be as straightforward. Governments were able to borrow management practices from the private sector, but they could not borrow performance indicators or accountability requirements. They had to improvise. Assessing performance became necessary because when you do away with centrally prescribed rules on financial and human resources management, you need something other than financial audits to see if requirements have been met and to measure performance. Imposing centrally prescribed rules and processes did clarify accountability requirements because it could be determined, albeit only after the fact, whether managers and their staff respected them. Managers in line departments and agencies applauded the government's decision to embrace private sector management practices because it gave them more freedom to manage. However, many long-serving former career officials also saw the challenges – how do you empower managers in a command and control culture? how do you measure performance? and how do you hold staff accountable in government?

Managers in line departments and agencies applauded the shift because it was in their interest to do so. Who likes dealing with centrally prescribed rules? Many also embraced the new approach with enthusiasm because it would provide them flexibility to manage operations, much like their private sector counterparts enjoy. A long-serving senior career official explains, to his chagrin, the enthusiasm with which public servants embraced the new approach and the transition to a private sector ethos in the federal government. He writes: "Without blushing or even without a second thought we now talk about our 'customers' or 'clients' in a way that would not have occurred to public servants three or four decades ago. And this is just the tip of the iceberg." He adds: "Sometimes the results of this attempt to reinvent the public sector into the private sector are quite bizarre. I recently visited a well-meaning colleague who proudly presented to me the organizational renewal efforts of a high-priced foreign consultant that consisted in, among other things, the translation of all terms of public administration and parliamentary democracy into private sector equivalents, including the reinvention of members of Parliament as the shareholders of the corporation and Cabinet as the Board of Directors."[6] Nothing is said about where Canadians and voters fit into this scheme of things.

Public servants in line departments knew and still know that they could fudge performance reports but not when dealing with clearly spelled out rules and regulations and financial audits. And fudge reports they did and do. Other than line department managers perhaps, no one is satisfied with the federal government's program evaluation and performance reports. The auditor general, for example, has consistently been highly critical of Ottawa's efforts to evaluate its programs.[7] No matter, centrally prescribed rules and procedural accountability are viewed as dated and out of step with efforts to dress the public sector in private sector clothes. The call to let the "manager manage" dates back some sixty years and Ottawa has been moving in this direction ever since, albeit in fits and starts.

No one, however, has also ever been able to answer the question – why would a line department manager ever provide information to produce a performance or evaluation report that would cast their department, program, or performance in a negative light? Doug Hartle, a former senior TBS official, put his finger on the problem when he wrote: "It is a strange dog that willingly carries the stick with which it is to be beaten."[8] In short, it is asking too much of government line department managers to think that they would report that their programs are not meeting expectations, however they are defined. It is also asking too much for them to report that their units and programs are too rich in either human or financial resources or for them to inform central agencies that their units could deliver the same level of service with fewer resources. That is not now how government works. Managers do not want to tell staff that they could not protect the department or their unit's interest before senior departmental officials and central agencies. This would be a sure sign that the manager is weak.

One could ask the question – are government programs and government bureaus immortal? I am hardly the first to ask the question. Herbert Kaufman asked this very question in 1976.[9] He argued that government organizations tend to persist, though he identified challenges as they went about their work. He did conclude that not all government organizations and government programs and positions are immortal. This is also true in Canada. One only needs to look to Ottawa's program review exercise of the mid-1990s to make the case that not all government programs are immortal. The review produced cuts in some programs and in the public service. However, those did not come from line department managers. They were told to cut spending and did as they were told. Central agencies only kicked into action after the prime minister and the minister of finance gave them clear marching orders. Regardless of new approaches to budgeting and the addition of numerous policy specialists (poets) in recent years, government managers still have no reason, no incentive to identify overstaffing in their organizations or to point out flaws in their programs to outsiders. The problem, however, is that they are the only ones who know or should know when departments have too many resources for current service levels.

## EVIDENCE-BASED DECISIONS ARE FOR OTHERS

Public servants only sing the praises of evidence-based and objective data when shaping public policy and making important decisions. They point out that "the use of evidence in policy-making is very powerful and entails a profound shift in the way that" government should "make decisions and engage various stakeholders." They add that evidence-based decision making is not subject to partisan political considerations or outside influences.[10] Michael Howlett explains that when evidence-based policy making hinges "on the idea that better decisions are those that incorporate the most available information, it is expected that enhancing the information basis of policy decisions will improve the results flowing from their implementation."[11] No one can argue against this line of thinking, least of all public servants. Recall that public sector unions representing federal public servants took aim at the Harper government's decision to cut science positions in the federal government, arguing that it would weaken policy making because it would denigrate the importance of sound scientific evidence.[12] How does evidence-based decision making apply when it addresses the institution that matters to government career officials and public sector unions – the public service?

I believe that the federal public service is overstaffed, that it is providing a lower level of service to Canadians, and that Canadians are losing trust in the institution. I argue that it is the responsibility of the public service to provide evidence that I am wrong, not the other way around. A number of Canadians, including public servants, perhaps because of my work, have contacted me on many occasions by email to report some of their dealings with federal government departments. I recognize that this hardly constitutes a representative survey and that few Canadians would take the time to report their positive experiences with government. But the message is clear and there is evidence that public opinion surveys support it.[13] It is also a message that former senior public servants have voiced in recent years.[14]

As an example, a mother reported that she accompanied her daughter to renew her passport at the local Service Canada office in June 2022. The Service Canada staff told her that she needed an appointment. She responded: "Well, I am here and there is no one in the lineup." They argued that she still needed an appointment while she insisted on staying to process her daughter's passport application. The staff then began speaking French to one another, saying that they had an annoying client, unaware that the woman spoke French. She asked to meet their manager. The employees told her that there was "no manager on site." The woman replied that she "would sit and wait until one arrived." In the end, because of her tenacity, she won the day.

She is a lawyer and told Service Canada employees that she "pays a lot of taxes, half of her salary and expected good service." She added that she did not appreciate public servants sitting and watching television, while she was waiting for service. She went on to say that it was also highly inappropriate for Service Canada staff to switch to French, thinking that she would not understand, to criticize a Canadian looking for service from a government agency. She revealed that others have reported similar experiences at the Passport Office. One individual told her, for example, that he had been waiting for two weeks for someone to return his call to set up an appointment.

A non-lawyer or someone less versed in the ways of government might not have won the day. For Canadians, accountability takes place at the point of contact with government. They do not have access to the officers of Parliament, TBS, or to senior career officials in head offices in Ottawa to hold staff at Service Canada to account. They can ask to meet the relevant manager but this is not always possible. They can contact their members of Parliament and ask for help. But this is a slow cumbersome process with limited chances of success. The chain of command from the minister, the deputy minister, and through several management layers, has to be respected when a question about front-line government services is put to a member of Parliament before an answer can be given.

I was in Ottawa on 21 October 2022 with some free time in the afternoon, before a late evening flight to Moncton, so I called the War Museum at 1:45 p.m. to plan a visit. I asked if I could leave my luggage at the door, thinking that I would go directly to the airport from the museum. I was strongly encouraged not to come. The museum agent explained that I would need to buy a ticket at one door and leave my luggage at another. She explained that the museum was closing at 4:00 p.m. and that I would not have enough time to go through the museum and that it would be preferable to visit it on another day. I note that Ottawa is at least a twelve-hour drive from Moncton. I then imagined the museum being managed by the private sector, thinking the experience would have been much different. The private sector employee would have made every effort to accommodate me, to sell tickets, and see to it that as many people as possible would come to the museum. The private sector operates under one set of rules and expectations, while the public sector operates under different ones.

Front-line workers in government know from experience the importance of the unwritten code – never be critical of your department, its programs, and its operations. Public servants operate a monopoly and those who look after passports or the War Museum know that clients simply cannot go to another office to secure their passports or walk through a museum. They also know that clients have no choice but to put up with the level of service being provided. As Albert Hirschman explained, clients have choices when dealing with a poor level of service in the private sector – exit, voice, and loyalty.[15] Hirschman underlines in three words the difference between the public and private sectors – government deals with "voice" while the private sector deals with both voice and, more important, exit. In the private sector, customers can easily move from one firm to another in search of better service. Clients have no such opportunity with the public sector. They have to stick with the government unit that provides the service. They can try voice, but voice has its limits. They can vote, they can write to their members of Parliament, they can voice their criticism to the media, and they can join a pressure group. They can also voice their concerns to the front-line public servant who is providing the service and later, if necessary, to the front-line manager. Surveys and studies, however, suggest that voice is not very effective and is no match for exit – this speaks to the difference between government and the private sector.[16]

When voice becomes loud enough to create political problems, the government will react with plans to address the problems. In light of the problems the federal government had in delivering services in the summer of 2022, the prime minister established a ten-member task force with a mandate to "improve government services."[17] If history is any guide, the task force will generate numerous meetings and provide contracts for consultants, and in the end, table a report. Will it lead to an improved quality of services? Time will tell but the past suggests that it is unlikely. Several months later, the prime minister decided to appoint a minister responsible for "Citizens' Services."[18]

A former senior federal public servant wrote to say that I was overly critical of the federal government's approach to service delivery, making the point that there is a difference between "service reputation" and "service experience." The argument is that the federal government has generated some successes in program delivery and that there is empirical evidence to support this claim.[19] The retired public servant also made the point that barely two months after COVID-19 hit, Ottawa's support programs were able to deposit funds directly into the bank accounts of Canadians – this is an incredible success story.[20] I made this point in a conversation with a federal deputy minister. Her response: "Yes, absolutely but remember that this success story was driven by the Privy Council Office – otherwise,

I do not think that it would have happened."[21] This, however, also speaks directly to the single most important challenge confronting the federal machinery of government – when the PMO-PCO reacts and directs, the system responds. The centre, however, can only respond to a very limited number of issues.

## COLLECTIVE BARGAINING

In 1967, the Public Service of Canada embarked on what was then described as a "profoundly significant" course based on a "new statute enacted without precedent or premeditation" when collective bargaining was introduced in Ottawa and when Parliament passed the *Public Service Staff Relations Act*.[22] The Act meant that public servants were now paid as a "matter of right" rather than as a "matter of privilege of the Crown."[23] Though the move has fundamentally changed government operations and management practices in government, the public administration literature has not given it anywhere near the amount of attention that it deserves.

Before collective bargaining, the federal government acted unilaterally in fixing salaries, simply relying on the guidance of the Civil Service Commission, advisory groups, and its Pay Research Bureau. The bureau established broad compensation benchmarks for public sector employees based on some, albeit limited, private sector comparisons. The Diefenbaker government in 1963 rejected a pay increase recommended by the Civil Service Commission, a recommendation prepared after consulting employee associations. The rejection led two of the employee associations to ask all political parties, before the next general election, if they supported collective bargaining for federal government workers.[24] The die was cast as all three major political parties agreed to support collective bargaining where compulsory arbitration would be used to resolve negotiation impasses.[25]

The newly elected Liberal government headed by Lester B. Pearson, a former senior federal public servant, agreed to pursue collective bargaining, and a preparatory committee made up of senior government officials was established. The committee did not explore the "underlying political issue of whether public servants should be permitted to engage in the process of collective bargaining."[26] That was simply taken as a given. The committee saw its mandate as a technical one, concerned only with implementing collective bargaining in federal government departments and agencies.

Until the 1960s, collective bargaining in Canada was limited to employees in the private sector. The resistance to collective bargaining in government was based on the view that it was "unnecessary, impractical and illegal." The question about legality was based on the view that a "sovereign state cannot be compelled by lesser bodies, in this case, public sector unions."[27] There has been very little debate about the legality of collective bargaining in the public sector over the years and it is now firmly entrenched in Ottawa and provincial capitals. I note that the Supreme Court ruled in 2007 that collective bargaining is now also protected under section 2(d) of the Canadian Charter of Rights and Freedoms.[28]

Collective bargaining in the public sector is unlike bargaining in the private sector because the push and pull in government depends not on a bottom line of revenues, expenses, market share, and profits or on how well the firm and its employees are doing in a competitive environment, but on political and policy considerations and the state of public finances. There is a world of difference between the two. For one thing, public servants work in a non-competitive field. For another, public sector managers and employees do not have financial incentives, as the private sector does, to minimize labour costs. If anything, incentives work the other way around. Public sector managers, for example, have no incentive and no interest in moving their operations to jurisdictions or communities with lower labour costs, as can happen in the private sector. Some Ottawa-based private sector firms may look to lower cost jurisdictions, including wages and housing, and decide to move their operations to these communities. The federal government has no such incentives. In recent years, it has done the opposite and built up its presence in the National Capital Region.

Collective bargaining in the public sector is an in-house or inward-looking bargaining process that takes place separate from outside influences such as market forces and other competitive requirements. Collective bargaining in the private sector is an economic process tied to determining what costs the business can bear. In the public sector, it is a political process dependent on political forces and the level of taxes voters are willing to assume. In the private sector, the negotiation process is quick because management has the last word, with no need to answer to a higher authority – here management owns what it says, what it does, and what mistakes it makes. In the public sector, the process is often drawn out.

Negotiators for the management side have to comply with government regulations and answer to several levels of higher authority.

Senior public sector managers, from deputy ministers down to the lowest executive officer level (typically at the director and manager levels), do not belong to a union and are not part of the collective bargaining process. However, they benefit directly from the process, in that it is understood that senior executives and their managers should enjoy the same as or better employee benefits than unionized public servants and that their salary levels need to be higher.

Public sector unions, for their part, maintain that it is unfair for the employer to have a dual role – as employer and as legislator.[29] They simply make the point without offering solutions. They argue that the government, as the employer, can override the collective bargaining process whenever they confront difficult economic issues or see a substantial drop in revenues. However, it is important to note that when the government limits its role to "employer," which is nearly always, the process is one of push and pull, with public sector unions able to push against political and policy considerations, not against a bottom line or market forces or the work of competitive firms.[30]

On some occasions the government decided to act beyond its employer role. For example, around 1975, the government imposed wage controls in its attempt to deal with inflation. In the 1990s, as employer, it went further and froze the salaries of public servants (a one-year freeze in 1991 and a two-year freeze in 1995) to bring order to its expenditure budget. In 1996, the employer went event further and temporarily suspended collective bargaining.

It is worth repeating the point that collective bargaining and the work of public sector unions have had and continue to have a profound effect on government operations and management practices, far more than all new public management measures combined. The absence of a bottom line or market test of appropriate compensation makes it difficult for governments to resist wage settlements that might not be warranted.[31] It is rarely good politics for politicians to see public servants go on strike. And senior government executives sitting on the other side of the negotiation table from public sector union representatives know that whatever concessions they make will also benefit them.

Even when the government, as employer, turned to legislation to impose a salary freeze, public sector unions were still able to gain better pension benefits. *The Public Service Superannuation Act* was amended in 1999 to reduce the salary-averaging period from six to five years. In addition, the Pensioners' Dental Services Plan was introduced in 2001. Wage restraints also fuelled "classification creep" in the federal public service. Senior executives and managers did, in many cases, turn to reclassifying positions to give their employees salary increases and there is evidence to suggest that this became common practice. A growing number of new "associate" positions were created in the post-program review period between 1995 and 2001.[32] This also enabled deputy ministers to bypass the wage freeze. It is important to underline the point, once again, that all federal public servants, whether members of a public sector union or not, including senior executives, benefited from these developments.

No one in the federal government, neither politicians nor career officials, has any interest in making classification creep or generous dental plans known to the public. Best to give these and other benefits a low profile in the media. Even public servants performing oversight functions, either in a central agency such as TBS or in the Office of the Auditor General (OAG), have no interest in launching a review of the size of the public service or compensation levels and employee benefits from salaries to indexed pensions. Such reviews would also shine a light on their own operations and staff benefits. The OAG has produced numerous studies on government mismanagement and waste over the years. However, I know of no OAG study on the size of the public service or on classification creep and its cost. For public servants and their managers, it is best to keep looking at the shadows in Plato's cave than have a well-documented public debate about the effect of collective bargaining on government operations or on what ails their institution.

There is a sharp difference in union coverage between the public and private sectors. From a dead start in the mid-1960s, most government workers now have a union to look after their interests. The union coverage in the public sector in 2021 stood at 77.2 per cent, whereas in the private sector, union coverage was only 15.3 per cent. Union coverage in the public sector has been on the rise in recent years, in contrast to the private sector, which has seen a decline of six per cent between 1997 and 2021.[33] Government executives and managers have to learn to work with collective bargaining, public sector unions, and even the courts, an environment that is largely foreign for their private sector counterparts. Because the courts have been drawn into management issues, many government managers have simply given up trying to dismiss employees on the basis of non-performance, fearing either lengthy dealings with the unions, limited chances of success, or having to defend their action in court. As Jeffrey Simpson writes, rights are "fundamentally about me and responsibility is mostly about us."[34]

The role of public sector unions is to gain concessions for their members and the more concessions they can secure the better. During the COVID-19 pandemic, some 135,000 federal public servants were granted paid leave because they had to cope with workplace closures and children displaced from schools and daycares. The TBS asked that employees make use of their accumulated credits before they applied for a discretionary paid leave, known as "699" leave. The Public Service Alliance of Canada (PSAC) challenged the guidance, while the government argued that the "699" leave was intended for short-term situations, such as a snowstorm, and were to be decided on a case-by-case basis by the managers. The Federal Public Sector Labour Relations and Employment Board ruled in favour of the union, prompting PSAC to declare that it had won "a major victory" for its members.[35] Government managers had little to say in this case.

## PUBLIC SECTOR UNIONS

The work of public sector unions tends to reinforce the unwritten code: that the unions will go to bat for their members whenever disciplinary actions against them are taken or even contemplated or when cuts to the public service are contemplated. In addition, government managers have little say in setting salaries, working conditions, or the process for declaring employee surpluses. That belongs to collective bargaining, led by the TBS and public sector unions. Even if collective bargaining does not always stop a manager from making a tough decision, it becomes a convenient cover for executives and managers to avoid doing so. It has never been easy to deal with non-performers in government, but it is even more difficult today, given that employees and their union representatives can go to court to counter disciplinary actions, including removal for non-performance. No manager wants the hassle. Senior executives in head offices and line department managers in the field always have more important things to deal with, at least from their perspective, than address staff who are unwilling to provide an acceptable level of service to clients.

Letting the manager manage may make sense in a royal commission report or in speeches by politicians and senior public servants. But how can government let managers manage when the most important human resources decisions are taken out of their hands? Government managers, for example, have no say about salary levels and employee benefits. When the president of the TBS announced in December 2022 a return to office two to three days a week by 31 March 2023, the public sector unions strongly opposed the decision, calling it "disingenuous" and served notice that they would include the "right to work remotely" in future collective agreements. TBS explained that the directive "will be applied to the entirety of the core public administration"[36] – so much for letting managers manage. I have often heard senior public sector executives point the finger at public sector unions to explain what ails government operations. I hasten to add, however, that I have not often heard them say this in public.

The unions served notice that they would fight the government's attempt to have public servants return to the office in post-COVID-19. They made it clear that "it will be a top issue at the bargaining table," and it was, in the 2023 negotiations. However, as Kathryn May argues, many Canadians "see public servants asking for the freedom of an independent contractor or entrepreneur to work when and where they want while keeping the job security, pay and benefits few other Canadians enjoy."[37]

There are reasons why management want their employees back in the office. Senior private sector executives insist that there are important downsides, particularly for managers and younger employees working from home.[38] One explained that it is particularly important to bring productive employees back to the office. It also helps to promote team building and cooperation between different teams working toward a goal.[39] Research carried out in the post-COVID-19 period confirms the advantages of working in the office. It reveals that full-time work from home lowers workers' productivity by 10 to 20 per cent compared with working in the office. Working in the office also promotes spontaneous conversations among colleagues, creating connections that spark creativity and innovation. But, in the case of the federal government, the debate with the unions about working from home was mainly about the give and take in the negotiation process under collective bargaining.[40]

Management served notice that the decision regarding where public servants work belongs to the employer. The unions did not agree, and they were able to make their argument win the day. One senior public servant made the point that: "The union has wind in their sails for a strike mandate. Treasury Board may say (remote work) is not a bargainable issue, but come on, people are out on strike over it and you won't bargain that?"[41] For the unions, the issue belongs to collective bargaining, nowhere else, and their role is to promote the economic interests of their members.

Collective bargaining is an ongoing process. Both management and the unions readied for a new round of negotiation in early 2023. The unions signalled a difficult road ahead as both sides sat at the negotiation table to strike agreements with unions representing more than 300,000 federal public servants. Wage increases, inflation, and place of work dominated the discussions. The TBS took the unusual step of issuing a statement accusing the unions of negotiating in bad faith. The statement reads: "From the start of negotiations in June 2021, the Public Service Alliance of Canada (PSAC) has flooded the bargaining tables with costly proposals – over 500 across its five bargaining units. At the same time, they have refused to prioritize their requests, refused to move on their initial proposals, and did not respond to the employer's comprehensive offers."[42] The unions were quick to disagree and to blame the TBS for the problems, insisting that it was using "stalling tactics" to deny its employees proper compensation, since it had been in talks with the employer for eighteen months.[43]

The unions won an important concession on working from home during the 2023 negotiations. The president of the TBS's commitment that where public servants work is a "right of the employer" proved to be short-lived.[44] PSAC came to an understanding with TBS that calls on managers to review work from home on an individual basis, rather than as a group. In addition, PSAC also secured an understanding to continue studying telework with TBS.[45]

The 2023 TBS-PSAC agreement provides a 11.5 per cent wage increase to the 120,000 PSAC members over four years, retroactive to 2021. The agreement also provides for a one-time payment of $2,500 and a number of other group-specific improvements over the life of the agreement.[46] Media reactions suggest that PSAC won the day in its negotiations with the TBS, with one observer arguing that "it is hard to conclude anything else" and also noting that only one-third of the members voted on what type of job action the union would take.[47]

Both the public and private sectors continue to debate the merits of remote work. A well-known senior private sector executive maintains that it is "perfectly reasonable" for those whose work involves researching, coding, or working on a book but that it does not "work for young" employees, for "management," and for "spontaneity."[48] Others argue that working from home has important disadvantages: it hampers teamwork, hurts motivation, gives rise to unmonitored performance, promotes frequent breaks, and poses a risk to productivity.[49] The Royal Bank of Canada instructed its employees to return to their offices three to four days a week and other private firms have introduced a similar policy.[50] It is easier to embrace a hybrid work culture or a combination office–work-from-home model for firms able to measure productivity, which is a great deal easier for many private sector firms than it is for governments. Jane Fraser, CEO of Citigroup, reports that the "less productive ones are being called back into the office for coaching."[51] A number of private sector firms have simply decreed that employees must return to the office, insisting that the employer has the right to decide where employees work.[52]

The Government of Canada's decision to allow public servants to work from home and to study the issue further with the unions has not been well received by many Canadians. Linda Duxbury, a professor in management and strategy at Carleton University explains why: "What about those people who don't have the luxury to even work one day a week from home? What about teachers? What about nurses? What about doctors?" She adds that PSAC "forces an uphill climb gaining the wider public's sympathy."[53] She also adds that remote work is "a privilege not a right" and explains: "I can't tell you who won this deal, but I can certainly tell you who lost; the front-line and middle-level managers."[54] Poets will be able to make the case that they can work from home but the same is not true for many plumbers, who have to be physically present to provide services to Canadians, including, for example, Canada Border Services officials.

The perception is that federal public servants enjoy a number of advantages not available to other Canadians in the private sector – job security, generous pension plans, the ability to retire earlier than other Canadians, special leaves (14.9 days compared with 9.8 days for the private sector), higher salaries for similar private sector jobs (8.5 per cent higher than their private sector counterparts) and strong memberships in public sector unions when compared with the private sector.[55] Collective bargaining plays a critical role in managing human resources and has added to the cost of government operations.[56]

## EVALUATING PERFORMANCE

The pattern of employees seldom being dismissed for misconduct or incompetence has not changed in recent years. In 2007–08, forty-nine employees were terminated for misconduct and another thirty-five for incompetence. In 2010–11, the numbers were fifty-four and forty-five, respectively. In 2015–16, ninety-two employees were terminated for misconduct and another seventy-seven for incompetence and incapacity.[57] I was not able to find the numbers for the most recent years. The more recent TBS documents on the public service no longer provide data on employees being terminated because of incompetence. The 2021 document, however, breaks down departures under three headings: retirement, resignations, and all other reasons. It adds, however, that, since 2014, "there has been a steady decrease in departures from the federal public service workforce."[58]

The TBS provides a document to managers titled: *Guidelines for Termination or Demotion for Unsatisfactory Performance; Termination or Demotion for Reasons Other than Breaches of Discipline or Misconduct; and Termination of Employment During Probation.* The guide is no more user-friendly than its title. It begins: "These guidelines support the principles set out in the *Policy Framework for People Management.*" It then outlines a "to-do" list for managers to consider, including: determine the required level of job performance; communicate to the employee the level of performance required; provide the employee with reasonable levels of supervision and instruction; allow the employee a reasonable period of time to meet the required level of job performance; provide the employee with reasonable warnings about the consequences of their continued failure to meet the required level of job performance; and once these measures have established the employee's inability to meet the required level of job performance, consider reasonable alternative employment within the government and within the employee's competence.[59]

The onus is on managers to document all the above. In some cases, it may be possible to document that "the required level of job performance is determined," notably in machine-like organizations or in government units processing applications, but not in other cases. How, for example, can one document the required level of job performance when dealing with policy analysts or public servants working in coordination and liaison units? Why would managers even want to try? Managers, to get through the process involved in terminating employees for incompetent work, need to be tenacious and to allocate hours to it, always with no guarantee of success. They can easily find more rewarding things to do for themselves and their units.

The above may explain why the great majority of public servants do not take annual performance evaluations seriously. Carroll and Siegel write that "virtually everyone" laughed when they asked public servants in the field about the performance appraisal system, suggesting that performance appraisal is largely a matter of going through the motions of the process and that neither supervisors nor subordinates take it very seriously. One front-line worker observed, "There hasn't been anyone in the last seven years come and tell me I've ever done anything wrong. Nobody ever comes to look ... They don't tell you you've done something right; and they don't tell you you've done something wrong. There's no review of the operation."[60]

An assessment of the *Public Service Modernization Act* returned a negative verdict on government managers' ability to deal with non-performers. Some 65 per cent of respondents recorded a "not at all" or "to a moderate extent" answer when asked about the capacity of managers to deal with their employees, including non-performers.[61] Terminating anywhere between twenty-two to no more than 100 employees a year for incompetence out of a workforce of 300,000-plus raises a number of questions. Peter Wallace, a former Treasury Board secretary, answered some of them when he said that "the barriers to firing public servants over mistakes were too high." Former TBS president Tony Clement argued that the executives involved in the "Phoenix fiasco should have been fired."[62] They were not, though it was a fiasco for all to see inside and outside the federal government. It is still ongoing.

Harrison McCain, one of Canada's leading business executives in his day, often said that there was no shame in hiring the wrong person – mistakes are often made, he said – but there is shame in keeping them.[63] Most private sector executives have a relatively free hand in turfing out or reassigning non-performers. The same is not true in government. In the great majority of cases, non-performers are isolated, placed outside the mainstream, so that they are out of the way and left to their own devices or assigned to tasks that are of little importance. Difficult decisions are thus avoided. Executives and managers point to the courts as another hurdle to deal with, making the process too unwieldy to even try.

It has never been easy to deal with non-performers in government. It is even more difficult today, given collective bargaining and the possibility that employees and their union representatives will go to the courts if management initiates an action to remove anyone for non-performance. It requires documenting, in minute detail, the causes for dismissal and numerous meetings with superiors, human resource specialists, and legal advisors to see the process through until it is completed before the courts. To avoid the hassle, managers focus on things over which they have more control. But such things are often designed to enlarge the scope of their programs or units rather than deal with non-performers. In any event, they have little incentive to engage in what would likely be at least a two- to three-year process to terminate an employee for non-performance. Many managers do not remain in the same position for much more than two years, moving on to a promotion or a lateral position with better prospects for advancement. Best to leave the problem for the next manager to deal with, and on and on it goes.

Again, even if managers think they have a solid case, there is no guarantee of success. For example, an arbitrator instructed a government department to rehire six public servants in Ontario who had been fired for exchanging pornographic emails at work that included graphic and violent images. The arbitrator ruled that the government lacked cause to dismiss the men. His decision made it to the front pages of Canada's national newspapers. To be sure, the message was not lost on government managers.[64] If the manager could not make the dismissal stick in this case, how could any manager make anything stick in other cases?

There have been cases, however, where a government department terminated employees because the circumstances clearly called for it. Employment and Social Development Canada, the department that oversaw the Canada Emergency Response Benefit (CERB), designed to help Canadians who stopped working because of reasons related to COVID-19, terminated forty-nine employees who claimed the benefit while employed in the department.[65] The Canada Revenue Agency also terminated 120 employees and investigated another 600 for "inappropriately" receiving CERB payments while they were implementing the program.[66]

There is strong evidence to suggest that many federal public servants are also underemployed. A senior analyst in the then Department of Citizenship and Immigration spent more than half his working day looking at news, sports, and porn websites from his desk while working at head office. The department took the highly unusual step of firing him for committing "time theft" by claiming that he was accepting pay while surfing the Internet. The employee appealed to the Public Sector Labour Relations and Employment Board (PSLREB), arguing that he wasn't given enough work to keep him busy, and that, in any case, he had met every deadline and had received positive performance appraisals. The PSLREB ruled in favour of the employee and ordered the department to reinstate him immediately. The Board argued in its ruling that it was surprised "that an employee could spend the amount of time that he did on non-work-related activities for months without his supervisors noting a lack of production or engagement."[67] Again, this ruling was not lost on other public sector managers: why bother even trying to discipline or fire an employee? It explains why a TBS study on compensation concluded that "it is relatively rare for public servants to be fired, with the greatest number of involuntary departures resulting from dismissal while on probation." The study pointed out that of the 4,883 separations of indeterminate employees that took place in 2002–03, only twenty-two were released for incompetence.[68]

A senior Government of Canada executive explained that public servants are handed golden handcuffs the moment they join the public service.[69] Their benefits range from parental leave to sick days, to vacation days, to generous health care benefits, and to a highly generous pension plan at the end of their career. The benefits make it difficult for public servants to leave the federal government. Public servants have few or no incentives to perform better or to leave government to pursue other opportunities. This outdated approach to human resource management has, in the words of a senior federal public servant in a private conversation, created too many "takers" in government. She suggested that government is now home to three types of public servants: leaders, bureaucrats, and takers.[70]

She maintains that it is more difficult for public service leaders to lead, and she went over the reasons, outlined above. Many public servants are solid workers, conscientious performers doing what they are asked to do. She maintains that they respect bureaucratic processes, always making sure that the "t's are crossed and the i's dotted." They continue to perform and deliver what is being asked, often under trying circumstances. Takers, meanwhile, are the non-performers, and once in, she insists, they take advantage of whatever is made available to them by collective agreements. They also demoralize other public servants, as it is virtually impossible to demote or fire non-performers and takers.

Government departments and their managers are left asking for still more resources whenever there are new demands or changes to their programs. Reallocating human resources away from low-priority activities is never part of the equation. When the government hints that it plans to introduce some spending cuts, it is met with pushback. The TBS, for example, announced in April 2023 that it was calling for cuts in the government's travel budget, making the point that technological improvements allowed for increased use of virtual platforms. The Board was told that cuts to the travel budget could well compromise the ability of the Department of Global Affairs to successfully pursue Canada's foreign policy objectives.[71]

Line managers will also make the case that feeding the "beast" or responding to demands for information from central agencies is increasingly eating up human resources. Those who would be expected to starve the beast are precisely the ones whose work is tied to the well-resourced beast – central agencies and oversight bodies. This, in turn, often explains the sharp difference in government between what is conceived, what is intended, and what is, in the end, implemented. And what is implemented very rarely squares with what was intended.

### LOOKING BACK

The unwritten code of "see no waste, talk no waste" explains in no small measure the behaviour of federal public servants, from the most senior level down to those on the front line. All incentives for public servants point in that direction. Some federal public servants, like many other Canadians, are motivated by their own economic self-interest. The economic benefits of saying nothing far outweigh saying something. Saying that a government department or a unit is overstaffed would mean that public servants would have to do something about it. But, when it comes to human resources management, executives and managers will turn away from difficult decisions and focus on other things, things that are within reach in getting done.

Beyond their economic self-interest, executives and managers have any number of reasons for not addressing the issue. They can argue that: the prime minister and ministers have a limited interest in human resources management; that there is never a shortage of more important issues to deal with; that it would require an inordinate amount of time and resources; that public sector unions would invariably fight the effort at every turn; and that all the efforts would amount to nothing if the courts decided against them. They could also make the case that, in the end, responsibility for doing something about it belongs to someone else – to the prime minister, to central agencies, to public sector unions, and to the courts – never to managers. Removing a number of centrally prescribed rules and adding human resource management levels in the federal government contributed to the unwritten code of see no waste, speak no waste, and never be critical of government operations with those outside the government. In making the case that responsibility for human resource management belongs to everyone, one can only conclude that when it comes to running their units federal managers cannot own what they say, what they do, and what mistakes they make.

## 5

## BOLTS OF LIGHTNING

It is not too much of an exaggeration to write that, if most politicians were free to produce expenditure budgets without constraints, we would see a constant stream of shiny spending measures drawn from what one politician calls: "whiz bang" ideas. Politicians would come up with new initiatives or introduce tax cuts and unveil them with great fanfare before the media.[1] If public servants were also free to shape budgets without constraints, we would see the status quo roll on, year after year, and the size of the public service growing endlessly. Public servants would continually add resources to existing programs and to government operations. This, in many ways, describes how the federal government's budgeting process works.

There are, however, days of reckoning when governments cannot avoid spending cuts. On several occasions during the past forty years, we have seen Ottawa reduce spending. In most cases, the impetuses for the cuts came from outside government, and in all cases, prime ministers were the architects and the driving forces behind the exercises. So much so that, in one case, the minister of finance and the president of the Treasury Board, like everyone else, only learned of the proposed cuts from the media.

To be sure, it is far easier for both politicians and career officials to add to the expenditure budget than to introduce spending cuts. This is not to suggest that politicians are always unaware of the difficult decisions that should be made. As the former prime minister of Luxembourg once observed: "We politicians all know what to do, we just don't know how to get re-elected after we have done it."[2] The task of cutting spending is made far easier when political leaders are able to blame outside forces for the cuts, notably the financial markets. Whatever the reason to introduce them, implementing spending cuts invariably requires strong political will at the top.

## THE ROAD BACK FROM BONN

The Pierre Trudeau government wrestled with inflation for much of the 1970s. When inflation ratcheted up to 10.9 per cent in 1975, the government responded by introducing several measures to deal with the problem, such as wage and price controls, in carefully identified segments of the economy. The initiatives, however, failed to arrest inflation and the decade gave us a new word, "stagflation," a combination of high inflation and low rates of economic growth.[3] Government spending also consistently outpaced budgetary revenues, given the slow economic growth throughout the decade, which was combined with increased government spending. As a result, the cost of servicing the public debt became a major concern for the Department of Finance.

When Trudeau attended the Bonn economic summit in July 1978, inflation was still running at 10 per cent. Inflation was also evident in much of the Western world and was the main item of discussion at the summit. A consensus emerged that growth in government spending was the main culprit. Trudeau returned to Ottawa determined to cut spending and announced that $2 billion would be cut from the federal government budget. He declared that the government "must have a major re-ordering of its priorities. We must reduce the size of government."[4] By most accounts, he came up with the $2 billion figure out of thin air.

We know that the number did not come from either the Department of Finance or the TBS, since Trudeau had consulted no one, other than his own advisors, before making the announcement.[5] It was a good round number to sell to Canadians. Trudeau simply declared that specific cuts would be unveiled in the coming weeks and he turned to the minister of finance and the president of the Treasury Board to get the job done. The two ministers, with the support of the prime minister, directed departments to come forward with spending cuts amounting to at least $2 billion, to be identified over the next few months. The cuts were to include eliminating 5,000 federal public service jobs.

The TBS did as it was told. It identified a series of cuts without involving line departments, their ministers, or deputy ministers. TBS did not even outline to the departments how it was able to identify the cuts. Departments were simply told to accept the cuts or, failing that, to come back with spending reductions of an equal value. The expenditures reduction process was not well planned and the minister of finance admitted as much, saying that: "the spending cuts were handled in a 'ham-handed way.'" He also acknowledged that the way they had been announced and implemented could well lead to the conclusion that the government was "in a state of crisis management." He explained, however, that "if you stayed with the orderly sort of process... the thing is that you will build up such a resistance and such a justification not to do it."[6] Because central agencies dictated the pace and scope of the exercise, departments openly criticized the process. To make matters worse, central agencies were never asked to cut their own spending or eliminate positions.

In the end, a number of large cuts were made across the board, and some federal public service positions were eliminated, but the number never amounted to 5,000. We also know that important cuts ($500 million) were made to federal-provincial programs. The political effect of these cuts was downloaded to provincial governments, far away from Ottawa and with limited political cost to the federal government.[7]

Some departments welcomed the "ham-handed approach" and took full advantage of it. The then Department of Regional Economic Expansion (DREE), for example, contained a Council on Rural Development in its portfolio, which reported directly to the minister rather than the department. Its purpose was to "advise the minister on the scope, direction and continuity of the federal government's policies and programs for rural development."[8] From time to time the Council was critical of DREE's policies and the department's lack of concern about the limited resources for rural development. When the department was asked to cut spending, it happily jumped at the opportunity to offer the Council to the TBS. DREE argued, and the Board agreed, that the Council could be easily abolished with little effect on government policies or operations and that Council staff could easily be reassigned to other departments. Other departments had similar examples.

Some departments suggested cuts in their capital budgets rather than in their operations and the TBS agreed. The Public Works Accommodation Program, for example, was cut by almost $100 million and some reductions to "fine art" purchases were announced.

These and a number of the other cuts would prove to be only temporary, and had a minimal effect on government departments and their staff.

When the Trudeau government went down to defeat in 1979, the new government showed little interest in pursuing the Bonn-inspired spending cuts. Joe Clark's Progressive Conservative party had formed a minority government and had little appetite to attack the expenditure budget. The Clark government served notice that it would look to tax increases to address the government's deficit. John Crosbie, the finance minister, used the phrase "short-term pain for long-term gain" in the 1979 budget, as he sought to sell the tax increases as a temporary measure. He had little to offer in spending cuts at that time.[9]

The Clark government went down to defeat after only nine months. Returned to power, Trudeau decided that he had more important issues to attend to than tackling the government deficit, so any bolts of lightning from above would have to deal with other issues. He introduced a highly controversial initiative to unilaterally patriate the *British North America Act* to Canada and entrenched a Charter of Rights and Freedoms in the Constitution with an amending formula. The initiative dominated the prime minister's agenda until April 1982. In 1980, the Trudeau government introduced another controversial issue – the National Energy Program (NEP). The program generated new revenues for Ottawa but at a very high political cost in Western Canada. Trudeau had little interest in attacking the government's expenditure budget in his last years in office, explaining: "We cannot cut expenses to the tune of some $14 billion [equivalent to 4.6 per cent of GDP]. Therefore, if we want to reduce the deficit, at some point there will have to be an increase in taxes."[10] The Trudeau government (c. 1980–83) had a number of other priorities, and the budget, notably dealing with government spending, took a back seat.

## MULRONEY TRIES FOR A SHORT WHILE

After the Liberal party went down to a resounding defeat in 1984, Brian Mulroney came to power, determined to deal with Ottawa's budget deficit. At the outset of his first mandate, he declared: "That we must deal with the deficit urgently is beyond dispute."[11] Unlike the Clark government, Mulroney's government would look to spending cuts to get Ottawa's fiscal house in order. Briefing books prepared by the PCO and the finance department to welcome his government to office showed that, after Italy, Canada was dealing with the worse deficit and debt situation among the G7 countries. The message to the incoming government could not be clearer – an urgent need to straighten Ottawa's fiscal house was in order.

The day after being sworn in, Mulroney established a ministerial task force to review all existing programs, to eliminate those that no longer served a purpose and consolidate the others, in the hope that not only savings but also better and more efficient government would result. The prime minister explained that he was asking the task force to review government programs to make them "simple, more understandable and more accessible to their clientele" and that the decision-making process would be "decentralized as far as possible to those in direct contact with client groups."[12] Mulroney is not the only politician to pledge to decentralize decision making by bringing it closer to client groups – however, the opposite has happened over the years, and this is on federal public servants, not on politicians.

Mulroney appointed deputy prime minister Erik Nielsen, a veteran of Ottawa politics widely viewed as "tough minded," to chair the program review exercise. Nielsen established private sector advisory groups at several levels inside government to help with the review. Three other senior federal ministers were also added to help Nielsen: the ministers of finance and justice, and the president of the Treasury Board. Mulroney looked to Britain and the United States to shape the Nielsen Task Force. Both those countries had also turned to input from the private sector to pursue the spending cut mandates that the British and American governments had given to the Rayner and Grace reviews in the early 1980s.[13] The Nielsen Task Force did the same and invited 100 private sector participants to the exercise – about the same number as the federal public servants working on the exercise.

The task force was directed to work quickly. The thinking was that ministers should be able to challenge their departments on their continuing programs early, or before the programs were "captured" by their senior career officials. The task force began its work by preparing an inventory of existing programs, encompassing both spending programs and tax expenditures, and then divided about 1,000 programs into "nineteen program families." Only a few of these "families" were limited to single departments, with the others crossing departmental lines. Once the inventory was done, a series of "study teams" combining both private sector and government officials were established to carry out the review of all programs.

The study teams produced a series of reports that were later made public. The reports sought to reduce the scope of some programs and eliminate others. None recommended that programs be expanded or that new ones be introduced. All study teams asked questions such as "Why is the federal government in this field?" or "What should be its role?" The teams were well aware of the new government's desire to downsize government and to reduce its spending. They responded by identifying programs that could be cut back or eliminated, or by looking at other possibilities, including devolving programs to the provinces, privatizing some of them, and contracting out others. Once the work was done, the private sector participants loaned for this exercise, with only a few exceptions, returned to their firms.[14]

The task force did generate some decisions, though not nearly as many or as consequential as initially envisaged. Several Crown corporations were privatized as a result of the Nielsen task force. In addition, the government cut about $500 million from programs and eliminated some public service positions. Many of these cuts, however, proved to be short-lived and the more ambitious recommendations were never pursued.[15]

The Nielsen Task Force efforts resulted in an exercise in search of support in government. In the end, it had very little political – and no bureaucratic – support and thus had very little lasting effect. As was expected, line departments strongly resisted. The fact that the task force decided not to review the work of central agencies led departments to label it a "biased" exercise. One senior departmental official explained: "If Nielsen was really serious about cutting back spending, eliminating waste in government and improving program delivery, then the first place you should look at is central agencies."[16] The fact that three of the four ministers on the task force did not have any departmental responsibilities confirmed their worst fears. It also explains why departments continually downplayed the Nielsen exercise and its recommendations and did everything they could to ignore its findings when dealing with their ministers and central agencies.

The Nielsen recommendations were turned over to the TBS to be implemented. The prime minister lost interest in the exercise and turned to what he felt were far more important issues, such as national unity (the Meech Lake Accord), undoing the National Energy Program, with a sense of urgency and pursuing a free trade agreement with the United States. Attending a series of meetings to explore possible spending cuts was no match for a free trade agreement or a possible constitutional accord, at least in establishing a legacy. When the prime minister lost interest in the exercise, ministers and the machinery of government soon followed, resulting in the Nielsen exercise leaving government without much of a trace.

The exercise, however, contributed a few lessons learned. The Nielsen Task Force itself summed up the challenge when reviewing Ottawa's expenditure budget. It reported on the "pervasive force of the status quo... as the most intractable issue of all ... Even where a given program is proven demonstrably useless, perverse or excessively expensive, abrupt termination often proves to be impossible."[17] The task force had nothing to say about who should be held to account for this state of affairs. It made the case that, when important spending cuts have been achieved, the prime minister's hand had to be present, highly visible, and firmly committed until the end of the exercise. When prime ministers lose interest in securing spending cuts, the effort dies. But there is more to it, because when prime ministers lose interest in cutting back the expenditure budgets, it is a signal for departments to start putting forward proposals again, to come up with "whiz bang" ideas and to expand their programs and operations.

## WHEN WALL STREET CALLS

In January 1995, the *Wall Street Journal* sent shockwaves through Canada's political and economic circles. In an editorial, it described the Canadian dollar as a "basket case" and added: "Mexico isn't the only U.S. neighbour flirting with the financial abyss." The editorial's title "Bankrupt Canada" made the case that "if dramatic action isn't taken in the next month's federal budget, it's not inconceivable that Canada could hit the debt wall and have to call in the International Monetary Fund to stabilize its falling currency."[18] David Dodge, then deputy minister of finance, described the editorial as a "seminal event" in the politics of the 1995 budget.[19]

It was the *Wall Street Journal* editorial, not the work of central agencies, that laid the groundwork for Ottawa to address its growing deficit and debt problem. The political parties referred to the challenge in the 1993 election campaign, but their solution to get Ottawa's fiscal house in order emphasized economic growth and job creation, not spending cuts. The Chrétien government only made passing reference to the government's deficit and debt problem in its 1994 speech from the throne. Finance Minister Paul Martin, however, was more forthcoming. He declared in his first budget plan that he would review: "all aspects of departmental spending to ensure that lower priority programmes are reduced or eliminated and that the government's diminished resources are directed to the highest priority requirements."[20] He did not elaborate, however, on how he would go about getting this done and had little to offer about where spending cuts could be made or which tax could be increased.

Martin did not live up to this commitment when he tabled his first budget in 1994, at least in part because it was tabled only three months after the government was sworn in. The budget was viewed as business as usual and the media were highly critical. The *Wall Street Journal* was hardly the only media outlet raising deep concerns about Canada's fiscal position. Media criticism was one thing, but when the bond market began to shy away from buying Canadian bonds it was quite another, at least for the Finance Department. The situation became "scary" in Ottawa's senior political and bureaucratic circles and Prime Minister Chrétien decided to act.[21] He said: "There would have been a day when we would have been the Greece of today. I knew we were in a bind and we had to do something." He added: "I said to myself, I will do it. I might be prime minister for only one term, but I will do it."[22] True to his word, Chrétien led his government into an ambitious program review that has since been described as the gold standard by which all program reviews should be measured. The international community took note and leading representatives of several countries came to Ottawa to see how program reviews should be carried out.[23]

The public service had some advice for the prime minister and the finance minister in dealing with government deficits. First, across-the-board cuts and budget freezes do not work. Second, efficiency measures and the notion of doing more with less do not offer "viable solutions."[24] I have never seen documented evidence that government departments could not do more with less or that it was not possible to squeeze greater efficiency out of government departments and agencies. The public service simply states this, time and again, as fact, leaving politicians with little basis on which to challenge the advice.

To be sure, the 1994–99 Ottawa program review was highly ambitious and involved all departments and agencies, including central agencies. The exercise also deliberately sought to involve all ministers and deputy ministers directly. It was a collective effort with the centre of government holding firm on the task at hand. Ministers and their departments were free to consult their clients as they saw fit to seek their views on where cuts could be made, but regardless, cuts would be made. All departments and agencies were told to test their policies and operations against six questions:

1. Does the program or activity continue to serve a public interest?
2. Is there a legitimate and necessary role for government in this program area or activity?
3. Is the current role of the federal government appropriate or can the program be realigned within provincial jurisdiction?
4. What activities or programs should, or could, be transferred in whole or in part to the private or voluntary sector?
5. If the program or activity continues, how could its efficiency be improved?
6. Is the resultant package of programs and activities affordable within the fiscal restraint? If not, what programs or activities should be abandoned?

The program review exercise was coordinated by committees of ministers and deputy ministers from carefully selected departments – some large and some small – to make the exercise as representative as possible. Departments had to generate answers to the six questions and produce departmental plans on how to implement the cuts. A program review secretariat was established to encourage open consultations between central agencies and departments. In turn, departments were instructed to designate a senior official responsible to ensure strong two-way communications between the department and the centre of government. In adjusting the machinery of government to meet the task at hand, the prime minister served notice that the program review exercise was to be taken seriously by everyone, including his most senior ministers, and that he would stay the course, come what may.

Ministers, deputy ministers, cabinet committees, and the minister of finance all played an important role in unfolding and managing the program review exercise. The prime minister was the key player, the one who ensured its success, but there were other reasons for the review's success. It took place at a time when there was a kind of perfect storm in reverse. The economy was growing again, after a short-lived but deep recession, and the political environment had never before been as conducive to an ambitious program review – nor, for that matter, has it been since. In addition, a significant part of the spending cuts was downloaded to provincial governments, in effect downloading political problems to the provinces.

The program review laid bare the failure of the federal government's continued efforts and its substantial investments in program evaluation and in producing a scientific approach to government budgeting. Arthur Kroeger, a widely respected senior deputy minister, assessed the program review exercise at the urging of the PCO and concluded: "It is universally acknowledged by those who participated that this process was utterly unscientific."[25] This speaks to the inability of public servants to make the "scientific approach," introduced some twenty-five years earlier, work. Program evaluation units operated at a different level throughout the program review exercise, uncertain of its practical value to decision making and essentially standing on the sidelines as the review ran its course. No one was held to account for the review process being "utterly unscientific" in spite of the substantial financial and human resources invested over the previous thirty years or so in trying to make the expenditure review process more scientific.

In laying the groundwork for the review, senior government officials were highly critical of across-the-board cuts and spending freezes. Regardless of the advice, the review exercise divided the expected spending cuts into three categories of across-the-board cuts – large or 25 per cent, substantial or 15 per cent, and token or 5 per cent – all three to be implemented over a three-year period. The results of the exercise had to be ready by the next budget and senior policy makers decided that there was no alternative to across-the-board cuts. They made certain that the large, substantial, or token categories would be respected. Initially, departments and agencies resisted and the first round of cuts only generated about 50 per cent of the required expenditure reductions.[26] But the review exercise did not let up, if only because the prime minister and the minister of finance never gave up.

A number of ministers tried to do "end runs" around the review process by going around the finance minister and appealing directly to the prime minister to reverse proposed spending cuts. Chrétien stood firm and never gave in once, knowing that if he did, it would open a floodgate of demands from other ministers. This was the decisive factor in making the exercise work. Chrétien was well versed in the Ottawa decision-making process, having served as minister in several large departments and as finance minister during the Bonn spending cuts exercise.

A number of other factors also helped the exercise. The PMO kept a close watch on public opinion by commissioning a series of public opinion surveys and they consistently showed support for the program review exercise.[27] In addition, in the 1993 election campaign, two opposition parties, the Reform and Progressive Conservatives, had run on the need to eliminate the deficit and were thus in no political position to criticize the initiative and its results.

On the face of it, the results of the Chrétien-Martin program review were impressive. The 1995 budget plan contained twenty-one pages of specific cuts, covering virtually all areas of government activities. These included replacing the $2 bill with a $2 coin; reducing the subsidy paid to dairy producers by 30 per cent; having regional development agencies rely on loans and repayable contributions rather than on direct subsidies; reducing subsidies to cultural industries by 8 per cent; terminating freight rate assistance; and reducing international assistance spending by 21 per cent.[28] Also, the size of the public service was to be reduced by 14 per cent or 45,000 positions, not the 50,000 as initially envisaged.

The review led to new user fees in various departments. For example, an immigration fee was introduced. Several departments, from Environment to Indian Affairs (as it was then called), were instructed to implement new cost-recovery measures tied to the cost of their services. It is important to note that the Mulroney government's decision to introduce a Goods and Services Tax (GST) in 1991 was also a key factor in dealing with the government's deficit problem (generating 13 per cent of total government revenues for 1995), replacing a hidden 13.5 per cent manufacturers' sales tax. The government maintained that the new tax would be revenue-neutral. It was not. Shortly after coming to office in 1993, the Chrétien Liberal party broke its campaign promise to get rid of the tax or replace it.

One large spending cut was made in the Transport Department. The government decided to no longer own, operate, or subsidize large parts of Canada's transportation system, focusing its efforts instead on its core policy and regulating functions. The control of airports (all twenty-five) was devolved to local airport authorities. With the transfer came all of the financial responsibility, both for operating the airports and for any capital improvements. The local airport authorities are not-for-profit corporations and are governed by boards of directors, and airport staff are employed by local authorities. The airports' staff are now not counted as federal public servants and they are no longer a drain on Ottawa's expenditure budget. Similarly, responsibility for operating Canada's ports was also devolved to local authorities. The seventeen port authorities were destined to become "commercially viable enterprises."

User fees, rather than parliamentary appropriations, now support the operations of all Canadian airports and ports. As a result of these cuts, full-time equivalents at Transport Canada fell from 19,881 in 1993–94 to 4,258 in 1998–99, and departmental spending fell by over 50 per cent, from $3.9 to $1.5 billion.[29] The burden of financing the operations of airports and ports moved from taxpayers to those who use the facilities. I note, however, that in 2021–22, Transport Canada's staff was 6,460, an increase of over 2,000 over a twenty-three-year period, during which it did not re-assume responsibility for airports and ports.[30]

The program review, meanwhile, did have a significant effect on program spending, spending that excludes all expenditures except interest payments on the public debt (see figure 5.1). It declined by over 10 per cent between 1994–95 and 1996–97 and also fell from 16.8 per cent of GDP in 1993–94 to 12.1 per cent in 1999–2000, the lowest level since 1949–50.[31] No small achievement to be sure when compared with other program review exercises.

A number of points colour the results of the Chrétien-Martin program review exercise. Though federal government politicians and public servants with a direct hand in the program review have made little mention of it, federal transfers to the provinces were cut by nearly $6 billion between 1994 and 1997. Provincial governments hold jurisdictional responsibility for health care, post-secondary

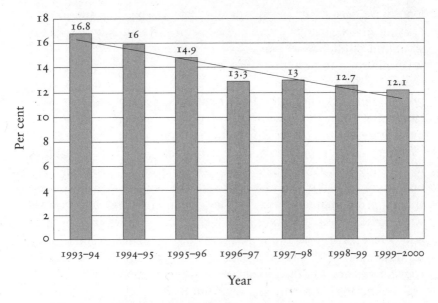

Figure 5.1 | Program spending, 1993–1994 to 1999–2000
Source: Federal Government Public Accounts, 2008

education, and social services, but historically they have benefited, and continue to benefit, from federal transfers to fund these programs. The cuts had a profound effect on provincially delivered programs: British Columbia, for example, saw federal transfers decline from 32 per cent in 1986 to 14 per cent of its health, post-secondary education, and income assistance in 1997. In 1980, federal transfers (both in cash and tax points) for health care represented about 44 per cent of provincial health expenditures but by 2000 this had fallen to 29.3 per cent. Provincial politicians made the case that while the Chrétien government was claiming full political credit for getting Ottawa's fiscal house in order, it was left to the provinces to actually grapple with the cuts in the politically sensitive areas of health care, social services, and education programs.[32]

The review generated a total of $29 billion in savings over a three-year period. Some $4 billion came from new tax revenues, and another $6 billion from cuts in transfers to the provinces and the territories. The government shifted away from business subsidies and cash grants toward repayable loans. We now know that not all such loans have been or are being repaid.³³ Defence spending and foreign assistance were cut by another $2 billion.³⁴ As already noted, the size of the public service was cut by 14 per cent, or 45,000 positions. It is important to note that some 6,000 of the positions eliminated were actually transferred to the private sector or local airport or port authorities. The bulk of the remaining 39,000 positions were eliminated through attrition and generous financial packages to public servants to entice them to leave the public service.

The 1994–99 program review exercise made clear the difficulties in carrying out a thorough review of government programs and operations. When it was able to do so, the Chrétien-Martin review sidestepped a number of issues. They favoured "stealth cuts," those with limited effects on taxpayers, such as cuts in foreign assistance and defence. Airports and ports were not shut down; responsibility for their operations was simply shifted to their communities. Cutting transfer payments to the provinces held limited political cost for federal politicians. This may well explain, in part, why Jean Chrétien won a majority mandate in the 1997 election, winning 155 seats, with the Reform Party becoming the official opposition, with 60 seats, leaving the sovereigntist Bloc Québécois with 44 seats.

It is important to underline the point that the exercise was an ad hoc initiative. Once it got the job done, the machinery of government reverted to its old ways. Chrétien himself dismissed the review's "Federalism Test" question when he made the Millennium Scholarship Fund his pet project a few years after the program review was finished. This fund provided financial assistance to university students, despite the fact that education falls clearly within provincial jurisdiction. Gilles Paquet and Robert Shepherd correctly pointed out that both the "federalism test and the partnership test would appear to have been essentially removed from the program review objectives" by the fall of 1997.³⁵

The government, at both the political and bureaucratic levels, began to push for new spending as soon as the review exercise came to an end. The same can be said about provincial governments who came calling on Ottawa to spend more. For example, the federal government signed a ten-year healthcare agreement with the provinces in 2004 that provided for an annual increase of 6 per cent, regardless of the state of the national economy.³⁶ The federal public service also went on a growth spurt in the immediate aftermath of the program review. The bulk of the new positions were created at senior levels, in policy, coordination, and evaluation units, in the National Capital Region, rather than in program delivery in regional or local offices.

It is worth repeating the point that today, over 41.1 per cent of federal public servants work in the NCR compared with only 25 per cent forty-five years ago.[37] Ironically, on the one hand, senior public servants applauded their work in shaping the program review exercise, while on the other they pointed to the exercise to explain why things went off the rails later in both the policy advisory and program implementation functions. Senior government managers have long argued that the program review had a negative effect on their policy advisory role. Senior government officials, including Jocelyne Bourgon, a key architect of the program review exercise, argued that cuts in key groups had weakened the capacity of public servants to produce strong policy advice. A senior finance official who had a direct hand in shaping the program review pointed to the need to strengthen policy units in departments after they had been "weakened" in the program review.[38] However, he and other senior public servants have had little to say about the review's effect on the federal government's capacity to deliver programs.

Another senior public servant argued that cuts in the public service resulting from the program review exercise led to scandals in government, notably the widely publicized sponsorship scandal. Alex Himelfarb, clerk of the Privy Council and cabinet secretary under both Chrétien and Martin, claimed that the program review cuts in the public service were one of the reasons for the high-profile sponsorship scandal. Scandals also occurred in the pre-program review era, but he had nothing to say about those and was not able to assign blame for them. The sponsorship scandal dominated the Canadian media for several years and ultimately brought down the Liberal government.[39] Himelfarb argued that more public servants ought to have been occupying oversight functions in such areas as internal audit or financial management, but that they became easy targets for elimination under the program review.[40]

The sponsorship scandal happened because government officials, including a senior public servant, broke the law. Surely, public servants should not need oversight bodies to tell them not to break the law. Charles Guité, a director-general–level official who had received highly positive performance reviews from his supervisors, was convicted of all five charges of "defrauding the federal government."

He was found to have committed fraud and ignored the *Financial Administration Act* and he was sent to prison. One could argue that the sponsorship scandal pointed to a breakdown of values and ethics in some quarters of the public service and officials in the PMO getting directly involved in program delivery decisions, rather than to a lack of oversight bodies. Many former federal public servants have long argued that government managers have to contend with too many oversight bodies, starting with officers of Parliament and ever-growing central agencies.[41]

The program review process also enabled provincial governments and senior public servants to engage in the blame game or blame avoidance for several years. Provincial governments insisted that responsibility for cuts in health care should be laid at the door of the federal government whenever a service or a hospital had to be reduced or eliminated. Provincial premiers made the case that, given cuts in transfer payments, they had no choice but to close or merge hospitals. Ontario's Mike Harris government, for example, announced the closure of three hospitals in 1997, including the Montfort Hospital, which serves the francophone minority community in the NCR. The announcement led to a heated political exchange between Harris and Prime Minister Chrétien. The local francophone community took the matter before the courts and won. The federal government subsequently announced a $10 million infusion of funds to Montfort.[42]

Though the 1994–97 Chrétien-Martin program review process had flaws, it generated important spending cuts and led the way in getting Ottawa's fiscal house in order. The initiative ranks at the very top compared with other program review exercises. But the review also exposed some important shortcomings. First, it was ad hoc and, once the job was done, things went back to constant pressure for new spending. Second, it was unscientific, in that ongoing efforts to evaluate programs contributed very little to the exercise. It was a political exercise. Third, across-the-board cuts became the go-to approach to generating spending cuts in short order. Fourth, it fuelled the blame game for public servants and provincial governments. Fifth, it proved that the strong hand of the prime minister needs to be present for a program review exercise to have any chance of success.

## THE HARPER CUTS

I recall federal public servants telling me in late 2005 and early 2006, as they were readying to receive the newly elected Harper government to power, that they were expecting sweeping spending cuts and a sharp reduction in the size of the public service. The fear proved unfounded. Harper had only won a minority mandate, making a program review or significant spending cuts difficult. In addition, Canada, like other Western countries, had confronted a serious financial meltdown in 2008. A consensus emerged that government spending cuts would only make things worse. But the pressure on politicians "to do something" was intense and OECD countries, Canada included, decided that the "best remedy" to deal with the financial crisis was to increase spending.[43] The Harper government thus launched an ambitious "Economic Action Plan" that included new spending for infrastructure, for housing, for business, and for community support.[44]

Though the Harper government launched four program reviews during its stay in office, it substantially added to Ottawa's expenditure budget between 2006 and 2011.[45] In 2006, Paul Martin's final year in power, federal government program spending stood at $175 billion compared with $245 billion under Harper by 2009–10. Several departments saw sharp increases in their spending plans under Harper – a 21 per cent increase for the Department of National Defence and a 45 per cent increase for the Royal Canadian Mounted Police (RCMP). The federal public service also grew during the Harper years, adding thousands of staff to the Canadian Armed Forces, to the RCMP, to Health Canada, to Human Resource and Skills Development Canada (8,000 new staff members); and the list goes on – an overall increase of 33,023 employees, or more than 13 per cent, over five years.[46]

After Stephen Harper won the 2011 general election, he quickly served notice that things would be different. The 2008 financial crisis was over, the economy was growing, and he had finally won a majority mandate. The Harper government launched its own program review in 2011 to deal with a growing deficit and, once again, to reduce the size of the federal public service, which had added 70,000 positions since 1998, since the end of the Chrétien-Martin program review exercise. Finance Minister James Flaherty committed the government to a balanced budget by 2015–16, pledging to carry out a comprehensive review of government spending. However, at the same time, he unveiled a new spending package, including funding for a new national park, $2.2 billion to Quebec to compensate the province for harmonizing its sales tax with Ottawa's GST, and a $4.2 billion loan guarantee for a Newfoundland and Labrador hydroelectric project.[47]

The Harper government was still able to announce in its 2014 Economic Action Plan that it was "on track to return to balanced budgets in 2015." It did this, it argued, through a "careful management of direct programs – specifically government administration" and explained that "direct program spending is projected to remain broadly in line with its 2010–11 levels over the forecast horizon – direct program spending had declined for three consecutive years ... in 2012–13, it was over $5 billion lower than in 2009–2010."[48] The government recorded a $1.9 billion surplus for fiscal year 2014–15. It also projected a $1.4 billion surplus for fiscal year 2015–16, adjusted later by the newly elected Justin Trudeau government to a $1.0 billion deficit, to the end of March 2016.[49]

Harper's 2011 budget commitment to reduce the $55 billion deficit resulted in several measures to get the job done. The government put an end to stimulus spending, froze operational budgets, and cut 5 per cent from departmental budgets.[50] The government also targeted some agencies, including the CBC, for deeper cuts. When Harper came to power, parliamentary appropriations to the CBC were $1.07 billion (in 2014 adjusted dollars) but by 2014–15 this figure had dropped to $929.3 million. It forced the CBC to cut 1,000 to 1,500 employees from its ranks by 2020, this from a workforce of 7,000, which it did largely through early retirements and buyouts.[51] Things took a different turn with the change of government in 2015. Today, CBC has a total workforce of 7,743 employees.[52]

The Harper government did get pushback from senior career officials when it decided to cut the operating budgets of line departments. Like previous prime ministers, Harper was warned that across-the-board cuts would "hurt public service morale, productivity and citizen satisfaction." Harper was told by the PCO that a better approach would be a series of "efficiency audits" of departments by asking line departments to identify more effective and efficient ways to deliver programs and services.[53] There is little evidence to show that this approach has ever been successful – it is an idea whose time never comes. One can also ask why public servants need to be told by politicians to carry out "efficiency audits." There is nothing to stop them from doing this on a continuing basis but there is little evidence that efficiency audits were ever carried out in the past. It is a case of public servants telling politicians that it is their responsibility to call for efficiency audits, not senior executives or managers. It also makes the case that it is easier for public servants to speak truth to politicians than to themselves.

Though it constituted a key component, the Harper government's ability to move to a balanced budget was due to factors other than the 5 per cent across-the-board cuts. After the 2008–09 financial meltdown, it benefited from strong economic growth, a $7.4 billion decrease in federal transfers to provincial governments, a $2.6 billion reduction in employment insurance to individuals, and a $3.4 billion drop in the cost of servicing the debt.[54]

## TRUDEAU FILS AT THE HELM

In his party's 2015 election platform, Justin Trudeau pledged that "the federal government will have a modest short-term deficit of less than $10 billion in each of the next two fiscal years ... After the next two fiscal years, the deficit will decline and our investment plan will return Canada to a balanced budget by 2019–20."[55] That did not work out as planned. The Parliamentary Budget Officer predicts that, without a fiscal course correction, Ottawa may only attain a balanced budget by the year 2070.[56] Finance Minister Chrystia Freeland, however, maintained that the federal government would see a balanced budget by 2027, when she spoke in 2022 of a new commitment to fiscal responsibility.[57]

Much as Stephen Harper could point to the 2008 financial meltdown to explain the growth in government spending, Justin Trudeau could also point to the new spending needed to deal with COVID-19. But the Trudeau government had opened the spending tap before the pandemic hit and projected a $20 billion deficit in its 2019–20 budget.[58] The government also introduced a number of costly new spending measures to deal with the pandemic and added new resources to existing programs. In addition, the Trudeau government introduced a series of tax increases, including a luxury goods tax, a tax on foreigners who own vacant homes, higher taxes for banks and insurance companies, and a tax on share buybacks to ensure that large corporations pay their fair share of taxes. Regardless of these tax increases, the government's debt passed the $1.2 trillion mark in 2022, nearly double what it was when the Justin Trudeau government came to power in 2015. The government spent $452 billion in 2022–23, $90 billion above pre-pandemic spending. Growth in government spending has been very broad – fifty-three out of fifty-eight federal departments and agencies expanded their staff count between 2015 and 2021. By one measure, the size of the federal public service went from slightly less than 200,000 when Trudeau came to power to 254,309 in 2022.[59] By another measure, it grew from 257,000 in 2015 to 319,000 by 2022.[60] TBS, meanwhile, reported that the federal public service grew by more than 35,000 people over a two-year period, between April 2020 and April 2022, a 12 per cent increase.[61]

With COVID-19 coming to an end by spring 2023, the Trudeau government began to talk about fiscal discipline. It had some help from inflation, which had boosted government revenues by $30 billion in 2022–23. By that time, government spending had also dropped by 21 per cent compared with peak COVID-19 spending in 2020–21. But federal spending was still up in 2022–23 by 35.9 per cent when compared with 2019–20, the fiscal year pre-COVID-19.[62] The government also committed new spending for health care, clean energy initiatives, $30 billion for a new childcare program, Old Age Security and the Guaranteed Income Support, and eliminated interest on the federal portion of Canada Student Loans and Canada Apprentice Loans.[63]

The minister of finance announced in the 2022 budget that the Treasury Board president would lead a "comprehensive strategic policy review" to generate $7 billion in savings over five years and $3 billion in annual savings by 2026–27. The review asked all departments and agencies to answer three questions: Is spending aligned with government priorities? Is every program working well? and Is this program the most efficient way to achieve the desired effect?[64] One could ask, why were central agency officials at Finance and the TBS as well as the various policy and program evaluation units in line departments not already asking these questions before or on an ongoing basis? It is also déjà vu, as similar questions were asked in previous program review exercises. One can only conclude that the questions are only taken out of storage when the government is forced to launch a program review.

The public service unions were quick to express concerns about the review. The president of the Public Service Alliance of Canada said: "It is very concerning for PSAC to see this. For there to be a specific amount hints that they know exactly what they are doing." The president of the Professional Institute of the Public Service of Canada said: "I would like to know where those numbers are coming from. I'm hoping it comes from moving to a hybrid working model because we'll need less real estate and less flying (travel) because more things can be done virtually."[65] Nothing was said about the growth in the size of the federal public service – by 35,000 people between 2020 and 2022, and by about 25 per cent between 2015 and 2022 – and its effect on the expenditure budget.[66]

The Justin Trudeau government unveiled a new series of spending cuts in August 2023, this time looking for $15.4 billion in savings over five years. Treasury Board president Anita Anand gave her cabinet colleagues less than two months to identify cuts. Public sector unions were quick to oppose the call for spending cuts, arguing that "you can't cut $15 billion in public service budgets without cutting services to Canadians." A TBS representative responded by insisting that the government "does not expect any cuts to affect the services Canadians receive and the plan is aimed at waste elimination."[67] The representative did not answer the question – why wait for the prime minister and senior ministers to unveil spending cuts to eliminate waste in government? In her letter to colleagues, Anand asked her colleagues and their departments and agencies to "review their programming to identify where there might be duplication, programs with lower value for money, or programs that do not address top priorities of the government."[68] Again, no one ever answers the obvious question – why do prime ministers have to announce spending cuts from above and what do the many public servants in policy and evaluation units and in central agencies do if not review programs for duplication and identify those with lower value for money on a continuing basis? Why is it not possible for the machinery of government itself, starting with central agencies, to identify on an ongoing basis duplication and programs with lower value for money?

LOOKING BACK

If the objective is to cut government spending, bolts of lightning from on high work. Nothing else seems to. The machinery of government has little to offer in reducing government spending – it has to be kicked into gear and the prime minister is the one to do it. Public servants have little to offer to politicians whenever there is a need to reduce government spending. Rather than looking to government operations, they will point to cuts in capital spending, which means kicking the can down the road. If cuts in government operations have to be made, they will look to cuts in regional or local offices or to blue-collar workers before other public service groups. They will, however, tell the prime minister and ministers not to look to them or to government operations to cut spending. They will also warn against across-the-board cuts, insisting that it is bad for public service morale and leads to weak policy units and even scandals in government operations. Politicians, meanwhile, will want to look to the government bureaucracy, convinced that there is always fat to be cut but they are never in a position to pinpoint where – hence they turn to across-the-board cuts. Public servants have not been able to recommend or make anything work better than across-the-board cuts to get the job done.

Public servants invariably look to politicians, their inability to make difficult political decisions and their desire to make spending announcements, to explain growth in government spending. A review of the growth in federal government spending over the past fifty years reveals that no political philosophy tied to either the Liberal or Conservative party affected, to any discernible degree, government spending levels. A former senior Finance Department official explains: "If I showed you a chart of government expenditure from 1997 and I asked you to mark when the government changed, you wouldn't have a hope of getting it right. They're indistinguishable. The Liberals cut expenditures for three years, then they let the barn door fly wide open. And the Conservatives just kept it wide open. Both parties ran program spending at about six-per-cent growth until the recession, then the Conservatives put it up to double digits. But the Liberals probably would have done the same thing."[69] Public servants, however, do not own up to their own failures in making various approaches to budgeting introduced since the 1960s work. Politicians are not fully to blame for funding program evaluation units that generate vapid reports, for the many policy shops in Ottawa unable to challenge the effectiveness of government programs and operations, and for determining the appropriate size of the federal government to do what it does. The public service does not take responsibility for the continued growth in the size of the public service, for constantly adding management levels and new executive positions. So who is accountable?

Parliament, meanwhile, has fallen far short in assuming its role of holding government to account for its spending. Lowell Murray, a highly respected cabinet minister in the Mulroney government, observed: "Parliament – specifically the House of Commons – over a period of more than forty years, has allowed its most vital power, the power of the purse, to become a dead letter, their Supply and Estimates process an empty ritual."[70] Sheila Fraser, former auditor general, said that members of Parliament are "failing Canadians" in one of their most important roles, reviewing the yearly spending estimates.[71] Walter Bagehot, arguably the leading authority on the Westminster parliamentary system down through the ages, looked to holding the government to account for its spending as one of members of Parliament's most important responsibilities.[72]

Members of Parliament are expected to approve the spending estimates – no questions asked – and Opposition members of Parliament are expected to oppose them – no questions asked. Thousands and thousands of pages are tabled every year in Parliament for review – they go largely unread and little, if anything, ever comes out of this process. In one case, TBS forgot to include pages for a highly controversial program – the firearms registry – and no one noticed.[73] Public servants recognize the problem. A senior TBS official said as much in a paper he gave to a public sector conference: "We did a lot of reporting that was not widely read (and produced) a large quantity of low-quality performance information."[74]

The government now looks to the budget process to load all manner of things that it wants done, whether they are related to the budget or not. This adds to the difficulties for MPs when the government's expenditure budget is tabled in Parliament. Both major political parties, when in opposition, have been highly critical of packaging many measures, at times unrelated to the expenditure budget, into an omnibus budget bill. Justin Trudeau pledged to end the practice when he was in opposition, as Stephen Harper had done before when he was leader of the opposition. They both changed their minds once in power. The 2015 Liberal Party platform read: "We will not resort to legislative tricks to avoid scrutiny … Stephen Harper has used omnibus bills to prevent Parliament from properly reviewing and debating his proposals. We will change the House of Commons Standing Orders to bring an end to this undemocratic practice."[75] The Trudeau government did no such thing – it simply continued the practice, including the 392-page 2019 budget implementation bill. Several measures were introduced in the bill, notably changes to the *Food and Drugs Act* and to the borders of national parks, and establishing a new government department. The *Toronto Star* argued that the budget omnibus bill makes "for accountability that is skin-deep."[76] In 2011, veteran member of Parliament Pat Martin summed up the general problem: "It provides the opportunity to hide a lot of spending that would never fly if given the light of day."[77]

Not only is Parliament unable to perform its historic function of exercising control of the public purse, it is not at all clear that members of Parliament have the necessary or accessible information available to enable them to ask penetrating questions about the budget. In a study prepared for the Commission of Inquiry into the Sponsorship Program and Advertising Activities, Ottawa's Parliamentary Centre concluded that Parliament only gives a "weak parliamentary attention to the Estimates." Members of Parliament told the Centre that "they did not pay much attention to the Estimates and that they had only a weak idea of what level of resources was expended to achieve program results."[78] In the 2023–24 Main Estimates, five House of Commons committees and a joint Commons-Senate committee did not even carry out a review of over $30 billion in spending. This is a long-standing problem and, as Lori Turnbull points out, if there is no rigorous process to review spending plans "then there's a problem in terms of the accountability for government."[79]

The Estimates are reviewed by parliamentary committees, where both the chairs and members often change, inhibiting the development of expertise at the committee level. Committees have, over the years, shown very limited interest in examining the Estimates. They are submitted by 1 March and committees have to report back by 31 May. Regardless of whether committees spend any time looking at the Estimates, they are deemed to have been approved by then. The Estimates contain thousands of pages and they are submitted in parts: Part I of the Estimates describes the Government's expense plan and provides an overview of federal spending. Part II, the "Main Estimates," identifies the spending authorities (Votes) and the amounts to be included in appropriation acts. Part III, the departmental expenditure plans, is further divided into two components. If you find this confusing, try going through the Estimates. I do, from time to time, in search of a specific item. They are very confusing to read and beyond the help of even the most competent copy editor.

The prime minister, cabinet ministers, and MPs on the government side prefer it this way because there is no advantage in seeing penetrating questions asked about the government's spending plans. Senior public servants also prefer it this way. There is no advantage in seeing MPs asking penetrating questions about government operations. The result is that Parliament has been turned into little more than an inconvenient obstacle for the government in getting its expenditure budget to the finish line. Canadians looking to Parliament to hold the government to account through the budget are left with questions rather than answers and everyone on the government side prefers it that way.

# 6

# TRY GRABBING SMOKE

Elmer MacKay, who served as a member of Parliament from 1971 to 1993 and was a minister in both the Joe Clark and the Brian Mulroney cabinets, said that, while in opposition, he found it very frustrating that, no matter how hard he tried, he could "never find the culprit." Things would be different, he thought, when he made it to government. However, once in government, he found it no less frustrating because he could still never find the culprit when things went wrong, no matter how hard he tried.[1] MacKay is not the only one who has made this observation. Justice Gomery, chair of the Sponsorship Inquiry, observed that in the federal government: "no one seems to be responsible" and that when incompetence is found "nothing is or can be done about it."[2] Thomas Axworthy, former chief of staff to Prime Minister Pierre Trudeau, writes that the "lack of attention to accountability, as an overriding goal of our political system, has resulted in many citizens choosing to opt out of the political process."[3] Sheila Fraser, former auditor general, maintains: "I think the great frustration of Canadians, quite frankly, is they have a sense that no one in government is accountable ... I think there is a sense that someone has to be responsible for these things when they go wrong, they have to be held to account and there has to be consequences."[4]

In the introduction, we saw that accountability in our Westminster-inspired parliamentary system calls for the following: public servants are accountable to ministers, ministers are accountable to Parliament, and members of Parliament are accountable to their constituents. This, in turn, requires both giving an account and being held to account. How does that chain of accountability now work? Where in the chain was MacKay not able to get answers or find the culprit and what led Sheila Fraser to argue that Canadians now believe that no one in government is accountable?

## PUBLIC SERVANTS TO MINISTERS

Accountability in the federal government starts at the bottom and works its way up to Parliament and from Parliament to Canadians. In theory at least, all public servants have obligations to render accounts to superiors, so that everyone is accountable to someone else at a higher level.[5] To make accountability work, a structure of subordinates to superiors is required, where superiors delegate authority to subordinates and assess subordinates' performance to decide on appropriate awards, corrective actions, or sanctions.

These processes in turn require hierarchies. There was a time when the hierarchies were simple, straightforward, and easily accessible. Today, many complex hierarchies come into play. It is increasingly difficult, in many cases, for superiors to assess the performance of subordinates, let alone establish a basis for rewards or sanctions, because hierarchy in government is no longer simple. It may have been possible at one time to separate, to some extent, politics-policy from administration. No more. The line now separating politics, policy, and administration is blurred and, in some cases, unrecognizable.

Luther Gulick had a simple question to guide the machinery of government: Is there a "little bleeding?"[6] Though departments were never watertight and completely self-contained, they could go about their work with limited concern for the work of other departments because, until the 1970s, there was little bleeding between boundaries separating departments. Departments, even at the level of individual public servants, were able to protect their turf, given that they occupied fairly well-defined boundaries which made it easy to determine who was responsible for what. They could also operate in relative isolation from one another. Today, by contrast, departments and even governments "bleed" profusely, and government policies and programs are increasingly linked. And, given the level of federal-provincial cooperation in virtually every sector, the boundaries separating the two levels of government are also collapsing.

The federal government has two fairly distinct organizations: machine-like organizations (where the plumbers work) and policy-coping organizations (where the poets work). In the case of machine-like organizations, it is still possible, in some cases, to draw boundaries around them and offer a visible understanding of how things work, as well as who is responsible for what. For the manager running a program at the Canada Revenue Agency, in a correctional facility or at Immigration, the Max Weber view of government operations still applies to some extent: government is organized "in a clearly defined hierarchy of offices."[7] The work, behaviour, and loyalty of public servants in machine-like organizations is markedly different from those working in policy-coping organizations. Those organizations are rarely in the line of fire because their work does not require the kind of controversial decision making or missteps that machine-like organizations can generate. If the work of machine organizations can be observed and measured, but that of coping organizations, with any degree of precision, cannot, then we need to ask if accountability requirements should be different for the two.

## MACHINE ORGANIZATIONS

Machine-like organizations are relatively self-contained and perform tasks that are fairly stable and predictable. Their managers and their staff have to look in two directions – at times up, but mostly down, and they prefer looking down, to citizens, clients, their unit's level of service and managing staff, and their financial resources. They also have to look up to head office, senior executives, the minister, and the political staffers in ministerial offices. A call from senior executives or the minister's office is never a good sign. Indeed, not getting a call means that the manager and staff have been able to get the job done, and avoided drawing attention, in the media or in political circles, to their programs or themselves.

A retired senior federal government public servant, who worked in Ottawa and in the Montreal and Halifax regional offices for the departments of Employment and Social Development and Fisheries and Oceans, explained the difference between working at head office and in a regional office: "In Ottawa it is all about politics, who is up and who is down and who has influence. In a regional office it is about getting things done."[8] A study published by the Public Policy Forum points in the same direction: "Regional executives felt they had more autonomy and authority over their immediate work environment than did their counterparts in the national capital region. This circumstance was attributed mainly to their further proximity from deputy ministers and ministers."[9] Program managers and their staff tend to group deputy ministers and ministers together – that is the Ottawa system.

In recent years, program managers have also learned the art of delegating up decisions that have the potential to hit the media or cause political problems. Richard Dicerni, a long-serving deputy minister with the federal government, maintains that front-line managers have mastered the art of "upward delegation" or pushing some decisions up to the most senior levels for resolution. He argues that what is urgent, what is important, at times what is not important, and what may become controversial is moved up to deputy ministers, ministers and, on occasion, to the PMO to handle.[10] Managers can sense what is politically sensitive or what will draw media attention and when it is best to move the issue up the organization to have higher ranked officials deal with it.

Program managers, the plumbers, are always ready when their services are required by senior executives to launch task forces and produce accompanying reports to promote empowerment, reduce red tape, and improve services to the public. These exercises, more often than not, come from central agencies. The plumbers see these efforts as little more than paper-pushing exercises, essentially just stating what they do and their ongoing efforts to improve the level of service. Many front-line public servants have been puzzled by Ottawa's emphasis on service quality in recent years, since a good number of them have spent most of their careers trying to convince senior departmental and central agency officials of the importance of delivering quality service to citizens.

In their exhaustive study on implementing programs and providing services, Barbara Carroll and David Siegel report on the frustration of public servants in the field with their head offices because they have, over the years, been "tirelessly inserting as many obstacles as possible to prevent them from providing good customer service. After this history, it is easy to imagine how field staff feel when they see large amounts of scarce funds spent on expensive consultants and glossy publications to convey to them exactly the same message they have been struggling in vain to convey to head office for years." And they go on to write, "Despite 'empowerment,' 'decentralization,' 'Total Quality Management (TQM),' and a myriad of other buzz words, acronyms, and improvements in communication technology, the gulf between head office and the field remains."[11]

I have, over the years, often heard federal public servants in line departments and agencies saying that "feeding the beast" eats up a lot of their time. By feeding the beast, they mean dealing with the constant demand for information and detailed reports about their activities from central agencies, political staffers in ministerial offices and officers of Parliament – the "Ottawa system." Two retired senior deputy ministers detail the constraints with which program managers must contend. They quote a "highly respected manager" who told them that having to respond to the accountability framework, to changes in management initiatives, and to provide paperwork to central agencies meant that he and the departmental staff "were spending less than 45 per cent of our time on actually delivering the various programs for which we were responsible."[12] In one of its audits of the evaluation function at Environment Canada, the Office of the Auditor General discovered that officials in the unit spent "about 40 per cent" of their time on tasks other than evaluation, without reporting what the other tasks may have been.[13] The two retired senior deputy ministers have no problem seeing the issue after they retire, but it is not at all clear that they saw it during their tenure as deputy ministers. I note that one served as Treasury Board secretary where he was in a strong position to reduce the need to feed the beast.

Front-line managers and their staff make every effort to "depoliticize" issues in their work. The prison warden has an operation to run and the more they can isolate staff from sources outside the institution, the better. Wardens operate in a high-stress environment and their focus is ensuring that staff and inmates are safe. Their work is both observable and measurable. They are also able to draw some boundaries around the work of the institution. They know the number of inmates, the cost per inmate, and the number of staff required to run the institution. They also know that senior management can compare the operational cost of other institutions of similar mandate and size.

Managers at the Canada Revenue Agency (CRA), for example, have a clear mandate and operate in a relatively self-contained organization. CRA is home to accountants and auditors and many of its employees often deal directly with Canadians. The agency is legally protected against political intervention. Senior executives can observe the activities and assess the productivity of staff down the line. The agency can also show, for example, that adding one tax auditor will generate revenues ten times their salary.[14] Such concrete advantages or benefits can hardly be demonstrated when adding a new staff member in the PCO, or in a policy or program evaluation unit in a line department.[15]

The federal government is home to many machine-like organizations. Think of Parks Canada, a separate agency that runs forty-seven national parks and 171 national historic sites. The agency is highly decentralized, operating in numerous communities in every region during peak season.[16] Park superintendents have considerable management authority to run national parks. It is also possible to observe their work and establish performance criteria because of the nature of their work and their ability to isolate, to some degree, their operations from other government departments.

One can consult the Government of Canada website and identify the departments and agencies that are home to machine-like organizations. Most departments have both machine and policy-coping units. We know, for example, that Employment and Social Development divides its activities into two headings: external programs and internal services. The department's four external programs are: Income Security and Social Development Branch; Learning Branch; Program Operations Branch; and Skills and Employment Branch. Its eight internal programs are: Chief Audit Executive; Chief Financial Officer; Corporate Secretary; Human Resources Services Branch; Innovation, Information and Technology Branch; Legal Services Branch; Public Affairs and Stakeholder Relations Branch; and Strategic and Service Policy Branch. The fact that the department has twice as many internal programs as external ones speaks to the importance of back-office work in the federal government and to the numerous oversight bodies that look over the shoulders of program managers.

Though it is never clear cut, a review of the various branches and the department's plan for fiscal year 2022–23 reveals that external programs are staffed largely by plumbers, while the internal ones are staffed by poets. The Employment and Social Development department (ESDC) also manages the Old Age Security (OAS) program and a guaranteed income supplement and allowance benefit to the spouse or survivor for low-income Canadians aged sixty to sixty-four. In addition, it delivers a number of other programs that target, among others, Canadians dealing with disabilities, student loans, and community development. In these cases, the work is again observable and often measurable. Front-line staff in the OAS program can measure the speed with which claims are being paid to beneficiaries.[17] Managers and their staff in these programs also produce observable work and can report on performance, however incomplete the report may be.

The department knows the percentage of seniors receiving an OAS pension at age seventy "in relation to the estimated total number of eligible seniors aged 70 and over;" the rate of Canadians approved for the disability tax credit, at 99 per cent; and also the ratio of Canadians who have a registered disability savings plan to encourage private savings, at 35 per cent. In other cases, Employment and Social Development can also establish targets and then report on results. For example, it established a percentage target of seniors living in poverty – set at 6.1 per cent – and then reported the results at 6.1 per cent in 2018. Though it is not clear how they were able to link their programs to the target or how the target was established, what is clear is that establishing a target and meeting it avoids political controversies. We also know that the ESDC department established the Service Canada agency in 2005 to provide a single point of service for the most subscribed federal government programs, including employment insurance, old age security, the Canada Pension Plan, and the delivery of Canadian passports. Managers of these programs do report on performance, though reports on the levels of success of programs have been spotty.[18]

Given that it is possible to observe and, at times, measure the work of machine-like organizations, their missteps are more visible than those of the policy-coping organizations. For example, when Passport Canada is experiencing problems and delays in processing applications, the media, opposition MPs, and the central agencies know where to point the finger – the passport offices, because their work is measurable and assigned to a unit. But this is not always the case, even for machine-like organizations.

For example, the media reported that the government had awarded $54 million to consultants to produce the ArriveCAN app. The project began as an $80,000 expense but the cost grew and grew. IT specialists insisted that the app could have been produced for a fraction of the cost. The media looked to the minister responsible for the Canada Border Services Agency (CBSA) for answers. But they soon realized that responsibility for ArriveCAN was shared between several departments: CBSA, Public Services and Procurement, and Health Canada. The media reminded the procurement minister that the prime minister had, a few years earlier, directed her to modernize federal procurement practices to provide value for money.[19] The minister did not respond to media inquiries. The point – even when the work is observable and the responsibility falls to machine-like organizations, it is still not possible, in many cases, to hold an individual or individuals accountable because often several departments and many public servants are involved in delivering the programs, so finding the culprit when things go wrong is now very difficult, if not impossible.

Things are even less clear when it comes to the federal government's internal programs. The ESDC department allocated nearly 5,000 full-time equivalents and about $1 billion for internal services for 2022–23. Total departmental spending was nearly $174 billion in 2022–23, with $157 billion allocated to statutory transfer payments to Canadians including, among others, employment insurance, Canada student loan programs, and the Canada Pension Plan. The department has produced performance indicators for its $1 billion in internal programs, but they are of little value because the department did not provide detailed information on its eight internal programs and said little about how it put together its accompanying performance indicators.[20] In the case of the corporate secretary, the report simply reads: "The Corporate Secretary supports the Department by providing portfolio coordination, executive and ministerial services, coordination of Cabinet and parliamentary affairs, and management of Access to Information and Privacy Act requests."[21] No information is provided on how the department is able to assess whether its human resources are well run. The same can be said about the Strategic and Service Policy Branch. Part II of the government's spending estimates also provides little additional information on its eight internal programs. I note that in years past these estimates, in particular part II, were much more forthcoming on the overhead cost of departments.[22] Because the nature of the work in these units is not easily observable or will rarely produce media interest, the internal programs are unlikely to draw the attention of anyone outside the department.

## DEPARTMENTS STAFFED BY POETS

Some departments and agencies have few or no external programs. They may be well known in government circles in Ottawa but enjoy little to no profile outside of the federal public service. These departments prefer it that way and would prefer to downplay their activities to outsiders. I consulted the Government of Canada website listing of its organizations to see how many such organizations existed. I counted twenty-nine policy-coping organizations.[23] There may be more depending on how one defines those organizations. This is not to suggest that their work is unimportant. Some, like the International Development Research Centre and the Canadian Intergovernmental Conference Secretariat perform important work. But they do not deliver programs or services directly to Canadians and, for several reasons, it is unlikely that they will be called to account for missteps by MPs: they operate in the background, they deal with issues that do not give them visibility in the media or in Parliament, and they have few to no dealings with Canadians. Though they are able to fly under the radar of public scrutiny, they do spend public funds and questions need to be asked about their performance. However, most have avoided difficult questions because the media and politicians have little interest in their work.

One such organization is the Canada School of Public Service. I have a special understanding of the school and I am able to write about it because of my inside knowledge of its birth and early development. While serving on a temporary assignment as assistant secretary at the Treasury Board Secretariat in 1987–88, on loan from my university, I was asked to write a report that led to the establishment of its forerunner – the Canadian Centre for Management Development. The then Treasury Board secretary, Gérard Veilleux, asked me to write a proposal that he could submit to the then clerk of the Privy Council, Paul Tellier, and to the prime minister, as well as to Don Mazankowski, the deputy prime minister, and arguably the most powerful member of Mulroney's cabinet. At the time, Mazankowski was also president of the Treasury Board and Veilleux's minister. Veilleux knew that if he could sell the proposal to them, it would be a done deal.

I produced a nineteen-page document – *The Canadian Centre for Management Studies* (CCMS) – arguing that the centre was necessary for two main reasons. First, the federal public service required a "strong, unifying and confident corporate culture," and the provinces and universities could not provide it. I quoted from the most recent annual report of the Public Service Commission (PSC): "The sense of pride in service that was the glory of the Public Service not all that long ago is being eroded."[24] Second, the government already had a training facility at Touraine, Quebec, but it had problems. It was more like an "orientation" centre for newly appointed managers. It had no research capacity and I argued that it did not "enjoy the reputation and prestige of a nationally recognized centre of excellence either in teaching or research."[25]

The solution – it was time to establish a dedicated centre for teaching and research in public sector management. In doing so, I stressed a number of caveats. First, I argued that the centre should stand alone, apart from any government department, and enjoy an independent status. I also argued that "it must have the capacity to bring together practitioners and leading academics in a centre known for its rigorous standards, especially in teaching, but also in its efforts to push back the frontier of knowledge in public sector management." This, I insisted, was necessary if the centre was to be more than a training centre and to gain credibility both inside and outside government. It must be seen to operate at arm's length from the pressures, both political and bureaucratic, of the federal government."[26]

I argued that the new centre "need not be costly." I reminded readers that for Canadians to appreciate the work of the public service, it had to be known for its "objectivity, its frugality and its value to society as a whole." I made the following case: "Experience tells us that the key element in establishing a centre of excellence is getting the right people. There is no correlation between the money made available to a new centre of excellence and its chances of success." I added, "Every effort should be made to limit spending, at least in the initial stages, to no more than what is now available at Touraine (i.e., forty-four person-years and $4.3 million annually)."[27]

I concluded with a series of recommendations on the curriculum (a combination of courses in management, communications, history, economics, political science, and constitutional and administrative law). The ideal faculty member would be "a mix of two people – a top flight broadly experienced university professor and a top flight broadly experienced practitioner. There are few such people and, if they can be found and attracted year by year, then the problem of finding faculty members will have been solved." I urged that every effort be made to "attract experienced academics, on contract, who could develop courses" in collaboration with experienced practitioners.[28] I stressed, however, that the centre had to be independent of government if it was to attract leading academics and promote rigorous research. I explained that solid academics will see their research interest go into areas where it needs to go and hence could, at times, be critical of the government of the day. This is why I insisted on giving the Centre an independent status.

I had a number of discussions with senior TBS officials. They accepted the paper but made important revisions to it. The Centre was renamed the Canadian Centre for Management Development, the words "independent" and "able to operate at arm's length" were removed, and the section on funding was adjusted to read "not much more than what is now available" from "no more."[29] An important distinction, as time would reveal.

I was asked to accompany Mazankowski to Toronto for the announcement and helped write his speech, which he delivered as drafted. The occasion – a public policy dinner held on 14 April 1988 to honour four Canadians who had contributed to public service: Ted Newall, Allen Lambert, Bob Bryce, and Paul Tellier. Mazankowski's speech read, "It is a great pleasure to announce the establishment of the Canadian Centre for Management Development … Our vision is a credible, nationally and, perhaps in time internationally, recognized centre of excellence in teaching and research in public sector management."[30] Mazankowski also introduced the centre's first principal, Jack Manion, a long-serving, highly respected deputy minister in Ottawa, who he called "an individual whose managerial skills are among the most highly respected in Ottawa."[31] He then announced that Paul Tellier had agreed to act as chairman of the centre's advisory board.[32] The fact that the Centre was guided by an advisory board rather than a board of directors revealed that it would not enjoy independence from the government of the kind that I had envisaged.

I was asked if I could go to the Centre as deputy principal for one year and serve as acting principal. I agreed. The PCO announced that Jack Manion would move over to the Centre in a year. But from the moment I stepped into the new centre, I felt pressured by the central agencies and senior departmental officials to take on some of their senior staff. They argued that the public servants in question had served the system well, were loyal, and had a wealth of management experience that they could share with aspiring senior managers. I thought – how could that "wealth of management experience" no longer be good enough for their departments, but somehow fine for the whole of the public service? These officials also often said that the individuals in question did not fit into the reorganization or that they could not adapt to new ways of doing things. In many cases, the central agency or department offered to carry their salary for a year or so. Their argument – these individuals had been very loyal to the system and it was time for the system to be loyal to them. The idea of building "a credible, nationally and perhaps in time internationally, recognized centre of excellence" was not on their agenda. They needed to move someone out of the department who were past their best-by date and the new centre provided a convenient out. I resisted, but when the clerk, associate clerk, or secretary to the Treasury Board call, it is not always possible to say no, especially when they have offered to carry the individual's salary for at least one year. But it is a slippery slope because when you say "yes" once, it becomes difficult to say "no" the next time.

The legislation establishing the Centre breezed through the House of Commons without problems or even questions. The Senate was a different matter. Michael Pitfield, former clerk of the Privy Council and now senator, had important concerns. Manion explains, "In Committee, it became clear that Pitfield opposed the very idea of the Centre and was just talking to obstruct. He kept asking the same questions of me over and over again. Finally he objected to the Chair that I was repeating the same answers. Unwisely, I blurted out 'when you stop repeating the same question, I will stop giving the same answer!' All hell broke loose. My staff hid their faces and the Senators went on about disrespect to the Senate. Ultimately I left, but it took two years to get the bill through the Senate."[33] As Manion explains in his autobiography, Pitfield could never accept the federal government undertaking activities that he felt more properly belonged to the universities.[34]

I have since seen the Centre grow. It sits in a beautiful heritage building opposite the National Gallery on Sussex Drive in downtown Ottawa. It is also home to several regional offices. The Centre moved away from fundamental research to what its officials labelled "action research." I have never understood what action research means nor have I seen any. Perhaps it is the academic in me, but I saw action research as the kind of research that could never get accepted in peer-reviewed publications. To be sure, action research generates a lot of meetings and a lot of discussions, but few publications. It also has no lasting value to the literature. It is, however, not critical of federal government policies or management practices.

In 2004, the government decided to change the name of the Canadian Centre for Management Development to the Canada School of Public Service. It was never made clear why the name was changed. I suspect that the word "school" brands the organization as more of an institution of higher learning than does the word "centre." The school reports to TBS and has all the trappings of a typical government department. It has also embraced other terms associated with universities, including referring to staff as faculty members and using emeritus to describe a former president.

Little research takes place at the School, which has a team of fourteen distinguished fellows and twenty-three faculty members. I know of no publication produced by these faculty members and the School's 2022–23 departmental plan has very little to say about research. It is not for a lack of resources – the School has a $111 million annual budget and operates with a staff of about 670 full-time equivalents, including 176 in internal services. I note that the plan says nothing of substance about evaluation or performance.[35]

The school's resources are a far cry from the day it was established and from the commitments Mazankowski had made to the prime minister. In September 1987, I wrote: "The objective is to develop a nationally and over time and internationally recognized centre of excellence in teaching and research in public sector management."[36] What about accountability? Prime Minister Mulroney is no longer there to ask questions, nor Mazankowski to provide answers. In any event, one can easily speculate that the new management centre quickly fell off the radar after Mazankowski announced its establishment. It has been left to senior public servants to manage the centre-cum-school with very limited intervention from politicians.

I do not hear anyone suggesting that the Canada School of Public Service is a nationally recognized centre of excellence, let alone an international one. It is not. I can write several 300-page books on Canadian public administration, as I have done, and not draw a single quote from the research carried out at the school. It is difficult even to determine if it is a good teaching facility. I note that the school is hardly the only learning institution funded by the federal government in full or in part, including the Ottawa-based Institute on Governance.[37]

I have watched over the years with interest as many senior central agency or department officials were transferred to the school. There is little evidence that they had ever entered a classroom to teach or undertaken substantial research before their new assignment. The school has simply become a convenient place to park senior public servants, mostly poets, while they wait for their retirement. But this is not without costs to taxpayers. The *Globe and Mail* called the school a "classic government boondoggle" in 2013. It is worth quoting at length from the article:

> The school hires retired, pensioned civil servants to teach other civil servants such things as "Writing Targeted Briefing Reports" and "Managing a Meeting." There are hundreds of courses available; some are online and cost nothing, while others, such as "How Ottawa Works," are taught in the classroom and have tuition fees as high as $1,650. The problem is that the retired civil servants teaching the courses are earning eye-catching fees. Records show one is making $82,500 a year for working a half week (22.5 hours). A former associate deputy minister gets $38,000 for 50 days work. Faculty members get as much as $760 per day to prepare and teach a class. They are also high fees compared to the average annual salaries of university professors in Canada. A full-time professor at the University of Toronto earns about $136,000 per year. One school faculty member earns $154,300 annually for not quite full-time work. The federal procurement ombudsman, Frank Brunetta, reported last month that he found evidence the school directed contracts to favoured clients and violated its own procurement policies in doing so. This came after Treasury Board President Tony Clement wrote in a letter to the school last year that he is concerned about the possibility of "inappropriate contracting with former public servants in receipt of pensions, either because contractors are being chosen preferentially or because contractors are being hired to provide work of dubious value."[38]

The *Globe and Mail* published this article over ten years ago, and salaries and per diems are much higher today. It could have added that the University of Toronto professor is expected to produce peer-review research. It could have also added that retired public servants enjoy many benefits, including an extremely generous pension plan and other employment benefits that are not available to faculty members at the University of Toronto. I suspect that if Mulroney and Mazankowski had known of this turn of events, they would not have signed on to the proposal. As it is, the *Globe and Mail* article did not generate many questions about the school in Parliament or anywhere else.

How could a *Globe and Mail* journalist uncover these lacunae, while several senior public servants at the school and the TBS with expertise in evaluating performance make the case that all was well with the school's performance or with the values and ethics of its staff? Officials at these two agencies, more so than those in line departments, should be at the leading edge of new management thinking in government and how to implement it. If these officials are not up to the challenge, one can hardly imagine what it is like for others. This also speaks to bureaucratic elites looking after their own economic interest and that of other bureaucratic elites. How else can one explain that retired senior public servants, who already enjoy generous pensions and other advantages, are able to enjoy $80,000-plus contracts for half-time work?

At my own university and at most other universities, a retired professor invited to teach a course to accommodate the department because of a sabbatical leave or another unforeseen development is paid $6,000 for the course. The $6,000 includes preparation and teaching time. I note that my university, unlike the federal public service, has never launched an elaborate values and ethics exercise.

I consulted a senior Canada School of Public Service official in February 2023 to test my views about the school. The official argued that I should not read too much into the school's decision to embrace academic terms such as "faculty" or judge its capacity to produce peer-reviewed publications, maintaining that the school is a "training" facility and that we should assess its performance on this basis. Before the centre was created and later turned into a school, there was a training facility at Touraine. The difference is that today the school that replaced the Touraine training institution operates under a different name and it is far more costly to run.

It is difficult to assess the school's performance as a training facility. Those who do find it wanting. Other than officials at the school and, at times, the TBS, precious few voices sing the school's praises. Writing some twenty years after the school was established, a retired deputy minister and head of the Public Service Commission maintains that senior public servants "don't have the training to handle the tough policy and management issues facing government today."[39] She adds that "the state of mind of executives has come to be tainted by a multitude of bad habits ... rewarding failure, punishing success, failure to confront."[40] She should know, having served as deputy minister in both a line department and in a central agency. Dominic Barton, the former head of McKinsey Consulting, recently told a parliamentary committee that the federal government is "weak in terms of training" its public servants.[41]

The School's annual budget is twice that of a small- to mid-sized university. Mount Allison University, for example, has an annual expenditures budget of $54.5 million. The university is home to about 2,500 students and its faculty are able to secure funding for research in arts, social sciences and natural sciences, and publish in peer-reviewed journals.[42] Some federal public servants that I consulted made the case that I should not compare the Canada School of Public Service with a university. They never explained why.

I looked at what other countries are doing in this field in an effort to compare an orange with an orange. Britain had a National School of Government but shut it down in 2010. The government transferred only a handful of its activities to the cabinet office under a new unit labelled Civil Service Learning.[43] The United States has a Federal Executive Institute that now operates under the Office of Personnel Management (OPM).[44] A proposal to expand the approach by creating a United States Public Service Academy has met with stiff opposition and remains on the drawing board, where it has been since 2007.[45] France did away with its École nationale d'administration (ENA) in 2021. ENA came under criticism because it was viewed as providing too narrow a focus on public policy and public administration issues and also for promoting in-breeding or group think.[46] France now has an Institut national du service public (INSP), located in Strasbourg, away from the capital. The Institute's mandate is geared to training and developing senior public servants and aspiring senior managers rather than research. It has a very modest budget, at least when compared with the Canada School of Public Service. The INSP only has a handful of government employees and looks to guest lecturers from the French public service, the universities, and elsewhere to teach and lead seminars.[47]

The question then is – why has no one in the Treasury Board, in Cabinet, or in Parliament taken the school to task? It would be disingenuous to argue that politicians should be held to account for the performance of the Canada School of Public Service. They can give the green light to launch the school and announce it publicly but it is beyond both their interest and ability to monitor its development over time. Public servants should be the ones held to account for the school's performance. However, to do so, public servants need to be willing to speak truth to one another or to other public servants.

The school is hardly the only example of federal public servants preferring what they desire over what is feasible. Determining what is feasible is always for someone else to decide – mostly the Finance Department, which is always strongly outnumbered by those wanting to promote what they desire over what is feasible. The Leaders' Debates Commission is another example of this. The federal government decided to set up a Leaders' Debates Commission in 2018 with a mandate to organize two debates (one in English, the other in French) for party leaders during federal election campaigns. Before the commission was set up, television networks had organized the debates. The cost for organizing the debates for the 2021 election campaign amounted to $4.4 million. However, the Commission continues to operate in nonelection years and spent $330,000, including more than $17,000 for performance bonuses, in a year when no election was held.[48]

The Commission released a report on the 2021 federal election accompanied by a series of recommendations. It began with its principal recommendations, followed by ten more: "We recommend the continuation and improvement of a permanent publicly funded entity to organize leaders' debates that is subject to periodic review." Other recommendations include: "The Commission should maintain sufficient permanent capacity between elections to ensure it can organize debates at short notice and to cultivate relationships between elections to foster discussion, both in Canada and in other countries"; "The Commission reaffirms it should ultimately be established through legislation (or similar mechanism) with a periodic review process, such as every five years, in order to prioritize greater continuity, transparency, and access to resources; and its institutional makeup should prioritize real and perceived operational independence, cost effectiveness, and administrative agility."[49] Why would the Commission's staff argue otherwise or that their work is done and that there is no need for a permanent organization or explore ways to get the same work done at less cost to taxpayers? The Commission submitted its recommendations to the minister responsible for democratic reform. The pressure on the minister and on the government to agree with their recommendations will be intense. The Commission will underline the point that it is desirable, given the state of democratic institutions in the Western world, and that the price tag will be only a drop in the bucket in a $400 billion-plus annual budget. If history is any guide, another drop will be added to the bucket.

The behaviour of both the Canada School of Public Service and the Leaders' Debates Commission is typical of government organizations. Once established, they will explore every opportunity, and advance every argument, to grow, to add to their responsibilities and to their resources. Their focus is on what they desire for their organizations, not for Canadians, and rarely, if ever, on what is feasible. The School and the Leaders' Debates Commission are only two of the agencies staffed by poets. There are many more.[50]

## LOOKING BACK

The federal government has become highly complex, making it more and more difficult to make accountability requirements work. It is now home to different organizations, in some of which their work can be observed and, to some extent, assessed. But this is less so, if at all possible, in the case of many other organizations, notably policy-coping organizations. We also know that their tendency is to focus on the present and the future because all the political incentives point in that direction. The result is that past experiences and what was promised when a government agency was established are never or rarely subjected to a systematic review. Thus, it it is no longer possible for MPs to find the culprit. It is also becoming impossible even for ministers. If ministers can no longer find the culprit and hold government units and individuals to account, then the chain of accountability from public servants to ministers, ministers to Parliament, and MPs to their constituents is broken.

It is not possible to determine if ministers, let alone MPs, have any interest, let alone the capacity, in holding either the Canada School of Public Service or the Leaders' Debates Commission to account. One can assume that it is unlikely. Few of them have raised any issue about their existence, let alone their performance. Canadians are simply told what the Canada School of Public Service or the

Leaders' Debates Commission cost to operate every year but only if one bothers to go through the government's spending estimates. Once established, such organizations have the ability to expand their operations. Nothing is hidden but no effort is made to review their cost or performance. These two organizations are not much different from many other government organizations. Canadians know that there is something not quite right with how the federal government operates and decides, and that Parliament is not up to the task of holding government officials to account.

Canadians have to rely on public servants, ministers, and MPs to hold hundreds of federal government departments and agencies to account for their activities and their spending. The media also have an important role to play but they need access to information to do so. MPs and Parliament are the ones who can make accountability requirements work. We saw earlier that MPs believe that they have more important things to attend to than holding government operations to account. In addition, few of them have the knowledge and skills to raise and pursue demanding questions. We also saw that, for various reasons, MPs are underperforming in their role of holding the government to account. We now need to look at the work of ministers and deputy ministers and their contribution to accountability. It is their responsibility to provide answers.

# 7

# MINISTERS:
# THE BUCK DOES NOT STOP THERE

Ministers lead incredibly busy lives, far more than those outside government can appreciate. I have had numerous dealings, over the years, with a number of past and present federal cabinet ministers as well as CEOs of large private sector firms. There are far more demands on a minister's agenda than for CEOs. For one thing, ministers constantly have to look to several places at once for direction and accountability. For another, they have numerous responsibilities that they need to attend to and, in many cases, their performance is in the eye of the beholder, not based on hard or objective data. The media have an ongoing interest in the work of all ministers while most CEOs can go about their work away from the public eye. Accountability requirements for CEOs are often straightforward with easy-to-understand perimeters. For ministers, accountability requirements are anything but straightforward.

Under our Westminster-inspired parliamentary system, ministers are the focal point of accountability, in essence constituting a single point of accountability. The very first sentence in the Privy Council's guide for ministers reads: "Clear ministerial accountability to Parliament is fundamental to responsible government, and to ensuring that Canadians have confidence that their government is acting in an open, honest and transparent manner."[1] This concentrated accountability makes ministers accountable for all things before Parliament, and if this does not work, they remain responsible or answerable no matter what the issue is. This is true even when Parliament confers authority directly to public servants. Accordingly, accountability should stop with ministers. In theory, it may. In practice, it does not.

## LOOKING HERE, THERE, AND EVERYWHERE

Ministers must look to the boss – the prime minister – for direction and accountability, before looking anywhere else. However, while their accountability starts with the prime minister, it does not end there. Accountability starts with the boss because the prime minister decides who is appointed to cabinet, who stays, who goes, and who gets promoted. In relatively rare cases, a minister will be dropped from cabinet. In some other cases, they will be demoted to a more junior portfolio. Being demoted to a junior portfolio sends an important message to the minister, to cabinet colleagues, and to the public service. If the boss is not happy with a minister's performance, word will quickly spread around Ottawa. Even if the minister remains in cabinet, they need to have the prime minister's confidence. If not, the minister's ability to get things done will be severely handicapped. The "Ottawa system" always keeps a watching brief on who, in cabinet, is close to the prime minister and who is not. This, as much as anything else, defines who has influence in Ottawa and who does not.

Ministers also know that they need to establish a strong working relationship with the PMO since they rarely get alone time with the prime minister, given that their chief of staff is very often in the room whenever the prime minister agrees to meet with a minister. I was informed, for example, that the former minister of finance, Bill Morneau, was not able to get a private one-on-one meeting with Prime Minister Justin Trudeau until days before he left cabinet. Morneau himself explained: "Virtually any topic you wanted to discuss with the prime minister – official or informal, strategy or gossip – had to be shared in the presence of members of his staff."[2] Stéphane Dion served as Justin Trudeau's foreign minister for over a year and he was also never able to secure a one-on-one meeting with the prime minister, despite multiple requests.[3]

I recall walking up Parliament Hill in the early 1980s with Pierre De Bané, the then minister responsible for regional economic development. We came across Jim Coutts, Prime Minister Pierre Trudeau's chief of staff, and De Bané told him: "You are not returning my phone calls." Coutts responded: "Don't take it personally, I don't always return ministers' phone calls." I suspect, however, that Coutts returned Allan MacEachen's and Marc Lalonde's phone calls, as both were senior ministers with close ties to Trudeau. The point is that not all ministers have the same degree of influence in Ottawa and thus a strong working relationship with the prime minister and the PMO is important. That matters a great deal when it comes to successfully pursuing priorities for themselves or their departments.

Ministers need to look to their cabinet colleagues for support, both in theory and in practice. The PCO tells ministers that: "All members of the Ministry are collectively responsible for carrying out the government's policies as established by the Cabinet. They are therefore expected to work in close consultation with their ministerial colleagues."[4] A cabinet that cannot speak with one voice will soon be experiencing serious political problems that could well threaten its survival. The PCO, in another document, instructs ministers to consult other "ministers, departments and portfolios" before they can proceed with a "submission to Cabinet."[5] Team players are highly valued in politics, particularly by the prime minister. The ability to sort out difficult issues quietly with one's colleagues will be noted and appreciated by the prime minister and the PMO.

There are also ministers who have more clout than others simply because of the portfolio they hold – the finance minister, for example, will invariably have more influence than the minister responsible for rural development. It is thus always in the interest of all ministers and their departments to invest time and effort in establishing a solid working relationship with the finance minister and their staff because it matters in pursuing departmental priorities.

Ministers also need to look to the government caucus for support. Those who are popular with caucus members tend to have more political capital to spend with the prime minister and the finance minister than those who pay little attention to them. Paying attention to caucus members requires time, commitment, and effort, but it is well worth it, notably for newly appointed ministers looking to establish political support within the party, with cabinet colleagues, and with the PMO.

Ministers have exempt staff, who always have important reasons, at least from their perspective, to see their minister. As we saw earlier, ministerial offices have greatly expanded in recent years. There are now anywhere between fifteen and twenty-five partisan officials on staff in a minister's office, with several occupying senior positions. Senior staff members expect to meet the ministers regularly and to be able to exert some influence. If they are not able to see their minister, at least on occasion, they will be unable to get things done and they may well look for employment opportunities elsewhere. In short, those who have access to the minister have influence, while those who do not are left on the outside looking in. Departmental officials know who on the minister's staff has easy access to and influence with the minister.

Ministers also have a constituency office to staff and they will want to remain in contact with that office because it represents an important link to their voters. Ministers have constituents to look after and they have reason to think that they are accountable to their voters because they have a say in their future. They are expected to defend the interests of their constituencies in Ottawa and to deliver projects for their ridings. They have to be present and be seen to be present in their constituencies. For some ministers, this often requires long waits at airports and days away from home, going back and forth from Ottawa. Weekends are not always reserved for family time and for many, travel time does not end on the weekend either. Travel around the constituency is very often required. Ministers know full well that strong ministers have gone down to defeat in their constituencies, even after their party was re-elected, and they understand that the greatest potential for ministerial casualties is at election time. Ministers are conscious of the fact that they became ministers and can only remain ministers by winning a seat, and keeping it, in the House of Commons.

The PMO always keeps a close watch on where and when ministers travel. It can, at times on short notice, schedule ministers to appear at certain events to speak on behalf of the government. The prime minister receives numerous invitations to attend community or party events and the PMO often needs to delegate such invitations to ministers. It is a balancing act because the government whip will want to make certain that there are enough ministers available for House votes or duties.[6] Travel time can thus eat up a lot of a minister's time. In addition, ministers always have a never-ending list of telephone calls to return and people to meet.

Ministers also need to pay close attention to the activities of their political parties. They must attend party functions and be available to speak at fundraising events for their constituencies and those of their colleagues. This requires still more travel commitments. They must pay special attention to the activities and demands of the government caucus, including weekly meetings when Parliament is sitting.

When appointed to cabinet, ministers are handed mandate letters from the prime minister that outline the government's priorities, what is expected of them, and how they should go about their work. They also establish expectations on how ministers should conduct themselves. The letters have proven effective for PMO staff to keep track of how well the prime minister's priorities and the party platform commitments are being pursued. Ministers always need to keep a close watch on their mandate letters. They are fully aware that the PMO can always look at the letters as a report card to assess how well they are doing in promoting the government's agenda.[7]

Ministers are assigned a parliamentary team to help them navigate the various parliamentary rules and requirements. Parliamentary secretaries can be young ambitious MPs, or veterans who know the ways of Parliament. It is important for ministers to establish a solid working relationship with them because they are appointed by the prime minister, they are members of the government caucus, and they can help them and their departments in dealing with Parliament and its committees. Meetings with members of the parliamentary team, however, take time from an already overloaded agenda.[8]

The media matter to all ministers – and well they should. In a world where "perception is reality," the media have a strong say in establishing who is a strong minister and who is weak. Having good press often determines how influential ministers are inside the government and in caucus. Ministers who are strong communicators and have an excellent rapport with the media are often called upon by the prime minister to deliver messages, particularly difficult ones, on behalf of the government. All ministers have a communications and public relations team to help them project a strong image and, whenever needed, to secure interviews both with local media in their constituencies and with the national media. A minister's PR team also needs to keep a close watch on what is being said about their minister on social media. Ministers can be rendered largely ineffective for their departments, for the government, and for the prime minister if they are constantly subjected to negative press.[9]

Ministers need to spend time with their departments, starting with their deputy ministers. Ministers who are able to establish a strong working relationship with senior departmental officials are also better able to navigate the Ottawa system to their advantage. Deputy ministers compare notes about ministers. If a minister is not working well with the deputy minister, the PMO-PCO may well conclude that the fault lies with the minister rather than the deputy minister. The PCO is aware of the ministers who work well with their departments and those who do not. Ministers should meet their deputy ministers at least once a week and whenever the need arises. They know that they should always accept or quickly return any calls from their deputy ministers because the calls are never about trivial matters – they could be about a negative story that will soon break in the media, a senior departmental official deciding or having to leave because of an issue that is about to hit the news, a growing conflict with another department and its minister, or the PMO-PCO raising objections to a departmental proposal.

Ministers, depending on their portfolio, also need to be accessible to senior provincial government officials, including premiers. Ministers will always want to meet or take calls from premiers, especially those from their home province. Provincial governments often need to be brought onside early, or at least informed, when Ottawa is planning new programs or initiatives that concern them. Premiers are closer to the local media than federal ministers are and, if a provincial government cannot be brought onside, the media will soon pick up on it.[10]

Ministers have families. Anybody who has spent time in Ottawa knows that politics is extremely demanding on families. It is not always possible for ministers to be with their families at key moments – graduations, wedding anniversaries, birthday gatherings, and the list goes on. I know a number of former ministers who have lost their marriages or who are estranged from their children and I often think that politics had a lot to do with it. Demands on a minister's time, either in Ottawa or in their home community, never end and the pressure on family life is also never-ending.

## SINGLE-POINT ACCOUNTABILITY IN PARLIAMENT AND MOTIVATION

The prime minister "expects ministers to place a very high priority on their House duties" and the PCO provides a "to-do list" that speaks to this priority.[11] Ministers are told to attend daily Question Period and that any "proposed absences must be cleared by the Prime Minister's Office."[12] They are told to take charge and be fully responsible for piloting their department's legislative projects before Parliament and its committees. The prime minister encourages ministers to "place a high priority on developing good relationships with parliamentary committees" and "to respond to questions on spending for which they are responsible."[13] The prime minister's to-do list adds that ministers are responsible for ensuring that "the government's management of the public purse is credible and avoids waste."[14] In addition, ministers must attend to Senate duties by being accessible when proposed legislation from their departments is brought forward. The PCO tells ministers how they should work with Parliament and its committees. It informs them that they are responsible for "deciding which question may be answered by officials speaking on their behalf," reminding them that public servants are there "to explain rather than defend or debate priorities." Ministers or their political representatives (parliamentary secretaries) are required to step in "if politically controversial matters are likely to arise."[15] These are the accountability requirements that the PCO lays out for ministers.

We now need to square these requirements with the several things that motivate ministers. Making accountability requirements better and more transparent is not anywhere near the top of the list. Ministers are members of Parliament and they know first-hand that they operate in a highly charged partisan political theatre. Putting aside PCO documents, they understand or will soon discover that they and the prime minister need to run Parliament rather than being accountable to it, because partisan politics requires it.[16] It is a question of political survival. Successful ministers know how to obfuscate or how to deal – or better yet, how to avoid dealing – with a politically sensitive issue, either in Parliament or with the media, at times without uttering a word of substance. Prime Minister Chrétien applauded former cabinet minister Ralph Goodale's ability to know how to circle an issue without landing or, failing that, knowing when to land.[17] One often hears in Ottawa that MPs should always remember that it is called Question Period, not Answer Period.[18] The objective is to avoid giving the opposition ammunition (read: information) to enable it to attack the government (read: government writ large), including the public service.

Ministers realize that Parliament is not where they get things done. It is an arena where they can score political points and deflect any criticism directed at the government and their departments and where the blame game is played out in full view. Jonathan Malloy sums it up best: "For the opposition, the purpose of scrutiny is always to nail the government to the wall, to embarrass and humiliate it, in the hope of electoral gain and replacing the government, or at least surpassing the other opposition parties. For the government, it is to defend its actions and to deflect and dilute criticism, and ideally squelch it entirely. For individual MPs on both sides, it is to build profiles and careers, whether as crusading opposition MPs or as dogged government backbenchers who nimbly defend the government to prove their loyalty and worthiness of promotion."[19] This is in sharp contrast to the British Parliament where MPs on the government side will often ask difficult questions in Question Period. In Canada, the scrutiny of government policies, activities, and spending belongs to opposition MPs.

Opposition MPs are able to score points from time to time, no matter what the issue is. For example, international minister Bev Oda was taken to task for staying at a five-star hotel in London and ordering a $16 orange juice. Oda later repaid a portion of the expenses to the government and resigned as a member of Parliament. However, holding the government to account for its $400-plus billion annual spending, managing 300-plus departments and agencies, and 320,000-plus employees requires a great deal more than catching a cabinet minister charging taxpayers $16 for orange juice.[20] Opposition MPs know that it is often easier to score political points over the purchase of an overpriced orange juice than over a multi-billion-dollar government program. If MPs have a choice between scoring points or working on refining accountability requirements over the budget process, they will opt for scoring political points.

Opposition members of Parliament have been able to turn to access to information legislation to give themselves an irresistible political advantage to damage a minister's political reputation. The legislation gives opposition political parties ammunition that would not otherwise exist or, at least, be available to them and has provided powerful fuel for the blame game.[21] No one knows this better than ministers and senior public servants.

Gordon Osbaldeston, former clerk of the Privy Council, penned a letter to cabinet ministers to advise them "on being a successful minister." Ministers are no different than individuals in other fields of work in that they are motivated by a desire to be successful. Osbaldeston wrote that one of the most difficult challenges for ministers "is controlling their time" all the while "working from

70 to 80 hours a week." He explained that ministers have to balance their roles as parliamentarians, as members of Cabinet and of a political party, and as constituency representatives. He added that ministers are unable to spend more than one-third to one-half of their time on departmental business and only have about three hours a week to spend with their deputy ministers. He warned that "an exhausted minister is a dangerous minister – both to himself and to the government."[22]

Ministers are also accountable, responsible, or answerable for more than their departments. They sit on top of several organizations and report to Parliament on their behalf. Osbaldeston reminded ministers that they became "legally and politically responsible for what is happening the moment you were sworn in."[23] The Canadian Heritage minister, for example, is responsible for the Heritage Department, three departmental agencies, eleven Crown corporations, and two administrative tribunals even though it is one of the federal government's smaller line departments – home to only about 2,000 employees – and spends about $1.8 billion a year.[24]

Former heritage minister (2021–23) Pablo Rodriguez's mandate letter was several pages and contained a number of standard paragraphs that are included in all mandate letters to ministers. They deal with such issues as post-COVID-19 recovery measures and reconciliation efforts with Canada's Indigenous communities. In the Rodriguez letter, the prime minister outlined eighteen objectives, four of them with sub-objectives.[25] The letter had nothing to say about the department's level of financial and human resources or whether a review of either was necessary. With respect to accountability – the prime minister tells Rodriguez that he needs "to work with the Deputy Minister ... and to turn to me, and your Deputy Minister early and often to support you in your role as minister." The prime minister adds: "To ensure we are accountable for our work, I will be asking you to publicly report to me, and all Canadians, on our progress ... on a regular basis." Parliament appears as an afterthought on accountability. The letter only suggests that the minister should "actively consider new ideas ... whether through public engagement, your work with Parliamentarians or advice from the public service."[26] Ambitious ministers need to pay attention to their mandate letters because they can point to them to show what they have accomplished. However, they may also come back to haunt them.[27]

Departmental briefing books offer a thorough overview of the portfolios' challenges and responsibilities. A number of departments now make their briefing books available to the public on their websites. The Canadian Heritage briefing books contain several sections and cover all aspects of its portfolio, policies, programs, and key departmental officials. Osbaldeston told ministers that "the first problem you are going to face is a truck load of briefings on issues you are vaguely familiar with. I understand from other ministers that this is a very humbling experience."[28] To have an effect on their department's policies, ministers need to understand the different policies and programs and departmental briefing books provide a solid start. However, establishing a strong working relationship with deputy ministers is a must.

I participated in a number of minister-deputy minister weekly meetings in the early 1980s, again in the late 1980s, and in 2004.[29] I also chaired the External Audit Committee at Canadian Heritage between 2008 and 2013. I did not see a set pattern in these meetings – they depended on the personalities of the ministers and deputy ministers, on the political issue of the day dominating the media, on the ministers' standing in the Ottawa system, the state of the departments' priorities, other ministers and departments that supported the departments' policies and those who were opposed and, on the departments' standing with the centre, notably the PMO-PCO and other central agencies. I do not recall any discussions about the level of financial and human resources being too high. I do recall, however, senior departmental officials making the point that departmental resources were stretched to the limit and that all new initiatives would require new resources. It is never in the interest of deputy ministers and their departments to launch a discussion with ministers to determine if they are oversupplied with financial or human resources. Ministers always have more important issues and priorities to discuss with their deputy ministers and deputy ministers have no incentive to raise the issue with their ministers. A former clerk of the Privy Council had a blunt warning for ministers: "You simply do not have the time to have problems with your Deputy Minister."[30] Challenging a deputy minister on how well they are managing the department's human and financial resources is a sure way to have problems.

I was not present at minister-deputy minister meetings whenever program reviews, in the form of bolts of lighting from above, were launched. I can speculate, however, that discussions would have revolved around how best to comply with demands from the centre for generating spending cuts, followed by debates on which measures should be put forward by the department to achieve the required spending reductions. But as soon as the reviews were done, things returned to normal, and the competition was back on between departments to secure new funding.

Why would ministers and deputy ministers ever want to make the case that they can do more, or the same, with fewer resources? If a minister and a deputy minister decided to sit down to go over their department's resources with the intention of reducing them, they would very likely be the only ones doing so, unless the prime minister had instructed all departments to do the same. Why would one minister-deputy minister team in one department launch a review of its financial-human resources when the other departments are not? Why generate savings only to see others make the case for more resources? This, in turn, explains why the government always turns to across-the-board cuts when launching program reviews or spending reduction measures. Nothing else works.

Ministers will also have their pet projects for their constituencies or regions to promote, while deputy ministers will have departmental projects to propose and programs to expand. I reviewed a number of mandate letters prepared after the 2021 election and I noticed that very little was said about the need to reallocate resources from low-priority activities to support new initiatives. Rather, the letters contained a to-do list of measures, many of which called for new resources. The letters were also thin on the ground when it came to accountability requirements – there was only a pro-forma clause on accountability that was simply added to all the letters.

Ministers have an overloaded agenda but so do deputy ministers. I say more about this later. Suffice to note here that deputy ministers have no reason to want to manage a smaller department or to lose financial and human resources. It is difficult to imagine a deputy minister telling the department's executive team that it is in their interest to convince the minister and central agencies that the department can do what it does with fewer resources or that they should reallocate resources from low-priority areas to support new measures.

What about ministers? They are being told that they are not the department's general manager – that responsibility belongs to their deputy ministers. There is also no advantage, political or otherwise, for ministers to take on the department's general manager role. In any event, if they ever tried, the department, central agencies, and the broader Ottawa system would oppose them at every turn, pointing to statutes that delegate responsibility for managing financial and human resources to deputy ministers. There is also simply no political merit in ministers telling the prime minister, the PMO, and their constituents that they were able to squeeze resources out of their departments. I cannot see ministers telling their constituents that they did not pursue projects for their region because they focused their efforts on ensuring that their own departments were doing more with less.

In January 2023, I was shown a federal minister's weekly agenda. There were no empty spots on it. I was told that if a spot should suddenly open up, it is very quickly filled with another meeting, a telephone call to return, or an event to attend. I was also informed that, on average, this minister's regular work week is seventy-plus hours. Ministers from the West Coast or Atlantic Canada have to allocate travel time back and forth to their constituencies. All ministers have to attend cabinet (Tuesdays) and cabinet committee meetings (Wednesdays), and weekly caucus meetings, and perform parliamentary duties, including Question Period when Parliament is sitting. Given the constant demands on the agenda of his ministers, Prime Minister Justin Trudeau underlined the importance of striking a work-life balance.[31] The balance, however, always tilts toward work. The point – ministers have to manage their agenda carefully if they want to have an effect. Spending time and effort to improve management or to determine a department's proper level of financial and human resources can never compete with other priorities that always fall on a minister's to-do list.

## MAKING IT TO CABINET AND STAYING THERE

Canadian political parties act as giant personnel agencies for recruiting members of Parliament. This remains one of their more important roles.[32] Being the official candidate of a political party gives the candidate a solid chance to make it to Parliament. It is rare indeed for anyone to be elected to Parliament as an independent. As a party's official candidate, it is easier to secure media interest and it provides access to the party's financial and human resources to help win the constituency.

Getting elected to Parliament is a prerequisite to making it to cabinet. Your party has to form the government and then the prime minister has to invite you to serve in cabinet. In January 2023, there were thirty-nine cabinet ministers, including the prime minister. A cursory look at the background of cabinet ministers before they entered politics reveals that eight had a law background, three worked in the medical field, five were consultants, eight worked in social work and community development, three were university professors, one was a farmer, two were police officers, two were former business executives, one was an entrepreneur, another was a former schoolteacher, and three were journalists. At least five would qualify as career politicians. I note that only one cabinet minister had had a career in the federal public service, serving for nearly ten years as a federal prosecutor. Federal prosecutors, however, fall under the plumber category and usually have limited knowledge of how the Ottawa system works.[33]

The constituencies and regions that ministers represent influence how they see their role. A minister representing University-Rosedale in Toronto will bring a different perspective and focus on different priorities than a minister representing a rural constituency in Atlantic Canada. A minister representing an Ottawa constituency will have more interest in machinery of government issues than a minister representing a Manitoba constituency. Ministers are also motivated by their own career aspirations and political interests.

Geography, regional interests, and language matter more than political ideology in shaping the policies of Canada's two "big tent" political parties. To be sure, party leaders also exert a great deal of influence on the policies of their party. Linguistic and regional cleavages, not ideology or economic class, at least until now, dominate Canadian politics. Richard Johnson maintains that "the brokerage image of Canadian parties does seem to be the dominant one" and Janine Brodie and Jane Jenson argue that political parties embrace principled positions only occasionally and, further, "these fragile constructions are easily reversed when conditions change."[34] David Herle sums things up nicely: "Parties don't run on what their members think and can't if they want to be successful. They run on what will get them the most votes. It is a strategic marketing exercise rather than a genuine contest of ideas."[35] Political ideology and the clash of ideas are no match for strategic marketing, political branding, public opinion surveys, and managing election campaigns at both the national and regional levels. Public servants understand this and have learned to navigate the political environment by accommodating, as best they can, the wishes of their political masters.

In an earlier publication, I grouped ministers under four broad categories – status, mission, policy, and process participants – to determine their motivation.[36] If anything, participants in two of those categories, mission and policy participants, face greater challenges today than they did, say forty years ago, including the rise of social media, 24-hour news channels, a stronger desire and capacity to govern from the centre, and the changing relationship between ministers, their offices, and the public service.

## Status Ministers

As always, there is never a shortage of status participants, those who seek positive visibility in the media, in the federal cabinet, in Parliament, inside government, and in their constituencies. They are highly valued by prime ministers, given the more dominant role of the media in recent years and the call for more transparency. To be sure, ministers have always known the importance of good press. As Maurice Lamontagne observed nearly sixty years ago: "If a minister enjoys a good press, he will be envied and respected by his colleagues. If he has no press, he has no future."[37] And a senior advisor to a cabinet minister argued in 2022: "If the media likes you, the P.M. (prime minister) will like you. If you want brownie points with the P.M., make sure that the media have an interest in what your minister is doing. The government needs the media onside to get things done and to get its message out."[38]

Status participants tend to work well with their departmental officials. If the department can regularly generate good material for the media, so much the better. They are the least troublesome ministers, in that they are never a threat to their departments, and they rarely question ongoing policies and programs or their resources levels. If anything, they are likely to encourage the department to do more of what it does, if only to capture media attention. Status participants and their staff are continually on the prowl in the department in search of new initiatives to announce. If Treasury Board approval is required, they will happily take up the challenge and lobby their colleagues on the Board to secure it. They will also happily volunteer to make announcements and give speeches.

Their main preoccupation is visibility. One senior official explained: "All my minister really cares about is getting good press. If we could orchestrate things so that his photo appears in a favourable light on the front page of the *Globe and Mail* and *The National* once a month, then we would have absolutely no problem with him."[39] Thus, the focus is almost always on appearances – promoting a high profile and positive visibility in the media. Status ministers emphasize not what they might do in government or what they might achieve, but how they appear to the electorate and to their colleagues. Sound public policy often takes a back seat to status.

Status participant ministers can never be counted upon to support cuts in expenditures or services. They may, in a general discussion in cabinet or in caucus, voice their support for controlled spending, but they will shy away from discussing specific program cuts. They will also strongly oppose any suggestion about cutting or even reducing their own programs. They only want to be the bearers of good news.

The personality of status participant ministers also usually inhibits them from challenging departmental policies and programs and accompanying financial and human resource levels. They will try to avoid confrontations with their own staff, their cabinet colleagues, or their departments. They will not want to jeopardize any opportunities to be cast in a favourable public light. A long-running debate with their department over policies and programs (over which they usually have only a limited interest in any event) could well divert attention away from initiatives involving the media and public relations.

## *Mission Ministers*

Mission participants make for quite different cabinet ministers. Like all politicians, they will certainly seek favourable press, but that is not their all-consuming purpose. They bring strongly held views to the debate and usually they do not avoid confrontation if their views are challenged. While their views are not always politically or ideologically inspired, they do seek to serve a cause. It is widely known, for example, in Parliament, in cabinet, and in the public service that Jake Epp, Brian Mulroney's minister of health and welfare, held strong religious views and that he would not hesitate to voice them; that Brian Tobin in Chrétien's government had strong regional views; that Joe Oliver in the Harper government had strong private sector-inspired views on the economy; and that Marc Miller in Justin Trudeau's government has strongly held views on Indigenous issues. Mission participants are particularly tenacious in pushing their causes or their point of view and they are likely to keep trying long after other ministers would have given up.

To be sure, there can be mission participants in both the spenders' (e.g., Brian Tobin) and the guardians' camps (e.g., Joe Oliver). Those in the latter camp, however, will find the going difficult. Mission participants who regard cuts in government spending as their principal reason for being in politics had better hope that they will be appointed to either Finance or the Treasury Board Secretariat. Mission participants seeking to reduce the role of government but who are heading spending departments will face a formidable challenge and a strong test of their tenacity. Their departments will inevitably resist cuts to their own programs or organizations. If the minister should persist, officials may well attempt to undermine their political direction by "providing incomplete information, by precooking among officials, by playing ministers off against one another."[40] They may attempt to delay any discussion with their ministers if departmental programs are threatened. With the many other demands on ministers' time, this is usually not overly difficult. They may also alert central agency officials that the minister is out to cut spending, which could well create political problems for the government.

Mission participants who have been successful in the past have been spenders, not those out to cut spending in their departments – great causes usually cost money. They are also often the ministers who have held the same portfolios for a long time. Eugene Whelan, Roméo LeBlanc, and Monique Bégin were all mission participants in the Trudeau administration, as was John Wise in the Mulroney government. Whelan continually pushed the interest of farmers and fishers, as did LeBlanc in promoting the interests of fishers.

It is much more difficult for mission participants in the federal government to be successful today than in years past. Perhaps for this reason, it is also much more difficult to identify mission participants today than it was in the days of those ministers. Bill Morneau explains why: "Policy decisions are now made on the fly, the need to react in the 24/7 news cycle and the willingness to securing political points over policy rationales. Important decisions are struck."[41] Governing from the centre has also made it difficult for mission participants to flourish because cabinet government in Ottawa is not what it once was. Mission participants now need to focus their efforts on the prime minister and their advisors to pursue a proposal, rather than cabinet colleagues. We saw earlier that it is rarely possible, even for the more senior ministers, to secure time alone with the prime minister. Those who maintain that cabinet government remains intact in Ottawa need to address the following: "Cabinet government – by way of a far from atypical illustration, two key decisions regarding Canada's deployment in Afghanistan – one by a Liberal government, one by a Conservative government – were made in the PMO with the help of a handful of political advisors and civilian and military officials. The relevant ministers of National Defence and Foreign Affairs were not even in the room."[42]

## Policy Ministers

Policy participants, meanwhile, have not fared any better in recent years than mission participants. Policy participants often have a specific area of expertise and arrive in government equipped with more than generalities. They are experts in their fields. However, there are not many of them in any given cabinet, if career politicians and their knowledge of how government works are excluded. One former deputy minister explained: "My experience as often as not was that the minister had no view (on policy)."[43] In any event, having a specific field of interest or expertise does not ensure that they will make it to cabinet, let alone be appointed to the post for which they are best suited. For example, Don Johnston, one of Pierre Trudeau's ministers, fell under the policy participant category. He had some definite policy views and was an expert in tax policy. He was never, however, appointed minister of finance or even of national revenue. Steven Guilbeault, on the other hand, brings a high level of expertise to his environment and climate change portfolio. Among other occupations, he served as a director of Greenpeace and co-founded the largest environmental organization in Quebec before going into politics.[44]

Having expertise in public policy is one thing; succeeding in partisan politics is quite another. The prime minister, PMO, and PCO keep a close eye on policy proposals so that they square with the government's broader political interests, and they have easy access to experts in all policy fields. Lobbyists are always at the ready to offer advice and they can argue all sides of an issue. In addition, knowing the policy process, how to connect the dots, and how to generate support from the "system" are now fields of specialization in their own right. It usually takes several years for public servant officials to fully understand the policy process. The result is that most ministers have to rely on their own departmental officials to help them through the maze. Officials are likely to argue that a single minister, however well connected and popular, can no longer make policy or launch major initiatives on their own. Permanent career officials will seek to dissuade both mission and policy participants from getting too far ahead of their colleagues or the "process" on any issue, insisting that it is in their own interest not to forge ahead without political and bureaucratic support, especially from central agencies.

Certainly, one would be hard-pressed to identify many major federal policy initiatives in recent years that were inspired by a single minister, unlike in years past with the likes of, among others, Clifford Sifton, C.D. Howe, Ernest Lapointe, Monique Bégin, and Allan MacEachen. All major policy developments or revisions in every sector, in recent years, have been the product of many hands guided by the centre. Policy participants who have been cabinet ministers and who have later written about their experiences often report on their disenchantment and deep frustration over their inability to have an effect on policy.[45] They point to officials in the PMO, the PCO, Finance, and elsewhere, who inhibited their efforts to introduce real change. One has to go back a number of years to see ministers who were able to claim some success on the policy front. Today, a minister has to have the ear of the prime minister and be able to go to extraordinary lengths to bypass the formal policy process to have any chance at successfully promoting a proposal. It is not possible for even the most determined and strong-willed cabinet minister to successfully challenge government spending in a department.[46]

## Process Ministers

The most numerous cabinet ministers are the process participants. Successful process participants know how to get things done and strike deals. Many of them are career politicians and they are able to establish solid working relationships with their senior departmental officials. They rarely question departmental policies and they understand how Parliament works. They enjoy parliamentary jostling, get along well with most of their colleagues, and take particular delight in striking deals. They are often politically partisan and willing to help one of their own who might be in some difficulty in their constituency.

Policy content, political ideology, government organization, management issues – and even government programs themselves – are all of limited interest to the process participants. The notion that government spending should be reduced may make for an interesting discussion, but it holds little real appeal for them. They are in politics to make a difference and projects are what matters, and the more the better. They will look to their own departments to come up with specific projects for their ridings or for the regions for which they are responsible.

Process participants are on the side of spenders and they view themselves, above all, as team players. They are the ones who will speak about the political importance of new spending announcements and are particularly popular with government backbenchers because they are the ones backbenchers will turn to for help on a particular project. It is rare to see a government backbencher who does not have at least one constituency project for which they are lobbying ministers. As one minister explains: "Backbenchers always have what I call a do-or-die project. They committed themselves in the election campaign to high-profile projects and when elected they must deliver or, in their opinion and that of their chief political organizers, they will be defeated at the next election."[47] There are spending departments that appeal to process participants, notably Housing, Infrastructure and Communities, Employment, Workforce Development and Disability Inclusion, National Defence, and Public Services and Procurement, as well as departments that have relatively flexible spending programs, such as Canadian Heritage and the several regional development agencies.

The above captures what motivates ministers, though not completely. There are also "departmental participants." I have heard ministers refer to some of their colleagues as suffering from "departmentalism" because of their interest in their own departments to the exclusion of other considerations, including their cabinet colleagues and government backbenchers. Departmental participants only need to spend a few weeks with their departments before they begin to espouse their long-standing policy lines. There is an important advantage for these ministers – they rarely get into political hot water or even political controversies when they embrace the departmental policies. According to them, talking about darting off in a new direction and openly challenging departmental advice is fraught with potential political problems. There is political safety in being departmental participants. They are almost always on the side of the spenders, they are willing to support their departments, and they are convinced that they have worthwhile ideas and projects to propose.

## LOOKING BACK

Ministers are constantly dealing with an overloaded agenda and serving in cabinet is more difficult now than in years past. The media are more present and more demanding; transparency requirements are also far more demanding; and ministers no longer own their agenda, their departments, and their departmental policies as they once did. All major initiatives, and even minor ones, are now the product of many hands, with the centre keeping a close eye on developments. The process soaks a lot of ministerial time and energy: In the fall of 2022, there were thirteen cabinet committees or subcommittees.[48]

There are legitimate reasons for the centre of government to exert more and more influence on government policies and operations because effective government measures now need to cut across departments. The omnipresence of the media is also forcing the hand of the prime minister and the PMO to exert greater control from the centre, for fear of not being seen to be in control. The 24/7 news cycle requires quick answers to questions. The prime minister's power of appointment is a strong lever to enable the centre to exert strong control. Prime ministers have always held the power to appoint deputy ministers, with some ministers having little to no say in the appointment.[49] Today, unlike in years past, the PMO also now appoints chiefs of staff to ministers, enabling the centre to exert still more influence. In more recent years, the PMO has gone further and now has a direct hand in appointing all senior positions in ministerial offices.[50]

Ministers are no less ambitious today than they were, say, sixty years ago. However, it is far more difficult for mission participants to identify visibly and strongly with a proposal, bring it to cabinet, and see it through the approval process. Examples of highly visible past mission participants include Allan MacEachen and medicare, Bryce Mackasey and reforms to Canada's employment insurance program, and Jean Marchand and regional development policy. This also explains why ministers no longer enjoy the high profiles that they had in the past. A public opinion survey reveals that two-thirds of cabinet ministers were "unknown to at least half the country" and that ministers "are so unrecognized that respondents were unable to render any opinion on whether these ministers of the Crown are doing a good or a bad job."[51] Whenever an issue of any consequence surfaces, calls are quickly made to directly involve the prime minister to deal with it.[52]

Even though ministers have a more demanding agenda than they did years ago, they exert less influence. The media are more intrusive, and the federal government is much bigger and more difficult to navigate at a time when ministers have to deal with a decline of deference toward them and politics both outside and inside government.[53] Social media, from X to Facebook, no longer has the gatekeepers that the old media had and still have. As Bill Fox points out, how "can rational actors 'manage' the media when even the billionaires who own the social media platforms insist the content that courses over them cannot, and should not, be managed?"[54] It is a free-for-all, and today some ministers spend half their time dealing with the media and coping with the public perception of how they perform. A century ago, ministers only had to let the right journalist know what the government intended to do and not much else was needed. Ministers and their advisors now need to keep a constant eye on the media before all hell breaks loose and, as Christopher Dornan points out, "the world of social media is one in which all hell breaks loose all the time."[55]

Ironically, ministers are still told that they are accountable, responsible, or answerable for everything that happens in their portfolio or for the collection of departments, agencies, and Crown corporations for which they are responsible. They still continue to represent the single point of accountability. This, at the same time as they are told that they should keep their hands off the management of financial and human resources because some authority for these areas is delegated directly by Parliament to deputy ministers. Ministers are also told that they have a collective responsibility. However, bolts of lightning and ideas that come from on high have, at least to some degree, replaced collective decision making and collective responsibility. Ministers have limited time available and lack the tools they need to hold public servants to account. Deputy ministers are appointed by the centre, by the prime minister, and by the clerk of the Privy Council and they are accountable to them more than they are to their ministers. In the next chapter, we look at the roles and responsibilities of deputy ministers.

# 8

# DEPUTY MINISTERS:
# ON THE INSIDE LOOKING EVERYWHERE

The Privy Council Office tells deputy ministers that they have to "manage a complex set of multiple accountabilities." In its guidance, it states, at the very outset, that deputy ministers "are appointed by the Governor in Council on the recommendation of the Prime Minister," making clear who their boss is. It then outlines the "multiple accountabilities" that deputy ministers need to navigate, including the prime minister, the clerk of the PCO, a performance management program, their minister, the TBS, and the Public Service Commission.[1] The *Handbook of Canadian Public Administration* adds that a deputy minister is also "responsible to Parliament and its committees for the work of his or her ministry" and concludes that "the accountability of a deputy minister can be both challenging and difficult to understand."[2]

Deputy ministers occupy a unique zone in government, where partisan politics and political power meet the permanent administration. The zone embodies the Romanov double-headed eagle, with the two heads representing the political and administrative worlds, much like it did for the Romanovs for whom it represented the dual sovereignty of the secular and the religious. A former senior federal public servant writes that "because deputies are the link between elected and non-elected officials, they not only draw the line between the public service and political authority, they embody it."[3]

They are expected to be loyal to their ministers and to the prime minister but need to be ready to switch allegiance whenever there is a change of government, and need to restrain themselves from applauding or criticizing their employers' policies. They also have to keep an eye on social media and their tendency to "name and shame" provincial governments, opposition parties, and several officers of Parliament.

We saw earlier that ministers lead incredibly busy lives. The same can also be said about deputy ministers, though they spend fewer days on the road and they do not always have to deal with the requirements of having a high visibility in Parliament and in the media, and they do not have to work with political constituencies. However, deputy ministers also put in seventy-hour work weeks and they are on call whenever the prime minister, the clerk of the Privy Council, or their ministers or senior staff need to talk with them.[4]

We have a growing body of literature on the work, career paths, and educational backgrounds of deputy ministers. Patrice Dutil and Andrea Migone, in their comparative study of the work of deputy ministers, identified five "time-allocation styles" of deputy ministers: operational, balanced, managerial, strategic, and HR-focused. The authors go on to divide the categories by tasks so that HR-focused deputy ministers, for example, will look to team building and professional development, while the managerial deputy ministers will focus on the various approval processes, among other activities. Dutil and Migone also reveal that deputy ministers, both at the federal and provincial levels, allocate more time to management, operations, and strategic activities than they do to HR issues.[5] They add: "Regardless of size of their department, they consistently are focussed on strategy and general managerial matters."[6] A public opinion survey reveals that newspapers remain their main source of outside information, followed by social media. It is important to note that federal deputy ministers scored the lowest of all respondents in the survey – only four out of thirty-six, 11.1 per cent, who were asked to participate, responded; compared with eight out of twenty-seven, or 29.6 per cent, for Ontario; and six out of fifteen, or 40 per cent, for Manitoba.[7]

The literature also suggests that federal deputy ministers attach less importance to management than their provincial counterparts. Jacques Bourgault has conducted several studies on the different aspects of a federal deputy minister's agenda and work. He also teamed up with Christopher Dunn to produce a collection of essays on provincial and federal deputy ministers, looking at who they are and how they see their work. They identified four roles – guardians, gurus, managers, and leaders. They write about the changing role of deputy ministers, making the point that "a role well-regarded in the 1950s, for example, may now be seen as too bureaucratic."[8] The collection of essays does not, however, explain how the federal government was less bureaucratic in the 1950s than it is today.

One can only ask – which role played by public servants in the 1950s is now regarded as too bureaucratic and what processes did they have to contend with to get things done? History tells us that they were able to get things done by learning to operate within rigid financial and administrative rules designed to prevent administrative wrongdoings. The 1950s were, in many ways, the golden years of the federal public service. Senior public servants were able to help their political masters plan and implement the welfare state.[9] Politicians, at least those on the government side, worked well with senior career officials, and said so. The public service also had a reputation for being parsimonious and public servants did not need a "values and ethics" exercise or code to tell them what they could not do. Long-serving senior public servants, including Clifford Clark, O.D. Skelton, Robert Bryce, Graham Towers, and Gordon Robertson, retired quietly with a modest public service pension, at least compared with what is now available to deputy ministers. Unlike many of their current-day counterparts, they did not join lobbying firms or sit on boards of major corporations, employing their knowledge of the machinery of government or their contacts with senior government officials, to influence decisions to benefit their firms.[10]

Some of the financial and administrative rules of years past have been done away with, in the hope of encouraging stronger management practices. If that is what is meant by being too bureaucratic, it is important to remember that those rules and regulations have been replaced by the need to produce numerous reports and deal with dozens of oversight bodies. Some public servants in Ottawa may well believe that the federal government is less bureaucratic than it once was. But others are not convinced, including member of Parliament Ted Falk, who writes: "In recent weeks, my staff have spent hours on the phone, trying to help constituents access basic government services – passports that never arrived, immigration applications that got deleted, travel chaos at airports."[11] Recently retired federal public servants are also making the case that the federal government is now overly bureaucratic.[12]

The doing away of a number of centrally prescribed or "bureaucratic" rules constitutes one of the most important changes in the federal government. Some public servants maintain that the government could go still further in decentralizing management authority to line departments by pointing, for example, to TBS imposing a government-wide policy on hybrid work arrangements in the aftermath of the COVID-19 pandemic.¹³ This debate, combined with the work of public sector unions and the collapse of boundaries separating departments and agencies, has reshaped the work of the public service, the delivery of government services, and how departments and their deputy ministers view their roles and responsibilities. The federal government has become, if anything, more bureaucratic and more cautious, not less. It is also more difficult for public servants to get things done than was the case in years past.

In his memoirs, Jack Manion explains how things worked in the federal government in the 1950s and 1960s. Manion spent much of his career in the Department of Citizenship and Immigration, going up through the ranks, eventually serving as its deputy minister. He describes how the Canadian government managed the Hungarian refugee crisis in the mid-1950s. It was the minister and senior departmental officials, not the prime minister or his partisan advisors, who ran the policy and the program. Manion and his peers would not have tolerated ministerial partisan staff "actually writing" the citizenship guide. More important, nor would the minister himself have accepted that his political staff would write the guidelines or the policy or questioned the work of departmental officials at every turn. And more to the point, the minister always turned to public servants, not his political staff, for policy advice. His political staff held junior positions and their role was to provide partisan political advice, deal with MPs, particularly those on the government side, and ensure that the office ran smoothly. Manion explained that the ministers often challenged senior public servants but the relationship worked very well in managing "one of the greatest refugee programs in Canada's history."¹⁴

Manion managed a "small" policy unit and later ran the operations side of the department before he became its deputy minister. His mandate was always clear and central agencies, interdepartmental committees, and outside policy networks were not much of a factor in his work. There were also no lobbyists to contend with. Central agency officials recognized that departments were not only a storehouse of knowledge about their sectors, but they also knew what worked in the field and what did not. Management levels were few and there were no "associate" positions attached to executive positions, as is the case today. J.W. Pickersgill, then minister of citizenship and immigration, together with his deputy minister, took charge of the file, owned it, and delivered the initiative. Nandor

Dreisziger, in his review of the Hungarian refugee crisis, concludes that Pickersgill was "the principal author of the vigorous steps the federal government had taken to bring Hungarian refugees to Canada."[15] Parliament also knew who was accountable, responsible, and answerable for the initiative – J.W. Pickersgill.

Things are vastly different today. This is not to suggest that the federal government can or should operate like it did in the 1950s. It cannot, for many reasons, including the fact that virtually all public policy issues cut across several departments and often involve provincial governments. Government officials now have to deal with a constant stream of lobbyists trying to influence decisions. Many of the lobbyists are former partisan political staffers or career officials and they know their way around the federal government.[16] In addition, the boundaries that separate departments from central agencies and other departments have collapsed, at least when compared with sixty years ago. The question is, have the federal government's accountability requirements been adjusted to reflect this change?

The challenge is to appreciate how deputy ministers now have to contend with a political-policy-administrative environment that is different, in all important ways, than was the case in the 1950s. Sixty years ago, federal government departments were largely staffed by plumbers. Deputy ministers worked within clear boundaries – they looked to their ministers for guidance, had clear rules that applied to all departments to ensure probity in managing financial and human resources and, for the most part, they had risen through the ranks of the departments that they were asked to lead.

Today, the departments at the senior levels are largely staffed by poets who rotate through central agencies and several departments before becoming deputy ministers. A strong knowledge of a department's history and programs matters a lot less than in years past, in part because line departments have lost standing over the years. A deputy minister can lead the Department of Indigenous Affairs one day and then lead Immigration, Refugees and Citizenship the next. The ability to understand the policy process, to work well with the PCO and ministers, to navigate through the Ottawa system, and to bring a government-wide perspective to policy issues is now key to going up through the ranks of the federal public service. Deputy ministers with the skills to keep bouncing ministers under control are highly valued by the PMO-PCO.

Now, deputy ministers remain in a department for about three years, even though many interested observers, including a former clerk of the Privy Council, have urged the government to make them stay longer.[17] Long-serving officials maintain that it takes more than a year for deputy ministers to learn how a department operates, its program structure, its challenges, and its history.[18] In January 2023, the Government of Canada listed twenty-four deputy ministers on its website. Nearly all had served in the PCO, in an associate deputy minister position, or as deputy minister in other departments before their current appointment. Only one, the deputy minister of Justice, had come up through the ranks of his home department – he has, however, since moved on.[19]

In many ways, the centre has become more important to deputy ministers than their departments. Bourgault writes that deputy ministers spend nearly 30 per cent of their working hours on interdepartmental management and corporate management and only spend 5 per cent of their time working with their ministers. Reading memoirs of long-retired former deputy ministers, one can conclude that the opposite was true sixty years ago, when deputy ministers spent a much smaller amount of time dealing with the centre. Deputy ministers now look to the centre because that is where the more important decisions are made and also because the centre is key for their future career opportunities. The clerk of the Privy Council is the lead player in assessing the performance of deputy ministers. In addition, as Bourgault argues, the PMO "has grown much more powerful than it once was." Prime ministers can, whenever they decide, get directly involved in the process to appoint deputy ministers. Reports reveal that the prime minister and his office were "responsible for the retirement of the Clerk of the Privy Council, Kevin Lynch, and the Deputy Minister of Transport, Louis Ranger."[20] Ranger wrote an email to Transport Canada employees to state that the prime minister had just announced his resignation, making clear that it was not his decision.[21]

It is important to underline once again the point that the Ottawa policy- and decision-making processes are operating within collapsed boundaries separating the centre from line departments as well as those between departments, between partisan political advisors, and career officials. The boundaries separating poets and plumbers in the same department have been weakened and the boundaries separating the political from the administrative have also been severely downgraded. Deputy ministers now have to manage a *ménage à quatre* between the centres of government, the minister, the minister's political staff, and their departments.

In public administration, boundaries are important. When you draw boundaries, you not only establish space within which people can operate, you also draw an understanding of how things work that is visible. When you remove boundaries, you remove this understanding, and without boundaries in government, you end up with "a big conceptual mess."[22] In a traditional bureaucracy, policy and decision making is top-down, consensus is established through acquiescence to higher authority, and smooth operations are ensured by respecting authority, rules, and traditions. For example, accountability, under the traditional bureaucracy model, also made it easier to ensure that J.W. Pickersgill and his senior department officials were able to manage issues for which they were both responsible and accountable. The plumbers, in the traditional model, were able to process refugee applications from Hungary efficiently because the lines of responsibility and accountability from the minister down to them were clear. Central agencies and the poets in the department were on the sidelines and not directly involved in managing files.

Things are vastly different today. Michael Hatfield, a retired senior economist with Human Resources and Skills Development Canada, writes, "Making sure that the director of every possible unit with the remotest interest in the policy areas has signed off on policy advice often becomes more important than subjecting that advice to real scrutiny by people with the knowledge and capacity for careful vetting."[23] Flipping documents between policy shops in Ottawa, always with an eye on what the prime minister and their courtiers are interested in, often ignores a key ingredient in shaping sound policy – how to best implement it. This may well explain why the government did not perform as well in managing the Afghan refugee crisis as it did managing the Hungarian refugee crisis.

Ottawa's response in the Afghan case has been widely criticized "for lacking efficiency and being too bureaucratic."[24] When the Taliban came back to power in August 2021, the federal government committed to bring 40,000 Afghans to Canada. However, ten months after the Taliban took over, only about 15,000 refugees had made it to Canada. Politicians and poets saw the need and had the ability to bring 40,000 refugees to Canada; however, the plumbers were only able to process 15,000. The director of a group dedicated to helping Afghan refugees reach Canada explained: "Getting someone out of Afghanistan, it's just a question of logistics. We can make it happen. The biggest challenges are the bureaucratic obstacles."[25] A special bipartisan parliamentary committee reported on the Afghanistan refugee crisis and was highly critical of the government's response. It questioned whether the federal government was "equipped, structured, and instructed to act in ... a timely manner in response to situations that require foresight and action."[26] The committee brought forward thirty-seven recommendations to strengthen Ottawa's capacity to deal with future refugee crises.

When boundaries are erased, a system of shared accountability must somehow come into play, and it becomes necessary to establish who does what and to define a new common language and concept. Governing without boundaries is far more complex than governing through a vertical axis, where the line of command is no different than the line of responsibility or accountability. Under a regime of shared accountability, accountability codes and requirements need to be adjusted, which is often done on the fly. When defining new measures, policy networks need to accept shared responsibility – and the more explicit this responsibility, the better for making politicians accountable for what is accomplished.[27] The question is – how?

Shared responsibility requires somehow blending vertical and horizontal accountability requirements with everyone accepting that they have to be accountable for their part. This is hardly a given. It also means ensuring there are enough staff available to fulfill those responsibilities. This is how it could work:

- Retain some elements of the traditional requirements and create new ones, such as pooling budgets and looking across departments to determine how to support a comprehensive program agenda;
- Dissect collaborative arrangements to determine how committed the government is to them: which departments are involved, what their roles are, and how to determine whether they are living up to their end of the bargain;
- Identify specific tasks and responsibilities for every collaboration so that all units, and individual public servants, have defined roles and responsibilities, an ambitious agenda to be sure.

It only takes a moment's reflection to appreciate that it is a lot easier to shirk accountability under a shared responsibility regime than it is under the traditional model.

Shared accountability may well require a different machinery of government, one that clarifies which are political interests and which are administrative interests and responsibilities. In the absence of creating such a regime, government officials are trying, as best they can, to answer which institution should hold whom accountable? Parliament can, at least in theory, hold the executive accountable but it cannot hold actors in broader relationships to account. For example, Parliament can hold the minister and Department of Indigenous Services accountable, but it cannot hold Indigenous Chiefs accountable, even though they may be responsible for spending an important part of the departmental budget. Governing by proxy poses many challenges for Parliament and ministers. This is the political-administrative environment in which deputy ministers now operate as they try, as best they can, to "embody" the line between the public service and political authority.

### THE DEPUTY MINISTER

The above illustrates the skills that are required of today's deputy ministers and why a deep knowledge of a department's history and program structure is no longer as important as it once was. As we noted earlier, the average tenure for deputy ministers was 12.2 years between 1867 and 1917 and 2.3 years between 1977 and 1987. In more recent years, the stay has been around three years. Going up through the ranks no longer works for those aspiring to become deputy ministers because these single-department career officials are considered to have too narrow a perspective to perform in an environment with collapsing boundaries. Deputy ministers need to be able to connect the dots, to work "the system" to move initiatives forward, to negotiate, and to understand the country's partisan political environment and how central agencies operate and decide.[28]

Today's deputy ministers are also expected to regularly introduce management reform measures, while making sure that implementing them does not create political problems for their ministers – in itself is no small achievement. In short, deputy ministers need to be competent negotiators, able to read the political tea leaves, be capable of leading their departments and their senior executives, to contend with different statutes, cooperate with other government departments and at times with other governments, all the while being able to represent their departments before the political class and interest groups, including lobbyists. Their success, to the extent that it can be properly determined, depends on a series of political and bureaucratic actors. Jacques Bourgault and Christopher Dunn summed it up in this fashion: "The public sector is a theatre with different plays presented all at the same time. Actors have different and simultaneous codirectors. Spectators sometimes have contradictory expectations."[29] To many, simply surviving in this demanding environment is a measure of success.

When deputy ministers go to work in the morning, they have to think about the expectations of many actors. Focusing on only one issue or one set of players is a luxury they no longer have. Here is a list, and not a complete one at that: at the top is the prime minister and then the clerk of the Privy Council because the prime minister is the boss and the clerk heads the public service. They are followed by the minister, the minister's political advisors, central agencies, the media, the department's senior executives, the department's clients, and the parliamentary officers, starting with the auditor general and what the opposition parties might be saying about their ministers and departments. Deputy ministers now need to know how to juggle several balls at once and they have to focus their efforts in several directions, in addition to their ministers and departments. They also have to keep an eye on any looming crisis that would put the department on the front page of Canadian newspapers.

One of the balls deputy ministers have to juggle is managing their departments. Deputy ministers hold considerable authority over their departments. We saw earlier that the *Financial Administration Act*, the *Public Service Employment Act*, and the *Official Languages Act* assign powers directly to deputy ministers. Two other acts – the *Interpretation Act* and *Departmental Acts*, also delegate authority to deputy ministers. The *Interpretation Act* allows that whatever power is granted to the minister by statute also includes the deputy minister. The deputy minister thus has the legal right to act for the Crown or for the government. However, they only enjoy a derived right. The minister needs to remain ultimately accountable, at least in theory. Deputy ministers make decisions that, constitutionally, are the responsibility of their ministers. If deputy ministers did not do this, the federal government would be turned into a never-ending series of bottleneck decisions or, rather, a lack of decisions. The point here is that the work of deputy ministers extends into the world of political decision making. The opposite is rarely true – ministers normally stay out of their department's management.

Senior career officials are far more present in the political arena than in years past – in some cases, willingly so. Alex Himelfarb, a senior public servant, declared at a symposium: "We will have Human Resources reform, we will have health reform and we will have an innovation agenda and we will have a skills and learning agenda, and we will reach out to Aboriginal people and poor people and we will make sure every kid has a good start in life."[30] This sounds like a political speech prepared for a partisan political crowd, not a speech by a senior public servant to career officials, which it was. Sixty years ago, such a speech would have been given by a politician, not by Gordon Robertson or Bob Bryce. Recently, a senior public servant, rather than a cabinet minister, told interested parties in Northern Ontario that a high-profile mineral project in the Ring of Fire region may never be developed because of several obstacles that will be difficult to overcome.[31] Ministers, meanwhile, do not often venture into their departments' management issues unless the issues come to dominate the media. The work environment for career government officials has changed a great deal in recent years. The same cannot be said about the government's accountability regime.

## WHAT ABOUT MANAGEMENT

Since the 1960s, we have seen numerous efforts to see senior career officials take a stronger interest in managing their departmental operations. These include two royal commissions (the Glassco and Lambert commissions), Increased Ministerial Authority and Accountability (IMAA) in 1986, Public Service 2000, Blueprint 2020, the introduction of the accounting officer concept, many new public management-inspired measures, as well as several management reform efforts launched by the Stephen Harper government, and the deliverology measures introduced by the Justin Trudeau government.[32] None have lived up to expectations. All were paraded in the Ottawa system with great promise but, within a few years, no one was referring to them. I have not heard, for example, anyone in Ottawa refer to IMAA and its accompanying memoranda of understanding (MOUs) in over twenty years. Regardless, all these efforts have had a hand in peeling away a number of centrally prescribed rules and regulations and turned the Public Service Commission into an audit agency, with little say in the staffing process.

There is little evidence to suggest that any of the above efforts have had a positive effect on management practices in the federal government. We have not, however, seen many efforts to bring back centrally prescribed rules and regulations. The result is that, when it comes to management, deputy ministers and their senior staff now perform the work of central agencies within their departments. However, because they are an integral part of the departmental team, it is very difficult for them to ask hard questions about financial and human resources.

My sense is that senior career officials knew from the start that the many management reform measures were more about announceables than about leading to lasting change. The observation of the former deputy minister of the Department of Defence, that politicians should heal their own institutions before trying to heal the public service, speaks to this point. Any federal public servant with a sense of history would have known, for example, that Justin Trudeau's deliverology initiative was essentially what the federal government had tried to implement with little success in the late 1960s and early 1970s – the Planning, Programming and Budgeting System.

Studies of the work of deputy ministers all point in the same direction when it comes to policy – as the centre has gained influence and as it consumes more time from line department deputy ministers, departments and management have lost standing.[33] Deputy ministers go where they need to go to get things done and focus on things that matter to them and their departments. Modern government, regardless of who the prime minister is, requires deputy ministers to look constantly beyond their departments in their work, even when pursuing their departments' interest. This is not a criticism of today's deputy ministers; it is, rather, a description of the political-administrative environment that they have to work in. Prime ministers, their advisors, and senior ministers do not value management skills nearly as much as they value the ability of senior government officials to steer departments away from political controversies, to pursue their political and policy agenda, and to generate announceables. Managing the blame game has also pushed deputy ministers to master the art of upward delegation. Issues that have the potential to spell political trouble are "delegated" up to the PCO-PMO to be resolved. It is safer this way for their ministers, for their departments, and for themselves.

Deputy ministers have to contend with many constraints to get things done, often outside their departments, that, in years past, deputy ministers did not have to deal with. The centre of government is now larger and more powerful; access to information legislation only dates back to the early 1980s; public sector unions were born in the mid-1960s; various affirmative action measures were created in the 1980s and 1990s; the work of various officers of Parliament, other than the auditor general, is relatively recent; the Charter of Rights and Freedoms was only introduced in 1982; social media and the 24/7 news channels are recent; privacy laws, and vision exercises that pop up from the centre, from time to time, are also recent. Deputy ministers have to manage this hodgepodge of contradictions and complexities because modern government requires it. The result is that they need to serve goals that are not always their preference or that of their departments and contend with policy actors that bring little to no value to their work.

Deputy ministers today also have to deal with judicial activism, something that was foreign to them sixty years ago. They have to come to terms with the fact that the judiciary is better at protecting rights than implementing programs or identifying resources to put new measures in place. They also have to accept that they now have limited say in managing human resources. They are not involved in collective bargaining negotiations, which have a significant effect both on departmental management and on the quality of the department's services to its clients.[34] This is one of several reasons why deputy ministers do not rank management skills high. The same is also true for "those who appoint and evaluate them."[35]

Unlike private sector executives, deputy ministers do not control the important policy and management levers. Control over departmental goals and revenues is given, to a large degree, to outside bodies, be they central agencies, politicians, Parliament, the courts, or interest groups. Goals are often vague and can work at cross purposes. The system favours incremental decision making because deputy ministers cannot depend on the prime minister, ministers, Parliament, or the courts to provide a solid, stable, and predictable foundation to guide future decisions. Long-term planning, at best, is geared to the next election. An unforeseen political development can reorient a department's policies or programs and deputy ministers are then expected to pick up the pieces.

The pull of deputy ministers toward the centre and away from their departments has never been stronger. Federal deputy ministers now spend nearly 40 per cent of their time on horizontal issues, that is, issues that cut across several departments, and we are told that "they are satisfied with this situation."[36] They attend weekly breakfast meetings chaired by the clerk of the Privy Council, participate in frequent discussion lunches, attend deputy ministers' retreats, and are members of various deputy ministers' committees. A former clerk explains that holding a deputy ministers' retreat once or twice a year constitutes "a tool for the clerk as the leader of the deputy minister community to help lead them and nudge them along."[37]

Deputy ministers are also frequently asked to take on special assignments outside their departmental areas of responsibilities. They are tasked to act as champions of selected communities, notably the information management-information technology community, the official languages community, values and ethics, and the list goes on. They are also asked to act as champions of selected programs or causes inside government, notably visible minorities. Here again, the list goes on. They are mandated to act as champions of Canadian universities, with the objective of "building relations between the Public Service of Canada and the universities in order to identify shared priorities, align and promote relevant research and build awareness of career opportunities in the public service."[38] They are asked to sit on several deputy ministers' committees, some permanent and some ad hoc. This, among other developments, supports David E. Smith's argument in a paper he wrote for the Gomery Inquiry that: "the old union of Ministers and Deputy has disappeared for reasons that are familiar. The range of complexity of government programs has multiplied."[39]

The traditional model was better at defining objectives, defining roles with specific responsibilities for the deputy ministers and managers down the line, establishing boundaries, and establishing more clearly who was responsible for what. The fact that deputy ministers no longer stay in one department for an extended period of time also amplifies the challenge. By the time a project or a major initiative is launched and implemented, often the deputy minister is no longer there to answer questions. It is becoming clear that we have moved away from Max Weber's classical model in which the individual bureaucrat was not allowed to "squirm out of the apparatus in which he was harnessed ... He is chained to his activity by his entire material and ideal existence."[40] Governing without boundaries now allows or encourages public servants to squirm out of the apparatus because there are different harnesses available to them at different times, as they are strongly encouraged to establish new partnerships with non-government groups. The tendency, in recent years, in Ottawa to attach an "associate position" to many executive-level positions serves to muddle still more the lines of authority and responsibility. The ability to squirm out of one's harness makes it more difficult to hold someone accountable for policy planning and for program spending. It also adds still more fuel to J.E. Hodgett's "doctrine of mutual deniability."[41]

The above has affected how the performance of senior public servants is assessed. Politicians often say that in politics, perception is often reality. The same can now be said about the work of senior career officials. So many variables have an effect on the success of a policy, a proposal, and a government program and its implementation, that it is impossible to single out one or even several officials to document the success or lack of success of a policy or even of departmental operations. The result is that the head of a government department or agency is now judged on the appearance or perception of success. James Q. Wilson explains that success in government: "can mean reputation, influence, charm, the absence of criticism, personal ideology or victory in policy debates." He adds that many government employees "often produce nothing that can be measured after the fact, making it very difficult to assess performance from an objective perspective." Michael Blumenthal is much blunter. He argues that, in government "you can be successful if you appear to be successful ... Appearance is as important as reality."[42]

Politics and administration now blend into one another far more than in years past. The problem is that hardly anyone agrees on how to measure the performance of senior public servants, in contrast to the private sector where measuring performance is often straightforward. Although governments have produced numerous papers on the attributes of competent career officials, there is still hardly any consensus on how to measure performance. One senior official in Ottawa spoke to this problem when he pointed out that for every ten people who approve the work of any deputy minister, ten others can easily be found to claim that the same person ought never to have been promoted to that level.[43] Unlike in business, sports, law, entertainment, and research in academe, there are no hard criteria to judge the success of the work of senior public servants. In the end, what truly matters in government is the centre, particularly the clerk of the Privy Council. If a deputy minister enjoys the confidence of the clerk, the Ottawa system is sure to follow.

A review process assesses the performance of deputy ministers, which the centre controls. Deputy ministers are also handed mandate letters by the clerk that outline corporate goals, as well as departmental objectives. The clerk initiates the review process by asking deputy ministers to prepare a "self-evaluation of performance during the previous fiscal year" and to come up with a proposed understanding for the next fiscal year. In some ways, deputy ministers are invited to write their own report cards. A retired deputy minister is hired to review the deputy ministers' self-evaluations. A Committee of Senior Officials is also asked to provide its views, as is the relevant minister.[44] The clerk then concludes the evaluation and makes a recommendation to the prime minister. In 2021–22, the federal government paid $190 million in bonuses to 89 per cent of senior executives. Executives in the department responsible for passports, which had a very difficult and controversial year in 2021–22, received $11 million in bonuses.[45] Senior officials in the Department of National Defence were awarded about $3.5 million in bonuses at a time when the department had come under heavy criticism for being one of the most over-ranked militaries in the world (i.e., ratio of generals to service members), massive cost overruns in major equipment purchases, and the number of sexual harassment cases.[46]

It is important to underline the point, once more, that the key player here in assessing the performance of deputy ministers is the clerk of the PCO, not the relevant minister. The clerk manages the deputy minister community on behalf of the government or, more specifically, on behalf of the prime minister. Ministers are often on the outside looking in throughout the review process. As noted, in some cases, ministers have no input in determining who their deputy minister will be. Francis Fox, for example, reports that he only learned of changes to the deputy minister community when reading the newspapers.[47] The clerk's responsibility in managing the deputy minister community is tied to the centre's responsibility for helping the prime minister manage the government and to promote a whole of government approach to governing. Deputy ministers are expected to alert the clerk when their minister is contemplating making a decision that goes against the public interest or is not in sync with the government's policy agenda. In turn, deputy ministers expect that the clerk will raise the matter with the prime minister to resolve the matter.

The prime minister is the final arbiter in assessing the performance of both ministers and deputy ministers – it is the prime minister's government and no one else's. Experienced ministers and deputy ministers need to think hard before approaching the prime minister to complain about the performance of the other. They are expected to work things out and recognize that both were chosen by the prime minister. Pierre de Bané, a minister in the Pierre Trudeau cabinet, told me that a colleague went to see the prime minister to ask that his deputy minister be removed from his department. Trudeau's response: "I know the deputy minister and he is very competent, more competent than you." I was told that the deputy minister remained in his position and so did the minister.

Deputy ministers are also expected to embrace the whole of government agenda, so that they will "put the interests of the government as a whole ahead of those of their departments."[48] This is laid out in the performance contracts, or agreements, that line deputy ministers sign with the centre. These agreements matter to deputy ministers because they may well determine their next promotion as well as their salary and bonus levels. The clerk recommends a performance rating and performance awards for deputy ministers. Salary levels in 2021–22 for federal deputy ministers ranged from $219,300 to $371,600 in addition to a performance program that can add up to 39 per cent in performance awards.[49] Deputy ministers also enjoy a more generous pension plan, indexed to inflation, than was the case sixty years ago. Their pension plan is also more generous than that of other senior career government officials – if a federal deputy minister serves at the deputy minister level for ten years, they will have a pension at 90 per cent of their salary over the last five years of service indexed for life.

The above should attract candidates from all sectors to serve as deputy ministers. However, it does not. We saw earlier that the federal deputy minister community is made up of career federal public servants who served in a central agency or in senior positions in several departments before being appointed deputy minister. They are known for their policy skills, for understanding the political dimension of policy making, and for their knowledge of the Ottawa system. This explains, for example, why a number of deputy ministers would have previously worked in a minister's office before joining the senior ranks of the public service.[50] It also explains why "prime ministers, ministers, even deputy ministers, pay little attention to operations or service delivery until there's a crisis. The focus is all policy and announceables, not execution."[51] It is difficult for private sector executives to navigate this environment, where everything is a moving target, where there are always many who have a say in one's work, and where hard objective data to assess performance is very difficult to generate. Few of those executives are recruited to senior public service positions and those who are only serve in government for a short period before returning to the private sector or elsewhere.[52]

## LOOKING BACK

Deputy ministers no longer relate to their departments to the extent that they once did. One can appreciate why – modern government and its requirements to promote a whole of government perspective are necessary because very few, if any, policy issues belong to a single department anymore. Modern politics also requires prime ministers to be in full control of their government. Prime ministers are in control when they are able to quickly answer any questions that the opposition or the media are asking. To do this, the centre has to be on top of issues so they can brief the prime minister. The point – nothing belongs to ministers and their departments anymore. Deputy ministers know this better than anyone else. They also know that their political bosses will invariably focus on "announceables" rather than execution or management and expect their departments not to create political problems for the government.

Accountability in the federal government still centres on the minister and deputy minister. The traditional model is simple – the public servant enters into an accountability relationship with their manager, under whom they agree on responsibilities and resource levels. From there, the responsible manager enters into an accountability relationship with their own manager and up the line it goes to the deputy minister. Given that there is a responsible manager at every level, the basis for accountability is established. However, the traditional model no longer works for a variety of reasons, no matter who holds political power. Today, both policies and decision making are the product of many hands. The challenge then is – how can accountability requirements be made to work?

It was easy for Parliament and the media to understand who was responsible for what in managing the Hungarian refugee crisis – the minister and his deputy ministers, together with their departmental officials, established the policy and the plumbers ran the program with little interference from the centre. Contrast this with the recent efforts to manage the Afghan refugee crisis. As noted, an all-party parliamentary committee slammed the government's implementation efforts because of its lack of proper planning and of its inefficient program delivery capacity. Themrise Khan, with wide experience in international development and global migration, writes: "What the Afghanistan situation most clearly illustrates is the absence of mechanisms with Canada's refugee policy to respond to complex emergencies on the ground."[53] The federal government fails on the ground, whether in delivering passports, Employment Insurance cheques, or providing assistance to veterans. This hardly constitutes a complete list.[54] While poets may have strong skills in delivering announceables, plumbers now have to deal with too many constraints to deliver programs and services effectively or perform to the level that they once did. The next chapter explores why.

# 9
# OWN WHAT YOU DO

In some sectors, managers and employees are able to own what they say, own what they do, and own their mistakes. I am one of the fortunate ones. I have always been free to own what I say and do and to be responsible for my mistakes. When I set out to write a book, I know that I will always own what I say. My publisher does have a say through the peer-review process. However, I always welcome it. The reviews have made my work better than it would have been without them. I often indicate, in the preface of my books, that I am answerable, responsible, and accountable for everything that I write. I would not have it any other way, nor would my colleagues at my and other universities. Books and articles in peer-reviewed journals are usually the product of one or only a few hands.

Entrepreneurs and senior private sector executives also own or should own what they say and do, and their mistakes. If their mistakes are not obvious to them, they are to others. They are able to measure their performance against telling data – revenues, profit, market share, and year-over-year growth. To be sure, luck also plays a role. The entrepreneurs who opened coffee shops two months before COVID-19 hit did not fully own their mistakes because they would not have known that COVID was on the horizon.

The prime minister can still own what they say but no one else in the executive can make the same claim with any degree of certainty. The former director of issues management for Stephen Harper explains: "In the current environment, the Prime Minister is accountable from a decision made by a low level public servant on a particular file to major issues to policy. My job was to make sure that we understand all those different issues and that we deal with them and managed these issues effectively."[1] He was right to stipulate the "current environment." Federal public service managers and their staff had a much better chance of owning what they said and did as well as their mistakes sixty years ago than they do today. If J.W. Pickersgill had failed to properly deal with the Hungarian refugee crisis, he would have owned it, no one else – not even the prime minister. Contrast this with Ottawa's documented failures in dealing with the Afghan refugee crisis. No one owns them because no one can own them – many hands had a say in developing and managing the effort. Parliament and the media will be looking to the prime minister and his office for answers because of the "current environment." Providing answers is one thing, but owning the failures and being accountable for them are another matter. Prime Minister Justin Trudeau may have accepted responsibility for the Canadian Security Intelligence Service (CSIS) not informing his office or a member of Parliament that he and his family were being targeted by the Chinese government. However, he did not hesitate to put the blame on CSIS by pointing out that the agency had not sent its report "up the chain of authority."[2]

Influence, real or perceived, not accountability, is what matters in Ottawa. Poets strive to appear to have influence, to have the clerk's confidence, to seem to have a safe pair of hands when it comes to managing difficult situations and ensuring that government operations run smoothly. Plumbers, meanwhile, seek to run programs without bringing attention to themselves or their work, particularly from the media. The saying "success has many friends but failure is an orphan" applies particularly well to modern government. Gaining visibility outside government, good or bad, is a sure way for plumbers to hurt their future career prospects. Success for plumbers is often measured by their ability to keep their heads below the parapet and to avoid bringing attention to themselves and their department.

Government is a theatre where almost everything now takes a back seat to managing the blame game. The arrival of permanent election campaigns, the 24/7 cable news channels, social media and access to information legislation have brought the theatre to all corners of the machinery of government. It only has one play – the opposition blames government for everything that goes wrong, while the government will only want to speak of things that go right and divert attention away from problems or political and administrative miscues.[3]

Public servants are an integral part of the government of the day. They are, after all, asked to be loyal to the government but must always be ready to change their loyalty when the power changes from one prime minister to another. Understanding how government operates for plumbers is to understand that the key to success for them is to see government programs operate without causing political problems for ministers and deputy ministers. The key to success for the poets, meanwhile, is to generate "whiz bang ideas" and announceables for the prime minister and ministers. The political theatre requires it, and ministers, as well as senior career officials, have become willing participants in producing announceables that cast the federal government in a positive light. This has brought leading academics in public administration to make the case that senior public servants have become "promiscuously partisan" in supporting the government of the day.[4]

I believe I am on safe ground when I write that more and more Canadians consider that the Ottawa system is not as competent as it should be, given the resources that it consumes. More and more Canadians are also of the view that government officials are out of touch with those living outside the National Capital Region. A declining number of Canadians are voting and joining political parties. The federal public service is not faring any better. As noted, public opinion surveys reveal that Canadians are losing trust in the federal public service, particularly in senior public servants.[5] The Parliamentary Budget Officer told the Senate Finance Committee in February 2023 that Canadians are not getting the level of service from federal public servants that they should expect and called on the government to "crack the whip" on Employment and Social Development Canada, arguing that there are pockets of "nonchalance" in the public service.[6] And Margaret Atwood told the media that federal bureaucrats "should not be telling creators what to write" and "should not be deciding what's Canadian."[7] This makes the point, once again, that federal public servants have few friends outside of government these days.

Government today does not lend itself to career officials owning what they say or do or their mistakes. The prime minister is the one government actor who can own all three. But this is not without problems even for the prime minister. In the summer of 2022, Prime Minister Trudeau was held responsible for problems at Canadian airports, flight delays, and lost luggage.[8] The prime minister is many levels removed from those running Canadian airports but he is the one who Parliament and the media will turn to for answers. He somehow became responsible for the problem, not the minister of Transport or the local airport managers.

The prime minister also took the blame when things went wrong with the Afghan refugee crisis, not the minister responsible for Immigration. Prime ministers can point the finger at others when things go wrong but, in the end, the buck stops with them, no one else. In the process, we are moving further away from the traditional chain of accountability: public servants accountable to ministers, ministers to Parliament, and members of Parliament to their constituents. If accountability is the hole in the doughnut, it is getting bigger at a time when disenchantment with federal government operations is growing.

In the summer of 2022, we saw the federal government struggling with refugee resettlement; airport delays; processing passports, visa applications, and Employment Insurance claims; and the list goes on. Some pointed to the COVID-19 pandemic to explain these difficulties. But Paul Tellier, a former clerk of the Privy Council, was not buying any of it. He said: "Come on ... you did not need to be a genius to see that more Canadians would be applying for passports in the post-pandemic period."[9] But again, it was the prime minister who took responsibility for fixing several high-profile failures in program and service delivery. He decided to establish a ministerial task force to "improve government services for Canadians."[10] The prime minister is expected to take responsibility because the "current environment" requires it.

At the same time as Ottawa was struggling to improve the quality of its services, the media reported that the federal public service had grown by about 25 per cent between 2015 and 2022 – from 257,034 to 319,601.[11] In addition, as we already noted, Ottawa spent $8.4 billion in 2015–16 on outside consultants but by 2023–24 that amount had more than doubled to $17.5 billion.[12] Having consultants work in government adds more hands to the policy and decision-making process, makes accountability more difficult, and also makes it harder to determine who owns what was done and what mistakes were made.

As we saw earlier, news broke in the fall of 2022 that Ottawa had spent $54 million on the ArriveCAN app which began as an $80,000 expense. In this case, the prime minister was not willing to own the mistake further than saying that the app seemed "illogical and inefficient."[13] He directed the PCO to inquire into the "highly illogical" $54 million contract to build the ArriveCAN app. Executives in the tech industry labelled the price tag "outrageous," arguing that most apps are built for less than $1 million.[14]

It was never clear who in the federal government owned the mistakes made in the ArriveCAN app fiasco. One agency admitted that it had provided inaccurate information to Parliament about the contract and then committed to launching a "review" that would provide full information on the contract "in the coming days."[15] However, the agency missed a parliamentary committee-ordered deadline to hand over the information. The Canada Border Services Agency (CBSA) "apologized" and committed to "double check" that no other errors would be made and that no other deadline would be missed. In addition to CBSA officials working on the app, representatives from the Public Health Agency of Canada, Public Safety Canada, Shared Services Canada, Public Works, Government Services, and, likely, central agencies were also involved, along with political staffers in ministerial offices from the departments involved in bringing the ArriveCAN to life. Any notion that anyone in government could possibly own this mistake is out the window. I doubt that the clerk was ever able to tell the prime minister how things went off the tracks, or why, or who was responsible. In any event, as the media lose interest in the controversy, it will also fall off the radar of the PMO and, by ricochet, the PCO.

On policy, federal public servants have recently been saying, under the cover of anonymity, that they are "afraid to speak truth to power." A study produced jointly by the Ottawa-based Institute on Governance and the Brian Mulroney Institute of Government at St Francis Xavier University reveals that the federal public service has become too isolated from Canadians and not sufficiently independent from politics. The *Top of Mind* study was based on forty-two interviews with career officials and a survey of 2,355 public servants. It pointed out that public servants saw a strong emphasis on "announcements today rather than implementation." It also argued that federal government officials insist that the government is putting much more "energy" into communications than ensuring that "implementation is sufficiently factored in to achieve the outcomes envisioned." The report stated that senior public servants are now "unsupported in providing fearless advice" to their political masters and expressed concerns about a "cascading effect" down to the assistant deputy minister level and beyond.[16]

That public servants are now afraid of speaking truth to political power does not tell the whole story. I hold that they are now also afraid or unwilling to speak truth to themselves. They avoid challenging their own operations to see if they could be run with fewer resources. They point fingers at politicians for problems in government spending and program delivery while continuing to add more staff and new management levels to their operations. John Tait said as much in his seminal report on values and ethics, writing: "Some have suggested to us that over the past two decades the climate of support for honest discussion and dialogue within the public service itself has deteriorated, and that public servants are not as ready as once they may have been to put forth honest views or engage in critical debate for fear of being seen to be 'offside' or untrustworthy."[17] Public servants thus have many incentives to avoid asking difficult questions in their operations, while those who encourage challenging the status quo are few, if there are any.

There are 320,000-plus federal public servants and the number keeps growing. As we saw, it is very rare for anyone to be fired for incompetence.[18] In the rare instances of public servants being terminated, it is usually for gross misconduct, leaving the government with no other choice and union representatives with impossible cases to defend. Some examples: a federal prison guard was fired after he viciously raped a twenty-one-year old woman, three bodyguards were terminated for using their influence to help smuggle cocaine into Canada, and forty-nine federal employees were fired because, while employed, they applied for and received funds from the Canada Emergency Response Benefit (CERB), a program designed for Canadians who lost their jobs because of the COVID-19 lockdown.[19]

We also saw earlier that very few public servants – whether they are managers or employees – take the annual review performance process seriously. In most cases, it is simply one more, and all too often meaningless item on a manager's to-do list. We know that some 90 per cent of all the executives in the federal government received bonuses in 2022, including those in departments that saw a breakdown in services. In addition, we saw that the federal public service has shown a remarkable inability or unwillingness to reallocate employees from low-priority initiatives to new or high-priority measures. It is too simplistic to blame politicians for this. Public servants cannot argue on the one hand that they are responsible for managing human resources, with statutes to back up their claim and, on the other hand, point the finger at politicians for mismanaging human resources.

We also know that, whenever decisions to cut spending have to be made, they come like bolts of lightning from the prime minister. Leaving aside the period when program review exercises are in play, the public service grows through good and bad times. Loss of employment because of a recession belongs to other sectors, not the federal public service. The IT sector has helped the private sector make service delivery more efficient, enabled businesses to reduce spending in their operations or reallocate human resources to higher priority areas, and eliminated some management levels. The federal public service, meanwhile, has long promised that IT would improve productivity and the quality of public services, and Ottawa has invested substantial funds in IT in recent years. Government programs are home to many routine, manual tasks and back-of-fice functions, notably record-keeping and processing applications. Regardless of the investments in IT, public service executives and managers have still not been able to prune their organizations as private sector firms have.[20] Again, it is too easy to place the blame on politicians for this.

The government established Shared Services Canada (SSC) in 2011 to deliver mandated email, data centre, and network services to forty-three departments and agencies. Before the agency was established, each department managed its own IT infrastructure and services. The Office of the Auditor General (OAG) took stock of the progress in 2015; the findings were nothing short of damning. The OAG discovered that basic management practices were lacking on several fronts: the government did not establish clear service expectations, did not document service agreements with departments, did not plan properly, and did not communicate clearly the objectives it wanted to pursue.[21] It is not politicians who are responsible for the mismanagement of the federal government's IT infrastructure.

Whenever an initiative goes off the rails, like the Phoenix pay system, no one in the federal government is held responsible. As recently as early 2023, the government gave an additional $500 million to "stabilize" the system.[22] We have also seen the number of executives grow substantially over the past thirty years. No one in

Ottawa has ever explained why. And here again the responsibility lies largely with public servants, not politicians. Associate positions have been tagged on to many executive positions from the deputy-minister level on down but no one has explained why or taken responsibility for it. It is worth repeating the point that thirty years ago, the TBS launched an exercise to de-layer management levels, insisting that it would make government more efficient and improve morale. The government has since done the exact opposite. No one has ever been held responsible for this *volte-face* and no one has ever explained why the initiative failed. When politicians break a promise, we often hear about it. When public servants do not follow up on commitments, few even notice.

It seems that senior federal public servants have borrowed a page from their political masters in managing the blame game. Spinning good news is now what matters to everyone in government, be it politicians or public servants, speaking truth to anyone by anyone be damned. One has only to read the annual reports of the clerk of the Privy Council on the state of the public service to see evidence of this. A former senior federal public servant writes that, when it comes to the public service reform agenda, the clerk's annual reports are not "always based on actual evidence or evaluations," and they tend "to over-emphasize or exaggerate successes." He adds: "The annual reports made no mention of some major reform initiatives, which were unsuccessful and subsequently abandoned."[23] This is what political spin looks like. Not speaking truth to its own institution or to other public servants promotes a narrative that all is well inside Plato's cave.

## WHY IS THIS HAPPENING?

The question is – why this state of affairs? Governing has changed substantially in recent years, often by stealth, and the changes have pushed public servants to own less of what they say and do and the mistakes they make. Ironically, it is the very opposite of what was envisaged when Ottawa embraced new public management measures and launched a number of public service reform measures, from PPBS to deliverology and all the other management reform efforts in between. Federal public servants make the case that, in our parliamentary system, it is not for them to own their mistakes – the doctrine of ministerial responsibility makes ministers responsible for all things before Parliament. It should, however, be a different matter within the government. Management reform measures have a lot to answer for including the difficulty in holding anyone accountable for implementing these measures is one.

There is also more to it than management reform measures not living up to expectations. What else has changed? Canadians have become less deferential to political authority. The media, including both 24/7 cable news channels and social media, have forced the hand of governments to react quickly to developments – both important ones and less important ones – whether they have a very short shelf life or require more reflection. Access to information legislation was designed to open up government and provide a window on who is saying or doing what. Instead, it has, made career officials more defensive and pushed them to come up with ways to work around the legislation.

Though the media and many Canadians may well view access to information legislation as an important building block to a stronger democracy, for many senior public servants the legislation goes counter to traditional public administration values. Some may well ask – why would governments want to "pass laws that threaten their power" or make life more difficult for themselves?[24] Public servants turn to a number of well-established tactics to put obstacles in the way of citizens' access to the legislation. They can delay responding to information access requests, they can redact material, and they can point to the high cost of responding to requests. For example, the House of Commons law clerk insisted that public servants "went too far in redacting the WE Charity documents" released to members of Parliament.[25] We also know that public servants will avoid putting things down on paper on contentious issues, opting for oral briefings instead.[26]

On numerous occasions, I have met with government officials who were working with two smartphones – one accessible under access to information legislation, the other one not. The media continue to report on the ability of public servants to sidestep the access to information legislation and on "secretive" and "tight-lipped bureaucrats."[27] Members of Parliament are also taking public servants to task for undermining access to information legislation. One MP decided to file a complaint with the information commissioner because some public servants were determined to undermine "the intent and spirit of the Access to information Act."[28] The comptroller-general, hardly a front-line career public servant tasked with delivering services to Canadians, told a team of government officials to be "careful what they write down" on paper in reviewing the contracts Ottawa had signed with McKinsey and Company because it would be accessible under the Act.[29] Access to information legislation does not work without a written record. The same can be said for accountability requirements under our Westminster-inspired parliamentary system.

Public servants are avoiding putting things on paper for fear of reading their material in the press, hence why we no longer have management by written documents. The legislation has also generated a demand for "poets" and political "firefighters in Ottawa" to deal with controversies flowing out of the access to information legislation. It has also made public servants more cautious and less willing to own what they say and do. Giles Gherson, former policy advisor and later a journalist, explains, "To address the access to information issue ... I saw myself that officials are extremely leery of putting things on paper that they wouldn't like to see made public or find its way to the media, several months later, that could be embarrassing to the minister."[30] There is always the fear that anyone outside government could discover what public servants have said and make it public – public servants know full well that outside government, people play by different rules. One can assume that this leads to less disciplined thinking, as strong memoranda have given way to PowerPoint presentations and oral briefings. Ironically, because advice along the lines of "be careful," if given at all, is no longer committed to paper, the advice has become less transparent and less consequential.

The concern over the media's use of the access to information legislation has reached the point at which the government is actually directing public servants not to commit anything to paper. For example, one federal department told consultants in a $132,000 contract not to leave "a paper trail in government offices" and insisted that they deliver their findings through oral briefings.[31] As well, several months after Stephen Harper came to power in January 2006, his government launched a program review exercise designed to cut at least $2 billion from expenditures. Public servants were instructed to do everything "orally," including briefings for their ministers in identifying potential spending cuts, and to avoid putting anything down on paper.[32] When you write something on paper, you own what you say. Much less so when you voice your views and recommendations through oral briefings.

Many senior federal public servants have bought into the view that political leaders have been promoting since the early 1980s, that "bureaucrats" have too much power. They are less forceful, if not less certain, when advising politicians and their partisan advisors. Public servants now often bring forward what they believe politicians want to hear rather than what they should hear or what they can do rather than what they should do.

## COLLAPSING BOUNDARIES

We saw in the previous chapter that boundaries continue to collapse between departments, between departments and central agencies, and even between the two senior levels of government. Powerful personalities both at the political level (among many others, C.D. Howe) and the public service level (among many others, Bob Bryce), who stood and identified strongly with a policy position or a cause, are no more. The courts have now also carved out a role for themselves in government operations. Governing from the centre is today firmly entrenched in Ottawa. There may well be solid reasons for strengthening the centre to shape policy and oversee government operations. However, those who have made the case that modern government requires a strong centre have failed to define new accountability requirements to accompany the change.

Some things, however, do not change. members of Parliament and parliamentary committees remain far more interested in scoring political points than in pursuing opportunities to improve government operations or strengthen accountability requirements. Although not always successful, public servants continue to favour anonymity because it is one sure way to avoid compromising their career prospects. Except for clerks of the Privy Council and some deputy and assistant deputy ministers, public servants are still not able to pursue comparable employment opportunities outside the public sector when they leave government.

One would think that high flyers with a limited employment history in the department that they are asked to lead would be willing to challenge the status quo and take a critical look at the department's financial and human resources, at least when it comes to moving resources away from low-priority activities toward new or high-priority initiatives. But we have seen very little evidence of this, likely because senior career officials quickly become part of the team when they move into a department. Team members do not shoot their own members. And, notwithstanding the succession of management reform measures, deputy ministers still have no incentive to challenge whether the department could do with fewer financial or human resources. Because they have not worked their way up in the department and because they do not have a deep knowledge of the department they are asked to lead, they have to turn to their department's executives for advice, where they are likely told to deal with other more pressing challenges confronting the department.

The widely employed argument is that cutting into government operations will only generate nickels and dimes in a multi-billion expenditures budget, so why bother? The Parliamentary Budget Office has this to say on the issue: "The performance data for 108 organizations do not suggest that financial resources have been reallocated from low-performing to high-performing programs. Rather, low-performing programs were somewhat more likely, on average, to receive budget increases in the subsequent year than programs that met targets or did not present measurable performance data."[33] The PBO added that in a number of cases, the government did not even try to "provide the measurement data." In one case it identified, no effort was even made to generate measurement data, notably programs targeted to building "strong and independent democratic institutions, a transparent, accountable and responsive federal government and well-managed and efficient government operations."[34]

Michael Ferguson, who served as Canada's auditor general until 2019, made a number of damning observations at the midpoint of his ten-year term, in his November 2016 report. He wrote: "What about programs that are managed to accommodate the people running them rather than the people receiving the services?" He maintained that: various "public accountability reports" failed to provide a clear picture of what is going on and added that: "our auditors came across the same problems in different organizations time and again ... when we come back to audit the same area again, we often find that program results have not improved ... – in the immortal words of Yogi Berra, – 'déjà vu all over again'."[35]

## NOT OWNING WHAT YOU DO

In 2004, I was invited to serve in the TBS in Ottawa as a Simon Reisman Visiting Fellow. It was in the immediate aftermath of the auditor general's report on the sponsorship scandal, and my mandate was to give secretariat staff a hand in developing new measures to strengthen accountability requirements. I was, and still am, in the habit at my university of turning off the lights in my own and surrounding offices and in classrooms on my way out of the building at the end of the day – it is my way of saving on the university's electricity bill. TBS was then housed in a large sprawling office complex, L'Esplanade Laurier, in downtown Ottawa. I often worked there late into the evening, and the lights were always on. In my early days with the secretariat, I searched for the light switch on my way out the door but without success. One day I asked a public servant on my floor to show me where the light switch was located. He had "no idea" and asked: "Why would you want to know?" When I explained, he said: "That really has nothing to do with you – someone else is responsible for turning the lights on and off."

This explains, at least in part, why the federal government performs poorly in delivering services. Other than the prime minister, few have any sense of ownership or responsibility for what they do. One would have thought that, as the government grew, its operations expanded, and new measures to improve management were introduced, sustained efforts would have been made to move decision making further down the line. We have seen the opposite. Rather than having more decisions pushed down, we are seeing more decisions, large and small, moved up to be resolved. We have not seen any new measures to challenge the status quo inside government departments. It doesn't matter which government is in power, senior policy makers continue to rely on bolts of lightning from above or across-the-board cuts whenever there is a need to challenge the status quo.

Deputy ministers openly talk about the tendency to delegate issues that may create political problems up for resolution – eliminating programs or reallocating resources certainly qualifies. The practice also serves deputy ministers well because, by delegating decisions upstairs, it enables them to avoid dealing with difficult decisions inside their departments. The problem is that the prime minister and their advisors can only address a very limited number of issues. Whenever the prime minister is distracted by a looming scandal or an emergency at home or abroad, the Ottawa system freezes up and decisions have to wait. And there is never a shortage of looming scandals or emergencies to distract the prime minister. The scandals or potential scandals we have seen in recent years include: the Aga Khan affair, the WE Charity scandal, the SNC-Lavalin affair, the revelation that the prime minister stayed in a $6,000-a-night suite when he attended the funeral for Queen Elizabeth II, problems with the Pierre Elliott Trudeau Foundation, China's alleged interference in elections; and the need to deal with Roxham Road, a small road straddling the Canada–US border where migrants were crossing to claim asylum.[36]

A dominant prime minister, an enlarged PMO, larger central agencies, new public management measures, several new oversight bodies (including a substantially expanded Office of the Auditor General), and the thinning or in some cases the doing away with boundaries between departments and between governments, as well as between government and citizens, have made public servants even more hesitant about owning what they say and do. The risk of owning what you say and do is too high for any benefit it might entail. In addition, if nothing belongs to a single government department anymore, it follows that nothing can belong to its executives and managers either. This does not square with private sector management practices. Business journals frequently make the case that "taking responsibility is an essential element of leadership" and "leadership is taking responsibility while others are making excuses."[37] Government, at its core, does not encourage even senior departmental officials to take responsibility or to own what they say, what they do, and their mistakes. The fact that the federal government also no longer manages by written documents to the extent that it once did does not help matters.[38]

Central agencies, meanwhile, have failed to challenge, on a continuing basis, the work of departments and agencies. The Finance Department and the PCO are concerned about the broader fiscal framework, the country's economic circumstances, and the dominant political and economic issues of the day. The TBS, the poor cousin to the other two, has no track record to show that it is able to challenge ongoing government programs or spending. Its role is to add funds to existing programs to deal with inflation, to accommodate the cost generated by new collective agreements, and to add resources whenever a program is expanded, but, like everyone else, it sits on the sidelines waiting for bolts of lightning to strike.

Since the early 1980s, we have seen new oversight bodies established (as noted earlier, several offices of Parliament have been created). Under J.J. Macdonnell, the OAG grew by 300 per cent, after Macdonnell successfully led the charge to introduce "performance audits" in addition to carrying out "financial audits."[39] To be sure, performance audits and the push on departments to produce "evaluation reports" have generated numerous documents and work for all departments and agencies. While it has added substantially to the overhead cost of government, performance audits have had little effect on the management of government operations or on developing and implementing Ottawa's ambitious program review exercises of the mid-1990s. The auditor general now tables reports twice a year and they always generate media interest, but only for a day or two. The other officers of Parliament are also forcing the hand of departments to generate reports, again at a cost.

Officers of Parliament, like other bureaucratic agencies or units, often ask for more resources.[40] The auditor general has an annual budget of $117 million but argues that it is not enough. The current auditor general, Karen Hogan, maintains that her office has been forced to delay audits and maintains that "when you're depending on getting funding from an organization that you audit, then it has an ability to impact your independence."[41] Other officers of Parliament have made the same argument, and have been trying to identify a more independent source of funding, possibly a funding formula tied to total government spending. Thus, a formula and a process, rather than politicians or public servants, would own, in future, the decision to fund the offices of the officers of Parliament. Paul Thomas correctly makes the case that they "can't have open-ended budgets and spend as much as they think they need. The foundational principle of Canada's democracy is responsible ministers determine spending ... and you don't get free tickets even though you serve Parliament."[42]

There is little evidence to suggest that officers of Parliament have had much of an effect on departments other than forcing them, in the words of a senior federal public servant, to feed the beast.[43] It is indeed a rare occurrence for an officer of Parliament to report that all is well in government and that nothing needs to be done. It is not in their DNA to do this. They see it as part of their mandate to identify something, anything, that needs fixing. The Ethics Commissioner, for example, issued a statement in February 2023, calling for senior government officials to undertake "mandatory ethics training."[44]

Officers of Parliament are very rarely subjected to scrutiny for their own activities or level of funding. Seven of them even asked members of Parliament to scrutinize their work more thoroughly.[45] I note that it took an assistant auditor general, a principal, a lead director, two directors, five other OAG officials, and outside consultants to work on an OAG report on evaluating the effectiveness of programs, which became a chapter in a full report of the auditor general. It would have been revealing to find out the cost of the thirty-nine page report and what effect it had.

Officers of Parliament and the new media have added a new and more demanding dimension to managing the blame game. Naming and shaming has become an important component of the blame game and it is a sure career stopper for public servants. They may not be fired but their career progression can come to a stop if the blame game turns on them. They have long embraced anonymity and the work of new oversight bodies has, if anything, strengthened even more public servants' desire to be even more anonymous in their work. The result is that public servants have become more adroit at not owning what they say, what they do, and their mistakes.

The federal government today is less about departmental hierarchy and more about interorganizational networks, with prime ministers and their advisors carefully overlooking the government's agenda and, to the extent that they can, controlling the work of ministers and their departments. This, too, has made it less likely for senior public servants and even ministers to own what they say, what they do, and their mistakes. Most public servants go to great lengths not to take ownership.

### WHEN A CULTURE OF FORGIVENESS DESCENDS ON OTTAWA, CALL THE RCMP[46]

For federal public servants, owning what they do can mean trouble. They know that in government if someone is held to account, only two things can happen – when you do well, nothing happens other than the relevant minister perhaps taking credit, but when you do badly, "all hell can break loose."[47] Public servants do not view accountability as a way of improving performance. They have a point.

Associating naming and shaming with accountability is as old as Parliament. What is new is that whatever government now does is the product of many hands. A new policy moves through a number of government departments and, at times, other levels of government, before it goes to the implementation stage. Unless the prime minister requires quick action, all policy proposals now need numerous individuals to sign off on them before they can go forward. Implementing programs is now also the product of many hands looking for input from other departments, central agencies, ministerial political staffers and, at times, other jurisdictions. In addition, because senior public servants no longer remain in their positions, even in the department that they are asked to lead, for very long before they move on to other opportunities, they frequently leave before the policy is fully implemented and before flaws surface. Mark Bovens puts it well: "The conduct of an organization is often the result of the interplay between fatherless traditions and orphaned decisions."[48]

No one, and federal public servants are no exception, wants to fall on their swords. All incentives inside government for public servants point to the need to circle the wagons, to close ranks, and to protect their positions, their units, and their departments. When the federal comptroller-general told senior government officials to "be careful what you write down," in reviewing contracts awarded to McKinsey, he was urging them to protect themselves and their departments.[49] He did not think that Parliament or the media would look at what they would write from the perspective of improving performance in government – he saw the potential for Parliament and the media to engage in "gotcha" politics or journalism. For public servants, the more impenetrable they make government operations, the better they and their departments are served and one can understand why. When they look to accountability requirements, they look to their more senior managers, the deputy minister, the minister, central agencies, the prime minister and their office, a dozen or so oversight bodies, Parliament, opposition parties, and all or nearly all the media, who are always on the lookout for material to fuel the blame game. Why would any public servant want to raise their head above the parapet whether things go right or wrong?

In sum, accountability remains an unresolved issue in government and recent reform measures have only made things worse. These measures have sought to replace accountability through political and administrative authority from elected office and legal mandates in favour of an entrepreneurial or private sector-inspired style of leadership and accountability. The measures required relaxing administrative and financial controls by doing away with a number of rules and regulations, to transform government operations into organizations "whose only difference from private, for profit organizations is the nature of the product that is delivered."[50] However, wishful thinking does not work. Unless competition is introduced to government operations, if at all possible, there is no point in changing the management approach.

Here is what we are left with: career government officials have been asked to work like their private sector counterparts but cannot; public servants are losing sight of what makes government different from other sectors and have to work in a world of boundaries that are collapsing or growing thinner, where their units are not separating from other units, their department from other departments, their government from other governments, and themselves from other sectors. Accountability in government does not have much of a chance in this environment and, when accountability goes, trust is never far behind.

### LOOKING BACK

The federal government, like many other governments in the Western world, set out to introduce new forms of governance without fundamentally adjusting the requirements for accountability. The reform measures did not and still do not easily square with the long-standing organizational culture found in the public service. We know that the federal public service has lost ground in recent years. As we saw earlier, public opinion surveys report that only 6 per cent of Canadians express "a lot of trust in senior public servants;" only 11 per cent of federal public servants think that "unsatisfactory employee performance is managed effectively;" and only 25 per cent feel that they receive "meaningful recognition for work done."

Politicians, regardless of the party in power, have substantially expanded their own offices as a check against the influence of career officials; and Canadians have witnessed a series of program failures in recent years, from processing passports to Employment Insurance applications. Public servants have even failed to deliver initiatives designed by and for the public service, notably the Phoenix pay system, as well as the failed attempt to reform position classification and job evaluation systems, at a cost of $200 million between 1998 and 2001.[51] Public servants, not politicians, are responsible for this failure. Two leading students of government, in a comparative study of public management, concluded that "Canada suffers ... a significant implementation gap with many initiatives failing to meet anything like full expectations."[52] Some public servants may want to simply blame politicians for this state of affairs and leave it at that. It does not, however, tell the whole story.

Federal public servants do see the problem with government operations, but only in retirement. A former clerk of the Privy Council, Kevin Lynch, teamed up with another former federal public servant to answer why the federal government services "are not being delivered well today." They maintain that "it is clearly not due to a shortage of spending, public servants, consultants or debt." They reminded their readers that, "at the federal level from 2015 to 2022, the size of the public service grew by 30 per cent, the use of consultants shot up 40 per cent, government spending skyrocketed by 66 per cent and government debt almost doubled." They concluded: "The size of government expanded considerably, while the efficiency of government declined noticeably – not a good combination. Too many new programs, with too little prioritization, that are too quickly rushed to the 'press release stage' is a recipe for delivery problems, not only of the new programs but also for related existing programs."[53] They pointed to several reasons for the failures, among others, the "extreme centralization of decision making ... at the expense of ministers, cabinet and Parliament. Ministerial accountability and collective decision making, with fearless advice from an empowered, non-partisan public service, are central to our Westminster system of government. The sad fact is we have strayed far from that guiding ideal."[54] In an earlier op-ed, Kevin Lynch argued that there are "too many layers of management, and little clarity on accountability for results."[55] As clerk of the Privy Council, he saw that there were too many management levels in the Ottawa bureaucracy. Like other senior public servants, he never explains why he sees problems better in retirement. There may well be reasons why there are so many management levels in the federal government. If not, then senior public servants should report on why and who is or was responsible. It is too easy to say that politicians are responsible and leave it at that.

There are some of the questions that the public service needs to address. Why is the size of the public service growing year after year? Why is Ottawa's management cadre continually growing? Why is the number of contracts to outside consultants still growing, even when the prime minister made a commitment in 2015 to arrest the growth? Why are there so many management levels in the federal government bureaucracy? Why is the federal government losing ground in its ability to deliver quality service? Why are federal government managers unable to deal with non-performers? Why have federal public servants lost standing with Canadians?[56] The next three chapters seek to answer these questions.

## 10

# WHAT DO CANADIANS WANT THE FEDERAL PUBLIC SERVICE TO BE?

At the risk of stating the obvious, the federal public service is an important institution for Canadians. It provides advice to our political leaders and it generates numerous decisions every day that profoundly affect Canada's political economic, social, and even moral circumstances. It delivers essential services to Canadians and also provides employment for a large segment of the population. If we did not have a federal public service, who would control our borders, who would look after our national parks, and who would regulate the sectors of our national economy that require regulations? The question is not whether we need a national public service but rather – what do Canadians want their national public service to be?

All is not well with the federal public service, as earlier chapters make clear. I am hardly the only one with concerns. Even federal public servants themselves told the authors of the *Top of Mind* report that they are now afraid of "speaking truth to power" and that the public service is falling short in delivering services to Canadians. As we saw, hardly a week went by between 2021 and 2023 when the media did not take the federal government to task for its failings in delivering services or mismanaging contracts for government consultants. A public opinion survey reveals that three-quarters of Canadians believe that "governments are broken ... because of wasteful spending."[1] We also saw that the public service falls short even when it is implementing measures for its own organization, notably in introducing a new pay system and establishing a new classification system for its positions.

To fulfill its basic function successfully, we need to take stock of the federal public service with a view to strengthening its capacity to provide policy advice to the government of the day, to deliver services, and to administer regulations. That is the purpose of this book. But books of this kind do not often engage Canadians in a debate or grab media attention and when they do, it is only briefly. However, I hold that answering the question, "What do we want the federal public to be?" should concern not only public servants, politicians, and public sector unions. Canadians also need to take a stronger interest in their national public service to promote change.

I had this in mind when I told a journalist in late 2022 that the time had come for a royal commission on the role of the federal public service. I explained: "I reluctantly came around to a royal commission because I see no better option. I'm not a big fan of them. They're costly and, once launched, can go off on tangents. But what else can we do?"[2] To be sure, royal commissions have shortcomings but they also have strengths: they can launch non-partisan public debates, produce excellent research, and engage Canadians, if only because the media take an interest in their work. My point is that we need to open a public debate on the future of the federal public service, much like Pope John XXIII did for the Catholic Church in 1962. The pope allegedly walked over to a window in the Vatican, threw it open, and said: "I want to throw open the window of the Church so that we can see out and people can see in."[3] The pope opened the Second Vatican Council in October 1962, which had a profound effect on the Roman Catholic Church. A royal commission may well enable public servants to see out of their Plato's cave, not just the recently retired ones, and also allow Canadians to see in.

My suggestion met with some resistance. A former clerk of the Privy Council dismissed the suggestion of a royal commission, saying that "some turn out to be duds." However, he never identified any of the "duds." I would not call the Glassco Commission on the federal public service a dud. Its effects have been strong and lasting, and the federal public service is still permeated with its legacy. The Macdonald Royal Commission laid the groundwork for the Canada–US Free Trade Agreement. Instead of a royal commission, he recommended that the federal government create a "permanent Better Government Fund in the care of the Treasury Board." The word "permanent" applies well to federal government activities, once launched. This falls under the category of "whiz bang" ideas. The fund would be designed to support conferences, research, and the like. He explained that such a fund would only constitute a small investment considering the federal government "spends $360 billion across the board every year."[4] It is an argument that works well in Ottawa and it beats supporting the idea on its own merit. It also speaks to what is desirable, not what is feasible or doable. A lot of new spending can be justified with this argument – support this modest proposal because the federal government spends $360 billion on everything else. One can also easily imagine cabinet ministers and MPs making the same case in promoting a modest project for their constituencies. Asking the TBS and its 2,500 employees to manage the fund would also not be without challenges. The role of the TBS, in theory at least, is to act as a guardian of the public purse, to challenge what departments do and how they do it, and to oversee how departments manage operations. Asking the TBS to manage the fund would be asking it to be judge and jury of its own activities. As earlier chapters point out, the TBS has had limited success in overseeing how departments manage operations – it is not at all clear how granting it a permanent fund would improve things.

As a former clerk, he would also have known all about the Canada School of Public Service. The school has an annual budget of $111 million and is home to about 670 full-time equivalents.[5] If the government should ever decide to contribute $20 million a year to a "permanent Better Government Fund," why not ask the school to take it on and reorient some of its activities and spending to support and manage the fund? There is, however, no assurance that the school could make the Better Government Fund work, given its track record. But that is the problem with "whiz bang" ideas. Once created, they are allowed to drift and no one takes anyone to task demanding answers.

The above speaks to one of the federal public service's important shortcomings, the reason why it has lost standing with politicians and Canadians, and why it is afraid to speak truth to power, either to politicians or to itself. This is why we need a process to enable public servants to see out of their institutions and to allow Canadians to see in. As we have seen, the federal public service has a limited capacity and little interest in challenging ongoing government activities. A theme that we have returned to time and again in this book is that senior government executives and managers only ask gruelling questions about government operations after they leave government.

Another former clerk of the Privy Council, in an op-ed, sees too many management levels in Ottawa. But, again, he only saw the problem after he retired. It is not clear why he did not see the problem while he was clerk and, if he did, why he decided not to do anything about it. As clerk, he had the influence to deal with the issue and he could have owned the problem with the cooperation of the secretary of the TBS and the blessing of the prime minister. A former senior finance official expressed in February 2023: "My concern about the bloat of the bureaucracy is that we're not improving outcomes, we're just adding more people." He added: "You can't just ask departments to downsize – it never works."[6] He is right, as we made clear in this book. The question that needs an answer is, why?

Leaving aside deputy ministers, program evaluation units, and their staff, it is also true that the federal government lacks the capacity to review programs or to make the case to reallocate resources from low-priority activities to high-priority areas. Michael Wernick, former clerk of the PCO, argues that he would be "extremely surprised if there's any kind of serious effort at either cutting back from the public service or trying to reform it," in part because "there's just not enough people to think about these things or work on these things."[7] It begs the question – what are the nearly 320,000-plus federal public servants thinking about or working on? More specifically – what are the poets working on, given that there are now nearly as many poets as there are plumbers, those actually delivering programs and services?

This brings us to a second theme of the book, a theme that I first wrote about twenty-five years ago: the growing concentration of power in the hands of the prime minister, the PMO, and central agencies. It is a theme that has since been picked up by many others. When I published *Governing from the Centre*, a number of cabinet ministers and senior public servants called to say that I'd got it right. They all said this, however, in private conversations. I accept that those who did not agree did not call me. One cabinet minister told me in private that I was right but then told the media that I had misread the situation.[8] One senior partisan advisor with the Chrétien government also argued that I had misread how government works but then wrote a book explaining in some detail why and how the prime minister is able to govern from the centre.[9]

It is now widely agreed that governing from the centre is firmly entrenched in Ottawa. The literature increasingly points in that direction and senior public servants themselves, including two former clerks of the PCO who served two different governments, are now speaking out about the centralization of power in the PMO. Both point to the negative aspects of governing from the centre, with Kevin Lynch calling on the government to "reverse the extreme centralization of decision-making within government."[10] After the centralization of power started in earnest under former prime minister Pierre Trudeau for reasons that I outlined earlier, no prime minister has ever turned back the clock, though some pledged to do so during election campaigns. Even the one who had committed to turning back the clock quickly changed his mind shortly after he was sitting in the prime minister's chair.[11]

The justification behind the centralization of power is straightforward. It is the prime minister's government, and when they leave, lose an election, or lose the confidence of the House of Commons, a new government has to be sworn in. Prime ministers are thus free to manage their government as they wish because it is their government. They are free to manage their government as they wish because they enjoy full control over both appointments and the machinery of government and decide the government's agenda. The requirements of modern government and the machinery of government have also strengthened the prime minister's hand. As we saw, the logic is that no or precious few policy issues can now belong to a single minister and their department and no one is in a better position to bring a whole of government perspective to government policies and operations than the prime minister and their advisors.

The only person able to limit the extent of the prime minister's reach into government operations is the prime minister and there is no reason why they should, at least from their perspective. Gordon Robertson put it well when he wrote, if "moderating the power of the Prime Minister is desirable, who to do it? Obviously, it would be the Prime Minister himself. However, admission of error is not common by prime ministers."[12] Prime ministers have continued to strengthen their hand over the past fifty years. We have reached the point where Justin Trudeau's chief of staff now has a direct say not only in staffing all ministerial chiefs of staff but also in staffing virtually all other senior positions in ministerial offices.

I appreciate that there are reasons why the prime minister would want to strengthen their hand in governing and why the PCO would be called in to help the process. It does, however, create problems for government operations. That is tied to the third theme of this book: If private sector management practices are to be introduced in government, then strong executives and managers should be able to own what they say, own what they do, and own their mistakes.

## WHEN GOVERNING FROM THE CENTRE MEETS NEW PUBLIC MANAGEMENT MEASURES

What is often overlooked is that the heavy hand of the prime minister, the PMO, and the PCO are not only felt when shaping policies but also in government operations. An assistant to former prime minister Harper explained why – it is because "the prime minister is accountable for anything from a decision made by a low level public servant."[13] This runs headlong into Ottawa's sustained effort to make management in government look like management in the private sector. It is important to underline the point that the effort to import private sector management measures (the Glassco Commission and its call to let managers manage) started at about the same time as Trudeau *père* decided to centralize more and more power in his own hands and office. The two clashed because it is not possible to make the theoretical underpinnings of the two approaches work together. The two cannot easily co-exist.

The federal public service, meanwhile, has to navigate, as best it can, between the two. It has also had to deal with a constant barrage of bureaucracy bashing, with some arguing that government bureaucracy is too lethargic and others insisting that public servants are too powerful. One senses that senior public servants decided, at one point, to turn the wheel over to politicians and say "OK, now you drive but stay away from the public service, its size, its cost and the number of management levels." A new bargain was struck – senior public servants would tell politicians in power what they wanted to hear rather than what they should hear and the public service would be left on its own to manage human resources. More to the point, politicians are discouraged from poking into financial and human resource management issues or trying to run government operations. As we noted earlier, there are also statutes that limit ministers from managing several areas of government operations, notably staffing and financial resources. Public sector unions have also made it difficult for politicians to poke into human resource issues.

Deputy ministers have to contend with an overcrowded agenda, where, as one senior federal deputy minister told me, "the urgent always crowds out the important."[14] There is never a shortage of urgent, delicate, and important issues for deputy ministers to attend to and dealing with a "bloated bureaucracy" is never one of them. Private and public sector differences are too pronounced for them to use the same management practices. Responsibility is a moving target in the public service – the boundaries separating who does what barely exist now and, as James Q. Wilson argues, performance is about appearance, not results. Businesses have hard objective data on performance. In most cases, that does not exist in the federal government.

John A. Hayes, formerly with the deputy prime minister's office, wrote a report to review programs in the aftermath of the Nielsen Task Force, an exercise that teamed up private sector representatives with federal public servants.[15] The private sector representatives felt that the task force accomplished little of substance. Federal public servants, meanwhile, felt that the business representatives were "too business oriented and bogged down in detail." However, they did think that private sector members on the study teams could "ask more easily awkward questions and questions that may not occur to public servants, who are conditioned by the government milieu" and "that pressure from the business representatives allowed the team to make punchy comments on programs." Hayes adds that private sector members had an attitude of: "Why can't the government do things the way we do them?"[16] It is a question that keeps coming up time and again. I also hear it often from friends in the business community.

The answer that Wallace Sayre uttered in the 1950s still applies: "Public and private management are fundamentally alike in all unimportant respects."[17] Federal public servants, for example, are comfortable working with a Treasury Board document on risk management that urges managers to "recognize, understand, accommodate and capitalize on new challenges and opportunities."[18] They would willingly attend numerous meetings to discuss the finer points in the above sentence or any other policy challenge. Private sector executives would see little merit in that sentence and would ask, as they did with the Nielsen Task Force, for more "details" and pose difficult or punchy questions for managers to answer.

Students of government have documented important shortcomings in Ottawa's various attempts to assess performance. For one thing, managers have every reason to game evaluation reports by highlighting the ones that cast their programs in a positive light. For another, reports are generated to meet reporting obligations, with little or no practical value or effect. It is worth quoting Robert P. Shepherd at length as he sums up the problem: "In Canada, the enthusiasm for results and performance management has waned since the 1990s because these functions have not kept their promises for improving accountability for results despite moves to decentralize performance management to departments and agencies. A central challenge is that implementation of the performance regime has tended to be complex and contestable, including coming to a common understanding of the purpose of performance management, measurement and reporting, how performance is understood across multiple disciplines and domains, how performance for results can be measured that serves multiple audiences each with differing purposes or aims, and how performance can be reported in ways that serves multiple audiences and purposes while also being digestible."[19] Serving multiple audiences and purposes lessens the ability to speak truth to both politicians and the public service. This does not, however, take anything away from the important role financial audits play in holding government officials accountable. Shepherd may well be right when he writes that "enthusiasm for results and performance has waned since the 1990s" but funding for this function has not waned.

The literature on private sector management has one theme that comes up time and again – empowering managers is key to organizational success.[20] One of *Time* magazine's top twenty-five most influential business management books is titled *First, Break All the Rules*.[21] Could senior federal public servants even think of doing this? They acknowledged that the private sector representatives on the Nielsen Task Force could more easily "ask awkward questions ... that may not occur to them." Senior public servants could break all the rules only if we did away with Parliament, several oversight bodies, the PMO and PCO, cabinet ministers, and the TBS.

Public servants have been caught between two diametrically opposite worlds. They can and do fudge reports on performance, not only because it is in their interest to do so, but it is also in the interest of the politicians they serve. Public servants, with a sense of the history of their institution and with an appreciation of their institution's values, know that importing private sector management practices to government would not work. Being told that their management measures were inferior to those in the private sector also hardly helped public servants gain confidence in their institution, in their management practices, and in themselves. In addition, federal public servants now work with a decision-making structure in which the centre runs too many things and deals with too many issues, leaving, in the process, too many decisions unattended and running the risk that no decision is a bad decision. Public sector unions, unlike their private sector counterparts, are able to push against politicians and bureaucrats, who are much more pliable than market forces. It is anything but an ideal situation for Canadian politicians, for public service executives and managers, for front-line public servants, and for Canadians.

However, the various management reform measures have had an effect. Departments and agencies now submit fewer than a thousand requests a year to the TBS to secure authority for financial or human resource transactions, compared with more than 6,000 some forty years ago. Departments now enjoy greater authority to classify and reclassify positions and to initiate financial transactions than they once did, and they are relatively free of centrally prescribed rules.[22] It is less and less possible to determine if government managers are respecting rules and regulations and to hold them to account because the federal public service continues to move away from this approach. The TBS's language has also changed to promote a private sector perspective. Executives and managers have taken note. When the secretary to the Treasury Board described how the government was able to address its deficit in the mid-1990s, he said that the board did not focus only on "the costs of inputs" because that would "not lead to a rethinking of our business and business processes."[23] He did not specify who now deals with "the costs of inputs," perhaps thinking that somehow the language of private sector management would take care of things. Nor did he explain how or when the government and public administration had been transformed into a business guided by business practices without assessing the implications for accountability.

The Public Service Commission, meanwhile, has been stripped of its role in recruiting public servants, with staffing authority delegated to departments. The result, as Jonathan Malloy explains, is that the federal public service now recruits "most of its members through word-of-mouth hiring for short-term contracts. These openings are rarely advertised, and are never widely circulated. Most are filled through managers' personal connections with individuals and temp agencies. The practice has become rampant, so much so that the auditor general concluded in 2001 that "short-term hiring has emerged as the main hiring practice in the federal government." Malloy adds: "The reliance on word-of-mouth hiring means that Canadians outside Ottawa have few chances at jobs in their own national capital – unless they know the right people and they don't mind moving to Ottawa for a contract job that may or may not be renewed.[24] Politicians refer to this as bureaucratic patronage and they have a point. Public servants in Ottawa also do not share the same frustrations as the rest of Canadians in accessing government programs and services. They know how the system works, how to walk through the maze of government programs, and how to look after their application processes. They also likely have contacts in the relevant departments to help them access information and employees.

## DEMOCRACY REQUIRES ACCOUNTABILITY

Democracy requires accountability and accountability is not simply about political institutions, electoral laws, processes, and procedures. It is also about government effectiveness, effective program and service delivery, and responsible public spending. While politicians and senior public servants are preoccupied with generating announceables and managing the blame game in the era of permanent election campaigns and social media, Canadians assess government performance on the basis of how they experience accessing programs and services. There is now a disconnect between the point of service and Canadians trying to navigate and access the maze of government programs and the federal government decision-making process.

The federal government has a serious program delivery problem. Politicians are not the only ones to blame for this state of affairs. In the past, most program and service decisions were made by public servants who worked across the country rather than solely in the NCR, so they knew which programs to deliver to Canadians. The federal public service, rather than locating more staff in the field, has done the opposite by concentrating more and more employees in the National Capital Region. Instead of simplifying the machinery of government to focus on program delivery, it has done the reverse by adding management levels and establishing "associate positions" in virtually all senior positions, with nearly all of them located in Ottawa. This has made the federal public service more risk averse and hidebound. It has also hindered its capacity to deliver programs and services in the rest of the country.

## WHEN APPROACHES CLASH

Max Weber's theory of bureaucracy has long held sway among public servants and, for some, it still applies. The theory calls for clearly defined responsibilities, clear lines of communications, accountability requirements working from the top of departments to the bottom, public servants selected on the basis of merit, and promotions based on seniority and performance. Weber defined his theory before public opinion polls began to shape new policies, before a whole of government perspective became necessary, before public sector unions were born, before the modern media were invented, and before access to information legislation was passed.

The Weber theory is hardly the only force that has shaped the behaviour of public servants and the organizational culture found in government departments and agencies. Under the Westminster-inspired parliamentary system, public servants are still told to work under the cover of anonymity, to be non-partisan, to provide advice to ministers without fear or favour, to accept procedural rules and regulations, to ensure results are measured so that citizens have equal access to government services, and to look to the doctrine of ministerial responsibility to underpin accountability requirements. To this day, the federal government insists that the personality of the public service is not distinct from the government of the day. Public servants are accountable to the prime minister and ministers in all things, and, in turn, the prime minister and ministers are accountable to Parliament. If this were not so, the result "would be government by the unelected."[25]

The theory falls down in practice because neither politicians nor public servants are willing to operate under these rules and requirements anymore. Ministers no longer want to take responsibility for errors that they haven't made. For example, in 2023, both Public Safety Minister Marco Mendicino and Prime Minister Justin Trudeau made it clear that they had no knowledge that departmental officials had decided to transfer serial killer Paul Bernardo to a medium-security prison.[26] This is hardly the only case where ministers decide to point the finger at public servants when things go off the track.[27]

Ministers and departments are no longer the centre of accountability requirements, given the arrival of a whole of government perspective when developing policy and, at times, multi-government or multi-jurisdiction perspectives and the shift to governing from the centre. There was a time when ministers shaping policy only had to look to public servants in their own departments for advice. Today they can turn to a substantially enlarged cadre of partisan political staffers, central agencies, think tanks, and public opinion specialists. If partisan political considerations are at play – and they very often are – politicians are best served by looking to their favourite pollsters for policy advice rather than public servants.

The age of certainty has come to an end for public servants. That era had important advantages – a clarity of roles, rules, and expectations. The behaviour of public servants could be predicted, both in serving their political masters and in how they executed their work. The biographies of Gordon Robertson, Bob Bryce, and Jack Manion reveal their influence in shaping policy, their capacity to work well with ministers, and their ability to work under the cover of anonymity. Front-line managers knew that they had to operate within prescribed rules and regulations and that their work was subject to financial audits and to the wishes of the prime minister, cabinet, and their ministers.

Public servants now work in a free-for-all environment, where prime ministers dominate everything they want to dominate, where the PCO continues to tell ministers that they are responsible for all things – except that several statutes insist that they are not – where boundaries separating departments and even governments are collapsing, where departments have two fairly distinct organizational cultures – one where poets flourish and the other where plumbers are viewed as the less talented administrative class – and where deputy ministers, like ministers, are assigned to departments only temporarily. Uncertainty is also being fuelled by hyperfast changes in society and by the global economy, by hyperactive partisanship, by the media's short attention span, and by a volatile electorate, all of this at a time when public servants are being told that their management capacity does not measure up to that of their private sector counterparts. This, in turn, has made it difficult for the public service to hold on to its distinct set of values and the organizational culture that sets it apart from other sectors – impartiality, equality, fairness, objectivity, strong values and ethics, and clear accountability requirements.

Uncertainty is also profoundly affecting the behaviour of public servants. Some, like others in society, are motivated by self-interest – although now more so than in years past. Collapsing boundaries, the substantial growth in the size of the federal public service in recent years, and the constant churn of deputy ministers have all contributed to a weaker public service as an institution. Public servants are no longer identified with nor can they identify with "a cause" like their predecessors: Bob Bryce (promoting Keynesian economics), Simon Reisman (fiscal discipline), Al Johnson (social policy), Huguette Labelle (official languages), among others. In addition, public servants do not easily identify with departments and agencies nowadays because departments are no longer the focal point in shaping policies. The government's engine room, where responsibility for delivering government programs and services is located, has also lost standing, for reasons outlined earlier. Public servants know this better than anyone.[28]

The problem is that in today's environment, it is highly unlikely that a Bob Bryce or a Simon Reisman could promote a cause as they did fifty or so years ago. There are reasons why policy issues cut across many departments and even governments and why prime ministers believe that they have to govern from the centre. The problem is that, though we saw a constant stream of reform measures, they left the machinery of government and its accountability requirements virtually intact.

The central purpose of the management reform measures introduced over the past forty years in the federal government was to empower public servants to manage government operations. But that can only be half of the equation. The other half, and the more important one, is how to make accountability work within the ambit of the doctrine of ministerial responsibility while empowering managers. J.E. Hodgetts maintains that what we have now is a "doctrine of mutual deniability whereby no one claims to be accountable in the end."[29] The inability to update accountability requirements has contributed to the degradation of the federal public service.

Public servants decided to batten down the hatches and wait for the storm of reforms to pass. Governments appear to have given up trying to make management in government look like management in the private sector because we no longer see a constant stream of new reform measures as we did some twenty or thirty years ago. The storm may have passed but it is leaving a markedly different public service: less confident in what it can do, where senior public servants are now afraid to speak truth to power (by their own admission), and where there is a disconnect between poets and plumbers.

Public servants are responding by circling the wagons, by applying the unwritten code of hear no problem, see no problem, and speak no problem. The code applies until they leave government. This behaviour becomes necessary because everything in the federal government is a moving target, where goals are adjusted on the fly and where the prime minister can get involved in the most minute of issues. An email sent by a PMO official speaks to this point. A partisan assistant in the PMO took the Public Health Agency of Canada to task, writing that the agency "posted PPE guidance for essential workers ... quite detailed ... None of us were aware."[30] How can anyone make the case that front-line managers can own what they say and do, working under these circumstances or when many issues, large and small, have to move up the line, at times to the PMO, to be resolved?

We are encouraging public servants to put self first. The government has noted the shift and responded by launching "values and ethics" exercises and by appointing "champions" of values in government departments. The exercises and champions have sought to underline the importance of the traditional values of public service, including the desire to serve the public interest and to take pride in their work and their institutions. However, at the same time, public servants are still being told that they should emulate their private sector counterparts. No one should then be surprised that, at least for some public servants and in some circumstances, the public interest will take a back seat to self-interest.

Prime ministers and ministers believe that, to impress, they must be seen as taking the initiative, unveiling new measures, promoting change, and producing announceables. We have seen a veritable alphabet soup of management reform measures over the past fifty years: PPBS, PEMS, IMAA, PS2000, the accounting officer concept, and deliverology. The list goes on. No one, including politicians, should be surprised that the departmental collective memory and core values are now barely visible, even to those on the inside. Senior public servants have learned to cope with the moment by looking up to the fashion of the day, by coming up with "whiz bang" ideas for their political masters, rather than looking down and strengthening the government's capacity to deliver programs and services.

Public servants maintain that it is the politicians, not them, who add to Ottawa's institutional complexity by pointing to the *Federal Accountability Act*, establishing external audit committees, and by accepting that, though the doctrine of ministerial responsibility still applies, they are not willing to live by its requirements. This too has only served to muddle accountability requirements and to encourage public servants to look inward, to circle the wagons. There is little risk for them when they focus inward. Reaching out to individuals or groups on the outside entails risks because those on the outside play by different rules.

Public servants are well aware that their standing in society has fallen sharply in recent years. Politicians have told them as much, as have numerous public opinion surveys and the media. A major study, based in part on a public opinion survey of Canadians, public servants, and focus groups sponsored by the federal government, delivered a harsh verdict on the state of the Canadian public service, concluding that Canadians see public servants as "disconnected, lazy and overpaid."[31]

Public servants in central agencies and line departments hold an important card because, leaving aside the occasional bolts of lightning, only they can decide on the level of financial and human resources they need. Executives and managers also know that they can count on the support of public sector unions at the first sign of possible cutbacks in government departments. Everyone inside government has an interest in see-no-evil and speak-no-evil when it comes to resources and accountability. While politicians on the government side are busy looking for "announceables," senior public servants have little in the way of incentives to motivate them to take a hard look at their operations and find ways to reduce costs, and public sector unions, for their part, are in the business of always asking for more benefits for their members. Public sector union representatives, for example, offered a simple solution to the problem that plagued the Phoenix pay system when, in some cases, it was overpaying public servants – the solution: forgive and forget. A union representative explained that, after seven years trying to make the system work, "chasing after overpayments is only creating a massive backlog for a system that still hands out paycheque errors every week."[32] The unions are paid to promote the economic interest of their members and they only have to push against political will. It will be recalled that the auditor general had earlier called on the government to collect over $500 million in overpayments to more than 100,000 employees.[33]

## WHAT ABOUT THE POLITICIANS?

Parliament is failing to hold the government to account on several fronts but nowhere is it more evident than in how financial and human resources are managed. Members of Parliament on the government side are there to defend and support the government, not to create problems by holding it accountable. Opposition MPs, meanwhile, are no match for the almost unlimited resources the government can marshal to defend the administration of any of its programs. Parliamentary committees, meanwhile, lack the resources to undertake penetrating reviews of government programs and their resources.[34] The review of the government's estimates has become an empty ritual. Efforts to "fix" the process have failed for several reasons, including the reality that "changing the estimates process makes for lousy social media clips."[35]

Accountability for MPs is about partisan politics, scoring political points, and generating fuel for the blame game. The role of MPs on the government side is to defend the executive, no questions ask, at least in Parliament. The role of opposition MPs is to find fault by turning to access to information legislation and the media, rather than undertaking a thorough review of government activities. Opposition MPs would need access to resources and experts to do such reviews, resources that are not available to them. This explains the value of going after a minister for ordering a $16 orange juice but not pursuing how the spending estimates are prepared; not delving into why the government sees the need to add 35,000 new positions to its public service over a two-year period; or why the government seems incapable of moving resources away from low-priority activities to support new measures.[36] MPs are not experts in the great majority of government activities for which they are expected to provide oversight and form a judgment. They also often lack the skills to pose penetrating questions to public servants appearing before parliamentary committees, who can prepare for hours to deal with anticipated questions. Neither the government nor the public service has any interest in helping politicians by giving them resources. Public servants have the ability and knowledge to ask penetrating questions, but they choose not to – why would they?

Ministers are key to making accountability work in a Westminster-inspired parliamentary system. But here again there are serious shortcomings. The numerous management reforms have looked to politicians to steer the ship of state, to define goals, and set priorities but then let the public service do the rowing. This is in the interest of ministers because they have insufficient time to plan their departmental activities in any detail and look after all their political commitments. In any event, ministers are unable to exercise a strong influence on their departmental operations because of the complexity in both planning and delivering programs, the need for coordinating different department and agency activities, and the number of actors involved in different parts of the federal public service and, at times, from the public services of other jurisdictions. Ministers are always outsiders to how things work in the bureaucratic world. The problem with letting public service executives manage their units, without anyone asking penetrating questions, is that it overlooks the point that the public service has a vested interest in its own growth.[37]

Royal commissions and commissions of inquiry, as well as a number of my colleagues, have been making the case that deputy ministers should now be called to account directly for their assigned delegated responsibilities before parliamentary committees. The Lambert Commission, for example, argued that having deputy ministers before the Public Accounts Committee would be "replacing myth with reality."[38] This and other similar suggestions have gone nowhere. The PCO sees little merit in having public servants becoming accountable to Parliament and its committees. Ministers also see little merit in making public the advice of their public servants, particularly after they have made a poor or costly decision. Opposition MPs, meanwhile, want to keep their focus on ministers because there is more political mileage to be gained in criticizing a minister than a public servant.

Ministers have reasons to sidestep traditional accountability requirements. They could well ask why a minister is ordering a $16 orange juice but say nothing if a senior public servant does it. In addition, the pervasive influence of prime ministers and their offices in both shaping polices and overseeing government operations have made ministers less responsible for their departmental activities. Governing from the centre has never addressed the reality that no human being, together with a handful of senior partisan advisors, can possibly direct, let alone control and be responsible for the behaviour of an organization as large as the federal government.

This also explains the inertia in federal government operations: delegating decisions upstairs leads to delayed decisions and, all too often, no decision. No one has ever been able to answer the question – how do you hold inertia accountable?

## WHAT DO WE WANT THE FEDERAL PUBLIC SERVICE TO BE?

Canadians and their politicians need to answer this question. Leaving it to prime ministers, the ones who can call for change and make it stick, essentially means leaving well enough alone. For one thing, the status quo serves the interest of prime ministers. If the status quo made life difficult for prime ministers, we would see change. For another, bringing meaningful change to the machinery of government and accountability requirements and making it stick would require prime ministers to commit an important part of their agenda to the task. This is easier said than done. As we have seen, the various efforts have not only failed, they have made government operations less efficient, more costly, and less accountable. And yet some government officials always stand at the ready to try to make them work, albeit often only giving the appearance of pursuing change. The point – if the goal is to make managing in government look like managing in the private sector, the solution is to move those government activities that can be moved to the private sector.

Canadians can also leave the federal public service well enough alone. It still works and it still delivers programs and services, though they are seriously lacking in a number of areas. Canadians could conclude that, by definition, governments can never be as efficient as the private sector and simply leave it at that. But that is akin to kicking the can down the road, deciding that not much can be done to improve government operations. It also leaves the federal public service looking for support and credibility outside its own ranks, no small ask if the status quo prevails.

Canadians and federal public servants would be better served by engaging politicians in efforts to improve government, to make sure public servants are not afraid of speaking truth to their political masters, and to make government operations both more efficient and less costly. Accountability still remains the unresolved issue. The challenge is as straightforward as it is difficult to pursue. The federal public service needs to change its organizational culture and employee behaviour patterns. There is a reason why senior federal public servants are only happy to speak truth to everyone after they retire, including to public servants, but not when they are in government. Unless public servants are able to speak truth to one another, they will find it difficult to speak truth to politicians or to Canadians when it comes to the deteriorating levels of services to Canadians and the cost of running government operations.

The behaviour of federal public servants is shaped by constraints, institutional expectations and, for some, also by a desire to "maximize their own power, income and prestige."[39] These behaviour patterns are firmly ingrained in the federal public service. Changing the organizational culture and behaviour patterns requires a strong and sustained wrench of the wheel because there are no economic forces forcing the hand of senior executives and managers to introduce change and make it stick. Because of this, inertia sets in. The onus is on public servants to promote change within their institution. The choice is clear – either they do it or, at some point, others will come in to do it. More to the point – they can either do it or expose their institutions to a barrage of bolts of lightning. The federal public service also needs to rebuild the credibility it has lost in recent years among Canadians.

Changing behaviours requires a capacity inside government to review ongoing programs systematically and continuously. It also requires a capacity to provide policy advice that resonates outside the Ottawa bubble. This calls for decentralizing not just government operations but also moving policy advisory units outside the National Capital Region. The federal public service needs to strengthen the merit principle when filling positions. Changes to the mandate of the Public Service Commission has promoted "who you know" rather than merit in staffing positions in the federal government and this continues to affect the public service's organizational culture and employee behaviour patterns. This issue is largely outside the reach of politicians.

In the past, centrally prescribed rules and regulations, clearly defined legal mandates, holding down the number of levels in a hierarchy, having relatively clear boundaries separating departments, and being able to work in relative anonymity have shaped not just how public servants went about their work but also how accountability functioned and served to shape the overall behaviour patterns of career government officials. When you move away from these defining characteristics, you create new behaviour patterns. When public servants are less able to see these characteristics in their institution, they will look to other forces to guide their behaviour. Federal public servants now operate in a vague and fluid environment where, in many cases, loyalty to superiors and to self trumps everything else. This environment also leads to a disconnect between officials at the top and those on the ground delivering programs and services.

We now have a government of individuals in Ottawa, not a government of laws or established processes and institutions. Too many issues in the federal government now revolve around the prime minister, partisan political staffers, a handful of powerful ministers and the clerk of the Privy Council, and deputy ministers. The thinking all too often is that things that matter to the prime minister or the centre of government need to be pushed up and pulled aside formal processes, so that the relevant officials can get on with the task at hand. Anything perceived not to matter as much to the prime minister is left in limbo. One casualty is the quality of service and program delivery. Those inside the Justin Trudeau government report that "there is a traffic jam" in the PMO because of its "insistence on running everything."[40]

If we now have a government of men and women for whom the written word matters less, where hierarchy no longer holds the place in the machinery of government that it once did, where boundaries separating departments and even governments are collapsing, and where government operations are being divided between poets and plumbers, then we need to look at the behaviour of public servants. If the Weber model and institutions now matter less, we need to identify the forces that shaped the new behaviour patterns of public servants. Understanding what motivates public servants will help to strengthen accountability requirements. The next chapter explores this issue.

# 11

# ATTITUDES, VALUES, AND BEHAVIOURS

For generations, public servants put on a harness as they went to work. They operated under established rules and regulations that told them how to deliver programs and services, in the hope that all Canadians would be treated in the same manner. Centrally prescribed rules and regulations made clear how government departments and agencies should operate and spend public funds. Departments and agencies were in the driver's seat both in shaping policy and in delivering programs. Hierarchy and accountability worked hand in hand and everyone knew their place in the decision-making process. The focus was on ministers and on administrative and financial inputs tied to accountability requirements. Ministers and their officials were handed an annual budget with the expectation that they would spend public funds with care. Public servants were frugal and sought to ensure that public funds were being spent for their intended purposes and reached the intended recipients.[1] The work of public servants, whether in policy units or in units delivering programs and services, and the relationship between politicians and public servants were anchored in an institutional setting that was easily understood.

The behaviour of public servants was shaped, at least in part, by the knowledge that rules existed and, if they were not respected, financial audits would identify the culprits. Public servants answered to their ministers and ministers answered to Parliament. This traditional bargain allowed public servants to be anonymous, to be politically neutral, to gain experience in their fields or jurisdictions, and to provide advice to their ministers without fear or favour in exchange for permanent employment and generous employment benefits. Ministers, meanwhile, could count on a dedicated public service, loyal to the government of the day. The number of executive and management levels was limited, as was the role of central agencies. The clerk of the PCO was, above all, secretary to the cabinet. Since 1989, the clerk has worn three hats: deputy minister to the prime minister, secretary to the cabinet, and head of the public service – and the one that matters the most is deputy minister to the prime minister.[2]

The federal government began to jettison the harness by the late 1960s, convinced that it was too cumbersome on public service managers for modern government. The Glassco call to "let managers manage," made in 1962, resonates to this day. The arrival of public sector unions in the mid-1960s also had and continues to have a profound effect on the behaviour of public servants. Public servants are no longer servants of the Crown to the extent that they once were. They are now members of an institution with rights. Luc Juillet and Ken Rasmussen explain that public servants became "less a part of a great chain of responsibility leading to Parliament" and instead became "possessors of rights and interests of their own, a development that would bring them into conflict with the other institutions of government."[3]

Public opinion surveys also report that public servants no longer enjoy the standing in society that they once did.[4] Forty years ago, public servants understood that both the private sector and the public sector had their place. The government's role was to ensure peace, order, and good government; to provide public goods; to implement measures to ensure that the disadvantages of the disadvantaged were mitigated; and to assist sectors, businesses, communities, and individuals to flourish. Public servants understood that their work demanded institutional requirements that were different from those that guided the work of their private sector counterparts.

Coincidentally or not, the public administration literature was turned on its head when the federal government started to abandon the institutional harness put on departments and agencies and public servants were told to emulate their private sector counterparts. Public choice theory and its variants look to forces that explain the behaviour of individuals in the marketplace and apply them to collective decision making and public administration.[5] Public choice theory, however, runs headlong into Weber's "ideal type" public service, where hierarchical layers of authorities, a rule-based procedure, and a qualified and salaried staff are expected to make decisions impersonally and disinterestedly. Public choice theorists hold that public servants seek to maximize their personal advantages whenever they can, drawing a parallel between a businessperson and a public servant: "Just as businessmen compete for share of market, so bureaucrats compete for share of budget: part of any increase can be taken as private benefits, an expansion in work means enlargement of staff, which in turn multiplies supervisory posts and enhances promotion prospects, and so on."[6]

On many occasions, I have sought to engage federal government officials in discussions about theories that explain their behaviour and that of politicians. I have never been able to engage either federal or provincial government officials in a lengthy discussion about public choice theory or, for that matter, any other theory tied to the motivation and behaviour of politicians and public servants, including neo-institutional theories. They do not engage, not only because they may not be aware of the literature, but also because they always see more important and timely issues they want to discuss and have more important things to do than debate theories that, in their view, have little to do with their work. The few who pursued the discussions argued that the theories, such as public choice theory, were too simplistic and could never provide the full picture. One federal public servant reflected the view of many when he said: "So, self interest in government like everywhere else is obvious, but do you really need a theory to tell us that?"[7] Some public servants have told me that, for a theory to be useful, you would need one for every government unit, for every department, and for every central agency because their requirements are vastly different. You would also need a theory for the relationship between every deputy minister and minister because the personalities of both often define how decisions are made.

Politicians hold similar views, convinced that the theories, to the extent that they are familiar with them, have an out-of-this-world perspective and are of no value to them. I recall asking Bernard Valcourt, a minister in the Mulroney and Harper governments, for his views on public choice theory after outlining its more salient points. His response: "Do we really need a bunch of academics to tell us that politicians are motivated by self-interests?" He added, "Show me a politician who does not look for ways to help win an election and I will show you a politician who will not be successful at anything. Why on earth should this be an important discovery for academics?"[8]

I accept that practitioners, at both the political and public service levels, have very rarely seen any merit in public choice theory and its variants or in neo-institutional theories. I maintain that no case study can ever trump a theory, however narrow.[9] Lessons learned from a case study all too often only apply to the case under review. I also recognize that political and economic theorists are making progress in explaining why and how political actors and permanent government officials go about their work. Public choice, rational choice, and neo-institutionalist theories have all made important contributions in gaining a better understanding of the behaviour of individuals and groups. But their work is not done.

We still know too little about the motivations and attitudes of federal public servants in the post-bureaucratic world. But we know that the link between politicians and public servants control, at the heart of our representative democracy, is operating under stress and strain. Through fits and starts, Ottawa has sought to see "managers free" for the past fifty years or so. The federal government has in effect sought to have it both ways: set managers free, but at the same time, draw more and more power to the centre. It is a case of everything should stay the same but everything should change. For federal public servants and politicians, including ministers, it is a case of *ne pas savoir sur quel pied danser*. Until they know on which foot to dance, accountability and government operations will remain broken, and it will continue to be impossible to find the culprit. And, unless we continue to make progress in gaining a better understanding of what motivates public servants, we will not make much progress in fixing federal government operations and its accountability requirements. They all go hand in hand.

## SOME THEORIES, SOME OF THE TIME

I recognize that some theories explain the behaviour of career government officials some of the time and in some situations, but not for all public servants all of the time and in all situations. However, it is also difficult to argue that public choice theory and its variants are completely missing the mark. Politicians and public servants will seek to maximize their individual self-interest under certain conditions and there are instances of both groups using their positions to work toward private ends and their own economic interests.

The problem is that the theories cannot "account for all instances of individual behaviour."[10] In many cases, individual politicians and public servants have made contributions beyond the call of duty knowing that they would receive few, if any, economic benefits.[11] Public choice and rational choice theories and their variants tend to understate the power of motives, such as one's sense of duty, concerns about the reputation of the agency one works for, and one's commitments to co-workers.[12] In addition, theories inspired by the economistic approach, the idea that public servants are economic men and women, are tied to individuals, and offer very little to explain collective behaviour or a collective mindset. While the prime minister need not be overly concerned with a collective mindset, virtually everyone else in the federal government is or should be. Collapsing boundaries and the need to pursue a whole of government approach, both in developing policy and in implementing programs, leave public choice theory and its variants wanting.

The neo-institutional theory does provide an understanding of organizational behaviour. It has merit. We saw evidence of the theory in earlier chapters where we noted that path dependency, tied to historical institutionalism, explains a lot about how and why the federal government decides.[13] However, the theory also has weaknesses, including its inability to account for establishing new institutions and understanding organizational change.

Though different behaviour patterns can be found throughout the public service, earlier chapters make the case that public servants, regardless of whether they are poets or plumbers or what agency or department they work in, prefer to remain in Plato's cave. That is what public servants do to protect themselves, their units, and their departments. They know that they operate in an unfriendly world, in a political theatre where the media and opposition parties only want to focus on things that go badly. It is a very rare occurrence when the media, both traditional and new, have positive things to say about the federal public service.[14] Public servants also know that they can no longer rely on politicians on the government side to come to their defence and that the several newly established officers of Parliament are there to find fault with government operations. As we saw, only when they leave the public service are federal public servants prepared to ask difficult questions about government operations, about the number of management levels in government departments, or about the power and influence of the prime minister and partisan political advisors.

I also recognize that the nature of government operations and the protection given to public servants by human resource policies and processes and by the work of public sector unions make it particularly difficult to understand why some public servants shirk responsibilities, while others outperform. I know public servants who welcome important challenges and take pride in their sense of duty to public service and others who value job security above everything else.

## THE EFFECT OF RECENT DEVELOPMENTS

A number of recent developments, which we outlined in previous chapters, are profoundly affecting the behaviour of public servants. A series of management reform measures, the widespread belief that career officials have too much influence in government, the need to bring a whole of government approach to policy making, the arrival of new media, and decisions made by a series of prime ministers to govern from the centre or from their own offices are also all having a profound effect on the behaviour of public servants. The more senior public servants no longer identify with a cause like their predecessors did, for example in developing the welfare state or implementing hybrid or highly flexible federalism.[15] Knowing how to navigate increasingly complex policy and decision-making processes is today a highly sought after skill for those who aspire to the most senior levels in the public service; and senior executives and managers can point to several reasons for their unwillingness or inability to ask difficult questions about government operations that include the work of public sector unions and partisan political advisors. While moving to a whole of government perspective in developing policy and even when implementing programs, governments have not defined an accountability regime to accompany the new approach.

We need to recognize that there are now two public services, one populated by poets, the policy specialists, and the other populated by plumbers, the public servants delivering programs and services. The differences between the two are sharp. It is not too much of an exaggeration to write that we now have two public services "warring in the bosom" of a single institution, with obvious implications for the behaviour and attitudes of career government officials.

The intensity of the criticism directed at government operations, the variety of sources generating the criticism, and the unwillingness of politicians on the government side to come to the defence of public servants make life inside government difficult. At times, public servants are defined by politicians as the "enemy within" that has to be held in check by substantially expanding the offices of the prime minister and ministers.[16] The result is that, more so than in years past, federal public servants are looking inward and unwilling to open up on the challenges confronting the federal public service.[17] One also has only to read the annual reports tabled every year on the state of the federal public service by the clerk of the Privy Council, head of the public service. They are replete with "feel good" stories – the public service version of political spin. If the goal is to fix what ails the public service, then one needs to look elsewhere than these reports. This explains one aspect of the behaviour and attitudes of federal public servants – see no problem, report no problem, look inward, and circle the wagons to protect the institution. However, that does not tell the whole story, largely depending on whether you are a poet or a plumber.

### THE POETS

The work of policy specialists has evolved substantially in recent years. Forty years ago, no one was making the case that senior public servants were promiscuously partisan. By their own admission, senior officials in policy units in Ottawa now report that they are afraid to speak truth to politicians. They also report that they are spending too much time and resources on "political and policy firefighting" on behalf of their ministers and deputy ministers and not enough working on long-term policy issues. To be sure, there is now a strong market for political and policy-fighting specialists. Policy firefighting provides important opportunities for the more ambitious public servants and they are successful when they are able to meet the expectations of, first, the deputy minister and, second, the minister. Because there is little in the way of measurable results, the personal relationship between the deputy minister and senior policy personnel "is an absolutely critical ingredient for success."[18] This observation was made in a document produced by TBS officials in 1984 and is even more evident today.

Policy firefighters are in demand because the urgent always drives out the important, even more now than it did in years past. They, for the most part, work out of Ottawa, close to deputy ministers, central agencies, and the political class. Those outside the public service likely do not appreciate the highly charged political environment in which the policy communities work. Politics is a tough business where politicians try to hurt opposing politicians before they are hurt. The notion that politics can be separated from administration was never completely possible, and is even less so today.

The centre, notably the prime minister and their office, looms larger and larger in the work of policy firefighters. There are far more partisan political advisors in the PMO and in ministerial offices than in years past. This not only adds political and policy firefighters to the machinery of government and promotes a competition for influence, it also puts pressure on career government officials in policy units to produce what politicians on the government side are looking for or want to hear. A senior PMO official has more clout than the most senior policy advisor in any department, something that ministers and deputy ministers are well aware of. Both former public servants and respected academics have been ringing the alarm bell over the growing influence of partisan political advisors, who "have absorbed new powers, and in some cases, even cut ministers out of what they're doing."[19] Political staffers, unlike in years past, now attend caucus and cabinet committee meetings and have become an important part of the policy and decision-making processes. The omnipresence of pollsters in the prime minister's court also adds more pressure on career policy people to perform or deliver on behalf of the prime minister, ministers, and deputy ministers. This, in turn, also serves to further erase the line that separates politics from administration.

Policy advisors and analysts focus on the urgent because that is where the market is for their work and there is never a shortage of political controversies. Some of the controversies are known to the media and opposition MPs, while others loom in the background. Being able to manage difficult political or policy issues gives one influence, with the result that policy units in both central agency and line departments are no longer able to do long-term planning, cutting-edge work, or participate effectively in the resource allocation process simply because there is less demand for this line of work than for political or policy firefighters.

Policy units and their staff should perform ten functions. They provide policy advice; they work on policy development by reviewing options; they have a challenge function; they carry out research and analysis activities; they undertake long-term strategic planning; they are responsible for liaison and coordination within their departments, in other departments and agencies, and in outside groups; they evaluate and audit; they provide information and communications services; they brief ministers on cabinet documents or initiatives prepared by other departments; and they carry out political and policy firefighting services for ministers and deputy ministers by dealing with controversial issues and preparing speeches or speaking notes. Policy staffers who excel as political or policy firefighters are the ones with influence and stand a greater chance of being promoted. Dealing with urgent matters, managing controversies, and promoting the interest of ministers and their departments easily trump all other responsibilities because the interest of ministers and deputy ministers has to do much more often with the short term. Ambitious public servants who make it to the highflyer list know that they are not judged on their ability to manage government units or operations but on their capacity to show that the files or initiatives they are working on are viewed as a success.

Deputy ministers are drawn from a highflyer list and, as we saw, are very rarely the product of the departments they are asked to lead. Their stay as deputy minister in a department is also short, on average three years, before they move on to another appointment. Their historical ties to the departments that they are asked to lead are often about the same as their ministers.

Public servants in policy units understand what gives them influence, which in turn has a profound influence on their behaviour – and why not? They have few rewards – having influence, making a contribution, and feeling personal satisfaction by promoting the interests of their departments and their ministers – stand at the top of the list of possible rewards. Policy specialists know that prime ministers and aspiring prime ministers often paint themselves into a corner during election campaigns and that they and their ministers will need help getting themselves out of difficult situations. No ambitious public servant wants to be perceived as being irrelevant or completely lacking in influence. In the federal public service, employees identify their own opportunities, and opportunities belong to those who can manage controversies for their political masters and deputy ministers.

What about looking to the long-term planning and the challenge functions? A long-term perspective for the prime minister, ministers, and their partisan political advisors is, at best, four years. This explains why the market for a long-term perspective is weak. The challenge function is particularly difficult to pursue. Few rewards are attached to it because there is little demand for it. In any event, departmental colleagues may well refuse to share relevant data or information because feeding the challenge function only generates bad news. Why would they ever share information that may cast a negative light on their work or on their unit's level of resources? Who wants to ask difficult questions if the units responsible for answering them are unwilling because there are no incentives to do so?

Not only are poets reporting that they are afraid of speaking truth to power or to politicians, there are signs that many have embraced the political-policy firefighting role on their behalf. There are signs that they are also unwilling to speak truth to one another. Ruth Hubbard and Gilles Paquet explain: "The most elusive sense that permeated the discussions was one of latent fear. This had nothing to do with any sort of edicts but rather some form of self-censorship that has become habitual, it would seem, as a survival instinct in a world where critical thinking and sharp exchanges are no longer valued as they used to be."[20] Hubbard was a former deputy minister in a line department and later headed the Public Service Commission. Ralph Heintzman writes that "in the two decades since the Tait report, both anecdotal and more solid evidence suggest that the honest expression of views is now more difficult than ever, especially at more senior levels in the public service." Heintzman explains that this is the result of a "climate of fear and self-censorship that is internally self-generated by the structure of motivation within the public service itself." He quotes a federal public service executive arguing that "people are planning their next career move, and trying to find out what the DM wants to hear before saying anything. This is dysfunctional."[21]

Size does not always matter in government. The most powerful and prestigious departments in Ottawa are relatively small both in size and financial resources. The more ambitious public servants in Ottawa would prefer working in the PCO (close to the prime minister) and the Department of Finance (together with the prime minister, this department decides which new measures will be funded and establishes the government's fiscal framework), than in a large line department with more opportunities for promotion. Both the PCO and the Department of Finance offer few opportunities for their most senior public servants to expand their offices. This challenges theories based on the view that bureaucrats are always on the lookout to grow their units by adding human and financial resources.

The theories based on the economic man are used to explain growth in government rather than cuts in spending and government operations. However, if public servants pursue self-serving interests when the government grows, one may also assume that when it pursues cuts in spending, public servants will go to the "wall" to save "thyself."[22] In earlier chapters, we looked at how Ottawa went about cutting expenditures when outside forces and the prime minister decided that the time had come. We saw that public servants were not able to make the scientific method work and produce evaluation reports that had any effect on program review processes, because they were unwilling or unable to identify cuts to their departments. In virtually all cases, the government relied on across-the-board cuts, albeit, at times, wrapped around a series of questions to guide the effort. Across-the-board cuts have one important advantage – they promote an "equal misery" approach, which is easier to sell politically and in the public service.[23]

In all cases, the prime minister and the finance minister laid down the broad outlines of what needed to be done. Public servants (the poets) along with their deputy ministers and ministers then came forward with recommendations. We also saw that the behaviour of public servants in the era of cutbacks mirrored their behaviour in periods of growth. Public servants with more power and influence looked after their own operations and interests. This explains why regional operations lost ground in relation to Ottawa head offices. Blue-collar workers at airports and ports were also much more vulnerable to cuts or transfers out of the federal public service than were the poets in policy shops in Ottawa or central agencies. Reductions in top level public service positions or senior management ranks were not as prominent as in middle and lower levels. We also saw that efforts were made to cut capital spending rather than operations, which are largely made up of salaries, postponing decisions that have to be made sooner or later. Operations that draw revenues from user fees were also less vulnerable to cuts and efforts were made to identify which operations could be turned over to user fees for financing. Ottawa also looked to cuts in transfer payments to the provinces and, in doing so, downloaded the political cost to provincial governments. We noted that arm's length organizations with high research and development spending saw deeper spending cuts than was the case for other organizations (recall, for example, the Harper program review).[24]

Past program reviews suggest that public servants tended to put forward anything except cuts in staff, suggesting that the public choice theory and its variants hold some merit. But there is more to it. Cuts in human resources are never easy for a number of reasons. Senior public servants are well aware that the public sector unions will oppose cuts at every turn. In addition, senior public servants saw merit in moving operations and responsibilities for program delivery to outside groups and community organizations, such as those managing airports. This runs counter to the view that public servants will opt for well-staffed in-house delivery units to deliver services because in-house operations generate strong economic benefits to government bureaucrats and their managers.[25]

We saw that governments, regardless of their political ideology, have no difficulty in establishing organizations, at times piece by piece, but have little capacity to tear them down as a whole or piece by piece. Government departments and agencies may not be immortal but their ability to carry on in whole or in part is remarkable.[26] We also saw that the moment program review exercises come to an end, government spending rises very quickly. As spending goes up, there is also a spike in the hiring of public servants, for the most part in head offices in Ottawa. This is in line with the public choice theory and its variants. But again, there is more to it.

## THE PLUMBERS

Plumbers who occupy senior positions in the federal government only have to look at the position classification system to understand that they are the poor cousins. Public servants in central agencies with no program responsibilities and very limited staff enjoy more-senior classifications and higher pay than line department executives responsible for complex and costly programs employing thousands of employees who deliver services to Canadians. Those who come up through policy work also far outnumber program executives in making it as deputy ministers. In addition, policy specialists in central agencies and line departments hold another important advantage – they are never held responsible or accountable for program failures.

Plumbers do not enjoy the influence and credibility that they once did. Responsibility for implementing policies and programs is now spread over several departments. Still, since plumbers are the ones expected to emulate their private sector counterparts, they should be able to own what they say, what they do, and own their mistakes. The opposite has happened. Today's plumbers know better than anyone that program decisions are often the product of many hands. They have also learned the art of delegating decisions upstairs rather than making them their own. This is the way of today's politics and public administration – politics require it because the prime minister needs to be seen as being in charge of all decisions that have the media's attention and public administration requires it because implementing programs now usually involves many departments and agencies.

Front-line managers and their staff, who deliver programs and services, operate in a vastly different political and administrative environment than poets or policy analysts. Again, the differences between the two are far greater than was the case forty years ago. Theories on the behaviour and attitudes of public servants do not underline these differences but they are sharp. I have had numerous discussions with federal public servants in recent years – those working on policy and those in program delivery units. I had a lengthy conversation with the recently retired warden of one of Canada's prisons. This conversation was vastly different in every way from the conversation I had with an Ottawa-based assistant deputy minister responsible for policy in a line department. During these and other discussions, I kept in mind Weber's bureaucratic theory and the more recent theories, including public and rational choice theories, as well as the several efforts to introduce new public management measures.

I found the discussions about the theories with these two practitioners lacking in some areas and confusing in others, particularly over how the new public management measures were being implemented. The assistant deputy minister focused his observations on the Ottawa system, on the role and growing influence of partisan political assistants, on the work of the PMO and the PCO, and on the inability of departments to "get things done." In short, he looked up in his work, rarely down to those delivering programs and services, and did not raise any program and service issues.

The retired prison warden focused his observations on the demanding work involved in managing Canada's prisons, dealing with his peers, and supervising his staff. He made the point that working in Canada's prisons is both dangerous and difficult. He has a point – for example, in 2020, there were five murders in Canadian prisons and correctional officers had to deploy force over 2,000 times.[27] The warden underlined the importance of his department's role in ensuring the safety of Canadians. I saw a sense of pride in his department's history and in the work of his peers and staff. He did not report on political interference from the minister responsible for the department or his partisan political advisors. He did, however, talk at some length about the "Ottawa system" and its never-ending calls for information and its constant desire to introduce new approaches. He also insisted that the work of public sector unions made his work difficult and challenging.

I asked him if he and his peers would accept being held accountable outside of government. He was quick with an answer: he saw no merit in being accountable to Parliament. He said: "Parliament is only about politics and why would any of us agree to be involved in politics?" He made the case that no matter how well he, his peers, or his staff perform, little will be said about it in political circles, in the media, or even in his community because only failures attract attention. He argued that if something goes wrong at the prison or if someone has a misstep, then "the world hears about it." When I observed that there is a tendency in the federal public service to "circle the wagons" and an unwillingness on the part of senior career government officials to ask fundamental questions about the public service, he responded that he and his staff were too busy running a prison to go around asking questions that had little relevance to their work, including whether his operations were getting too many resources. He insisted that at no point did he think that he had too many staff. He added that he had to deal with a multitude of human resource issues, including seeing some of his staff go on stress leave or turn to alcohol or drugs to cope with the stress of the job.

He identifies with an institution that has deep historical roots and a clear mandate. He spoke about his department's "strong culture," about the distinctive competencies it offers, as an organization where public servants have a strong belief in their work and the contributions they make to Canadian society. He said that he and his staff looked to their work with a sense of pride and considered their contributions to society as their rewards. He recognized that prison wardens and their staff have lost standing in society. The reasons – he pointed to the media, to the perception that federal public servants enjoy employment benefits that few others enjoy, and to Ottawa's never-ending appetite for information, for introducing new approaches that do not always work out; and for the lack of understanding of how difficult and demanding it is to run a prison. He acknowledged that both the public service and his department have lost standing and prestige in recent years.

I posed a series of questions about new public management measures. He recognized that he was not very familiar with the measures, though he had to give them some attention from time to time. He reported that it "was an Ottawa invention that added little value to his work." He did report that he had had some discussions about them at departmental meetings and went along with the efforts to keep the Ottawa system at bay. He spoke, for example, about the challenges in identifying clients – were his clients the Canadian citizens they were ensuring the safety of or the prisoners they were trying to rehabilitate? He explained that new public management issues never made it to the top of his agenda simply because he was too busy running a prison.

I highlight this conversation because it speaks to the work of front-line managers and their staff – the plumbers. One conversation does not, to be sure, make a case that applies to all situations. However, the literature also supports the points made above.[28] It makes the case that some public servants, notably those on the front line delivering services, behave in a way that does not always square with the findings of rational choice or public choice theorists. It also differs from those in Ottawa working on policy or head office functions.

Front-line managers are responsible for everything that happens inside their units and for their programs. Prison wardens are captains of their ships and know that they are responsible for everything that happens under their watch. Prison wardens also know that they do not have access to all the levers to guide the ship because key management decisions are made elsewhere, in collective agreements or at the TBS. They can take some satisfaction, however, in the fact that Canadians and advocacy groups have a much more positive view of their work than is the case for elected officials or senior public servants: 45 per cent of Canadians have a positive view of front-line workers in contrast to only 34 per cent for senior public servants.[29]

## THE BEHAVIOUR OF PUBLIC SERVANTS

Are policy specialists motivated by self-interest? Wanting to have influence and to make a contribution are powerful motivating forces for public servants. Ottawa's policy world is what matters to the prime minister, to the clerk of the Privy Council, and senior ministers, and to senior political advisors and deputy ministers. These officials do not work in a purely administrative environment but in a highly charged political environment fuelled by the new media, interest groups, political parties, what is said in Parliament, lobbyists, the next general election, opinion polls, and public sector unions. The challenge is to translate political and policy choices into government action and manage political controversies. Prime ministers, senior ministers, and their political advisors have an overriding objective: manage the blame game, score political points, hurt the opposition parties before they get hurt, and win the next election.

Senior public servants have a choice – to be relevant or not. Is being relevant self-serving for a senior public servant? Yes, because it may well lead to promotions. Being relevant also brings job satisfaction and a sense that one is making a contribution by helping politicians on the government side deliver on their commitments and manage the affairs of state. Being relevant requires senior public servants working on issues that matter to prime ministers, senior ministers, and their senior political advisors. A federal deputy minister summed things up well when he described himself and his fellow deputies as "serially monogamous in our loyalty to the government of the day."[30] Those who decide not to be relevant or not to engage in issues that matter to Ottawa's political and policy elites are left turning cranks not attached to anything.

Senior public servants will also influence the attitudes and behaviours of public servants below them. Public servants delivering programs and services on the front line know that their work can cause political problems. They know that they do not fully control their work, or own what they say and do, and own their mistakes, for many reasons: because of the omnipresence of partisan political advisors in government, because many departments and many hands are now involved in developing and delivering government programs, and because a number of important management decisions are struck elsewhere. They also know that failure attracts media attention.

Political power and bureaucratic influence have shifted in recent years, away from front-line offices that deliver programs, line departments, and even ministers, and toward the centre of government and key partisan political advisors. This explains, in part, why the federal public service has concentrated more and more of its human resources in the Ottawa-Gatineau region. Public servants have adjusted. They know, particularly those in line departments, that they have lost influence and that their ministers have lost power. Being in charge of anything is increasingly difficult. New public management measures have done away with "some" centrally prescribed rules, but little else. Senior managers have little say in managing human resources – key decisions are made elsewhere in various collective agreements, program decisions are now the product of many hands, and some decisions are kicked upstairs because they may be politically sensitive and best left to senior politicians and their partisan advisors to resolve. Ironically, the ability of senior executives and program managers to run their operations has been drained by the loss of centrally prescribed rules. To be sure, they were cumbersome and bureaucratic but to a certain degree, they also isolated line department managers from outside forces, including partisan policy advisors, oversight bodies looking over their shoulders, and, to a certain extent, collective agreements.

Poets know that to have influence, to be in the game, they have to become part of the prime minister's "court government" or act as courtiers. Deputy ministers, their senior staff, and aspiring deputy ministers work for one audience – the prime minister, the clerk of the Privy Council, and senior political advisors. There is no market for poets to ask difficult questions about the prime minister's agenda, government operations, the relevance of ongoing government programs, or anticipating problems that do not appear important or urgent today but very often become important tomorrow or next year. Being relevant for policy specialists means fixing political or policy problems, whereas being relevant for front-line managers means avoiding fuelling the blame game.

The political power that ministers once had and the influence that senior public servants once had have been largely drawn up to the centre. The behaviour of career officials is now shaped by several forces, including economic considerations, status, organizational culture, and highly respected role models. It is possible to discern one behaviour pattern that applies to both. Both poets and plumbers have lost confidence in their institution and in their departments or agencies and the public service has been knocked off its moorings. Public service morale has fallen and policy units are less certain about their role in a post-positivism world. In their search for relevance, public servants have become overly operational, focusing their work on political and policy firefighting while leaving unattended the challenge function and long-range policy planning. The federal public service continues to be plagued by morale problems: almost half of all federal public servants have seriously considered leaving their jobs. Public servants realize that they are witnessing a "devaluation of the work of the public service and many public servants ... resent the fact that their hard work is perceived as not good enough for government work."[31]

How then can one explain the behaviour and attitudes of federal public servants? Public choice theory or theories based on the economic man provide an answer, but the answer is not complete. The economic man concept applies far more to poets than to plumbers. It also applies to public servants in organizations that do not deliver programs and services to Canadians or to units that only serve other public servants. We saw examples of organizations that serve other public servants. The Canada School of Public Service comes to mind. The poets have a lesser sense of duty to their agencies and clients than the plumbers and a lesser sense of pride in their departments and their departments' history.

Plumbers tend to look up to role models who served in their departments more than poets do. Plumbers can point to countless examples where they performed admirably in difficult moments without seeking self-interested economic gain. Among many other examples: federal public health workers during the COVID-19 epidemic, public servants carrying out search and rescue operations, wardens running prisons, and military personnel serving in highly dangerous missions.

The challenge for students of public administration is to explore further what motivates public servants. The answer to this holds the key to resolving problems with Ottawa's accountability requirements. If accountability cannot be fixed, government operations cannot be fixed. Canadians see the problem – it is worth revisiting the recent public opinion survey that we highlighted in the introduction: 20 per cent of Canadians are "very unsatisfied" with the level of services they receive from the federal government. Another 26 per cent say they are "unsatisfied." This is in contrast to only 8 per cent who are "very unsatisfied with the level of services from provincial governments.[32] Canadians also point to being "more accountable" as the single most important change governments need to make.[33]

# 12

# WHAT NOW?

What conclusions can we draw from earlier chapters? We documented a number of challenges and shortcomings: the failure to control growth in the federal public service, the inability to establish performance, prime ministers having to resort to bolts of lightning to control spending, an unwillingness to ask penetrating questions about government operations, too many decisions being delegated up rather than down, and the government's inadequate accountability requirements.

## THE CENTRE IS EVERYWHERE

There are reasons why the centre wants to have a hand in all kinds of decisions: it is the prime minister's government, policy issues now cut across government departments and, in some cases, involve other governments, social media requires answers in a timely fashion, and the buck only stops with the prime minister. Central agencies, notably the PMO and the PCO, have grown in recent years and are staffed by highly educated and ambitious officials. They want influence and do not hesitate to intervene whenever they see a need.

The clerk of the Privy Council now wears three hats: deputy minister to the prime minister, secretary to the Cabinet, and head of the public service. All three hats give them influence with the prime minister, ministers, and the deputy ministers community. Ambitious public servants know that the clerk often determines who becomes a deputy minister. However, the deputy minister to the prime minister hat has come to dominate. Two former clerks came under criticism for turning the PCO into a "propaganda" machine serving the partisan political interest of the prime minister.[1] No one ever accused Gordon Robertson, clerk between 1963 and 1975, of turning the PCO into a propaganda machine. He saw his role as secretary to the cabinet, not as a deputy minister to anyone.[2]

The centre's omnipresence in all things has become an integral part of Ottawa's political-administrative and media culture. When Anthony Rota, speaker of the House of Commons, invited a former member of the Waffen-SS to attend a joint session of Parliament to hear Ukraine president Volodymyr Zelenskyy speak, the incident made news around the world and Rota accepted blame and resigned. The media and opposition parties also pointed fingers at Prime Minister Trudeau and his office. One journalist wrote: "A lot of people asked 'how the control freaks in the Prime Minister's Office had missed this.'" He added that things will be different next time with the PMO asking to vet "the Speaker's guests and presumably speeches would have to be vetted too."[3] Governing from the centre inside government is one thing but extending the approach to the House of Commons is quite another. The point is that important decisions, difficult decisions, controversial decisions, potentially controversial decisions dealing with events that grab the media's attention, and decisions that need the participation of several departments, are delegated up to the centre. The centre simply cannot cope with all those decisions, thus leaving many unattended – no decision also constitutes a decision.

The prime minister and the clerk of the Privy Council have an incredibly busy agenda – there are few, if any, open periods, and holidays are a luxury for both. Prime ministers have hundreds of people, from ministers, deputy ministers, heads of Crown corporations, and government agencies, as well as political advisors and assistants, who can lay claim on their time. The prime minister and the clerk meet most mornings and both have a demanding to-do list and issues to resolve. Neither one – as former clerk Paul Tellier explained – tolerates surprises easily so there is never a shortage of briefing notes floating around the PMO or the PCO that require their attention.

Issues discussed at the morning meetings vary – keeping a bouncing minister under control, dealing with the political crisis of the day, developments dealing with post-COVID matters, the war in Ukraine, trade issues with the United States, appointing deputy ministers and heads of agencies, and the list goes on and on. There is also never a shortage of urgent or difficult decisions to be made. It only takes a moment's reflection to appreciate that neither side has any interest in discussing the size of the public service, how many management levels a government department should have, or how to sharpen the government's capacity to establish the performance of public servants or government programs. When the media take an interest in these issues, the prime minister, their chief of staff, and the clerk of the Privy Council do focus on them, but the moment the media lose interest, so will they. There is no incentive on either side to delve into these issues. There are always issues more urgent or more interesting to discuss.

How, then, does the government decide on budget matters or the size of the public service? A set pattern now emerges whenever spending cuts are necessary: the cost of servicing the debt becomes too high, the media ring the alarm bell, financial or currency markets force the federal government to act, or the belief that the rise in government spending fuels inflation. In all cases, the prime minister decides on the size of the cuts and then unveils a process to get the job done. This has been Ottawa's modus operandi since former prime minister Pierre Trudeau, with no forewarning, unveiled spending cuts on his return from the Bonn Economic Summit in 1978.[4] Trudeau *fils* embraced the same approach in August 2023 when he called for $15 billion in spending cuts, as did the prime ministers between Trudeau *père* and *fils*.[5]

The same can be said about the growth in the size of the federal public service. The federal public service grew by about 25 percent between 2015 and 2023. No one has made a convincing case for why growth in the public service was needed, other than making reference to the need for new staff to deal with COVID-19.[6] There is also little evidence that the government is able to shed positions unless it is struck by bolts of lightning from above. Adding new staff has hardly improved the delivery of government programs or the level of service. Kathryn May asks: "Why, with all this hiring, are services not any better? For months, people have been waiting for passports, immigration applications and veteran benefits to be processed."[7] Jason Kenney, a former senior minister in the Harper government, may have the answer: "Often, especially in Ottawa, you just get redundant layers of bureaucracy... the profusion of new agencies and quangos, quasi-non-government organizations, and procedures that eat up public resources that deny those resources from the front-line services. So, I do think that is a real problem. It's not just my anecdotal observation."[8] Kenney was speaking about the work of poets, not plumbers.

## PLUMBERS ARE THE POOR COUSINS

Whether or not anyone is or has been willing to own the problem, the federal government has a problem delivering program services. It fell far short in delivering the Phoenix pay system to its own employees. As we saw earlier, the federal government also fell short in processing passport applications and in delivering several high-profile programs, including employment insurance and delivering veterans' benefits.[9] Efforts to improve service delivery have never lived up to expectations. Justin Trudeau's "deliverology" initiative to strengthen program service delivery "obviously didn't pan out" and again no one owned the failure.[10] As a result, Trudeau decided in August 2023 to establish a new cabinet position with a mandate to strengthen the government's service delivery after he had established a task force to identify ways to improve service delivery. Pollster Greg Lyle explained the prime minister's motivation: "There's a lot of alienation going on with the ineffective service of the federal government."[11]

The first question to be answered is how much of the machinery of government actually delivers programs and services. Ottawa does not provide information on this point. One former senior Cabinet minister maintains that "with a few exceptions like Defence, Immigration and Indigenous services, Ottawa is not really a service delivery government; it is a funding and policy government."[12] Ottawa spends about $400 billion annually.[13] The annual cost of servicing the debt is $24 billion and transfer payments to the other two levels of government and to individuals amount to $243 billion, or 61.1 percent of the government's expenditures budget. This includes $95 billion in transfers to provincial governments. Servicing the debt and managing transfers to the provinces (about $120 billion out of the $400 billion) requires little in the way of human resources. We saw earlier that only 40 percent of federal public servants deal with the public as one of their responsibilities, even if it amounted to only 10 percent of their work. But this number has likely gone down in recent years, given the greater concentration of public servants in the National Capital Region.

Poets are highly valued in Ottawa for their political and policy skills and for pursuing an agenda defined by the prime minister or the clerk, plumbers much less so. The signs are everywhere: poets enjoy a higher classification, they benefit from faster promotions, and they, not plumbers, make up the bulk of the deputy minister community. The system rarely, certainly far less than it once did, promotes public servants with a strong program delivery background. Plumbers are on the front line, far from Ottawa's political and policy circles, delivering programs and services. They know first-hand that Canadians see the federal government is not up to standard in delivering programs. For Canadians, this is where accountability takes place because for most of them, this is their only point of contact with the federal government.

Accountability in the federal government is now anything but clear. Two former clerks of the Privy Council made this plain when they could not even agree on one of accountability's basic requirements – determining who is responsible for what. We saw earlier that one former clerk argued that "authority can be delegated, but accountability can't" while another insisted "where authority resides, so resides accountability." Neither one bothered to answer the question – where does authority now reside when policy and program decisions are the product of many departments, many hands, and, at times, many governments?

Things do happen when the prime minister and the clerk decide to focus on an issue because they hold most of the political and bureaucratic authority in the government. This explains why the federal government was able to deposit funds directly into the bank accounts of Canadians barely two months after COVID-19 hit. The PCO drove the initiative and kept a close watch on its implementation. When it turned its attention to other priorities, COVID-19 measures did not run as smoothly.

The federal government has a crippling overload problem, creating a bottleneck at the centre of government. Everything of any consequence goes there, this at a time when, as we saw, prime ministers and clerks value error-free government and no surprises. Public servants in departments and agencies know that it is best to run on their tracks, avoid controversies, and avoid risks. Ministers also know that the key to success is to stay out of trouble, particularly with the media. The PCO tells them: "[R]esponsibility is honed by the ever-present possibility that in particular circumstances ministers may be embarrassed, suffer loss of prestige weakening themselves and the government, jeopardize their standing with their colleagues and hence their political future, or even be forced to submit to public enquiry possibly resulting in censure and loss of office."[14]

The above explains why not enough attention is given to problems with delivering programs and services. It also explains why so many issues do not get the attention they deserve. This includes the size of the federal public service, efficient management practices that work in government, keeping an eye on the number of management levels in departments, evaluating the effectiveness of programs and the performance of public servants, ensuring that the merit principle in staffing is respected, and seeing that accountability requirements are followed because they have to compete with the issues that crowd the prime minister and the clerk's agenda.

## EVERYTHING MUST CHANGE BUT EVERYTHING MUST STAY THE SAME

Prime ministers come to office with promises to change government operations. They commit to greater transparency and more efficiency in government operations (for example, Brian Mulroney's commitment to give pink slips and running shoes to bureaucrats, Stephen Harper and the *Accountability Act*, Justin Trudeau's commitment to move away from governing from the centre). However, after only a few months in power, they all saw things differently. In explaining the difference between opposition and government, Jean Chrétien made the point that, as a politician on the government side, you have to learn "to walk with your back to the wall, your elbows high ... It's a survival game played under the glare of light ... The press wants to get you. The opposition wants to get you. Even some bureaucrats want to get you. They all may have an interest in making you look bad."[15] Suddenly, greater transparency, stronger access to information legislation, reports that reveal flaws in government programs, and the need to ask difficult questions about government operations all lose the strong appeal they once had while in opposition. Why would a prime minister, a minister, or a senior public servant reveal the percentage of federal public servants that serve on the front line who actually deliver programs. In government, prime ministers, ministers, and senior public servants equate greater transparency with accentuating political and bureaucratic failures, real or perceived, endless debates, and a tendency to oversimplify complex policy issues and government operations.

Those outside government can easily see the merit in importing private sector management practices to government operations. The private sector has a solid track record in running efficient businesses and providing first-rate levels of services to clients – if not, the business would not be able to compete effectively. Those inside government understand that applying private sector management practices in government only leads to muddying accountability requirements. In business, one can tell executives, managers, and front-line workers to own what they say and what they do, and own their mistakes. But in government, the prime minister is the only one who can manage along these lines. The past forty years have demonstrated that importing private management practices to government has been little more than a fool's errand: they have made government operations costlier, more bureaucratic, and less accountable.

### WHAT ABOUT PARLIAMENT?

The role of Parliament is to hold the government to account. But no one, including parliamentarians themselves, is making the case that Parliament is able to hold the government to account when it comes to public spending or assessing the size of the public service. I can do no better than, once again, to quote Senator Lowell Murray: "Parliament – specifically the House of Commons, because over a period of more than forty years they have allowed their most vital power, the power of the purse, to become a dead letter, their Supply and Estimates process an empty ritual."[16] Many observers, including a former auditor general, former ministers, and former and current MPs have echoed Murray's view.[17]

No one has been able to explain why MPs on the government side would have any interest in holding the government to account, in asking penetrating questions about government programs, growth in the public service, or why the public service sees the need to move more and more staff into the National Capital Region. It would be akin to shooting themselves in the foot. Opposition MPs, meanwhile, have an interest in asking such questions, but not the knowledge or access to timely information to enable them to do so. They are not equipped, nor do they have the staff, to sift through the government's expenditure budget and to ask questions that need to be asked to hold the government and the public service to account on government spending.

Parliament is now all about political theatre and the ability to generate thirty-second clips for the evening news steals the stage. Scoring political points is what matters. We saw in an earlier chapter that public servants manage their appearances before parliamentary committees very carefully. The less they say, the better. Public servants are told that they are loyal to the government of the day. It is left to them to decide what that means. When they appear before Parliament, they do so on behalf of their ministers and, though they answer before Parliament, they are not accountable to it. This, even though in several cases Parliament has delegated authority to public servants, not ministers, leaving unexplained the point made by an earlier clerk of the Privy Council: "Authority can be delegated, but accountability can't."

## THE PRIME MINISTER AND THE CLERK CAN ASK AND SECURE ANSWERS TO PENETRATING QUESTIONS

Two individuals have the authority to ask piercing questions, introduce changes, and make them stick: the prime minister and the clerk of the Privy Council. When they sit in the prime minister's chair, prime ministers have few friends – not the media, not the opposition, not disenchanted MPs on the government side not invited to sit in Cabinet, and not officers of Parliament. Given that public servants are expected to be loyal to the government of the day, the public service is a friend. Prime ministers develop a close working relationship with the clerk of the Privy Council. Clerks serve at the pleasure of the prime minister and, if the relationship does not work for the prime minister, a change is made. Unlike ministers and their deputy ministers, prime ministers are always free to retain or remove the clerk, no questions asked.

Why would prime ministers want to ask penetrating questions about the size and growth of the public service, about the appropriate number of management levels in line departments, or how best to assess the performance of public servants? This would be akin to shooting on their own troops. Not only do they always have more important things to attend to, prime ministers need both the clerk and the public service to pursue their policy agenda, to ensure that ministers and their departments run on their tracks, to promote error-free government, and to minimize surprises.

Clerks of the Privy Council are also head of the public service and understand that they have a role in protecting the public service and its members. Clerks meet deputy ministers every week and at special retreats to go over challenges ahead – they are colleagues working on the same team. Clerks also always have more pressing issues than asking about the size of the public service, how many management levels a line department requires, and why the public service is increasingly Ottawa-centric. They have no incentive to ask such questions and, as we saw, only in retirement do they feel the need to do so.

## QUESTIONS NEED TO BE ASKED

Many questions remain unanswered. Why do prime ministers, no matter what party is in power, have to rely on bolts of lightning to reduce government spending? This approach has important shortcomings – it is a one-shot deal, with the usual suspects getting cut: new staff, capital budget, some consultants, however temporarily, or delaying major spending commitments. The approach does not deal with Parliamentary Budget Officer Yves Giroux's point, that when a government spends half a trillion dollars a year, there should be "lots of room for trimming." Others also argue that the bolts of lightning approach always overlooks the "many inefficiencies rooted in a risk averse culture that is bogged down by rules, structures and processes built for another era ... Why do you need five people in the office of a deputy minister or assistant deputy minister in a digital world?"[18] When it comes to accountability, why should the prime minister be "accountable for anything from a decision made by a low level public servant on a particular file to major issues on policy"?[19]

Still more questions remain unanswered. Who is looking at the question of "kids in short pants" in the PMO or in ministerial offices destroying the public service? It is difficult for clerks of the Privy Council to do so because it is outside their mandate. There are other questions that need to be answered. Why do departments need so many management levels? How should public servants be held to account, given recent developments in the media and the arrival of the digital world? What are the best management practices for government operations, given the public sector's distinct culture and democratic requirements? What is the best way to structure an internal capacity to challenge the status quo in government operations and to ask penetrating questions? What should be the proper ratio of public servants working outside the National Capital Region to those working within it? How does the government deal with information asymmetry between line departments and central agencies? Is there a need to update accountability requirements when boundaries between departments and, at times, between governments, are collapsing? Why are senior public servants, as we saw earlier, now saying that it is not possible to speak truth to power? Can program evaluation efforts be made stronger and more relevant to decision making? Is there a need to revisit collective bargaining and its effect on delivering government services? Does the merit principle in the federal public service still apply? Should it? If so, should it be strengthened? Is there a need to update the role of Parliament in reviewing the government's expenditure estimates? Is there a need for a Charter of Public Service Values outlining the constitutional position of the public service, including its relationship with the political sphere of government, as some observers have recommended?[20]

## WHO SHOULD ASK AND WHO SHOULD ANSWER?

After they come to power, politicians, and senior public servants, have shown little interest in asking the above question or in providing the incentives for pursuing difficult questions about government operations. For politicians on the government side, it is better and easier simply to blame bureaucrats for poor management and leave it at that. Public servants, in turn, can point the finger at politicians, telling them to heal their institutions before they set out to heal the public service. There is no incentive on either side to focus on management, to ask about the size of the public service, and why it is not possible to deal with non-performers in government, why public servants have to be told from time to time to look for duplication in government programs, and to identify duplications and low-priority programs. Amanda Clarke went to the heart of the issue when she wrote: "Discussions on federal public service management have unfolded in elite and insular circles."[21] The view in Ottawa public service circles is that government management issues are very complex and that it is best to leave these issues to them to sort things out. Earlier chapters, however, make clear that their track record on this front is lacking.

Experience tells us that leaving these questions to prime ministers, their courtiers, and senior permanent government officials and public sector unions will only let things continue running on their tracks. The future of the federal public service, its ability to provide advice without fear or favour, to deliver programs and services effectively and efficiently and its cost, should not be of concern only to a handful of actors who have an interest in leaving well enough alone. If change is in order, then a public debate that engages a cross-section of Canadians is required. Until now, management practices in the federal government have barely captured the attention of Canadian voters. No one knows this better than the leaders of political parties and their pollsters. But things may be changing, given the federal government's deteriorating fiscal framework, the problems with the government's capacity to deliver programs and services, and its realization that campaign commitments can only be delivered by a well-functioning public service.

Still, waiting for politicians to take a strong interest in management issues or for senior public servants to open up to outside scrutiny about government operations is much like waiting for the Greek Calends, a time that never comes or does not exist.[22] Things will change only if Canadians take more than a passing interest in the workings of government. Politicians will react if Canadians demand it and public servants will respond if the prime minister and the clerk ask for change and both keep an eye on the efforts. I return to a point I made earlier about the need for a royal commission to answer questions that have been left unanswered for too long. A royal commission, or a comparable process, is needed to open the windows of government operations so that federal public servants can see out and other Canadians can see in. Pursuing difficult questions and providing answers are in the interest of the federal public service, public servants, Parliament, and Canadians.

The questions that need answers go to the heart of how our democratic institutions operate. They deal with relations between politicians and public servants and between Canadians and their national government. Two distinct perspectives will shape the debate and how we can go about answering the questions noted above. One is seeing both politicians and public servants making every effort to reinvigorate the workings and accountability requirements of the founding institutions of our system of government. The other is to separate the constitutional modes of accountability by establishing separate spheres of responsibilities, one for politicians and another for public servants.

Over the years and in my publications, I have favoured the traditional approach. Clearly, however, the traditional approach is being pressed on all sides – some ministers are no longer willing to accept responsibility for the work of their public servants and senior public servants are sending out mixed messages on accountability. Embracing this approach would require prime ministers to restore cabinet government and for Parliament to rediscover its role of holding the government to account. Or, to quote Sheila Fraser once again, to have Parliament "stop failing Canadians" in reviewing the yearly spending estimates,[23] for federal public servants to provide advice to the prime minister and ministers without fear or favour under the cover of anonymity, for strengthening the hand of front-line managers and their staff (the plumbers) in delivering programs and services to Canadians, and for developing an in-government capacity to ask difficult questions to both central agencies and line departments about their level of financial and human resources.

Changing constitutional modes of accountability, meanwhile, is not without far-reaching consequences. This explains why governments have danced around the idea but never fully embraced it. New public management measures have never lived up to expectations because public servants have been told to manage the same way the private sector is managed but never compromise the accountability requirements of the traditional approach. This was and remains an impossible task. Proponents of the approach need to pursue it to its logical end and ask public servants to own what they say and what they do, and own their mistakes. This means Canadians could no longer look to Parliament and politicians for all the answers since public servants would have their own separate and unambiguous spheres of responsibility and would then be held accountable for their activities outside of the government. Public servants would not only lose their anonymity but would also become political actors. This, in turn, would mean the formal end of a merit-based non-partisan public service.

Answers to the series of questions and carefully identifying the merits and drawbacks of both approaches require a well-informed debate. The debate should not be the preserve only of politicians, public servants, public sector unions, or interest groups. The future of the public service is of interest to all Canadians.

# NOTES

## PREFACE

1 Aaron Wildavsky, *Speaking Truth to Power: The Art and Craft of Policy Analysis* (Boston: Little Brown, 1979).
2 Sir Robin Butler, quoted in Donald J. Savoie, *What Is Government Good At? A Canadian Answer* (Montreal: McGill-Queen's University Press, 2015), 206.

## INTRODUCTION

1 Emmanuel Macron made this observation on *The Lead with Jake Tapper*, CNN, 22 September 2022.
2 *Trust in Government* (Paris: OECD, 2021), 1.
3 The surveyors asked 1,536 Canadians about their trust in leaders and institutions. See "'All-time low': Report finds Canadians don't have much trust in government," *Daily Hive*, 9 February 2022.
4 "Opinion: 67% Agree Canada Is Broken – and Here's Why," *National Post*, 5 February 2023.
5 *The Report of the Knight Commission on Trust, Media and Democracy* (Washington, DC: The Aspen Institute, 2019).
6 Donald J. Savoie, *What Is Government Good At? A Canadian Answer* (Montreal: McGill-Queen's University Press), 205.
7 "Canadians More Positive about Their Encounters Accessing Services from Cities, Provincial Governments," Angus Reid, 10 June 2022.
8 Anthony Downs, *A Theory of Bureaucracy* (Santa Monica: Rand Corporation, 1964).

9 Donald J. Savoie, *Government: Have Presidents and Prime Ministers Misdiagnosed the Patient?* (Montreal: McGill-Queen's University Press, 2022).
10 Donald Trump is hardly the only politician to employ the term. See, "Does the Deep State Exist? Journalist Bruce Livesey Investigates," CBC, 18 November 2019.
11 Christopher Hood and Martin Lodge, *The Politics of Public Service Bargains: Reward, Competency, Loyalty – and Blame* (Oxford; Oxford University Press, 2007).
12 John Greenaway, "British Conservatism and Bureaucracy," *History of Political Thought* 13, no. 1 (Spring 1992), 135.
13 *Report on the Organisation of the Permanent Civil Service* (London: House of Commons, printed by George E. Eyre and William Spottiswoode, 1854).
14 See, among others, Paul P. Van Riper, *History of the United States Civil Service* (Evanston, IL: Row Peterson, 1958).
15 Niccolò Machiavelli quoted in Andrew R. Murphy, "Longing, Nostalgia, and Golden Age Politics: The American Jeremiad and the Power of the Past," *Perspective on Politics* 7, no. 1 (March 2009), 125.
16 See, among others, Harold Macmillan, *At the End of the Day, 1961–1963* (London: Harper and Row, 1973); and Lester B. Pearson, *Mike: The Memoirs of the Rt. Hon. Lester B. Pearson, Volume Three: 1957–1968* (Toronto: University of Toronto Press, 2015).
17 "Public Trust in Government: 1958–2021," Pew Research Center, 17 May 2021; and "2021 Edelman Trust Barometer," Edelman, https://www.edelman.com/trust/2021-trust-barometer.
18 "Trust in Government – Total, Percentage, 2022 or Latest Available," OECD, accessed on 18 May 2023, https://data.oecd.org/gga/trust-in-government.htm. See also "2022 Results Report," Proof Strategies-Can Trust Index, https://proofagency.wpenginepowered.com/wp-content/uploads/2022/12/Proof-Strategies-CanTrust-Index-2022.pdf.
19 See, among others, *Top of Mind* (Ottawa: Institute on Governance, 2022).
20 Canada, *Task Force on Public Service Values and Ethics: A Strong Foundation* (Ottawa: Canadian Centre for Management Development, 2000), 60.
21 Ralph Heintzman, "Establishing the Boundaries of the Public Service: Toward a New Moral Contract," 124.
22 Ralph Heintzman, "Border-Crossing: The PBO, PCO and the Boundary of the Public Service," *Canadian Public Administration* 59, no. 3 (2016), 358–78.
23 "Passport Delays Spur Some Canadians to Game the System with Fake Travel Plans," CBC, 15 August 2022; and "Majority say Canadian Airport

Delays 'a National Embarrassment,' Avoiding Travel: Poll," *Global News*, 15 July 2022.
24 See, for example, "Ottawa Acknowledges It Underestimated Surge in Demand for Passports," *The Globe and Mail*, 6 July 2022; and Kathryn May, "The Achilles Heel of the Federal Public Service Gives Out Again with Passport Fiasco," *Policy Options*, 29 June 2022.
25 Lord Gowrie on BBC Radio 4, quoted in Hugo Young, "The Vanishing Mandarins," 13 February 1985.
26 See, among others, Donald J. Savoie, *Democracy in Canada: The Disintegration of Our Institutions* (Montreal: McGill-Queen's University Press, 2019), chapters 12 and 13.
27 See, among others, James Sherk, *Tales from the Swamp: How Federal Bureaucrats Resisted President Trump* (Washington, DC: AFPI, 2022).
28 Robin V. Sears, "We Need to Rebuild Respect Between Politicians and Public Servants," *Toronto Star*, 22 April 2022.
29 "John Ivison: The Rot in Canada's Dysfunctional Government Is Coming from the Top," *National Post*, 8 July 2022.
30 Paul Tellier quoted in Kathryn May, "All Powerful PMO, Mistrust 'Destroying' the Public Service," *Policy Options*, 30 May 2022.
31 By machinery of government, I am referring to how agencies and departments support the government in developing policies, regulations, preparing funding proposals, and delivering programs and services.
32 See, among many others, Donald J. Savoie, *Governing from the Centre: The Concentration of Power in Canadian Politics* (Toronto: University of Toronto Press, 1999).
33 See *House of Commons – Public Service Committee – 313-1* (London: U.K. Government, Second Session, 1995–1996).
34 J.E. Hodgetts, "Royal Commissions and Public Sector: Personal Reflections," *Canadian Public Administration* 50, no. 4 (Winter 2007), 531.
35 Canada, *Royal Commission on Government Organization* (Ottawa: The Queen's Printer, 1962 and 1963), 5 volumes.
36 James Q. Wilson identified several government organization types in *Bureaucracy: What Government Agencies Do and Why They Do It* (New York: Basic Books, 1989).
37 Andrew Caddell, "Six Decades Later, We Are Overdue for a Study of the Public Service," *Hill Times*, 22 January 2022.
38 "A New Low for Global Democracy," *The Economist*, February 2022.
39 Charlie Senack, "Carleton MP Pierre Poilievre Endorses Downtown Anti COVID-19 Demonstrations," *Manotick Messenger*, 4 February 2022.

40 *Report on the 44th General Election of September 20, 2021* (Ottawa: Office of the Chief Electoral Officer of Canada, 27 January 2022).
41 "The Canada Bashers Have Got It Wrong about This Country," *The Globe and Mail*, 9 February 2022.
42 Nik Nanos, "Data Dive with Nik Nanos: Canada has joined the Club of Angry, Polarized Countries," *The Globe and Mail*, 15 October 2022.
43 Donald J. Savoie, *Thatcher, Reagan, and Mulroney: In Search of a New Bureaucracy* (Pittsburgh: University of Pittsburgh Press, 1994).
44 Based on information provided by Alfred Doucet, a senior advisor to Prime Minister Brian Mulroney, various dates.
45 See, among others, Savoie, *Thatcher, Reagan, and Mulroney*.
46 See, for example, Donald J. Savoie, *The Politics of Public Spending in Canada* (Toronto: University of Toronto Press, 1990).
47 Canada, *Treasury Board President Mona Fortier tables departmental plans for the 2022–23 fiscal year* (Ottawa: Treasury Board of Canada Secretariat, 2 March 2022).
48 Canada, Supplementary Estimates 2022–2023 (C) (Ottawa: Office of the Parliamentary Budget Officer, 2022); and Kathryn May, "Public Service Will Swell to 409,000 in Five Years, PBO Says," *Policy Options*, 21 November 2022 and "A Warning Sign of Government Bloat," *The Globe and Mail*, 20 January 2022.
49 Robert F. Adie and Paul G. Thomas, *Canadian Public Administration: Problematical Perspectives* (Scarborough, ON: Prentice-Hall, 1982), 141.
50 Quoted in Christopher Pollitt, *Managerialism and the Public Services: The Anglo-American Experience* (Oxford: Basil Blackwell, 1988), 97. See also Donald J. Savoie, *Democracy in Canada*.
51 See, among others, Canada, *Meeting the Expectations of Canadians: Review of the Responsibilities and Accountabilities of Ministers and Senior Officials* (Ottawa: Treasury Board of Canada Secretariat, 2005); and Peter Aucoin and Mark D. Jarvis, *Modernizing Government Accountability: A Framework for Reform* (Ottawa: Canada School of Public Service, 2005).
52 Canada, Royal Commission on Financial Management and Accountability, *Final Report*, 1979, 52–3.
53 *Top of Mind* (Ottawa: Institute on Governance and the Brian Mulroney Institute of Government, 2022).
54 See, among others, Caddell, "Six Decades Later, We Are Overdue for a Study of the Public Service."

## CHAPTER ONE

1 One Government of Canada website lists 130 organizations. However, another lists 207; see notes 13 and 14 below.
2 Donald J. Savoie, *Looking for Bootstraps: Economic Development in the Maritimes* (Halifax: Nimbus, 2017).
3 *Open and Accountable Government* (Ottawa: Prime Minister of Canada, 27 November 2015), 47.
4 J.L. Granatstein, *The Ottawa Men: The Civil Service Mandarins 1933–37* (Toronto: University of Toronto Press, 1952), 12; and Savoie, *Governing from the Centre*, 35.
5 The thirteen departments were Agriculture, Customs, Finance, Indian Affairs, Inland Revenue, Justice, Marine and Fisheries, Militia and Defence, Post Office, Public Works, Receiver General, Secretary of State for the Provinces and Secretary of State.
6 Donald J. Savoie, *Court Government and the Collapse of Accountability in Canada and the United Kingdom* (Toronto: University of Toronto Press, 2008), 38.
7 Dennis C. Grube makes a similar point in his *Megaphone Bureaucracy: Speaking Truth to Power in the Age of the New Normal* (Princeton: Princeton University Press, 2019, 146).
8 J.E. Hodgetts, *Pioneer Public Service: An Administrative History of the United Canadas, 1841–1867* (Toronto: University of Toronto Press, 1955).
9 See, among others, Donald J. Savoie, *Federal-Provincial Collaboration: The Canada-New Brunswick General Development Agreement* (Montreal: McGill-Queen's University Press, 1981).
10 See, for example, Donald J. Savoie, *Federal-Provincial Collaboration: The Canada-New Brunswick General Development Agreement* (Montreal: McGill-Queen's University Press, 1981).
11 Pierre E. Trudeau, quoted in George Radwanski, *Trudeau* (Toronto: Macmillan of Canada, 1978), 146.
12 Tom Kent, *A Public Purpose: An Experience of Liberal Opposition and Canadian Government* (Montreal: McGill-Queen's University Press, 1988), 225.
13 See, for example, Jacques Bourgault and Stéphane Dion, *The Changing Profile of Federal Deputy Ministers* (Ottawa: CCMD, 199).
14 *Open and Accountable Government* (Ottawa: Prime Minister of Canada, 27 November 2015).

15 "'Kids in Short Pants' Rule All Says New Samara Report," *Hill Times*, 5 November 2018. See also various publications on the issue at www.samaracanada.com.
16 David Zussman, "Stephen Harper and the Federal Public Service: An Uneasy and Unresolved Relationship," in Jennifer Ditchburn and Graham Fox (eds.), *The Harper Factor: Assessing a Prime Minister's Policy Legacy* (Montreal: McGill-Queen's University Press, 2016), 57.
17 See, for example, Donald J. Savoie, *Governing from the Centre: The Concentration of Power in Canadian Politics* (Toronto: University of Toronto Press, 1999).
18 Paul Tellier quoted in Kathryn May, "All-powerful PMO, Mistrust 'Destroying' the Public Service," *Policy Options*, 30 May 2022.
19 *Open and Accountable Government* (Ottawa: Office of the Prime Minister, 27 November 2015), 6, 7, 14, 30, 40, and 43.
20 Ibid., Annex C and pp. 15 and 16.
21 Canada, *Open and Accountable Government*, 38.
22 Canada, *Departments and Agencies*, https://www.canada.ca/en/government/dept.html.
23 Canada, *Population of the Federal Public Service by department*, Treasury Board Secretariat, https://www.canada.ca/en/treasury-board-secretariat/services/innovation/human-resources-statistics/population-federal-public-service-department.html.
24 Michael Wernick, *Governing Canada: A Guide to the Tradecraft of Politics* (Vancouver: On Point Press, 2021), 23.
25 Canada, *Departments and Agencies*, Canada.ca/en/government/dept.html, undated.
26 See, among others, Josh Dehaas, "Election Analysis: Most Common Occupations for Candidates in Each Party," CTV News, 9 October 2015.
27 James T. Pow, "Amateurs versus Professionals: Explaining the Political (in)Experience of Canadian Members of Parliament," *Parliamentary Affairs* 71 (2018): 633.
28 The information was compiled from the biographical notes of members of Parliament from the Library of Parliament website. See also, "Politicians Now More Likely to Be Businessmen Than Lawyers," *Toronto Star*, 1 February 2013.
29 Malloy, *The Paradox of Parliament*, 83.
30 Brent Rathgeber, *Irresponsible Government: The Decline of Parliamentary Democracy in Canada* (Toronto: Dundurn, 2014), 64.

31 "Former MPs Talk about the Tug of War between Personal and Party Politics on New Samara Centre Podcast," *Hill Times*, 20 March 2023, 3.
32 Michael Morden, ed., *Real House Lives: Former Members of Parliament on How to Reclaim Democratic Leadership* (Toronto: Samara Centre for Democracy, 2022).
33 Jonathan Malloy, *The Paradox of Parliament* (Toronto: University of Toronto Press, 2023), 207.
34 David C. Docherty, *Mr. Smith Goes to Ottawa: Life in the House of Commons* (Vancouver: UBC Press, 1997); and "The Canadian Political Career Structure: From Stability to Free Agency," *Regional and Federal Studies* 21: 185–203.
35 Sheila Copps, "Politics: The Only Job Where the More Experience You Get, the More People Want to Get Rid of You," *Hill Times*, 17 April 2023, 9.
36 Kelly Blidook, *Constituency Influence in Parliament: Countering the Centre* (Vancouver: UBC Press, 2012), 115.
37 Malloy, *The Paradox of Parliament*, 208.
38 Jody Wilson-Raybould, *Indian in the Cabinet: Speaking Truth to Power* (Toronto: Harper Collins, 2021), 116.
39 Rick Williams, who served as a deputy minister responsible for policy to the premier of Nova Scotia, makes a similar observation in his *Making Government Work*, October 2019, mimeo.
40 Jonathan Craft and John Halligan, *Advising Governments in the Westminster Tradition: Policy Advisory Systems in Australia, Britain, Canada and New Zealand* (Cambridge: Cambridge University Press, 2020), 2.
41 See, among many others, Peter Aucoin, "New Political Governance in Westminster Systems: Impartial Public Administration and Management Performance at Risk," *Governance* 25, no. 2: 177–99.
42 Sharon Sutherland, "The Al-Mashat Affair: Administrative Accountability in Parliamentary Institutions," *Canadian Public Administration* 34, no. 4 (1991): 595.
43 B. Guy Peters and Jon Pierre, *Politicization of the Public Service: The Quest for Control* (London: Routledge, 2004).
44 Wernick, *Governing Canada*, 91.
45 See, for example, B. Guy Peters, *Pursuing Horizontal Management: The Politics of Public Sector Coordination* (Lawrence: University Press of Kansas, 2015).

46 They include the Office of the Auditor General, Commissioner of Official Languages, Information Commissioner of Canada, Privacy Commissioner of Canada, Conflict of Interest and Ethics Commissioner, Commissioner of Lobbying of Canada, Public Sector Integrity Commissioner of Canada, and the Parliamentary Budget Officer. Michael Wernick writes that there are nine officers of Parliament without identifying them in Wernick, *Governing Canada*, 23.
47 This includes federal public servants, numerous reports, and the ongoing work of the Office of the Auditor General. See also, Savoie, *Democracy in Canada*.
48 Jacques Bourgault, "The Deputy Minister's Role in the Government of Canada: His Responsibility and His Accountability," in Canada: *Restoring Accountability* 1 (2006): 2.
49 Jacques Bourgault, *Profile of Deputy Ministers in the Government of Canada* (Ottawa: Canada School of Public Service, 2005), 11–12.
50 From a conversation I had with Mel Cappe.
51 Rick Williams, *Making Government Work*, October 2019, mimeo.
52 Quoted in "The Hole in Accountability," *Ottawa Citizen*, 18 November 2006, B4.
53 Jacques Bourgault, *Profile of Deputy Ministers in the Government of Canada* (Ottawa: Canada School of Public Service, 2005), 14.
54 See, among others, David Mitchell and Ryan Conway, "From the Deputy Shuffle to the Deputy Churn: Keeping the Best and Brightest in Ottawa," *Policy Options*, 1 May 2011.
55 Gordon Osbaldeston, *Keeping Deputy Ministers Accountable* (Toronto: McGraw-Hill, 1989).
56 Canada, *Royal Commission on Financial Management and Accountability* (Ottawa: Minister of Supply and Services-Final Report, 1979), 371.
57 Canada, *Accountable Government* (Ottawa: Privy Council Office, 2011), 1.
58 Canada, *Governing Responsibly: A Guide for Ministers and Ministers of State* (Ottawa: Privy Council Office, 2003), 3.
59 Among others, see cases from the Mulroney Government (see the Al-Mashat decision) to the Justin Trudeau government when the minister of national revenue declared that she was disappointed that her public servants struck a decision on tax benefits without her knowledge. The prime minister made clear his support for the minister. See Bill Curry, "Trudeau Rules Out Taxing Employee Discounts." *The Globe and Mail*, 11 October 2017.
60 For a more thorough discussion on these points, see Savoie, *Democracy in Canada*, chapter 8.

61 Canada, *Guidance for Deputy Ministers* (Ottawa: Privy Council Office, undated), 6.
62 Ibid., 9.
63 This development is not limited to Canada. See Richard A. Chapman, "The Next Steps," *Public Policy and Administration* 111 (1988): 3–10.
64 Keelan Buck, *Taking the Minister out of Ministerial Responsibility? Public Servants, Parliamentary Committees, and the Westminster Tradition in Canada, 1995–2021* (Ottawa: School of Political Studies, University of Ottawa, 16 August 2022), 35. I note, however, that Prime Minister Trudeau's chief of staff, Katie Telford, has testified before a parliamentary committee on several occasions.
65 Ibid., 42.
66 Ralph Heintzman, "Establishing the Boundaries of the Public Service: Toward a New Moral Contract," in *Governing: Essays in Honour of Donald J. Savoie*, ed. James Bickerton and B. Guy Peters (Montreal: McGill-Queen's University Press, 2013), 107.
67 Canada, Commission of Inquiry into the Sponsorship Program & Advertising Activities. *Restoring Accountability: Recommendations* (Ottawa: Her Majesty the Queen in Right of Canada, 2006), 109.
68 Canada, *Guidance for Deputy Ministers* (Ottawa: Privy Council Office, undated), 10.
69 Ibid.
70 Ibid., 26 and 27.
71 See, among others, Jacques Bourgault, "The Role of Deputy Ministers in Canadian Government," in *The Handbook of Canadian Public Administration*, ed. C. Dunn (Toronto: Oxford University Press, 2002); and Patrice Dutil and Andrea Migone, "Leadership on the Run: Time Management Among Deputy Ministers in Canada," *International Journal of Public Leadership* 18, no. 1 (2022): 57–76; and Jacques Bourgault, *Enjeux Contemporains de Gouvernance Pour Les Sous-Ministres Du Gouvernement Du Canada* (Montreal: JFD Éditions, 2021).
72 Luther Gulick and L. Urwick, eds., *Papers on the Science of Administration* (New York: Institute of Public Administration, 1937), 9.
73 See Canada, *Organizational Structure: Environment and Climate Change Canada* (Ottawa: Environment and Climate Change Canada, October 2021).
74 Audrey D. Doerr, *The Machinery of Government in Canada* (Toronto: Methuen, 1981), 91–4.
75 Quoted in *Top of Mind* (Ottawa: Institute on Governance and the Brian Mulroney Institute of Government, 2022), 14.
76 Various conversations with Gérard Veilleux, Ottawa and Montreal.

## CHAPTER TWO

1 See, among others, Donald J. Savoie, *Democracy in Canada: The Disintegration of Our Institutions* (Montreal: McGill-Queen's University Press, 2019), 282–3.
2 See, for example, John Doerr, M*easure What Matters* (London: Portfolio-Penguin, 2018).
3 David E. Lewis, "Presidential Appointments and Personnel," *Annual Review of Political Science* 14 (2011): 47–66.
4 *A Survivor's Guide for Presidential Nominees* (Washington, DC: Brookings Institution, 2000), 9.
5 James P. Pfiffner, "Political Appointees and Career Executives: The Democracy-Bureaucracy Nexus in the Third Century," *Public Administration Review* 47, no. 1 (February 1987): 57–65.
6 See, for example, June Burnham and Robert Pyper, *Britain's Modernised Civil Service* (London: Macmillan, 2008).
7 Nehal Panchamia and Peter Thomas, *The Next Steps Initiative* (London: Institute for Government, 2010).
8 *Executive Agencies: A Guide for Departments* (London: Cabinet Office – Public Bodies Handbook – Part 3, undated), chapter 3.
9 I am thinking, for example, of Jonathan Powell, chief of staff to Prime Minister Tony Blair.
10 *Improving the Federal Public Service Hiring Process; Report of the Standing Committee on Government Operations and Estimates* (Ottawa; House of Commons, June 2019, 42nd Parliament, 1st Session), 1.
11 *Values of the Public Service Employment Act* (Ottawa: Public Service Commission of Canada, undated).
12 Government of Canada website, geds-sage-gc.ca.
13 See, for example, Canada, *26th Annual Report to the Prime Minister on the Public Service of Canada* (Ottawa: Privy Council Office, March 2019).
14 See, among others, Donald J. Savoie, *Thatcher, Reagan, and Mulroney: In Search of a New Bureaucracy* (Toronto: University of Toronto Press, 1994).
15 See, among many others, "Crisis Exposes How America Has Hollowed Out Its Government," *Washington Post*, 16 May 2020.
16 "Bagehot: Gray Day, Gray Day," the *Economist*, 5 February 2022, 51.
17 See, among others, Douglas Yates, *Bureaucratic Democracy: The Search for Democracy and Efficiency in American Government* (Cambridge: Harvard University Press, 1982), 62.

18 Peter Losin, "Education and Plato's Parable of the Cave," *The Journal of Education* 178, no. 3 (1996): 49–65.
19 Consultations with Marc Rochon, Ottawa, various dates. Mr Rochon is a former deputy minister at the Department of Canadian Heritage and head of Canada Mortgage and Housing Corporation.
20 Consultations with Gérard Veilleux, Ottawa and Montreal, various dates. Mr Veilleux is a former deputy minister of federal-provincial relations, secretary to the Treasury Board, and president of the Canadian Broadcasting Corporation with the Government of Canada.
21 Donald J. Savoie, *The Politics of Public Spending in Canada* (Toronto: University of Toronto Press, 1990).
22 Amanda Clarke, *Opening the Government of Canada: The Federal Bureaucracy in the Digital Age* (Vancouver: UBC Press, 2019), 11.
23 M. Weber, "Bureaucracy," in *From Max Weber: Essays in Sociology*, eds. and trans. H.H. Gerth and C.W. Mills (London: Lowe and Brydon, 1970), 214.
24 Donald J. Savoie, "The Minister's Staff in Ottawa: The Need for Reform," *Canadian Public Administration* 26, no. 4 (Winter 1983).
25 See Canada, "Guidance for Deputy Ministers" (Ottawa: Privy Council Office, undated).
26 "Who's Who in Infrastructure and Intergovernmental Affairs Minister LeBlanc's Office," *Hill Times* (Ottawa), 16 February 2022, 16–17.
27 Richard Crossman, *The Diaries of a Cabinet Minister*, vol. 1 (London: Hamilton and Cape, 1975), 90.
28 Tony Benn, "Manifestors and Mandates," in *Policy and Practice: The Experience of Government* (London: Royal Institute of Public Administration, 1980), 62.
29 Flora MacDonald, "The Minister and the Mandarins," *Policy Options* 1, no. 3 (September–October 1980): 29–31; Jeffrey Simpson, *Discipline of Power: The Conservative Interlude and the Liberal Restoration* (Toronto: University of Toronto Press, 1996), 119–20.
30 See, for example, Savoie, *The Politics of Public Spending in Canada*.
31 Quoted in Derek Bok, "A Daring and Complicated Strategy," *Harvard Magazine* (May–June 1989), 49.
32 James Judd, a former deputy minister of defence, made this observation to me in October 1997.
33 For a discussion on different levels of organizational culture, see K.S. Cameron and R.E. Quinn, *Diagnosing and Changing Organizational Culture: Based on the Competing Values Framework* (New York: Jossey Bass, John Wiley and Sons, 2011).

34 One only has to read reports regularly produced by the Office of the Auditor General for evidence.
35 "Canadians Lack Faith in Upper Ranks of Public Service: survey," *Ottawa Citizen*, 7 September 2016.
36 Campbell Clark, "A Warning Sign of Government Bloat," *The Globe and Mail*, 20 January 2022.
37 Canada, Privy Council Office, *Constitutional Responsibility and Accountability* (Ottawa: Section VII, Accountability in Parliamentary Government – the Minister, 1993).
38 R. Armstrong, *The Duties and Responsibilities in Relation to Ministers: Note by the Head of the Civil Service* (London: Cabinet Office, 1985), 2.
39 London, House of Lords, Parliamentary-Debates-Hansard, vol. 679, no. 113.3, 3 March 2006, 470.
40 Canada, *Final Submissions of the Attorney General of Canada to the Commission of Inquiry into the Sponsorship Program and Advertising Activities* (Ottawa: June 2005), para.77, 16.
41 Josh Harris, *Following the Pound: The Accounting Officer in Central Government* (London: Institute for Government, 2013), 1.
42 Ralph Heintzman, "Can the Federal Public Service Fix Its Culture Problem?" *The Globe and Mail*, 22 June 2018.
43 Canada, *Federal Accountability Action Plan: Turning a New Leaf* (Ottawa: Message from the Prime Minister, 11 April 2006), 36.
44 Canada, *Notes on the Responsibility of Public Servants in Relation to Parliamentary Committees, Swearing of Public Servants* (Ottawa: Privy Council Office, December 1990).
45 Alex Himelfarb in testimony before House of Commons Public Accounts Committee, 3 May 2004.
46 Geoffrey Marshall, *Constitutional Conventions: The Rules and Forms of Political Accountability* (Oxford: Clarendon Press, 2001), 54.
47 Sidney Low, Sir Ivor Jennings, and Lord Morrison of Lambeth quoted in ibid., 61–6.
48 See, among others, Donald J. Savoie, *Court Government and the Collapse of Accountability in Canada and the United Kingdom* (Toronto: University of Toronto Press, 2008), chapter 11.
49 Quoted in Donald J. Savoie, *Governing from the Centre: The Concentration of Power in Canadian Politics* (Toronto: University of Toronto Press, 1999), 156.
50 See, among others, Peter Hennessy, *The Blair Centre: A Question of Command and Control?* (London: Public Management Foundation, 1999).

51 John Greenaway makes this point in his "British Conservatism and Bureaucracy," *History of Political Thought* 13, no. 1 (Spring 1992): 129–60.
52 Temur Durrani, "Shopify Cuts 10 Per Cent of Staff as CEO Tobias Lutke Apologizes for Big Bets on E-Commerce, Admits He 'Got This Wrong,'" *Globe and Mail*, 26 July 2022.
53 S.E. Finer, *The History of Government*, 3 vols. (Oxford: Oxford University Press, 1997).
54 See, for example, M. MacCarthaigh, "Public service Values," Committee for Public Management Research Discussion Paper Number 39, Dublin: Institute of Public Administration, http://wwwipa.ie/pdf/cpmr/CPMR_DP_39_Public ServiceValues.pdf (2008 and accessed July 2022).
55 See, for example, a former clerk of the Privy Council calling on Parliament to strengthen Access to Information legislation, "Prime Minister, Federal Ministers Should Not Be Exempt from Access Laws, Former Top Public Servant Says," *The Globe and Mail*, 21 November 2022.
56 Dennis C. Grube, *Megaphone Bureaucracy: Speaking Truth to Power in the Age of the New Normal* (Princeton: Princeton University Press, 2019), 139.
57 Ibid., 152.
58 Ibid., 42.

## CHAPTER THREE

1 Canada, Canadian Coast Guard, undated, https://www.ccg-gcc.gc.ca/index-eng.html.
2 Canada, *29th Annual Report to the Prime Minister on the Public Service of Canada* (Ottawa: Privy Council Office, 31 March 2022), 28.
3 Canada, "Population of the Federal Public Service from the Treasury Board Secretariat," last modified on 28 November 2022, https://www.canada.ca/en/treasury-board-secretariat/services/innovation/human-resources-statistics/population-federal-public-service.html.
4 Canada, "About the Canada Revenue Agency (CRA)," last modified on 22 March 2023, https://www.canada.ca/en/revenue-agency/corporate/about-canada-revenue-agency-cra.html.
5 "Staff in Canada Revenue Agency Unit Complain of Bullying and Harassment, Report Finds," *The Globe and Mail*, 27 April 2022.
6 Canada, "Collective Bargaining Update" (Ottawa: Treasury Board Secretariat, undated).

7 "Liberals Call for End to Harper's Wasteful Government Spending," www.liberal.ca, 21 May 2015.
8 Campbell Clark, "A Warning Sign of Government Bloat," *The Globe and Mail*, 20 January 2022.
9 See, for example, Canada, *Service Standards: A Guide to the Initiative* (Ottawa: Treasury Board of Canada Secretariat, n.d.).
10 Canada, *29th Annual Report*, 23.
11 Canada, *26th Annual Report to the Prime Minister on the Public Service of Canada* (Ottawa: Privy Council Office, 31 March 2019), 12.
12 See, among others, "What's Gone Wrong with Passports, Airports and Basic Federal Services? How a Perfect Storm Swamped Canada's Bureaucracy," *The Globe and Mail*, 6 November 2022.
13 See, among others, "An Absurd Choice Is No Choice for Canadians," www.psac-afpc.com, n.d.
14 For a discussion on this issue, see Donald J. Savoie, *Whatever Happened to the Music Teacher: How Government Decides and Why* (Montreal: McGill-Queen's University Press, 2013), chapter 6.
15 Andrew Griffith, "Disconnect between Political Priorities and Service Delivery," *Hill Times*, 14 July 2022.
16 "What's Gone Wrong with Passports, Airports and Basic Federal Services?" *The Globe and Mail*, 6 November 2022.
17 "Treasury Hopes Senior Cuts Will Boost Employee Morale," *Ottawa Citizen*, 18 April 1980.
18 Paul Tellier, "Public Service 2000: The Renewal of the Public Service," *Canadian Public Administration* 33, no. 2 (1990): 131.
19 Canada, *Eighteenth Annual Report to the Prime Minister on the Public Service of Canada* (Ottawa: Privy Council Office, 31 March 2011), 18.
20 Canada, *Twenty-Second Annual Report to the Prime Minister on the Public Service of Canada* (Ottawa: Privy Council Office, 31 March 2015), 19.
21 The number is now 7,972. See Canada, *Twenty-Ninth Annual Report to the Prime Minister on the Public Service of Canada* (Ottawa: Privy Council Office, 31 March 2022), Annex: key data.
22 Canada, "Infographic for Government of Canada," www.tbs-sct.gc.ca.
23 Ibid.
24 "Largely" because the federal government needs plumbers to deliver its transfer payments to Canadians, notably Old Age Security.
25 Jonathon Gatehouse and Albert Leung, "Ottawa's Pandemic Hiring Boom Adds Billions to Federal Payroll," CBC News, 24 October 2022; and

Canada, "Infographic for Government of Canada," (Ottawa: Treasury Board Secretariat, undated).
26 "Ottawa's Pandemic Hiring Boom Adds Billions to Federal Payroll."
27 Canada, Table 1 – Consolidated Per Capita Spending by Selected Canadian Classification of Functions of Government, 2020, Statistics Canada.
28 Canada, Canadian Classification of Functions of Government (CCOFOG), 2014, Statistics Canada.
29 Canada, Innovation, Science and Economic Development Canada, 2022–23, *Departmental Plans* and Our Organization.
30 Canada, Department of Finance Organizational Structure, https://www.canada.ca/en/department-finance/corporate/organizational-structure.html; and Canada, *Departmental Plan 2022–2023*, https://www.canada.ca/en/department-finance/corporate/transparency/plans-performance/departmental-plans/2022-2023/report.html.
31 Canada, *Treasury Board of Canada Secretariat, 2022–23, Departmental Plan.*
32 Canada, *2022–23 Estimates – Part I and II, The Government Expenditure Plan and Main Estimates*, 193.
33 Canada, *Population of the Federal Public Service by Department*, www.canada.ca.
34 Canada, Task Force on Public Service Values and Ethics, *Discussion Paper* (Ottawa: Privy Council Office, 1996), 57.
35 John C. Tait, *A Strong Foundation: Report on the Task Force on Public Service Values and Ethics* (Ottawa: Canadian Centre for Management Development, 2000), 36.
36 Richard Dicerni, "A Letter to a New Deputy Minister," *Public Sector Management* 25, no. 1 (2014): 6 and 7.
37 James Q. Wilson, *Bureaucracy: What Government Agencies Do and Why They Do It* (New York: Basic Books, 1999).
38 Ibid.
39 See, among others, Donald J. Savoie, *The Politics of Public Spending in Canada* (Toronto: University of Toronto Press, 1990).
40 Canada, *The Royal Commission on Government Organization*, vol. 1 to 4 (Ottawa: Privy Council Office, 1962).
41 Edgar Benson, "The New Budget Process," *Canadian Tax Journal*, May 1968, 161.
42 A.W. Johnson, "P.P.B. and Decision-Making in the Government of Canada," *Cost and Management*, March–April 1971, 14.

43 Robert F. Adie and Paul Thomas, *Canadian Public Administration: Problematical Perspectives* (Scarborough, ON: Prentice-Hall, 1982), 172.
44 Ibid., 171.
45 Canada, *Report of the Auditor General of Canada to the House of Commons for Fiscal Year Ended 31 March 1976* (Ottawa: Supply and Services, 1976), 10.
46 Savoie, *The Politics of Public Spending in Canada*, 69.
47 See, for example, Donald J. Savoie, *Democracy in Canada: The Disintegration of Our Institutions* (Kingston and Montreal: McGill-Queen's University Press, 2021), chapter 10.
48 Adam Radwanski, "Trudeau's 'Deliverology' on the Verge of Becoming Punchline," *The Globe and Mail*, 17 November 2017.
49 Aaron Wherry, "How Justin Trudeau Plans to Deliver on 'Deliverology,'" CBC *News*, 27 August 2016, https://www.cbc.ca/news/politics/wherry-trudeau-deliverology-1.3735890.
50 See, for example, Radwanski, "Trudeau's 'Deliverology' on the Verge of Becoming a Punchline."
51 Treasury Board of Canada Secretariat, undated.
52 Richard French, "Trudeau's Challenge: Turning Promises into Policy," *The Globe and Mail*, 20 July 2016, A11.
53 For a list of Cabinet committees from Mackenzie King to Chrétien, see Donald J. Savoie, *Governing from the Centre: The Concentration of Power in Canadian Politics* (Toronto: University of Toronto Press, 1999), 43–5.
54 Canada, *Chronic Homelessness: 2022 Reports 5 to 8 of the Auditor General of Canada to the Parliament of Canada, Report 5* (Ottawa: Office of the Auditor General, 15 November 2022), 7.
55 Ibid.
56 The Moncton executive is in the construction business and the comments were made on 24 August 2022.

CHAPTER FOUR

1 The former public servant made this observation over breakfast in Ottawa.
2 See, for example, Ken Rubin, "While the Charter Lets Us Dream, the Access Act Is a Nightmare," *Hill Times*, 9 June 2022, 12.
3 See, among others, Douglas Yates, *Bureaucratic Democracy: The Search for Democracy and Efficiency in American Government* (Cambridge: Harvard University Press, 1982), chap. 4.

4 David A. Good, *The Politics of Public Money* (Toronto: University of Toronto Press, 2007), 87.
5 Ibid., 168–9.
6 Ralph Heintzman, "The Effects of Globalization on Management Practices: Should the Public Sector Operate on Different Parameters?" (paper presented to the IPAC National Conference, Fredericton, New Brunswick, 31 August 1999), 7–9.
7 See, among others, Donald J. Savoie, *What Is Government Good At? A Canadian Answer* (Montreal: McGill-Queen's University Press, 2015), chap. 6.
8 Douglas G. Hartle, "The Role of the Auditor General of Canada," *Canadian Tax Journal* 23, no. 3 (1975): 197.
9 Herbert Kaufman, *Are Government Organizations Immortal?* (Washington, DC: Brookings, 1976).
10 Brooke Struck, quoted in "Open Evidence-Based Government," undated, https://open.canada.ca/en/idea/open-evidence-based-government.
11 Michael Howlett, "Policy Analytical Capacity and Evidence-Based Policy-Making: Lessons from Canada," *Canadian Public Administration* 52, no. 2 (June 2009): 157.
12 "Canadian Federal Scientists, Professionals Union Launches Anti-Harper Campaign," *Canadian Dimension*, 14 August 2015.
13 See, for example, "Service Please: Canadians Split Over Satisfaction When Accessing Federal Government Services," Angus Reid Institute, 10 June 2022.
14 See, for example, Kevin Lynch and Jim Mitchell, "Instead of Adding New Programs, Ottawa Should Focus on Proper Delivery of the Ones It Has," *The Globe and Mail*, 11 February 2023.
15 Albert O. Hirschman, *Exit, Voice and Loyalty: Responses to Decline in Firms, Organizations and States* (Cambridge, MA: Harvard University Press, 1970).
16 See, among others, "The Achilles Heel of the Federal Public Service Gives Out Again with Passport Fiasco," *Policy Options*, 29 June 2022. I note that in responding to problems in service delivery, the federal government established a ten-member task force to improve service delivery; also see Canada, "Prime Minister Announces New Task Force to Improve Government Services for Canadians" (Ottawa: Office of the Prime Minister, 25 June 2022).
17 Canada, "Prime Minister Announces."
18 "Meet the New Faces in Prime Minister Trudeau's Cabinet," CBC News, 26 July 2023.

19 See, for example, Citizens First 2020 (Toronto: Institute for Citizen-Centred Service, 2000).
20 A letter sent to the author by a retired senior federal public servant, dated 6 August 2023.
21 Consultation with a federal deputy minister, 28 August 2023.
22 H.W. Arthurs, "Collective Bargaining in the Public Service of Canada: Bold Experiment or Act of Folly?," *Michigan Law Review* 67, no. 5 (1969): 971–1000.
23 Audrey D. Doerr, *The Machinery of Government in Canada* (Toronto: Methuen, 1981, 63).
24 See "Our History," http://psacunion.ca/our-history, undated.
25 Arthurs, "Collective Bargaining in the Public Service of Canada," 976.
26 Ibid., 977.
27 Michael Farrell, "Collective Bargaining in Canada," *Journal of Collective Bargaining in the Academy* 0, no. 47 (2008), 2.
28 See Section 2(d) – Freedom of Association, www.justice.gc.ca, undated.
29 *Identifying the Issues: Final Report* (Ottawa: Advisory Committee on Labour Management Relations in the Federal Public Service, 2000).
30 Gene Swimmer, *How Ottawa Spends – Seeing Red – A Liberal Report Card* (Ottawa: Carleton University, 1997).
31 The Treasury Board acknowledges as much. See Canada, *Expenditure Review of Federal Public Compensation Policy and Comparability* (Ottawa: Treasury Board Secretariat, 2007), 1, 8.
32 See, for example, ibid., 1, no. 5, 15.
33 *Collective Bargaining Coverage Rate, 1997 to 2021* (Canada: Statistics Canada, 30 May 2022).
34 Jeffrey Simpson, "In A World Full of Rights: We Ignore Our Responsibility," *The Globe and Mail*, 23 January 2009, A7.
35 "Public Service Alliance of Canada Scores Major Victory," *Telegraph Journal*, 18 April 2022.
36 "Federal Public Servants Mandated to Return to Office 2–3 Days a Week by March 31," CBC News, 15 December 2022.
37 Kathryn May, "The Public Service's Biggest Disruption in Decades: Hybrid Work," *Policy Options*, 27 September 2022.
38 See, for example, Britney Nguyen, "JP Morgan CEO Says Remote Work Isn't Good for Young People and Managers, but Can Be 'Perfectly Reasonable' for Coders and Women with Caregiver Concerns," *Business Insider*, 21 January 2023, https://www.businessinsider.com/jpmorgan-ceo-remote-work-perfectly-reasonable-women-primary-care-concerns-2023-1.

39 See comments made by Jane Fraser, CEO of Citigroup in Allison Morrow, "Wall Street's Biggest WFH Advocate Is Bringing Underperforming Staff Back into the Office," CNN, 18 January 2023, https://www.cnn.com/2023/01/18/business/citi-work-from-home-jane-fraser/index.html.
40 "The Boss Was Right: Working from Home Full Time Really Is Bad for Business," *Financial Post*, 22 August 2023.
41 Quoted in Kathryn May, "The Biggest Public Service Union Prepares for the First National Strike in Decades," *Policy Options*, 3 February 2023.
42 *Statement on the Status of Negotiations with the Public Service Alliance of Canada* (Ottawa: Treasury Board Secretariat, 13 January 2023).
43 "Politics Briefing: Federal Government Accuses Canada's Largest Public-Sector Union of Bargaining in Bad Faith, Files Complaint," *The Globe and Mail*, 13 January 2023.
44 "Treasury Board President Calls Return-to-Office Plan Right of Employer," *Ottawa Citizen*, 27 December 2022.
45 *Government Reaches Tentative Agreements with the Public Service Alliance of Canada* (Ottawa: Treasury Board Secretariat, 1 May 2023).
46 Ibid.
47 Tim Powers, "PSAC Got Their Win, but We Don't Yet Know What It Means," *Hill Times*, 3 May 2023.
48 "JP Morgan CEO Says Remote Work Can be 'Perfectly Reasonable' for Women with Caregiver Concerns," *Business Insider*, 21 January 2023.
49 Susmita Sarma, "Top 7 Disadvantages of Working From Home," *Vantage Circle*, 18 October 2022.
50 "RBC Tells Employees to Return to the Office Three to Four Days a Week," *The Globe and Mail*, 21 March 2023.
51 "Wall Street's Biggest WFH Advocate Is Bringing Underperforming Staff Back into the Office," CNN, 18 January 2023.
52 "Bosses Mean It This Time: Return to Office or Get a New Job!" *Washington Post*, 3 September 2023.
53 "Is Remote Work A Perk or a Right? Depends Who You Ask," CBC, 29 April 2023.
54 Kathryn May, "A Whole New Conflict around Remote Work," *Policy Options*, 10 May 2023.
55 See, for example, *Comparing Government and Private Sector Compensation in Canada* (Vancouver, BC: Fraser Institute, 2015).
56 See, among others, "How Much Are Government Workers Making Compared to the Private Sector?," *HR Reporter*, 18 April 2023.
57 Canada, "Federal Public Service Indeterminate Employee Departures by Separation Type, Fiscal Years 2005 to 2006 until 2015 to 2016," Treasury

Board of Canada Secretariat, last modified on 13 June 2019, https://www.canada.ca/en/treasury-board-secretariat/services/innovation/human-resources-statistics/federal-public-service-indeterminate-departures-separation-type.html.

58 Canada, "Demographic Snapshot of Canada's Public Service, 2021," last modified on 17 August 2022, https://www.canada.ca/en/treasury-board-secretariat/services/innovation/human-resources-statistics/demographic-snapshot-federal-public-service-2021.html#toc02.

59 Canada, "Guidelines for Termination or Demotion for Unsatisfactory Performance; Termination or Demotion for Reasons Other than Breaches of Discipline or Misconduct; and Termination of Employment During Probation," last modified on 9 June 2011, https://www.tbs-sct.canada.ca/pol/doc-eng.aspx?id=22379&section=html.

60 Barbara Wake Carroll and David Siegel, *Service in the Field: The World of Front-Line Public Servants* (Montreal: McGill-Queen's University Press, 1999), 119.

61 Treasury Board of Canada Secretariat, *Report of the Review of the Public Service Modernization Act*, 2003, ch.5.7, December 2011.

62 Both quoted in Canada, "Guidelines for Termination or Demotion for Unsatisfactory Performance; Termination or Demotion for Reasons Other than Breaches of Discipline or Misconduct; and Termination of Employment During Probation," 28 June 2018.

63 Donald J. Savoie, *Harrison McCain: Single-Minded Purpose* (Montreal: McGill-Queen's University Press, 2012).

64 "Province Laments Reversal of Firings over Email Porn," *The Globe and Mail*, 12 July 2004.

65 "Federal Department Fires 49 Employees for Claiming CERB While Employed," CTV News-Ottawa, 3 February 2023.

66 "Hundreds of CRA Employees Under Investigation for Receiving Potentially Inappropriate Pandemic Benefits," *The Globe and Mail*, 30 June 2023; and "Canada Revenue Agency Fires 120 Employees Following Review of Inappropriate CERB Payments," *The Globe and Mail*, 1 September 2023.

67 "But Was It Time Theft," *The Globe and Mail*, 9 September 2010.

68 Treasury Board Secretariat, *Expenditure Review of Federal Public Sector* (Ottawa: Treasury Board Secretariat, 2007), 1:11.10, and 166.

69 Consultations with Ailish Campbell in Moncton, 15 August 2014. Ms Campbell was a director general with Industry Canada on an exchange with the Canadian Council of Chief Executives.

70 Ibid.

71 "Continued Public Service Travel Cuts Could Threaten Canada's International Engagement, Say Experts," *Hill Times*, 12 April 2023.

CHAPTER FIVE

1 New Brunswick Premier Blaine Higgs made this observation on several occasions when discussing budget matters.
2 Quoted in Christopher Hood, David Heald, Rozana Himaz (eds.) *When the Party's Over: The Politics of Fiscal Squeeze in Perspective* (Oxford: Oxford University Press, 2014), 11.
3 Ronald G. Wirick, "Wage and Price Controls, *The Canadian Encyclopedia*, 7 February 2006.
4 "Mr. Trudeau Tries Again," *The Globe and Mail*, 3 August 1978, 6; see also, "Fed-Up – PM Pledges Postal Shakeup," *The Globe and Mail*, 2 August 1978, 1.
5 See, Donald J. Savoie, *The Politics of Public Spending in Canada* (Toronto: University of Toronto Press, 1990), chap. 7.
6 "Are Cuts Real or Are They An Imaginary Total," *The Globe and Mail*, 9 September 1978, 1.
7 Ibid.
8 See, *Regional Poverty and Change* (Ottawa: Canadian Council on Rural Development, 1976), 1.
9 Canada, *Budget Speech – Delivered by the Honourable John Crosbie* (Ottawa: Department of Finance, 11 December 1979).
10 Canada, House of Commons Debates, 32nd Parliament, 1st Session, vol. 2 (3 June 1980), 1682.
11 Canada, Journals of the Senate of Canada, 33rd Parliament, 1st Session, vol. 128, part 1, 5 November 1984, 25.
12 Quoted in Canada, Task Force on Program Review, *An Introduction to the Process of Program Review* (Ottawa: Minister of Supply and Services Canada, 1986), 1.
13 Donald J. Savoie, *Thatcher, Reagan, and Mulroney: In Search of a New Bureaucracy* (Pittsburgh: University of Pittsburgh Press, 1994).
14 See Canada, Task Force on Program Review, Private Sector Advisory Committee, news release, Ottawa, 11 March 1986. See also Canada, "Letter to Members of the Private Sector Advisory Committee and to the Study Team Leaders of the Ministerial Task Force on Program Review from the President of the Treasury Board," dated 23 February 1988. The letter was made public on 8 March 1988 by the Treasury Board Secretariat.

15 Canada, Treasury Board of Canada, "The Management of the Public Service Restraint and Productivity: Fact Sheet No. 6," *News Release*, 2 March 1987.
16 Quoted in Savoie, *The Politics of Public Spending*, 140.
17 Canada, *An Introduction to the Process of Program Review*, 26.
18 Prime Minister Jean Chrétien often made reference to the editorial. See, for example, Michael Walker, "Canada, the Country That Keeps on Taxing," *The Wall Street Journal*, 27 March 1998.
19 Edward Greenspon and Anthony Wilson-Smith, *Double Vision: The Inside Story of the Liberals in Power* (Toronto: Doubleday, 1996), 236.
20 Canada, Paul Martin, *The Budget Plan* (Ottawa: Department of Finance, February 1994).
21 See, for example, Randall Palmer and Louise Egan, "Insight: Lessons for U.S. from Canada's 'Basket Case' Moment," *Reuters*, 21 November 2011, https://www.reuters.com/article/us-crisis-idUSTRE7AK0EP20111121.
22 Ibid.
23 Donald J. Savoie, "A Perfect Storm in Reverse: The 1994–1997 Program Review in Canada," in *When the Party's Over: The Politics of Fiscal Squeeze in Perspective*.
24 *Programme Review: The Government of Canada's Experience Eliminating the Deficit 1994–99, a Canadian Case Study*, ed. Christopher Hood et al. (Waterloo: Centre for International Governance Innovation, 10 September 2009), 12.
25 Arthur Kroeger, "The Central Agencies and Program Review," in *Managing Strategic Change: Learning from Program Review*, ed. Peter Aucoin and Donald J. Savoie (Ottawa: Canadian Centre for Management Development, 1998), 16.
26 Ibid.
27 See, for example, David Herle, "Poll-Driven Politics: The Role of Public Opinion in Canada," *Policy Options*, May 2007, 19–25.
28 Savoie, "The 1994–1997 Program Review in Canada," in Hood et al., *When the Party's Over*, 214.
29 Herman Bakvis, "Transport Canada and Program Review," in *Managing Strategic Change: Learning from Program Review*, eds. Peter Aucoin and Donald J. Savoie (Ottawa: Canadian Centre for Management Development, 1998).
30 Canada, *Transport Canada 2022–23 Departmental Plan* (Ottawa: Treasury Board Secretariat, 2021).

31 *Program Review: The Government of Canada's Experience Eliminating the Deficit 1994–1999: A Canadian Case Study* (Waterloo: The Centre for International Governance Innovation, 10 September 2009), 7, 19.
32 See, among others, Keith Banting, "The Social Policy Divide: The Welfare State in Canada and the United States," in *Degrees of Freedom: Canada and the United States in a Changing World*, eds. Keith Banting, George Hoberg, and Richard Simeon (Montreal: McGill-Queen's University Press).
33 See, among others, Donald J. Savoie, *Visiting Grandchildren: Economic Development in the Maritimes* (Toronto: University of Toronto Press, 2006).
34 Donald J. Savoie, "A Perfect Storm in Reverse: The 1994–97 Program Review in Canada," in Hood et al., *When the Party's Over*, 224.
35 Gilles Paquet and Robert Shepherd, *The Program Review Process: A Deconstruction*, Working Paper 26/15 (Ottawa: University of Ottawa, 1996).
36 Savoie, "A Perfect Storm," 224.
37 Donald J. Savoie, *Whatever Happened to the Music Teacher? How Government Decides and Why* (Montreal: McGill-Queen's University Press, 2013).
38 Don Drummond, "Personal Reflections on the State of Public Policy Analysis in Canada," in *New Directions for Intelligent Government in Canada: Papers in Honour of Ian Stewart*, ed. Fred Gorbet and Andrew Sharpe (Ottawa, Centre for the Study of Living Standards, 2011), 337–52.
39 "A Closer Look at the Sponsorship Scandal," *The Globe and Mail*, 22 July 2011, A3.
40 "Chuck Guité Found Guilty of Fraud," CBC News, 6 June 2006, https://www.cbc.ca/news/canada/ottawa/chuck-guit-233-found-guilty-of-fraud-1.578627.
41 See, for example, Savoie, *Democracy in Canada*, chap. 13.
42 Montfort Hospital, "Our History," formerly available at www.hopital-montfort.com/our-history.cfm.
43 *Structural Reform at a Time of Financial Crisis* (Paris: OECD, 2009).
44 Canada, *Canada's Economic Action Plan* (Ottawa: Department of Finance, 2009).
45 They were: an Administrative Service Review (ASR), a Strategic Review (SR), a Strategic and operating Review (SOR), and a Deficit Reduction Action Plan (DRAP).
46 For an excellent overview of budgeting under the Harper government, see Christopher Stoney and G. Bruce Doern, "Harper Budgeting in a New

Majority Government: Trimming Fat or Slicing Pork," in *How Ottawa Spends*, eds. Christopher Stoney and G. Bruce Doern (Ottawa and Montreal: The School of Public Policy and Administration, Carleton University and McGill-Queen's University Press, 2011), 3–38.
47 Ibid.
48 Canada, *The Road to Balance: Creating Jobs and Opportunities* (Ottawa: Department of Finance, 11 February 2014), 241–5.
49 Canada, *Annual Financial Report of the Government of Canada: Fiscal Year 2015–2016* (Ottawa: Department of Finance, March 2016).
50 Christopher Stoney and G. Bruce Doern, "Harper Budgeting in a New Majority Government," 9.
51 Charlie Smith, "Massive CBC Cuts Anger Canadian Media Guild and Friends of Canadian Broadcasting," *Georgia Straight*, 26 June 2014, https://www.straight.com/news/674771/massive-cbc-cuts-anger-canadian-media-guild-and-friends-canadian-broadcasting.
52 Canada, *Annual Report 2021–22* (Ottawa: CBC, 2022), 31.
53 "'Death by a Thousand Cuts' Memo to Harper Questions Across-the-Board Cuts," *National Post*, 26 November 2014.
54 Stoney and Doern, "Harper Budgeting in a New Majority Government," 9.
55 *Real Change: A New Plan for a Strong Middle Class* (Ottawa: Liberal Party of Canada, 2015), 76.
56 *Fiscal Sustainability Report 2022* (Ottawa: Office of the Parliamentary Budget Officer, 2022).
57 Nojoud Al Mallees, "Canada Projected to See Balanced Budget by 2027, Freeland Says in Fiscal Update," Global News, 3 November 2022.
58 Canada, *Budget 2019* (Ottawa: Department of Finance, 19 March 2019).
59 Patrick Brethour, "Ottawa's Hiring Spree Is Beyond Measure," *The Globe and Mail*, 9 September 2022.
60 Joanne Laucius, "Review Is a Matter of Making Government 'Smarter, Not Smaller,' Treasury Board President Says," *Ottawa Citizen*, 12 April 2022.
61 Jonathon Gatehouse and Albert Leung, "Ottawa's Pandemic Hiring Boom Adds Billions to Federal Payroll," CBC News, 24 October 2022.
62 "Federal Spending Down 21.6 Percent in 2021–22 after COVID-Fuelled High," *Hill Times*, 9 November 2022.
63 Canada, "Remarks by the Deputy Prime Minister for the 2022 Fall Economic Statement" (Ottawa: Department of Finance, 3 November 2022); and "A Money-Spending Liberal Version of Restraint, with Bigger Choices Coming," *The Globe and Mail*, 4 November 2022.
64 Joanne Laucius, "Review Is a Matter of Making Government 'Smarter, Not Smaller,' Treasury Board President Says," *Ottawa Citizen*, 12 April 2022.

65 Joanne Laucius, "'Strategic Policy Review' in 2022 Budget Could Lead to Job Cuts, Public Service Unions Warn," *Ottawa Citizen*, 8 April 2022.
66 See, among others, Campbell Clark, "A Warning Sign of Government Bloat," *The Globe and Mail*, 20 January 2022.
67 "Public Sector Union Warns of Rushed Plans to Cut Federal Spending," CBC, 15 August 2023.
68 Ibid.
69 Don Drummond quoted in Dan Gardner, "The Economy Doesn't Care Who Wins: In The Big Picture, Liberal and Conservative Economic Policies are Almost Indistinguishable," *Ottawa Citizen*, 1 March 2011.
70 Senator Lowell Murray, "Power, Responsibility and Agency in Canadian Government," in *Governing: Essays in Honour of Donald J. Savoie*, ed. James Bickerton and B. Guy Peters (Montreal: McGill-Queen's University Press, 2013), 26.
71 Quoted in "Feds Bring Down Legislative Hammer on Massive Budget Implementation Bill," *Hill Times* (Ottawa), 4 November 2013, 19.
72 Walter Bagehot, *The English Constitution* (London: Chapman and Hall, second edition, 1873).
73 Canada, *Government Decisions Limited Parliament's Control of Public Spending* (Ottawa: Office of the Auditor General, May 2006), 2.
74 Brian Pagan, "Connecting the Dots between Resources and Results" (paper presented to the CPA Canada Public Sector Conference, November 2016), 6.
75 *Real Change* (Ottawa: Liberal Party, 18 June 2015).
76 "Omnibus Bill Shows It's Still Politics as Usual for Trudeau Government," *Toronto Star*, 9 April 2019.
77 Quoted in "Prime Minister's Office Now Rolled into Privy Council Office," *Ottawa Citizen*, 20 June 2011, 1.
78 Canada, *Commission of Inquiry into the Sponsorship Program and Advertising Activities*, Volume 3 (Ottawa: Government Services Canada, 2006), 56.
79 "The System Is Broken: $30.7-Billion in Spending Estimates Not Reviewed by House Committees," *Hill Times*, 14 June 2023, 1.

CHAPTER SIX

1 Based on several consultations with the Honourable Elmer MacKay.
2 Quoted in David E. Smith, "Clarifying the Doctrine of Ministerial Responsibility as It Applies to the Government and Parliament of Canada," *Restoring Accountability. Research Studies Volume 1 – Parliament, Ministers and Deputy Ministers*, 114.

3 Quoted in ibid., 103.
4 Quoted in Kathryn May, "Our System Is Broken," *Ottawa Citizen*, 21 February 2004.
5 Peter Aucoin and Mark D. Jarvis, *Modernizing Government Accountability: A Framework for Reform* (Ottawa: Canada School of Public Service, 2005), 8 and 28–9.
6 Luther Gulick, "Politics, Administration, and the New Deal," *Annals of the American Academy of Political and Social Science*, September 1933, 61–7.
7 Max Weber, "Politics as a Vocation," in *From Max Weber: Essays in Sociology*, ed. and trans. H.H. Gerth and C. Wright Mills (New York: Oxford University Press, 1958), 91.
8 Consultation with a former senior executive with the federal government, 27 November 2022.
9 "Innovation in the Federal Government: The Risk Not Taken," paper prepared by the Public Policy Forum for the Office of the Auditor General, Ottawa, August 1998, 8.
10 Donald J. Savoie, *What Is Government Good At? A Canadian Answer* (Montreal: McGill-Queen's University Press, 2015), 195.
11 Carroll and Siegel, *Service in the Field: The World of Front-line Public Servants* (Montreal: McGill-Queen's University Press, 1998), 200–3.
12 Ian D. Clark and Harry Swain, "Distinguishing the Real from the Surreal in Management Reform: Suggestions for Beleaguered Administrators in the Government of Canada," *Canadian Public Administration* 48, no. 4 (2005): 458.
13 Office of the Auditor General, *Evaluating the Effectiveness of Programs*, Fall Report of the Auditor General of Canada (Ottawa: Office of the Auditor General, 2009), 24.
14 In the mid-1980s, it was established that adding one tax auditor would generate $75,000 in revenues.
15 See Savoie, *What Is Government Good At?*, 187.
16 Canada, Corporate Book, November 2019, parks.canada.ca.
17 Canada, 2022–23 *Departmental Plan* (Ottawa: Employment and Social Development Canada, 2022).
18 Canada, Service Canada, canada.ca.
19 Bill Curry, "Spending on ArriveCAN App Projected to Top $54-Million, Double the Amount Ottawa First Divulged," *The Globe and Mail*, 6 October 2022.
20 See, Canada, Reporting Framework, Employment and Social Development, Canada.ca, undated.

21 Ibid.
22 Canada, *2022–23 Estimates: Part 1 and 11 The Government Expenditure Plan and Main Estimates* (Ottawa: Treasury Board, 2022), part 11–67 to 72.
23 Canada, Departments and Agencies, www.canada.ca.
24 Quoted in Donald J. Savoie, *The Canadian Centre for Management Studies* (Ottawa: Treasury Board Secretariat, July 1987), 8.
25 Ibid., 2–3.
26 Ibid., 6.
27 Ibid., 10.
28 Ibid., 12.
29 These comments were written in the margin of my paper, and the document was revised to reflect these concerns.
30 "A New Commitment to Public Sector Management," notes for an address by Don Mazankowski to the Public Policy Forum, Toronto, 14 April 1988, 16.
31 Ibid, 17.
32 Ibid, 18.
33 Jack Manion, *How Lucky I've Been* (Ottawa: Luhn, 2012), 205–06.
34 Ibid, 205.
35 Canada, *Departmental Plan* (Ottawa: Canada School of Public Service, 2022–23). The figure includes $20 million for internal services.
36 Don Mazankowski, president of the Treasury Board, to Brian Mulroney, prime minister, 3 September 1987, 1.
37 *Leadership and Learning* (Ottawa: Institute on Governance, undated).
38 "Ottawa's Civil Service School Is Teaching the Wrong Lessons," *The Globe and Mail*, 2 April 2013, https://www.theglobeandmail.com/opinion/editorials/ottawas-civil-service-school-is-teaching-the-wrong-lessons/article10664421/.
39 Quoted in Kathryn May, "Federal Executives Lack Training, Flexibility, Expert Says," *Ottawa Citizen*, 17 June 2014.
40 Ibid.
41 Dominic Barton: "Training in the Federal Civil Service Is Weak," *Hill Times*, 6 February 2023.
42 *2023–24 University Budget* (Sackville, NB: Mount Allison University, 24 May 2023).
43 "Civil Service Learning," https://gcs.civilservice.gov.uk/external-resources/civil-service-learning/, undated.
44 "Center for Leadership Development," leadership.opm.gov/facilities.aspx?F-48, undated.

45 See, for example, David Van Slyke and Alasdair Roberts, "A Poorly Designed Solution for a Misdiagnosed Problem," *Administration and Society*, vol. 4 (March 2009), 127–9.
46 See, for example, "Suppression de l'ENA: une école dangereuse?," 23 October 2015, https://www.telerama.fr/idees/l-ena-est-elle-une-ecole-dangereuse,132669.php.
47 République française, Institut national du service public, insp.gouv.fr.
48 "Federal Debates Commission is a Waste of Public Money," *Telegraph Journal*, 10 March 2022.
49 "Leaders' Debates Commission Releases Its Final Report on the 2021 Federal Election Experience" (Ottawa: Leaders' Debates Commission, 10 May 2022).
50 See, Canada, *Departments and Agencies*, Canada.ca, n.d.

CHAPTER SEVEN

1 Canada, *Governing Responsibly: A Guide for Ministers and Ministers of State* (Ottawa: Privy Council Office, 2003), 1.
2 Quoted in "Morneau Says PM Favoured 'Political Points' Over Policy, Felt Like 'Rubber Stamp' ahead of 'Inevitable' Resignation," CTV News, 8 January 2023.
3 Jocelyn Coulon, *Un selfie avec Justin Trudeau: Regard critique sur la diplomatie du premier ministre* (Montreal: Québec-Amérique, 2018),
4 Canada, *Open and Accountable Government* (Ottawa: Privy Council Office, 2015), 7.
5 Canada, *Governing Responsibly*, 46.
6 Wernick, *Governing Canada: A Guide to the Tradecraft of Politics*, 137–8.
7 See, Mel Cappe and Yan Campagnolo, "Mandate Letters Should Be Kept Confidential," *Policy Options*, 7 April 2022.
8 Canada, *Guide for Parliamentary Secretaries* (Ottawa: Office of the Prime Minister, 5 January 2010).
9 Alex Marland, Thierry Giasson, and Tamara A. Small, eds., *Political Communications in Canada: Meet the Press and Tweet the Rest* (Vancouver: UBC Press, 2015).
10 David Cameron and Richard Simeon, "Intergovernmental Relations in Canada: The Emergence of Collaborative Federalism," *Publius* 32, no. 2: 49–71.
11 Canada, *Governing Responsibly*, 16.
12 Ibid.

13 Ibid., 17.
14 Ibid.
15 Ibid., 19.
16 Former MP Brent Rathgeber made this point in his *Irresponsible Government: The Decline of Parliamentary Democracy in Canada* (Toronto: Dundurn Press, 2014), 62.
17 See Edward Greenspon and Anthony Wilson-Smith, *Double Vision: The Inside Story of the Liberals in Power* (Toronto: Doubleday Press, 1996) and Donald J. Savoie, *Governing from the Centre: The Concentration of Power in Canadian Politics* (Toronto: University of Toronto Press, 1999), 239.
18 See, for example, "The Commons: Question Period, Not Answer Period," *Maclean's*, 1 December 2010.
19 Jonathan Malloy, *The Paradox of Parliament*, 209–10.
20 See, among many others, "Critics Blast Oda's Swanky Hotel Stay – $16 Orange Juice," CTV News, 23 April 2012.
21 See, for example, Ben Worthy, *The Politics of Freedom of Information: How and Why Governments Pass Laws That Threaten Their Power* (Manchester: Manchester University Press, 2017), 185.
22 Gordon Osbaldeston, *Dear Minister: A Letter to an Old Friend on Being a Successful Minister* (Ottawa: Association of Professional Executives of the Public Service of Canada, 22 January 1988).
23 Ibid.
24 Canada, *Departmental Plan 2022–23* (Ottawa: Canadian Heritage, 2023).
25 Canada, *Mandate Letter* (Ottawa: Canadian Heritage, n.d).
26 Ibid.
27 See, for example, Wernick, *Governing Canada*.
28 Osbaldeston, *Dear Minister*.
29 I served as senior policy advisor to the minister of Regional Economic Expansion (in the early 1980s), assistant secretary at the Treasury Board Secretariat in the late 1980s, and was a Simon Reisman Visiting Fellow at the Treasury Board Secretariat in 2004.
30 Osbaldeston, *Dear Minister*, 3.
31 "Canada PM Pushes Work-Life Balance, Cabinet Too Busy to Listen," Reuters, 14 June 2016.
32 Harold D. Clarke et al., *Absent Mandate* (Toronto: Gage Publishing, 1984), 110.
33 Canada, "Ministry (Cabinet) as of August 31, 2022," Members of Parliament, House of Commons, Parliament of Canada, undated, https://www.ourcommons.ca/members/en/ministries.

34 Richard Johnston, "The Ideological Structure of Opinion on Policy," in *Party Democracy in Canada: The Politics of National Party Conventions*, ed. George Perlin (Scarborough: Prentice Hall, 1988), 54–70 and 57; Janine M. Brodie and Jane Jenson, "Piercing the Smokescreen: Brokerage Parties and Class Politics," in *Canadian Parties in Transition: Discourse, Organization and Representation*, ed. Alain-G. Gagnon and A. Brian Tanguay (Scarborough: Nelson, 1991), 33.
35 David Herle, "Poll-Driven Politics – the Role of Public Opinion in Canada," *Policy Options*, 1 May 2007.
36 Donald J. Savoie, *The Politics of Public Spending in Canada* (Toronto: University of Toronto Press, 1990), 187.
37 Maurice Lamontagne, "The Influence of the Politician," *Canadian Public Administration* 11, no. 3 (1968): 270.
38 Consultation with a senior advisor to a federal cabinet minister, 20 August 2022.
39 Consultation with a senior departmental official, Ottawa, 12 March 1988.
40 Michael Pitfield, "Politics and Policy Making," Address to the Alma Mater Society Queen's University, Kingston, Ontario, 10 February, 1983, 5.
41 Bill Morneau, *Where To From Here: A Path to Canadian Prosperity* (Toronto: ECW Press, 2023).
42 Lowell Murray, "Power, Responsibility, and Agency in Canadian Government," in *Governing*, ed. James Bickerton and B. Guy Peters (Montreal: McGill-Queen's University Press, 2013). See also Janice Stein and Eugene Lang, *The Unexpected War: Canada in Kandahar* (Toronto: Penguin Random House, 2008).
43 Quoted in Timothy Plumptre, *Beyond the Bottom Line: Management in Government* (Montreal: McGill-Queen's University Press, 1991), 130.
44 Canada, "The Honourable Steven Guilbeault – Minister of Environment and Climate Change," www.pm.gc.ca/en/cabinet/honourable-steven-guilbeault.
45 See Donald Johnston, *Up the Hill* (Montreal: Optimum Publishing International, 1986) and Morneau, *Where To From Here*.
46 See, among others, Lloyd Axworthy, "Control of Policy," *Policy Options* 6, no. 3 (1985): 17–19.
47 Savoie, *The Politics of Public Spending in Canada*, 194.
48 See, pm.gc.ca/en/cabinet-committee-mandate-and-membership, undated.
49 Savoie, *Governing from the Centre*.
50 "Telford Shuffles Senior PMO Staffers and Chiefs of Staff to Cabinet Ministers," *Hill Times*, 7 February 2023.

51 "The Good, the Bad and the Unknown: Canadians Assess Cabinet Performance at the Two-Year Mark," Angus Reid Institute, https://angusreid.org/cabinet-performance/.
52 See, for example, "PSAC President Calls on Trudeau to Get Involved in Negotiations," CBC, 26 April 2023.
53 Neil Nevitte's book, *The Decline of Deference: Canadian Value Change in Cross-National Perspective*, published by the University of Toronto Press in 1996, resonates to this day.
54 Christopher Dornan, "Bill Fox Digs into How Social Media, Online Journalism Have Completely Transformed the Way We Do Politics," *Hill Times*, 19 December 2022.
55 Ibid.

CHAPTER EIGHT

1 Canada, "Guidance for Deputy Ministers" (Ottawa, Privy Council Office, undated).
2 Christopher Dunn, "The Role of Deputy Ministers in Canadian Government," in *The Handbook of Canadian Public Administration* (Don Mills: Oxford University Press, 2010), chap. 10.
3 Heintzman, "Establishing the Boundaries of the Public Service: Towards a New Moral Contract," 107.
4 See Jacques Bourgault and Christopher Dunn, eds., *Deputy Ministers in Canada: Comparative and Jurisdictional Perspectives* (Toronto: University of Toronto Press, 2014).
5 Ibid., 445.
6 Ibid., 446.
7 See, among others, Patrice Dutil and Andrea Migone, "The Time Management Styles of Deputy Ministers in Canada: Towards a Taxonomy," *Canadian Public Administration* 65, no. 3 (2022): 439–56.
8 Jacques Bourgault and Christopher Dunn, "Conclusion: Deputy Ministers in Canada – Evaluation of Deputy Ministers as Archetypal Figures," in Bourgault and Dunn, *Deputy Ministers in Canada*, 429.
9 See, for example, J.L. Granatstein, *The Ottawa Men: The Civil Service Mandarins 1935–1957* (Toronto: Rock's Mills Press, 2015).
10 I am thinking here of clerk of the Privy Council Michael Wernick resigning because he decided that opposition parties "don't trust him." Opposition MPs charged that he "overstepped his role" in managing the SNC-Lavalin affair. Kevin Lynch, a former clerk of the Privy Council, as chair of the SNC-Lavalin Board, had contacted Wernick to influence the

government's decision on "a deferred prosecution agreement" for the firm. See, "Privy Council Clerk Michael Wernick resigns after controversy over SNC-Lavalin testimony," *National Post*, 18 March 2019; and "SNC-Lavalin Chair Kevin Lynch sought Michael Wernick's help to secure deferred prosecution agreement," *The Globe and Mail*, 6 March 2019.

11 Ted Falk, MP, "Canada's Bureaucracy Is Broken," www.tedfalk.ca, 8 July 2022.
12 See, among others, Andrew Griffith, "Disconnect Between Political Priorities and Service Delivery," *Hill Times*, 14 July 2022.
13 See, for example, Michael Wernick, "The Pull and Push of the Centre That Haunts the Public Service," *Policy Options*, 24 January 2023.
14 John L. Manion, *How Lucky I've Been*.
15 Nandor Dreisziger, "The Biggest Welcome Ever: The Toronto Tories, the Ottawa Liberals and the Admission of Hungarian Refugees to Canada in 1956," *Hungarian Studies Review* 35, no. 1–2 (2008): 57.
16 See, for example, "Record-Breaking Lobbying Activity in November with Discussions about Economy and Federal Budget," *Hill Times*, 3 January 2023, 3.
17 Gordon F. Osbaldeston, *Keeping Deputy Ministers Accountable* (Toronto: McGraw-Hill Ryerson, 1989).
18 Jacques Bourgault, "Federal Deputy Ministers: Serial Servers Looking for Influence," in *Deputy Ministers in Canada*, eds. Bourgault and Dunn, 371.
19 See, https://geds-sage.gc.ca/en/GEDS/?pgid=016&fid=11, undated.
20 Bourgault, "Federal Deputy Ministers," 371 and 377.
21 Consultation with a former federal government employee, 2 September 2014.
22 James Q. Wilson, *Bureaucracy: What Government Agencies Do and Why They Do It* (New York: Basic Books, 1999), 57.
23 Michael Hatfield, "Public Service Not Irrelevant," *Hill Times*, Ottawa, 16 June 2014, 13.
24 *Honouring Canada's Legacy in Afghanistan: Responding to the Humanitarian Crisis and Helping People Reach Safety: Report of the Special Committee on Afghanistan* (Ottawa: House of Commons, June 2022, 44th Parliament, 1st Session), 26
25 Brian Macdonald quoted in "Parliamentary Committee Report Slams Government's Handling of Afghan Refugee Crisis," *ctvnews.ca*, 10 June 2022.
26 *Honouring Canada's Legacy in Afghanistan*, 26.

27 Mark Considine, "The End of the Line? Accountable Governance in the Age of Networks, Partnerships, and Joined-Up Services," *Governance* 15, no. 1 (January 2022): 22.
28 David Mitchell and Ryan Conway, "From the Deputy Shuffle to the Deputy Churn: Keeping the Best and Brightest in Ottawa," *Policy Options,* 1 May 2011.
29 Jacques Bourgault and Christopher Dunn, "Conclusion," in Bourgault and Dunn, *Deputy Ministers in Canada,* 438.
30 Alex Himelfarb, "The Intermestic Challenge: Notes for an Address at the APEX Symposium 2002" (Ottawa: Privy Council Office, 5 June 2002), 5.
31 "Top Federal Government Official Casts Doubt on Ontario's Ring of Fire Mining Development," *The Globe and Mail,* 29 November 2002.
32 See, among others, Donald J. Savoie, *Breaking the Bargain: Public Servants, Ministers, and Parliament* (Toronto: University of Toronto Press, 2003).
33 See among others, Bourgault and Dunn, eds., *Deputy Ministers in Canada*; Jacques Bourgault and Stéphane Dion, *Profile of Deputy Ministers in the Government of Canada 1867–1988* (Ottawa: Canadian Centre for Management Development, 1999).
34 See, for example, Canada, *Guidance for Deputy Ministers* (Ottawa: Privy Council Office, 2018), 11–12.
35 "The Responsibilities and Accountabilities of Deputy Ministers – Chapter 5," in *Restoring Accountability; Recommendations* (Ottawa: Commission of Inquiry into the Sponsorship and Advertising Activities, 2006), 106.
36 Bourgault, "Federal Deputy Ministers," 390.
37 "There's No Fixed Playbook: Deputy Minister Retreat," *Hill Times,* 23 January 2023.
38 Canada, "Deputy Minister Champions" (Ottawa: November 2022).
39 David E. Smith, "Clarifying the Doctrine of Ministerial Responsibility as It Applies to the Government and Parliament of Canada," Ottawa, Report of the Commission of Inquiry into the Sponsorship Program and Advertising Activities, vol. 1, 113.
40 Quoted in Louis C. Gawthrop, *Public Service and Democracy: Ethical Imperatives for the 21st Century* (New York: CQ Press, 1998).
41 J.E. Hodgetts, "Royal Commission and Public-Service Reform: Personal Reflections," *Canadian Public Administration* 50, no. 4 (2007): 527.
42 James Q. Wilson, *Bureaucracy,* and Michael Blumenthal quoted in Wilson, *Bureaucracy,* 155 and 197.
43 Consultations with a senior official with the Government of Canada, Ottawa.

44 Canada, "Performance Management Program for Deputy Ministers, Associate Deputy Ministers, and Individuals Paid in the GX Range," (Ottawa: Privy Council Office, undated).
45 "Unjustifiable: $190 Million in Bonuses to Public Servants," *National Post*, 27 September 2022.
46 "Steep Bonuses for DND Execs a Real Head-Scratcher," *Hill Times*, 11 August 2023.
47 Bourgault, "Federal Deputy Ministers," 367.
48 Ibid., 370.
49 Canada, *Salary Ranges and Maximum Performance Pay for Governor in Council Appointees*.
50 Bourgault, "Federal Deputy Ministers," 367.
51 Kathryn May, "The Achilles Heel of the Federal Public Service Gives Out Again with Passport Fiasco," *Policy Options*, 29 June 2022.
52 Arthur Kroeger, *Deputy Ministers Coming from Outside the Public Service: Challenges and Lessons Learned* (Ottawa: CCMD, 2004).
53 Themrise Khan, "The Incoherence of Canada's Refugee Policy," *Policy Options*, 19 January 2022.
54 See, for example, "Veterans Are Not Getting the Services They Need," *Hill Times*, 13 March 2023.

## CHAPTER NINE

1 Quoted in David Zussman, "Stephen Harper and the Federal Public Service: An Uneasy and Unresolved Relationship," in *The Harper Factor: Assessing a Prime Minister's Policy Legacy*, ed. Jennifer Ditchburn and Graham Fox (Montreal: McGill-Queen's University Press, 2016), 55.
2 "Trudeau Blames CSIS for Not Informing MP Chong about Being Target of China," *The Globe and Mail*, 3 May 2023, 1.
3 Andrew Coyne makes this point in "Everything Isn't Broken. The Government Is," *The Globe and Mail*, 1 February 2023, A6.
4 Peter Aucoin, "New Political Governance in Westminster Systems: Impartial Public Administration and Management Performance at Risk," *Governance* 24, no. 2 (2012), 189.
5 For a more thorough discussion of this point, see Donald J. Savoie, *What Is Government Good At? A Canadian Answer* (Montreal: McGill-Queen's University Press, 2015).
6 "Quoted in PBO Blasts CRA for Saying 'Not Worth The Effort' to Recover $15 billion in COVID Overpayments," *National Post*, 8 February 2023.

7 "Margaret Atwood on Bill C-11 and Why Bureaucrats Shouldn't Tell Authors What to Write," *The Globe and Mail*, 3 February 2023.
8 See, for example, "Trudeau Needs to Put a Stop to Airport Chaos," *True North*, 8 June 2022.
9 "Qu'est-ce qui cloche avec la machine fédérale?" *La Presse*, 3 July 2022. Please note that I translated Mr Tellier's observation.
10 Canada, "Prime Minister Announces New Task Force to Improve Government Services for Canadians," www.pm.gc.ca, 29 June 2022.
11 See, among others, Campbell Clark, "A Warning Sign of Government Bloat," *The Globe and* Mail, 20 January 2022.
12 Cal Bricker, "Not Just McKinsey: How Government Learned to Stop Worrying and Love Consultants," *The Globe and Mail*, 2 February 2023; and ibid. See also, Canada, *Supplementary Estimates (CC) 2022–23* (Ottawa: Office of the Parliamentary Budget Officer, 2022).
13 "ArriveCAN Appears Illogical and Inefficient, Says Trudeau," www.globalnews.ca, 24 January 2023
14 "ArriveCAN's $54-Million Price Tag Outrageous Tech Leaders Say," *The Globe and Mail*, 7 October 2022.
15 "Canada's Border Agency Launches Full Review after Listing Wrong Company in $1.2 Million ArriveCAN Contract," *The Globe and Mail*, 22 October 2022.
16 *Top of Mind: Answering the Call, Adapting to Change* (Ottawa and Antigonish: Institute on Governance and the Brian Mulroney Institute of Government, 2022), 21.
17 Tait, "A Strong Foundation: Report on the Task Force on Values and Ethics in the Public Service, 1996," 48.
18 Population of the Federal Public Service by Executive Level, www.canada.ca/en/treasury-board-secretariat/services/innovation/human-resources-statistics, 31 March 2022.
19 "Federal Department Fired 49 Employees Who Received CERB Though Employed," *National Post*, 2 February 2023.
20 See, among others, Donald J. Savoie, *What Is Government Good At? A Canadian Answer* (Montreal: McGill-Queen's University Press, 2015), 204.
21 *Report 4-Information Technology, Shared Services* (Ottawa: Office of the Auditor General, Fall 2015).
22 "John Ivison: If Anita Anand Wants Government Savings, She Can Try the Reckless Department She Ran," *National Post*, 20 September 2023.
23 Robert D'Aoust, *Federal Public Management Reforms Consolidated Views and Results* (Ottawa: University of Ottawa, Executive in Residence, July 2020), 3 and 4.

24 See, for example, Ben Worthy, *The Politics of Freedom of Information: How and Why Governments Pass Laws That Threaten Their Power* (Manchester: Manchester University Press, 2017).
25 "Commons Law Clerk Says Government Went Too Far in Redacting WE Charity Documents," CBC, 27 August 2020.
26 See, for example, Savoie, *What Is Government Good At?*, chap. 6.
27 "Secretive Bureaucrats Tight-Lipped on Two Prime Ministerial Promises," *Hill Times*, 10 February 2023, 7.
28 "Government Official Warns Subordinates to Be Careful about What They Write on McKinsey Audits," CBC News, 9 February 2023.
29 "Federal Comptroller-General Rebuked for Advising – Be Careful What You Write Down – in McKinsey Contract Review," *The Globe and Mail*, 10 February 2023.
30 Giles Gherson, "Public Opinion," *This Morning*, CBC Broadcast, 3 December 1997.
31 "Contract Specifies That Consultant Leave No Paper Trail in Federal Offices," www.macleans.ca, 10 October 2005.
32 Consultations with a deputy minister, Ottawa, 11 June 2006.
33 Canada, *Analysis of Performance Budgeting During Recent Fiscal Consolidation* (Ottawa: Office of the Parliamentary Budget Officer, 2014), 1.
34 Ibid., 4.
35 *Message from the Auditor General—2016 Fall Report of the Auditor General* (Ottawa: Office of the Auditor General, November 2016).
36 See, among others, "List of Scandals and Missteps Involving Canada's Trudeau," Reuters, 19 September 2019; and "Roxham: The Little Country Road that became a Big Political Headache for the Trudeau Government," CBC, 25 February 2023.
37 See, among others, Dina Denham Smith, "Are You Too Responsible?," *Harvard Business Journal*, 20 July 2022.
38 These attributes are in line with Max Weber's work on bureaucracy.
39 Based on information provided to the author by Brent White, a former auditor with the New Brunswick Auditor General's Office, in an email dated 22 June 2022.
40 Richard Dicerni, former deputy minister of Industry Canada, made this point in discussions I had with him, various dates.
41 Karen Hogan, quoted in "Canada's Parliamentary Watchdogs Struggle for More Financial Independence," *Policy Options*, 29 April 2022.
42 Paul Thomas, quoted in Kathryn May, "Canada's Parliamentary Watchdogs Struggle for More Financial Independence," *Policy Options*, 22 April 2022.

43 See, among others, Kathryn May, ibid.
44 "Ethics Commissioner Calls for Mandatory Ethics Training for All Senior Liberals After New Breach," *National Post*, 14 February 2023.
45 Donald J. Savoie, *Whatever Happened to the Music Teacher* (Montreal: McGill-Queen's University Press, 2013), 248.
46 James Q. Wilson made a similar observation about the US government in his "The 1994 John Gaus Lecture: Reinventing Public Administration," *Political Science and Politics*, December 1994, 671.
47 R.D. Behn, *Rethinking Democratic Accountability* (Washington, DC: Brookings Institution, 2001), 3.
48 Mark Bovens, "Public Accountability," in *The Oxford Handbook of Public Management*, ed. Evan Ferlie, Laurence E. Lynn Jr, and Christopher Pollitt (Oxford: Oxford University Press, 2007), 190.
49 "Federal Comptroller-General Rebuked."
50 B. Guy Peters and Jon Pierre, "Governance Without Government? Rethinking Public Administration," *Journal of Public Administration Research and Theory*, vol. 8 (1998), 232.
51 Kathryn May, "Canadians Lack Faith in Upper Ranks of Public Service: Survey," *Ottawa Citizen*, 7 September 2016; and Canada, 2017 Public Service Employee Survey (Ottawa: Treasury Board Secretariat, 2017).
52 Christopher Pollitt and Geert Bouckaert, *Public Management Reform: A Comparative Analysis into the Age of Austerity* (Oxford: Oxford University Press, 2017), 260–3.
53 Kevin Lynch and Jim Mitchell, "Instead of Adding New Programs, Ottawa Should Focus on Proper Delivery of the Ones It Has," *The Globe and Mail*, 11 January 2023.
54 Ibid.
55 Kevin Lynch, "Why Aren't Things Working as They Should? Policy Execution Is Key," *The Globe and Mail*, 22 April 2022.
56 As we saw earlier, some of these questions have also been asked by a clerk of the Privy Council Office and retired federal public servants.

### CHAPTER TEN

1 *Canadian Public Opinion on Governance and the Public Service* (Ottawa: The Environics Institute and the Institute on Governance, 2014), 12.
2 Kathryn May, "Canada Needs a Royal Commission to Fix Problems with the Federal Public Service," *Policy Options*, 6 December 2022.
3 Elizabeth Knowles, *The Oxford Dictionary of Quotations* (Oxford: Oxford University Press, 2001).

4   Michael Wernick, "These Practical Ideas Can Help Reinvigorate Canada's Public Sector," *The Globe and Mail*, 11 February 2023.
5   Canada, *Departmental Plan 2022–2023* (Ottawa: Canada School of Public Service, 2022).
6   "'New Normal' Provides Challenge to Public Sector's 'Strategic Policy Review,' Say Experts, as Feds Look to Save $6-Billion by 2026–27," *Hill Times*, 13 February 2023.
7   Wernick, "These Practical Ideas Can Help Reinvigorate Canada's Public Sector."
8   Brian Tobin told CBC that I had misread the situation but also told me in a conversation at the Halifax airport that my assessment was correct.
9   Eddie Goldenberg, *The Way It Works: Inside Ottawa* (Toronto: Penguin, 2005).
10  The two are Kevin Lynch and Paul Tellier. See also Jeffrey Simpson, *The Friendly Dictator* (Toronto: McClelland and Stewart, 2001), and Kevin Lynch and Jim Mitchell, "Instead of Adding New Programs, Ottawa Should Focus on Proper Delivery of the One It Has," *The Globe and Mail*, 22 February 2023.
11  Justin Trudeau made such a commitment during the 2015 general election campaign.
12  Gordon Robertson, "The Prime Minister and the Executive Power," a paper presented to the Canadian Study of Parliament Group – 1999 Fall Conference, mimeo, 5.
13  Quoted in Jennifer Ditchburn, "Duffy Trial Sheds Light on PMO Power, Hand-Holding of MPs," *Maclean's*, 26 August 2015, http://www.macleans.ca/politics/ottawa-duffy-trial-sheds-light-on-pmo-power-hand-holding-of-mps/.
14  Peter Harder made this observation in a conversation I had with him in 2016.
15  John A. Hayes, *Value for Money*, mimeo, April 1986, 3.
16  Ibid., 4.
17  See, among others, Graham T. Allison, "Public and Private Management: Are They Fundamentally Alike in All Unimportant Respects?," paper presented at the Public Management Research Conference (Washington, DC: Brookings Institution, November 1979).
18  Daniel J. Caron, Evert Lindquist, Robert P. Shepherd, "Critical Considerations for the Future of the Public Service," *Policy Options*, 14 February 2023.
19  Robert P. Shepherd, "Internal Governmental Performance and Accountability in Canada: Insights and Lessons for Post-Pandemic

Improvement," *Canadian Public Administration* 62, no. 3 (September 2022), 522.

20 See, among many others, Julie Zhuo, *The Making of a Manager: What to Do When Everyone Looks to You* (Edmonton: Portfolio Publishing, 2019).

21 Marcus Buckingham and Curt Coffman, *First, Break All the Rules* (New York: Galleys Press, 2016).

22 See, among others, Donald J. Savoie, *Court Government and the Collapse of Accountability in Canada and the United Kingdom* (Toronto: University of Toronto Press, 2008).

23 V. Peter Harder, "The Public Service of Canada: A Key Partner in Productivity," presentation to the SUMMA Forum on Productivity, Ottawa, 15 March 1999, 3 (mimeo).

24 Jonathan Malloy, "The Search for Merit Is Killing Canada's Civil Service," *The Globe and Mail*, 10 September 2002 and updated 28 April 2018.

25 Canada, *Restoring Accountability – Recommendations – Chapter 4* (Ottawa: Commission of Inquiry into the Sponsorship Program and Advertising Activities, 2006), 67.

26 "Bernardo's Prison Transfer Report Offers Rare Insights into Killer's Life Behind Bars," CBC, 22 July 2023.

27 See, for example, Sharon Sutherland, "The Al-Mashat Affair: Administrative Accountability in Parliamentary Institutions," *Canadian Public Administration* 34, no. 4 (Winter 1991): 395.

28 See, for example, Andrew Griffith, "Disconnect between political priorities and service delivery," *Hill Times*, 14 July 2022.

29 J.E. Hodgetts, "Royal Commissions and Public-Service Reform: Personal Reflections," *Canadian Public Administration* 50, no. 4 (December 2007): 538.

30 "PMO E-Mails Reveal Frustration with Public Health Agency as Pandemic Worsened," *The Globe and Mail*, 1 February 2021.

31 This dates back to 2006 and all indications are that the situation has deteriorated in recent years. See "Stop Talking about Fixing Government: Just Do It, Public Says," *Ottawa Citizen*, 21 April 2006.

32 "Forgive Phoenix Pay System Overpayments: Union," *Telegraph Journal*, 1 March 2023.

33 "Auditor General Says $500-Million in Overpayments to Civil Servants Needs to Be Collected," *The Globe and Mail*, 27 October 2022.

34 Canada, *Parliament and Government* (Ottawa: Commission of Inquiry into the Sponsorship Program and Advertising Activities – Chapter 4 of Restoring Accountability: Recommendations, 2006), 6.

35 Peter Mazereeuw, "Politics This Morning: PBO Takes Stock of 2023 and Beyond," *Hill Times*, 3 March 2023.
36 "Ottawa's Pandemic Hiring Boom Adds Billions to Federal Payroll," cbc.ca, 24 October 2022.
37 John Greenaway makes this point in his "British Conservatism and Bureaucracy," *History of Political Thought*, vol. XIII, no. 1 (1992), 129.
38 Canada, Royal Commission on Financial Management and Accountability, *Final Report* (Ottawa: Minister of Supply and Services, 1979), 57.
39 Downs, *Inside Bureaucracy*, 4.
40 "Katie Telford, Long-Serving Chief of Staff, Is the Last Woman Standing in Justin Trudeau's Inner Circle," *The Globe and Mail*, 16 September 2023, A13.

CHAPTER ELEVEN

1 Donald J. Savoie, *The Politics of Public Spending in Canada* (Toronto: University of Toronto Press, 1990).
2 See, among others, Canada, *The Role and Structure of the Privy Council Office* (Ottawa: Privy Council Office, October 1997), 1.
3 Luc Juillet and Ken Rasmussen, *Defending a Contested Ideal* (Ottawa: University of Ottawa Press, 2017), 99.
4 See, for example, *Canadian Public Opinion on Governance and the Public Service* (Toronto: The Environics Institute, 2014).
5 Paul Cairney, *Understanding Public Policy Theories and Issues* (New York: Red Globe Press, 2019).
6 Andrew Dunsire, Christopher Hood, and Meg Huby, *Cutback Management in Public Bureaucracies: Popular Theories and Observed Outcomes in Whitehall* (Cambridge: Cambridge University Press, 1989), 34.
7 Consultation with a senior federal public servant, Ottawa.
8 Consultation with Hon. Bernard Valcourt, Moncton, NB, 5 July 2011. The consultation was in French and I translated his points.
9 John D. Dilulio Jr, "Principled Agents: The Cultural Bases of Behavior in a Federal Government Bureaucracy," *Journal of Public Administration Research and Theory* 4 (1994): 282.
10 See, for example, Richard A. Epstein, "The Independence of Judges: The Uses and Limitations of Public Choice Theory," BYU *Law Review* 827 (1990): 830.
11 I have seen firsthand evidence of public servants carrying out selfless acts. One only has to look at federal health care workers during the COVID-19 pandemic to see evidence of this.

12 See, for example, John D. Dilulio Jr, "Principled Agents: The Cultural Bases of Behavior in a Federal Government Bureaucracy," *Journal of Public Administration Research and Theory* 4, no. 3 (1994): 277–318.
13 It is not possible to do justice to the Neo Institute in a few short paragraphs. For an excellent overview, see W. Richard Scott, *Institutions and Organizations: Ideas, Interests and Identities* (Thousand Oaks, CA: Sage Publications, 2013).
14 Public servants point to the media to explain falling trust in their institution. See, for example, Basyouni Hamada and Davis Vallesi, "Determinants of Journalists' Trust in Public Institutions: A Macro and Micro Analysis Across 67 Countries," *Journalism Practice*, 27 February 2023, 2–12.
15 When Michael Sabia was appointed deputy minister of Finance, it was widely believed that he would drive an economic growth agenda, given his experience in the private sector. The media now report that "he has not been able to deliver that agenda." See, "Michael Sabia Was Greeted as a Game Changer as Canada's Deputy Finance Minister. A Year Later, He Has Made Little Headway," *The Globe and Mail*, 31 December 2021.
16 I borrowed this view from John Hoskyns, *Just in Time: Inside the Thatcher Revolution* (London: Autumn, 2000).
17 This is not a Canada-only phenomenon. See, for example, Fernando Kleiman, Marijn Janssen, Sebastiaan Meijer, and Sylvia JT Jansen, "Changing Civil Servants' Behaviour Concerning the Opening of Governmental Data: Evaluating the Effect of a Game by Comparing Civil Servants' Intentions Before and After a Game Intervention," *International Review of Administrative Sciences* 88, no. 4 (2020): 921–2.
18 *Organization for Policy Development* (Ottawa: Treasury Board, Organization Policy Group, 28 March 1984), 16.
19 "Review of Democratic Processes Needed as Ministerial Responsibility Changes: Experts," *National News Watch*, 9 April 2023.
20 Ruth Hubbard and Gilles Paquet, *The Black Hole of Public Administration* (Ottawa: University of Ottawa Press, 2010), 43.
21 Ralph Heintzman, *Renewal of the Federal Public Service: Toward a Charter of Public Service* (Ottawa: Canada 2020, 2020), 20
22 Andrew Dunsire and Christopher Hood, *Cutback Management in Public Bureaucracies: Popular Theories and Observed Outcomes in Whitehall* (Cambridge: Cambridge University Press, 1989), 42.
23 Dunsire and Hood make the same point in ibid., 94.
24 See, among others, Peter Aucoin and Donald J. Savoie, eds., *Managing Strategic Change: Learning from Program Review* (Ottawa: Canadian Centre for Management Development, 1998).

25  See, for example, Albert Breton, *The Economic Theory of Representative Government* (London: Macmillan, 1974).
26  Charles H. Levine, "More on Cutback Management: Hard Questions for Hard Times," *Public Administration Review* 39, no. 2 (1979): 179.
27  It is a valid point. See, for example, *The Canadian Prison System: A Broken Institution* (Kingston: John Howard Society of Canada, 19 May 2021).
28  See, among many others, Carroll and Siegel, *Service in the Field*.
29  See, for example, *Canadian Public Opinion on Governance and the Public Service–2014*, 17.
30  Richard Dicerni quoted in Ralph Heintzman, "Border-Crossing: The PBO, PCO and the Boundary of the Public Service," *Canadian Public Administration* 59, no. 3 (September 2016): 370.
31  Thomas S. Axworthy and Julie Burch, "Crisis in the Ontario and Federal Public Services," *Policy Options* 31, no. 3 (2010): 24.
32  "Canadians More Positive about Their Encounters Accessing Services from Cities, Provincial Governments," Angus Reid, 10 June 2022.
33  The survey dates back to 2014 and one can only assume that the numbers have fallen further since, given the number of difficulties the federal government has had recently in delivering services, including, among others, passports and cheques to veterans. See *Canadian Public Opinion on Government and the Public Service–2014*, 11 and 22.

## CHAPTER TWELVE

1  See Ralph Heintzman, *Renewal of the Federal Public Service: Toward a Charter of Public Service* (Ottawa: Canada 2020, 2014).
2  Gordon Robertson, *Memoirs of a Very Civil Servant: Mackenzie King to Pierre Trudeau* (Toronto: University of Toronto Press, 2000).
3  "Anthony Rota Does the Inevitable, and Now Trudeau Must Pick Up the Pieces," *The Globe and Mail*, 27 September 2023, A7. The leader of the Opposition laid blame on the prime minister, his staff, and his government for not vetting Yaroslav Hunka before inviting him to Parliament. See "Trudeau Apologizes after Man Who Fought in Nazi Unit was Praised by Parliamentarians at Zelenskyy Event," CBC, 27 September 2023.
4  See, for example, "Mr. Trudeau Tries Again," *Globe and Mail*, 3 August 1978.
5  "Cabinet Ministers Given Oct. 2 Deadline to Cut $15 Billion from Spending Plans," *Globe and Mail*, 15 August 2023.

6 "Ottawa's Pandemic Hiring Boom Adds Billions to Federal Payroll," CBC, 24 October 2022.
7 Kathryn May, "Public Service Will Swell to 409,000 in Five Years, PBO Says," *Policy Options*, 21 November 2022.
8 "Making the Tough Calls: Jason Kenney and Kathleen Wynne on the Dying Art of Political Compromise," *The Hub*, 15 August 2023.
9 Veterans waited almost forty weeks for a decision on the first application for disability benefits, "Ottawa Struggling to Deliver Benefits to Disabled Veterans, Vulnerable Populations: AG Report," www.cbc.ca, 3 May 2022.
10 Darrell Bricker made this observation in "There's a Lot of Alienation Going On," *Hill Times*, 21 August 2023.
11 Greg Lyle quoted in ibid.
12 Hon. Jason Kenney quoted in "Making the Tough Calls," *The Hub*, 15 August 2023.
13 Canada, *2022–2023 Estimates* (Ottawa: Treasury Board Secretariat), https://www.canada.ca/en/treasury-board-secretariat/services/planned-government-spending/government-expenditure-plan-main-estimates.html.
14 Canada, *Responsibility in the Constitution* (Ottawa: Privy Council Office, undated), chapter 7, 2.
15 Jean Chrétien, *Straight from the Heart* (Toronto: Key Porter Books, 1985), 18.
16 Murray, *Power, Responsibility, and Agency in Canadian Government*, 26.
17 See chapter 6.
18 Kathryn May, "Cutting $15 Billion from the Public Service Won't Be Hard. But What's Next?" *Policy Options*, 7 September 2023.
19 David Zussman, "Stephen Harper and the Federal Public Service: An Uneasy and Unresolved Relationship," in *The Harper Factor: Assessing a Prime Minister's Policy Legacy*, eds. Jennifer Ditchburn and Graham Fox (Montreal: McGill-Queen's University Press, 2016), 55.
20 See, among others, Heintzman, *Renewal of the Federal Public Service*.
21 Amanda Clarke, "Who's Going to Finally Fix Federal Public Service Management?" *Policy Options*, 12 June 2023.
22 Amanda Clarke points out that federal government executives have "a crippling fear of external scrutiny," quoted in ibid.
23 Quoted in "Feds Bring Down Legislative Hammer on Massive Budget Implementation Bill," *Hill Times*, 4 November 2013, 19.

# INDEX

access to information, 198–9; and defensive values, 62; legislation, 25–6; media and, 148; opposition and, 224; and paper vs oral records, 198–9; transparency and, 62

accountability: and answerability vs responsibility, 18; associate positions and, 185; authority and, 59; and avoiding/diverting blame, 60; boundaries and, 178–9, 185; Canada School of Public Service and, 142, 145–6, 147–8; chain of, 11–12, 40–1, 130–1, 193, 219; changing constitutional modes of, 259; changing relationships and, 11; complexity and, 40–1, 147; consequences of, 205; consultants and, 193; customer vs political, 72; delegation of, 59, 252, 255; democracy and, 218; deputy ministers and, 19, 26, 35, 38–9, 40, 42, 58, 170, 171, 188–9, 225; domination of management of, 11–12; in external vs internal programs, 137; for failures/mistakes, 191; fault line and, 72, 74; in federal-provincial agreements, 22; financial audits and, 216; in financial/human resource management, 224; of front-line public servants, 252; governing from centre and, 200, 219–20; growth of government and, 11; growth of responsibilities and, 11; hierarchy and, 131, 229; homelessness and, 81; impenetrability of, 11–12; for inertia, 226; influence vs, 191; interdepartmental, 137; inward looking and, 18; lack of attention to, 130; lack of clarity in, 59; Leaders' Debates Commission, 147; in machine-like vs policy-coping organizations, 60, 132; management reform and, 198, 206, 207, 217, 221; media and, 41; in minister–deputy minister relationship, 180–1; ministerial responsibility and, 221, 223; in minister–public servant relationship, 60; ministers and, 19, 36–8, 149, 155,

159, 169–70, 188–9, 224–5; for missteps, 138; motivation and, 228, 246; MPs and, 28, 148, 224, 254; mutual deniability and, 221; naming and shaming in, 205–6; new forms of governance and, 207; and new public management, 259; new vocabulary of requirements, 18–19, 42; omnibus bills and, 128; in *Open and Accountable Government*, 25–6; and operations, 13; opposition and, 13, 224, 254; ownership of words/deeds/mistakes and, 190, 259; Parliament and, 19, 24, 26–7, 127, 129, 179, 242, 254, 259; partisan political advisors and, 256; in past, 22; performance management and, 216; PMO advisors and, 24; at point of contact, 89; of policy specialists, 240; political point scoring vs, 200; politician–public servant relationship and, 222–3; postwar, 22; in prime minister–minister relationship, 150; prime ministers and, 13, 26–7, 150, 190–1, 214, 226, 256; in private sector, 149; private sector management and, 15, 16, 40, 41, 85, 259; in public administration vocabulary, 11; public opinion on, 148, 247; of public servants, 57, 58; reinvigoration of requirements, 257, 258; replacement of, 206; responsibility for tasks and, 252; rules/processes, 85–6; shared, 178–9; traditional model, 177, 188–9, 193; and trust, 7,

12–13, 206; as unresolved issue, 206; as upward looking, 206; values and, 227–8; weakening of, 42; whole of government approach and, 219–20, 234; written vs oral records and, 199. *See also* responsibility

*Accountability Act*, 39, 222, 253

accounting officer concept, 39, 58, 60, 181

Afghan refugee crisis, 177–8, 189, 191, 193

Aga Khan affair, 202

agencies, 20, 26, 64; CRA as, 64–5

Anand, Anita, 125

announceables: management reform as, 182; ministers and, 192; poets and, 192; politicians and, 223

anonymity, 37–8, 59, 200, 205, 219, 229, 259

answerability: for failures/mistakes, 191; ministerial accountability vs, 36–7, 58; ministers and, 169; responsibility vs, 18; for words/deeds, 190

Armstrong, Robert, 57

ArriveCAN app, 136–7, 193–4

associate/assistant deputy ministers, 39–40; background, 46; numbers of, 46; senior public servants and, 70

associate positions, 70, 94, 185, 197, 218

Atlantic Canada Opportunities Agency (ACOA), 49

Atwood, Margaret, 192

auditor general (AG): budget, 204; on PPBS, 76; on program evaluation, 86–7; on short-term

contract staffing, 217–18. *See also* Office of the Auditor General (OAG)
Axworthy, Thomas, 130

Bagehot, Walter, 127
"Bankrupt Canada" (*Wall Street Journal*), 111
Barton, Dominic, 145
Bégin, Monique, 164, 166
behaviour: change in patterns of, 227; collective, 233; economistic approach and, 233, 246; effect of changes on, 19; forces shaping, 245–6; of poets vs plumbers, 246; of policy specialists, 237; public choice theory and, 230–2, 246; recent developments and, 234–5; rules and regulations and, 229; theories, 232–4; unions and, 230
benefits, 93–4, 96, 102–3, 143–4, 173, 187, 223
Bernardo, Paul, 219
blame/blaming, 7–8, 16–17; for Afghan refugee crisis, 193; avoidance/diverting of, 60; of "bureaucrats," 29; crises/miscues and, 31; deputy ministers and, 182–3; domination of management of, 11–12; front-line managers and, 245; management of, 191; naming and shaming in, 205; new media and, 205; by opposition, 191; within politician–public servant relationship, 195, 257; of politicians, 15, 196, 207; program review and, 120; senior public servants and, 197; for spending cuts, 106; taking vs accepting, 59–60; and upward delegation, 73. *See also* bureaucracy bashing
Blidook, Kelly, 29
Bloc Québécois, 118
Blueprint 2020, 181
Blumenthal, Michael, 185
Bok, Derek, 54
bond market, 112
Bonn economic summit, 106, 108, 250
boundaries: central agency–department, 174, 175; in central agency–line department relationship, 19; collapse of, 174, 176–7, 200–1, 206, 220, 233; between departments, 131; deputy ministers working within, 175; erasure, and sharing of accountability, 178–9; between federal and provincial governments, 131; importance in public administration, 177; and lack of accountability, 185; between machine-like and policy-coping organizations, 132; between poets and plumbers, 176; and policy/decision making, 176–7; and public choice theory, 233; and reshaping of public service, 174
Bourgault, Jacques, 34, 172, 176, 180
Bourgon, Jocelyne, 59, 119
Boven, Mark, 206
Bragg, John, xii
Brian Mulroney Institute of Government, 194
Brodie, Janine, 161
Brunetta, Frank, 143

Bryce, Robert (Bob), 140, 173, 181, 200, 220, 221
Buck, Keelan, 37–8
budget(s), 18, 68–9; 1995, 111; about, 31; accomplishments vs, 17; adding to, vs cutting, 105–6; balanced, 122, 123; freezes, 112; Harper and, 121; line-item process, 74; new approaches to, 81–2; numbers of staff, 71; omnibus bills, 127–8; PEMS and, 76–7; politicians and, 105; PPBS and, 75–6; program evaluation and, 114; scientific approach to, 114; spending on oversight of, 71; status quo and, 105; statutory items, 68–9; surplus, 122
*Bureaucracy* (Wilson), 73
bureaucracy bashing, 18; barrage of, 214; and defensive values, 62; and inward looking, 46–7, 55, 83; and morale, 46; and organizational culture, 56. *See also* blame/blaming
Butler, Sir Robin, xii–xiii

cabinet: appointments, 150; ministers and, 160; prime ministers and appointments to, 161; status ministers and, 162
cabinet committees, 23–4; partisan political advisors and, 236; PCO and, 79; and PEMS, 77; policy making, 37; and program reviews, 114; streamlining, 79
cabinet government, 25, 164–5, 259
Campbell, Kim, 27
Camp, Dalton, 49–50, 51

Canada Border Services Agency (CBSA), 136–7, 194
Canada Emergency Response Benefit (CERB), 101–2, 195
Canada Mortgage and Housing Corporation, 81
Canada Revenue Agency (CRA): employees receiving CERB inappropriately, 102; managerial mandate, 133–5; New Public Management and, 64–5; number of employees, 26
Canada School of Public Service (formerly Canadian Centre for Management Development), 138–40; accountability and, 142, 145–6, 147–8; behaviour typical of government organizations, 147; and Better Government Fund, 211; budget, 145, 211; *The Canadian Centre for Management Studies*, 138–40; as centre of excellence, 139, 140, 141, 142; establishment of, 138, 141; faculty, 139–41, 142, 143–4; funding, 139, 140; independence, 139, 140; media on, 143–4; as organization serving other public servants, 246; payment for teaching at, 143, 144; performance assessment of, 142, 144–5; renaming, 142; research, 139, 140, 141–2; resources, 142; TBS and, 142, 144, 145–6; as training facility, 144–5
Canada–US Free Trade Agreement, 111, 210
Canadian Heritage, 157, 158
Canadian Intergovernmental Conference Secretariat, 138

Canadian Security Intelligence
  Service (CSIS), 191
capital budgets: cuts to, vs
  operations, 239; spending cuts
  to, vs to operations, 107–8, 126
career officials. *See* public servants
Carroll, Barbara, 100, 133
caucus: ministers and, 151, 160;
  partisan political advisors and,
  236
causes: deputy ministers and, 221;
  mission ministers and, 163–4;
  policy issues and, 221; senior
  public servants and, 234
CBC employee reduction, 122
central agencies: balance of power
  shifting to, 24; boundaries with
  departments, 174, 175;
  challenging work of
  departments/agencies, 203;
  expansion of, 23; information
  demands from, 103; and job
  eliminations, 107; and miscues,
  34; and mission ministers, 166;
  Nielsen Task Force and, 110;
  OAG and, 34; organizational
  structure, 70; patronage
  appointments, 32; and PEMS, 77;
  and policy analysts, 23; and
  policy ministers, 166; and policy
  shaping, 30; and prime ministers,
  30; and program reviews, 87,
  113, 125; program reviews in, vs
  departments, 110; promotion
  through, 23; and red tape, 31–2;
  role of, 20; and service quality,
  133; size of, 22; and spending
  cuts, 107; spending cuts in, vs
  departments, 110. *See also*
  Department of Finance; Prime
Minister's Office (PMO); Privy
  Council Office (PCO)
central agency–line department
  relationship: boundaries
  between, 174, 175; boundaries
  in, 19; challenging by agency in,
  31; changes in, 17, 25;
  deliverology and, 78; information demands in, 23, 134; and
  job elimination, 106; monitoring
  in, 33; policy coordination in,
  32–3; and reports, 134
centralization of power. *See*
  governing from centre
centre of government: collapse of
  boundaries with line departments, 176–7; concentration in,
  228; delegation up to, 249; and
  deputy ministers, 39, 170, 176;
  influence of, 168, 248; involve-
  ment in decisions, 248, 249; and
  media, 168, 250; omnipresence
  of, 249; and policies, 168; and
  policy firefighting, 236; pollsters
  in, 236; strength of, 23
CEOs: decision making, 41; deputy
  ministers compared, 41;
  ministers compared, 149;
  prime ministers compared, 79.
  *See also* private sector
challenge function, 237–8, 246
Charter of Public Service Values,
  257
Charter of Rights and Freedoms,
  183; collective bargaining under,
  92; entrenchment in
  Constitution, 108
Chrétien, Jean, 27, 155; and
  accounting officer concept, 58;
  and cabinet committees, 79; and

GST, 116; and Harris, 120; and Millennium Scholarship Fund, 118; on opposition vs government, 253; program review, 68, 87, 112, 113, 120; spending cuts, 113–19
Civil Service Learning (UK), 145
Clark, Clifford, 173
Clarke, Amanda, 257
Clark, Joe, 53, 108
classification of positions, 94, 207
Clement, Tony, 100, 143
clerk of the Privy Council. *See* Privy Council Office (PCO) clerk
climate change strategy, 12
Co-Investment Fund, 81
collective bargaining: during 2023, 97–8; and benefits, 93; under Charter of Rights and Freedoms, 92; CRA and, 65; deputy ministers and, 183; front-line managers and, 65; and insulation of public sector, 56; introduction of, 91–2; as inward looking, 92–3; legality, 92; managers and, 95; and non-performers, 56, 101; number of units, 65; and organizational culture, 56; and payment as right vs privilege, 91; political parties and, 91; as political vs economic process, 92; in private sector, 92–3; senior managers and, 93; and strikes, 93; suspension of, 93; TBS and, 65
Commissioner of Official Languages, 33
Commission of Inquiry into the Sponsorship Program and Advertising Activities. *See* Gomery Commission (Commission of Inquiry into the Sponsorship Program and Advertising Activities
*Conflict of Interest Act,* 26
consultants: and accountability, 193; and ArriveCAN app, 136; costs of, 17; numbers of, 65; and service delivery, 133, 208; spending on, 65, 193; variety of, 65
controversies/crises: avoidance of, 252; and blame game, 31; debureaucratization and, 31; deputy ministers and, 180, 182; extra staff and, 80; line departments and, 37; media and, 180; minister–deputy minister relationship and, 40; ministerial responsibility and, 36; and ministers, 37; and policy firefighting, 236; politicians and, 56; responsibility vs, 252–3. *See also* missteps/mistakes; scandals
Copps, Sheila, 29
Coutts, Jim, 150
COVID-19 pandemic: and "699" public service leave, 95; and CERB, 101–2, 195; health workers during, 246; and hybrid work arrangements, 173–4; and new spending, 123; new staff to deal with, 250; and passports delay, 7–8; problems arising from, 193; return to office vs remote work after, 96–7; speed of implementation of measures, 252; support programs, 90–1
Craft, Jonathan, 31
Crosbie, John, 108

Crossman, Richard, 53
Crown corporations: number of, 26; privatization of, 110; role, 20; Second World War and, 20
cutbacks: and behaviour, 223; and blue-collar workers, 239; in regional vs NCR operations, 239–40; unions and, 223. *See* human resource cuts; spending cuts

De Bané, Pierre, 150, 186
debt, public, 106, 112, 124, 251
decision making: centralization of, 208, 213, 217; centre of government and, 248, 249; by CEOs, 41; collapsed boundaries and, 176–7; collective, 208; decentralization of, 32; deputy ministers and, 183–4; evidence-based, 87–8; "ideal type" public servant and, 230–1; incremental, 183–4; in minister-deputy minister relationship, 180–1; politicization of, 40; as top-down, 177; upward delegation in, 226; upward vs downward, 202
deficit: elimination, 115; Harper and, 122; political parties and, 112; tax increases and, 108; J. Trudeau and, 122, 123
delegation: of accountability, 59, 252, 255; to centre of government, 249; deputy ministers on, 202; to front-line managers, 44, 65; of machinery of government issues, 21; new public management and, 64–5; program managers and, 133; to public servants, 57; upward, 73, 133, 183, 202, 226, 241, 249
deliverology, 77–9, 181, 182, 251
*Departmental Act,* 180
Department of External Affairs, 21
Department of Finance: and bond market, 112; challenging programs and spending, 203; and desirability vs feasibility, 146; executives in, 70; human/financial resources, 239; minister's responsibilities, 71; organizational structure, 70–2; and PEMS, 77; poets staffing, 71; power/prestige of, 238–9; and program reviews, 71–2; and service of public debt, 106; and TBS, 71–2
Department of Fisheries and Oceans, 132
Department of National Defence: bonuses awarded in, 186; spending increase, 121
Department of Regional Economic Expansion (DREE), Council on Regional Development, 107
deputy minister–line department relationship: changes in, 188; and complexity of departmental organization, 39–40; management in, 38, 159–60, 180–1, 182; pull toward centre vs, 184
deputy ministers (DMs): and accountability, 19, 37, 38–9, 40, 42, 58, 170, 171, 188–9, 225; as accounting officers, 26; agenda, 40, 159, 172, 214–15; associate/assistant, 39–40, 46, 70; backgrounds, 34–5, 46, 176, 179,

187–8, 237, 240; and blame game, 182–3; and "bloated bureaucracy," 215; boundaries and, 175, 176–7; and causes, 221; centre of government and, 39, 170, 176; changes in environment, 174–5; and collective bargaining, 183; committees, 184; constraints upon, 183; and controversies/crises, 180, 182; and decision making, 183–4; on delegation of issues, 202; departmental management, 180–1; expectations of, 180; and financial/human resource reductions, 201; former public servants as, 34–5; in golden years of public service, 173; horizontal issues and, 184; HR-focused, 172; and human resource management, 183; and judicial activism, 183; literature on, 172; and lobbying, 173; in machinery of government, 38; and management reform measures, 179; managerial, 172; mandate letters, 186; and media, 41, 171, 172; *ménage à quatre* management, 177; numbers of, 46; and Parliament, 39; in partisan political environment, 40; and partisan staff, 174; PCO and, 38–9, 171; PCO clerk and, 176, 186–7, 230, 248–9, 256; pensions, 173, 187; performance assessment, 176, 186–7; poets as, 175; and policy, 38, 40, 52, 182, 188; policy specialists/poets and, 235, 237, 252; policy work and promotion to, 240; prime ministers and, 38, 80, 168; private sector executives compared, 41, 183, 188; and program reviews, 114; promotion through departmental ranks to, 179; provincial vs federal, 172; and Public Accounts Committee, 225; responsibilities, 38–9; retired, 186; retreats, 184; roles, 171, 172; salaries, 187; and senior public servants, 53–4; special assignments, 184; subject expertise, 35; tenure, 34–5, 175–6, 179, 237; time allocation, 172; turnover, 34–5, 221; upward delegation, 183; and whole of government approach, 187. *See also* minister–deputy minister relationship

Dewar, Bev, 54
Dicerni, Richard, 73, 133
Diefenbaker, John, and civil service pay increase, 91
Dion, Stéphane, 150
Docherty, David, 28–9
Dodge, David, 111
Doerr, Audrey, *The Machinery of Government in Canada*, 39–40
Dornan, Christopher, 169
Downs, Anthony, 4
Dreisziger, Nandor, 174–5
Dunn, Christopher, 172, 180
Dutil, Patrice, 172
Duxbury, Linda, 98

École nationale d'administration (ENA) (France), 145
Economic Action Plan (Harper government), 121
*Economist*: on British civil service, 47; on liberal democracy, 14

economistic approach, 233, 239, 246
efficiency: audits, 122–3; line departments and, 112–13; Macron on lack of, 3; of operations, 226; outside consultants and, 65; in private sector, 226, 254; size of public sector vs, 208; spending and, 65, 208
Employment and Social Development Canada (ESDC), 101–2, 132, 135–6, 137, 192
Epp, Jake, 163
Estimates: MPs and, 127, 128; opposition review of, 224; Parliament and, 259; parliamentary committees and, 128
Ethics Commissioner, 204
executives: associate positions, 197; bonuses, 195; and difficult decisions in human resource management, 104; in Finance vs line departments, 70; numbers of, 68, 196–7; ownership of words/deeds/mistakes, 214; in PCO vs line departments, 70; in regional vs NCR offices, 132–3. *See also* associate positions; CEOs; deputy ministers (DMs); senior public servants
exempt staff, 25, 52, 151–2. *See also* partisan political advisors
expenditure budget(s). *See* budget(s)
expertise: balance in appointments vs, 29; cabinet appointments vs, 29; and consultants, 65; deputy ministers and, 35; and Estimates, 165; MP turnover vs, 29; personal leadership vs, 165; of policy ministers, 165; politicians and, 29; politicization vs, in policy advice, 32

failures: accountability for, 191; media and, 244; PCO clerk's annual report and, 66; program, 207; in program/service delivery, 193; responsibility for, 5; successes vs, 5; understanding reasons for, 5; and visibility, 60. *See also* success(es)
Falk, Ted, 173
fault line: customer vs political accountability and, 72; between poets and plumbers, 18, 72, 73; between senior and front-line public servants, 74; upward delegation and, 73; and values, 72
*Federal Accountability Act*, 39, 222–3
Federal Executive Institute (US), 145
federal government: agencies, 26, 64; boundaries between provincial and, 131; Canadians' relations with, 258; citizens' concerns and, 3; cost of, 68–72; growth in, 22; machine-like organizations, 131–2; number of employees, 64; number of organizations within, 26, 64; outside experts in, 65; overload problem, 252; policy-coping organizations, 131–2; in postwar period, 6; role, 230; trust in, 3. *See also* machinery of government; size/growth of government

Federal Public Sector Labour Relations and Employment Board, 95
federal public service. *See* public service
Ferguson, Michael, 201
*Financial Administration Act*, 37, 57, 120, 180
*First, Break All the Rules*, 216
Flaherty, James, 121–2
*Food and Drugs Act*, 128
Fox, Bill, 169
Fox, Francis, 185
Fraser, Jane, 98
Fraser, Sheila, 127, 130, 131, 259
Freeland, Chrystia, 123
French, Richard, 79
front-line departments. *See* line departments
front-line managers: and blame game, 245; and collective bargaining, 65; delegation to, 44, 65; depoliticization by, 134; and line-item budgeting process, 74; relevance, 245; responsibility, 243; and service levels, 90; strengthening in program/service delivery, 259. *See also* managers
front-line public servants (plumbers): and accountability, 252; achievements, 246; behaviour vs policy specialists (poets), 246; centralization of power and, 245; emulation of private sector workers, 241; in ESDC internal programs, 135; fault line between policy specialists (poets) and, 18, 72, 73; influence of, 191; inward looking, 242; loss of influence, 245; and new public management, 243; new public management and, 245; numbers of, vs policy specialists (poets), 212; on organizational culture, 242–3; owning mistakes, 244; policy specialists (poets) compared, 67, 234, 241; PPBS and, 75; prison wardens, 241–3; in provincial governments, 69; public opinion of, vs senior public servants, 243; role, 252; and role models, 246; and service levels, 90, 133; success for, 191, 192; and two public services, 234; and unwritten code, 89–90; upward delegation by, 241; and visibility, 191; working from home, 98

Gherson, Giles, 199
Giroux, Yves, 256
Glassco Commission (Royal Commission on Government Organizations), 11, 34, 60, 75, 181, 210, 214, 230
*Globe and Mail*, on Canada School of Public Service, 143–4
Gomery, John, 130
Gomery Commission (Commission of Inquiry into the Sponsorship Program and Advertising Activities), 34, 58, 60, 128
Goodale, Ralph, 155
Good, David, 83–4
Goods and Services Tax (GST), 115–16
governing from centre: and accountability, 200, 219–20; and central concentration of power, 212–13; entrenchment of,

212–13; freeing of managers vs, 232; mission ministers and, 164–5; and movement of influence, 245; and NCR concentration, 245; and policy, 166. *See also* National Capital Region (NCR)
*Governing from the Centre* (Savoie), 212
governments: and large issues, 9; in postwar period, 6–7; during Second World War, 6; trust in, 6–7. *See also* federal government; size/growth of government
growth of government. *See* size/growth of government
growth of public sector. *See* size/growth of public sector
Grube, Dennis, 63
*Guidance for Deputy Ministers* (PCO), 38–9
*Guidelines for Termination or Demotion for Unsatisfactory Performance* (TBS), 99–100
Guilbeault, Steven, 165
Guité, Charles, 119–20
Gulick, Luther, 39, 131

Halligan, John, 31
*The Handbook of Canadian Public Administration*, 171
Harder, Peter, 67
Harper, Stephen: and *Accountability Act*, 253; and accounting officer concept, 58; and across-the-board cuts, 122; and balanced budget, 122, 123; and deficit reduction, 122; Economic Action Plan, 121, 122; and expenditure budget, 121; and management levels, 68; and management reform, 181; and omnibus bills, 127; program reviews, 121, 199; program spending, 121, 122; science position cuts, 88; and size of public service, 121; and spending cuts, 121; and surplus, 122
Harris, Mike, 120
Hartle, Doug, 86
Hatfield, Michael, 177
Hayes, John A., 215
Heintzman, Ralph, 7, 238
Herle, David, 161
hierarchy: and accountability, 131, 229; complexity of, 131; interorganizational networks vs, 205; and inward looking, 51; in line departments, 51; in Roman bureaucracy, 61–2; Weber and, 132
Himelfarb, Alex, 59, 119, 181
Hirschman, Albert, 90
Hodgetts, J.E. "Ted," 11, 185, 221, xiii
Hogan, Karen, 204
homelessness, 80–1
Howe, C.D., 22, 166, 200
Howlett, Michael, 87–8
Hubbard, Paul, 238
human resource cuts, 240; bolts of lightning and, 250; at CBC, 122; central agencies and, 107; central agencies–line department relations and, 106; Chrétien-Martin program review and, 68; cuts to, 240; globalization and, 4; Nielsen Task Force and, 110; program review and, 118; in science, 88

human resource management: accountability in, 224; deputy ministers and, 183; difficult decisions in, 104; by line department managers, 245; patronage vs, 32; politicians and, 214; resource reallocation, 103

Hungarian refugee crisis, 174–5, 177, 189, 191

hybrid work arrangements, 98, 125, 173–4

incompetence: dismissal for, 99, 100–1, 102, 195; inappropriate receipt of CERB, 102; management of, 207; responsibility for, 130; TBS on, 99–100; time theft, 102. *See also* non-performers

Increased Ministerial Authority and Accountability (IMAA), 181

Independent Advisory Board for Senate Appointments for New Brunswick, 9

inflation, 93, 106, 124

information demands, 23, 55, 103, 134

Innovation, Science and Economic Development Canada, 70

Institute on Governance, 142, 194

Institut national du service public (INSP), 145

International Development Research Centre, 138

*Interpretation Act*, 180

inward looking, 17–18, 62–3; and accountability, 18; accounting officer concept and, 60; bureaucracy bashing and, 46–7, 55, 83; career officials and, 10; collective bargaining and, 56, 92–3; hierarchies and, 51; line departments as, 61, 62–3; media and, 63; military command and control model and, 62; ministerial responsibility and, 223; partisan political advisors and, 55, 63; PCO and, 80; politician–public servant relationship and, 235; public opinion and, 54; public servants and, 242; self-protection and, 206; senior public servants and, 60; transparency and, 18, 83; unwritten code and, 222

IT sector, 196

Jenson, Jane, 161
job eliminations. *See* human resource cuts
Johnson, Al, 75, 221
Johnson, Boris, 10
Johnson, Lyndon B., "Great Society," 6
Johnson, Richard, 161
Johnston, Don, 165
John XXIII, pope, 210
Juillet, Luc, 230

Kaufman, Herbert, 87
Kenney, Jason, 250–1
Kent, Tom, 23
Khan, Themrise, 189
King, William Lyon Mackenzie, 27
Kroeger, Arthur, 114

Labelle, Huguette, 221
Lalonde, Marc, 150–1
Lambert, Allen, 140
Lambert Commission (Royal Commission on Financial

Management and Accountability), 11, 19, 34, 36, 60, 76, 181, 225
Lamontagne, Maurice, 162
Lapointe, Ernest, 166
Leaders' Debates Commission, 146–8
LeBlanc, Roméo, 164
Léger public opinion survey, 3
line departments: and across-the-board cuts, 112; assignment of responsibilities to, 21; "bleeding," 131; boundaries between, 131; boundaries with centre of government, 176–7; briefing books, 158; as closed shops, 51; complexity of organization, 39–40; controversies/crises and, 37; culture of secrecy within, 50–1; and doing more with less, 112–13; and efficiency, 112–13, 122–3; executives, 70, 240; financial/human resources, 158, 159; hierarchy in, 51; identification with, 221; as inward looking, 61, 62–3; loss of standing, 175; management, 33, 34, 173–4; managers, and performance evaluation reports, 86–7; military command and control model, 62; ministers and, 153, 157; mission ministers and, 164; as monopoly, 84; numbers of, 21; OAG and, 34; operating budgets, 122; organizational structure, 70; Parliament concentration on answers, 37; performance evaluation in, 63, 86–7; and policy advice, 52; and policy analysts, 23; policy making/shaping, 37, 221; process ministers and, 166, 167–8; program reviews and, 110, 113, 158–9; program/service delivery, 30, 33; role of, 20; self-protection, 83; as silos, 21, 33–4, 42, 50, 61; spending cuts, vs central agencies, 110; spending cuts and, 106–7, 158–9; spending plans, 74; status ministers and, 162; as taking lead on issues, 22; thickness of, 63; and welfare state, 22; and "whiz bang" ideas, 111. *See also* central agency–line department relationship; deputy minister–line department relationship
*Lobbying Act*, 26
lobbyists, 165, 173, 175
local governments, transfer of responsibilities to, 68
looking inward. *See* inward looking
loyalty: to government of day, 192, 230, 244, 255; in minister–deputy minister relationship, 171; in minister–public servant relationship, 229–30; of MPs to party, 28; as paramount, 228; of public servants to government of day, 192
Lutke, Tobias, 61
Lyle, Greg, 251
Lynch, Kevin, 176, 208, 213

MacDonald, Flora, 53
Macdonald Royal Commission, 210
Macdonnell, J.J., 203

MacEachen, Allan, 53–4, 150–1, 166, 168
Machiavelli, Niccolò, 6
machine-like organizations, 12, 132–7; and accountability, 60; plumbers in, 131; political world vs, 54–5
machinery of government: about, 17; agencies focused on internal vs external, 65–6; central agencies in, 30–3; cessation of function, 13–14; changing relationships and, 11; complexity of, 20, 30, 41; delegation of issues, 21; deputy ministers in, 38; four groups comprising, 20; history of, 21–3; "it depends" working of, 41–2; line departments in, 33–41; management of, 56–61; members of Parliament in, 27–8; ministers in, 29–30, 36–8; MPs and, 29, 30; and operations, 17; organizations within, 26–7; overload problem, 42; Parliament and, 20, 21; PCO and, 20–1, 60; PMO and expansion of, 23–4; prime ministers and, 20–1, 27, 226; in private sector, 41; and program reviews, 125; proportion involved in program/service delivery, 251; public servants in, 25–6; Second World War and, 22; J. Trudeau and, 24. *See also* federal government; operations
*The Machinery of Government in Canada* (Doerr), 39–40
Mackasey, Bryce, 168
MacKay, Elmer, 130, 131

Mackenzie, Alexander, 21
Macron, Emmanuel, 3
Malloy, Jonathan, 28, 29, 155–6, 217–18
management: best practices, 256; CCMS and, 139; centrally prescribed rules/regulations, 182; collective bargaining and, 91, 93; decentralization of, 75, 173–4; of line departments, 33, 34, 173–4; media and, 57; opacity of, 56; performance audits/evaluation and, 63, 204; politicians' interest in, 258; politicians and, 56, 57; senior career officials and, 181–2; theory, and location of public servants, 44; up vs down, 72–3; voter attention to, 258. *See also* human resource management; new public management; private sector management
management levels: de-layering of, 68, 197; numbers of, 67–8, 208, 210–12, 218, 230, 256; and numbers of poets, 67; PCO clerks on, 68; responsibility for, 126, 208
management reform(s): accountability and, 198, 206, 207, 217, 221; as announceable vs lasting change, 182; and authority of departments, 217; deputy ministers and, 179; effect of, 217; and financial/human resource levels, 84; Harper government and, 181; of line departments, 33; ministerial responsibility and, 17; opposite effects of, 15; and ownership of words/deeds/

mistakes, 197; PCO clerk's reports and, 197; and politicians, 85, 225; 85; private sector management and, 84–5; senior public servants and, 85; and values, 222
managers: and benefits, 96; and collective bargaining, 95; at CRA, 134–5; and difficult decisions in human resource management, 104; empowerment of, 216, 221; and incompetence, 100; and information demands from central agencies, 103; letting managers manage, 75, 86, 96, 214, 225, 230, 232; and non-performers, 95–6; oversight bodies and, 120; ownership of words/deeds/mistakes, 214; and private sector management, 85, 86; and salary levels, 96. *See also* front-line managers; senior managers
Manion, John (Jack) A., 49–50, 140, 141, 174, 220
Marchand, Jean, 169
Marshall, Geoffrey, 59
Martin, Lawrence, 14
Martin, Pat, 128
Martin, Paul, 27; and government spending, 112, 121; program review, 68, 113–19, 120
Massé, Marcel, 27
May, Kathryn, 96, 250
Mazankowski, Don, 138, 140, 142, 144
McCain, Harrison, 100–1
McKinsey and Company, 199, 206
media: and access to information, 148, 198, 199; and accountability, 41; and ArriveCAN app, 136–7; and blame game, 205; blaming of, 9; and bureaucracy bashing, 18; on Canada School of Public Service, 143–4; centre and, 168, 250; and controversies/crises, 180, 252; on CRA, 65; deputy ministers and, 41, 171, 172; and failures, 244; on failures vs successes, 5; frequency of criticism, 209; "gotcha" journalism, 206; on growth in public service, 57; and inward looking, 63; on management issues, 57; and ministers, 149, 153, 168, 169; mission ministers and, 163; and missteps, 51; opposition and, 224; party candidates and, 160; and performance improvement, 206; on positive vs negative, 233; and prime minister–minister relationship, 153, 162; prime ministers and, 241; provincial premiers and, 154; on public servants, 5; and royal commissions, 210; social, 62, 153, 169, 171, 172; on sponsorship scandal, 119; status ministers and, 162; and success stories, 51; on TBS vs PSAC, 98; and upward delegation, 133; *Wall Street Journal* on Canadian economic situation, 111–12
Meech Lake Accord, 111
members of Parliament (MPs): and accountability, 28, 148, 224; amateurism of, 28–9; constituencies, 29; and estimates, 127, 128; expertise vs cabinet appointments, 29; as former

public servants, 28; and government accountability, 254; loyalty to party, 28; motivation to become, 29; numbers of public servants for each, 21–2; political parties recruitment of, 160; responsibilities, 28; and scrutiny, 29; short-term perspective, 29; time demands, 28; turnover, 29
Mendocino, Marco, 219
merit principle, 32, 45–6, 227, 257, 259
Migone, Andrea, 172
Millennium Scholarship Fund, 118
Miller, Marc, 164
minister–deputy minister relationship: accountability in, 180–1; and controversies/crises, 40; decision making in, 180–1; and departmental projects, 159; disappearance of, 184; DM control of minister in, 175; and Hungarian refugee crisis, 174–5; loyalty in, 171; PCO clerk in, 186–7; policy advice in, 52; program reviews in, 158–9; and spending cuts, 159; weekly meetings, 158–9; working relationship, 153–4
ministerial accountability/responsibility: accounting officer concept and, 58; answerability vs, 36–7; controversies/crises and, 36; doctrine of, 41–2, 197–8, 208, 219; and inward looking, 223; Lambert Commission and, 36; PCO and, 60, 149, 155; PMOs/prime ministers and, 225; in politician–public servant relationship, 59; reform measures and, 17
minister–public servant relationship: accountability in, 60, 169–70; avoidance of addressing shortcomings in, 60; criticism by minister in, 53; loyalty in, 229–30; in *Open and Accountable Government*, 25–6; PCO and, 60; in UK, 53
ministers: and accountability, 19, 36–8, 169, 188–9, 224–5; agenda, 149, 159, 160, 168, 169; and announceables, 192; answerability of, 169; and answerability vs accountability, 58; avoidance of controversies, 252; backgrounds, 27, 161; and cabinet, 151, 160; and caucus, 151, 160; CEOs compared, 149; chiefs of staff to, 168; communications/PR teams, 153; constituencies, 152, 160, 161, 167; control over time, 156–7; crises/controversies and, 37; demotion, 150; as departmental general managers, 159–60; and departments, 153, 157; exempt staff, 52, 151–2; expansion of offices, 55; expertise vs cabinet appointments, 29; families of, 154; influence, 151, 169; long-term perspective for, 237–8; in machinery of government, 36–8; mandate letters, 153, 157, 159; media and, 149, 153, 168, 169; mission, 163–5, 168–9; offices, and demand for briefing material, 9; opposition and,

155–6, 225; organization memberships, 157; and Parliament, 155–6; parliamentary teams and, 153; and partisan politics, 155; partisan staffers and, 151; and PEMS, 77; pet projects, 159; and policy/policies, 158, 165–6; and political parties, 152, 161–2; portfolios and influence, 151; process, 166–8; profiles, 169; and provincial government officials, 154; Question Period attendance, 154, 160; before Second World War, 22; and Senate, 155; senior staff meetings with, 151–2; short-term perspective, 29; status, 162–3; as taking lead on issues, 22; telephone calls, 152; transparency requirements and, 168; travel, 152, 160; and work-life balance, 160. See also minister–deputy minister relationship; minister–public servant relationship

missteps/mistakes: accountability for, 138, 191; central agencies and, 34; dismissal for misconduct, 99; diversion of attention from, 191; front-line public servants (plumbers) owning, 244; machine-like organizations and, 132, 136; media and, 51; ownership of, 192–3, 194; policy-coping organizations and, 136, 138; in prisons, 242. See also controversies/crises

Montfort Hospital, 120
morale, 4, 46, 246
Morneau, Bill, 150, 164
motivation(s): and accountability, 228, 246; lack of knowledge of, 232; public choice theory and, 231; theories and, 233
Mulroney, Brian: and accountability, 16; and ACOA, 49; and cabinet committees, 79; and Canada School of Public Service, 138, 142, 144; and crises, 31; and deficit, 108; and GST, 115–16; and management levels, 67–8; overhaul of bureaucracy, 16; and private sector management practices, 16; program review, 109–11; and public service, 47, 253; and spending cuts, 109–11
Murray, Lowell, 127, 254
Murray Report, 6

Nanos, Nik, 14–15
National Capital Region (NCR): centralization of power, and concentration in, 245; concentration of federal public service in, 67, 119, 218, 251; concentration of public service in, 44; decentralization of policy advisory units from, 227; executives in, vs regional offices, 132–3; policy-coping organizations in, 67; ratio of public servants in vs outside, 257
National Energy Program (NEP), 108, 111
National School of Government (UK), 145

neo-institutional theories, 231, 232, 233
neutrality, political. *See* partisanship, political
Newall, Ted, 140
new public management, 197; accountability requirements vs, 259; and CRA as agency, 64–5; delegation in, 64–5; front-line workers and, 243; and line department workers, 245; and managing up vs down, 73; performance evaluation under, 65; plumbers/front-line workers and, 241
Nielsen Task Force, 109–11, 215, 216
non-performers: collective bargaining and, 56; courts and, 101; dismissal of, 95, 100–1; managers and, 95–6; in private sector, 101; takers as, 103; unions and, 95–6, 101. *See also* incompetence
Northcote-Trevelyn Report, 5–6, 13–14

Oda, Bev, 156
Office of the Auditor General (OAG): and classification creep, 94; and compensation levels/employee benefits, 94; growth of, 203–4; and IT, 196; and line departments, 34; monitoring by, 33; and size of public service, 94. *See also* auditor general (AG)
officers of Parliament: and blame game, 205; and departments, 204; fault-finding by, 233; funding, 204; information/report demands on departments, 134; resources, 204; scrutiny of, 204–5
*Official Languages Act*, 33, 37, 57, 180
Oliver, Joe, 163–4
*Open and Accountable Government* (Trudeau), 24, 25–6
operations: accountability and, 13; central agencies in, 214; centre of government influence on, 168; challenging status quo in, 256–7; changing relationships and, 11; collective bargaining and, 91, 93, 94; costliness of management of, 16; costs, and program/service delivery, 16; deregulation, 31–2; efficiency of, 226; impenetrability of, 206; line department operating budgets, 122; machinery of government and, 17; moving to outside groups vs in-home, 240; opening up to outside scrutiny, 258; Parliament, and changes to, 19; politicians and, 214; public servant responsibility for, vs politicians, 17; questions regarding, 129; reinvigoration of requirements of, 258; royal commission on, 258; spending cuts to, vs capital budgets/spending, 107–8, 126, 239. *See also* machinery of government
opposition: and access to information, 224; and accountability, 13, 224; blaming by, 191; and estimates, 224; focus on ministers, 225; holding government to account, 254; and media, 224; ministers and,

155–6; public service partisanship and, 36
Organisation for Economic Co-operation and Development (OECD) countries: and 2008 financial crisis, 121; spending increase, 121; trust in governments in, 3
organizational culture, 55–6, 139, 220, 226–7, 242–3
organizational structure, and roles, 73–4
Osbaldeston, Gordon, 35, 156–7, 158
"Ottawa system," 150, 188, 242, 243
Ouellette, Robert-Falcon, 28
outside contracts. *See* consultants
oversight/oversight bodies: addition of, 42; of budget, 71; and constraints on reviews, 94; establishment of new, 203–4; government managers and, 120; and program managers, 135; rules and regulations vs, 173; scandals and, 119; spending on employer role vs, 70–1
ownership of deeds/words/mistakes, 190, 259; and accountability, 259; anonymity vs, 259; and ArriveCAN app, 194; by career officials, 192–3; executives and, 214; managers and, 214; and paper vs oral records, 199; in past vs present, 191; risks of, 203; in service delivery, 202

Paquet, Gilles, 118, 238
Parks Canada, 135

Parliament: and accountability, 19, 24, 179, 242, 254; deputy ministers and, 39; and "gotcha" politics, 206; holding government to account, 26–7, 127, 129, 259; and line departments, 37; and machinery of government, 20, 21; ministers' accountability to, 36; ministers and, 155–6; and operational changes, 19; oversight role, 26; and PCO, 21; PMO advisors and, 24; as political theatre, 255; prime minister–minister relationship and, 154–5; process ministers and, 166–7; Question Period, 154, 155, 156, 160; and spending estimates, 259
Parliament (UK), Question Period, 156
Parliamentary Budget Office/Officer: on balanced budget, 123; on reallocation of program resources, 201; on service levels, 192
Parliamentary Centre, 128
Parliamentary committees: and program reviews, 224; public servants appearing before, 37–8
partisan political advisors: accountability of, 256; addition of, 52; criticism of career officials, 10; deputy ministers and, 174; growth of presence and influence, 51; influence of, 236; information/report demands on departments, 134; and inward looking, 63; long-term perspective for, 238; ministers and, 151; and monitoring, 33; and parallel

partisan bureaucracies, 55; PCO clerk and, 256; and policy advice, 52; policy firefighting and, 236; in US public service, 44–5
partisanship, political: deputy ministers and, 40; ministers and, 155; PCO, and propaganda, 248–9; policy ministers and, 165–6; in policy shaping, 220; process ministers and, 167; of public servants, 229; public servants and, 36, 37–8, 219, 259; senior career officials and, 181
passports, 7–8, 34, 88–90, 136, 251
Pay Research Bureau, 91
Pearson, Lester B., 22–3, 27, 91
*Pendleton Act* (US), 6
Pensioners' Dental Services Plan, 94
pensions, 94; deputy ministers, 173, 187. *See also* benefits
People's Party, 14
performance assessment: attitudes toward, 100, 195; audits, 203–4; of Canada School of Public Service, 142, 144–5; criteria in machine-like organizations, 135; of deputy ministers, 176, 186–7; empowerment and, 85; and inward looking, 63; line department managers and, 86–7; of ministers, 187; new public management and, 65; performance indicators, 135, 137; in private vs public sector, 185–6; of senior public servants, 185–6; shortcomings in, 215–16
Phoenix pay system, 196, 207, 221, 251

Pickersgill, J.W., 174–5, 177, 191
Pitfield, Michael, 141
Planning, Programming and Budgeting System (PPBS), 75–6, 78, 182, 197
Plato's cave allegory, 47–8, 57, 62, 94, 197, 210, 233
plumbers. *See* front-line public servants (plumbers)
poets. *See* policy specialists (poets)
Poilièvre, Pierre, 14
policy advice: and changing behaviours, 227; deputy ministers and, 38, 52; deputy minister–senior public servant relationship and, 53–4; line departments and, 52; in minister–deputy minister relationship, 52; partisan advisors and, 52; in politician–public servant relationship, 32; politicization vs expertise in, 32; program review and, 119; public servants and, 220
Policy and Expenditure Management System (PEMS), 76–7
policy-coping organizations, 12, 138–47; and accountability, 60; concentration in NCR, 67; and missteps, 136, 138; numbers of, 138; poets in, 131. *See also* Canada School of Public Service; Leaders' Debates Commission
*Policy Framework for People Management* (TBS), 99
policy making/shaping: addition of politically partisan officials and, 52; by cabinet committees, 37; career officials and, 4, 30; central

agencies and, 30; collapsed boundaries and, 176–7; evidence-based, 31, 87–8; line departments and, 37, 221; political partisanship and, 220; politicians and, 30; politicians vs career officials in, 31; promotion through, 23; public opinion in, 220; public servants and, 220; as top-down, 177; whole of government approach in, 19

policy/policies: career officials vs politicians in, 51–2; causes and, 221; centre of government influence over, 168; complexity of issues, 20, 234; coordination, in central agency–line department relationship, 32–3; deputy ministers and, 40, 182; deputy ministers' skills in, 188; firefighting, 235, 238, 246; governing from centre and, 166; implementation, 177, 189; issues as cross-departmental, 61, 175; linkages among, 131; lobbyists and, 175; ministers and, 158; mission ministers and, 164; policy ministers and, 165–6; as product of many hands, 205–6; provincial governments and, 175; silos and, 32; and speaking truth to power, 194–5; status ministers and, 163

policy specialists (poets): accountability of, 240; and announceables, 192; behaviour of, 237; behaviour vs plumbers, 246; as deputy ministers, 240, 252; deputy ministers and, 235, 237; in ESDC internal programs, 135; evolution of work, 235; fault line between front-line workers/plumbers and, 18, 72, 73; as firefighters, 237; front-line workers/plumbers vs, 67, 234, 241; functions, 236–7; influence of, 191; long-term planning, 237–8; numbers of, vs plumbers, 212; policy firefighting, 235–6, 238; PPBS and, 75; and prime ministers, 237, 245; problem avoidance, 245; relevance, 245; self-censorship, 238; self-interest, 244; senior management levels and numbers of, 67; speaking truth to one another, 238; speaking truth to power, 238; and success, 192, 237; in TBS, 71; value of, 252; "whiz bang" ideas, 192; working from home, 98

political parties: and collective bargaining, 91; and deficit/debt, 112; ministers and, 152, 161–2; recruitment of MPs, 160; and spending growth, 126

political partisanship. *See* partisanship, political

politician–public servant relationship: and accountability, 222–3; bargain in, 5, 214; and behaviour, 19; blaming within, 257; challenging within, 5; changes in, 25; criticism within, 8, 10–11, 53; defence of public service in, 233, 235; disconnect in, 9; influence in policy shaping, 31; institutional healing in, 54; and inward looking, 235; lack of support in, 10; managing programs/operations in, 17; ministerial responsibility in, 59; and organizational culture, 56; policy advice in, 32; policy shaping in, 31; in postwar period, 6; questions regarding, 258; speaking truth in, 123, 226; and spending cuts, 126; and spending growth, 126; stress within, 232

politicians: and announceables, 223; backgrounds of, 27–8; blaming of, 15, 196, 207; briefing books, 57; and crises, 56; criticism from, 46–7; expansion of offices, 207; and expenditure budgets, 105; and management issues/reform, 56, 57, 85, 225, 258; parallel partisan bureaucracies in offices, 55; and policy function, 30; PPBS and, 75–6; and private sector management, 85; and public choice theory, 231; public demands and, 258; strengthening of offices, 5

*The Politics of Public Spending in Canada* (Savoie), 49

populism, 14

Pow, James T., 27

prime minister–minister relationship: accountability in, 150; cabinet appointments in, 150; media and, 153, 162; meetings in, 150–1; and ministerial responsibility, 225; and ministers' performance assessments, 187; mission ministers and, 165; and Parliament, 154–5; PM appointment of ministerial staff, 168; PMO and, 150; and policy initiatives, 166; team players in, 151

prime ministers (PMs): and accountability, 13, 26–7, 150, 190–1, 214, 226, 256; agenda, 249; appointment powers, 168; balance of power shifting to, 24; briefings, 188; cabinet appointments, 161; central agencies and, 30; and centralization of power, 213; CEOs compared with, 79; control of government, 188; court government, 245; criticism of public service, 53; and deputy ministers, 38, 80, 168, 176, 202; focus on issue and action by, 252; former public servants as, 27; long-term perspective for, 237–8; and machinery of government, 20–1, 226; and media, 241; need for public service, 255; as paramount, 26; PCO clerk and, 230, 248–50, 255; policy specialists and, 237; and program reviews, 114, 120; promises of, 253; and red tape, 31–2; responsibilities, 24, 192–3; scandals and, 202–3; before Second World War, 22; and Senate appointments, 9; and spending decisions, 31, 80, 105, 108, 111, 125, 196, 250, 256; status quo and, 226

Prime Minister's Office (PMO): advisors in, 24, 26; balance of power shifting to, 24; centralization of power in, 25, 213, 228; and destruction of public service, 11; and expansion of machinery

of government, 23–4; growth of, 22–3, 55, 176; and ministerial responsibility, 225; ministers' relationship with, 150; and ministers' travel, 152; and PEMS, 77; and program review, 115; and Question Period, 154; system response to, 91; P. Trudeau as architect of modern, 22–3
Prime Minister's Office (UK), 45
prison wardens, 134, 241–2
private sector: accountability in, 41; admission of wrong in, 61; appointees in US public service, 44–5; collective bargaining in, 92–3; Crown corporations and, 20; emulation of, 4, 207, 230; executives compared to deputy ministers, 183, 188; globalization and, vs public sector, 4; hybrid work culture in, 98; and IT, 196; labour cost in minimization in, 92; machinery of government in, 41; moving activities to, 226; and Niesen Task Force, 215; non-performers in, 101; ownership of words/deeds/mistakes, 190, 213–14; performance assessment in, vs public sector, 185–6; positions transferred to, 118; and program reviews, 109; public choice theory and, 231; public sector differences from, 17, 230; public servant advantages over workers in, 98–9; and public vs self-interest, 222; ratio of service delivery to policy and, 67; responsibility and leadership in, 203; self-interest in, 231; service levels in, 90; and spending cuts, 109; staffing levels, 48; in UK, 109; unions in, 94, 217; in US, 109; War Museum compared, 89; working from office vs home in, 96–7
private sector management: and accountability, 15, 16, 40, 85, 259; belief in superiority of, 16; and efficiency, 226, 254; empowerment of managers, 216; emulation of, 214, 221, 226, 259; former career officials and, 85–6; line department managers and, 85, 86; and management reform, 84–5; performance indicators, 85; politicians and, 85; and program/service delivery, 254; public management vs, 215–16; and TBS language, 217
Privy Council Office (PCO): about, 21; and accounting officer concept, 58; advice for ministers, 149; advice to ministers, 36, 151, 154, 155; and ArriveCAN app, 194; and cabinet committees, 23–4, 79; and centralization of power in PMO, 213; and Centre for Management Development, 140; challenging programs and spending, 203; and COVID-19 support programs, 90–1; deliverology in, 77–8; and deputy ministers, 38–9, 52, 171; deputy ministers drawn from, 34, 46; and efficiency audits, 122; executives in, 70; expansion of, 23; functions, 79; *Guidance for Deputy*

*Ministers*, 38–9; human/financial resources, 239; inward looking, 80; and machinery of government, 20–1, 60; on ministerial accountability vs answerability, 36–7; and ministerial responsibility, 60; and minister–public servant relationship, 60; Parliament and, 21; and PEMS, 77; poets staffing, 71; political partisanship and, 248–9; power/prestige of, 238–9; secretariats, 79–80; system response to, 91

Privy Council Office (PCO) clerk: agenda, 249; annual reports on public service, 46, 66, 197, 235; deputy minister appointments, 38, 248; and deputy ministers, 176, 186–7; focus on issue and action by, 252; as head of public service, 256; on management levels, 68; meetings with deputy ministers, 256; and partisan political advisors, 256; prime ministers and, 249–50, 255; roles, 230, 248; vision exercises, 4

Professional Institute of the Public Service of Canada, 125

program delivery. *See* program/service delivery

program managers/management: delegation up, 133; and loss of rules and regulations, 245; oversight bodies and, 135; public servant responsibility for, vs politicians, 17; and service quality, 133

program review(s): as ad hoc, 118, 120; and blame game, 120; central agencies and, 87, 125; and changing behaviours, 227; departments and, 158–9; in departments vs central agencies, 110; effects of, 120; federal government capacity for, 212; Finance Department and, 71; and growth spurt, 118–19; Harper and, 121, 199; and job eliminations, 68, 118; Martin and, 68, 113–19, 120; in minister–deputy minister relationship, 158–9; Mulroney and, 109–11; and oral vs paper records, 199; Parliamentary committees and, 224; and policy advisory role, 119; policy and evaluation units and, 125; prime ministers and, 114, 120; private sector and, 109; and program cuts, 87; and program delivery, 119; and provincial governments, 120; public opinion on, 115; and repayable loans vs subsidies, 117–18; and scandals, 119; and senior managers, 119; shortcomings, 120; and spending, 87, 116, 118–19, 240; TBS and, 71–2

programs: auditor general on, 86–7; evaluation, 80, 81, 86–7; evaluation in program reviews, 114; failures, 207; growth in number of, 61; Harper and spending on, 121, 122; linkages among, 131; longevity of, 87; Nielsen Task Force and cuts to, 110; objectives, 76; as product of multiple sources, 36, 205–6; program review(s), and spending on, 116; reallocation of resources from low- to high-performing, 201

program/service delivery: and Afghan vs Hungarian refugee crises, 189; announcements vs implementation in, 194; central agencies and, 133; collective bargaining and, 257; consultants and quality of, 133; cynicism in, 10; deliverology and, 251; duplication in, 257; failures in, 66, 193; federal public servants on, 209; future of, 258; IT sector and, 196; lack of attention to, 253; line departments and, 30; low- vs high-priority, 77, 195–6, 200, 212, 257; moving to outside groups vs in-home, 240; numbers of public servants providing, 65–6, 250–1; operating costs vs quality of, 16; ownership in, 202; PCO clerk's annual report and, 66; percentage of public servants directly involved in, 67; as poor cousin to policy, 67; private sector levels, 90; private sector management and, 254; problems in, 8, 218, 251; program review and, 119; proportion of machinery involved in, 251; provincial government, 247; public opinion on, 4, 192, 246–7; quality of, 88, 90, 133, 208; responsibility for, 202; rules and regulations and, 229; and service reputation vs experience, 90–1; spending cuts and, 66–7; strengthening of front-line managers for, 259; successes, 66; task force on, 90, 251; time spent on, vs conflicting demands, 134

provincial governments: boundaries between federal and, 131; cost sharing with federal government, 22; and federal spending levels, 118; federal spending vs, 69; federal transfers to, 69, 116–17, 120, 239, 251; jurisdictional responsibility, 116–17; labour-intensive jurisdictions in, 69; ministers and officials of, 154; plumbers in, 69; and policy issues, 175; premiers, 154; program reviews and, 114, 120; program/service delivery, 247; and spending cuts, 107, 114; transfer of responsibilities to, 68

PS 2000, 34

public choice theory, 230–2, 233, 240, 241, 243, 246

Public Health Agency of Canada, 222

public opinion: and accountability, 148, 247; education/income and opinion of public service, 54; of front-line vs senior public servants, 243; in policy advice/shaping, 220; on program reviews, 115; on program/service delivery, 4; on provincial government service levels, 247; of public servants, 223, 230; of senior public servants, 56–7, 207; on service levels, 192, 246–7; on trust in Canadian government, 3; on trust in national governments, 3; on trust

in public service, 192; on wasteful spending, 209; on work of government, 14–15
Public Policy Forum, 132
Public Sector Labour Relations and Employment Board (PSLREB), 102
public sector unions. *See* unions
public servants: anonymity, 37–8, 200, 219; appearing before parliamentary committees, 37–8; budget expenditures on, 69; and bureaucratic patronage, 218; in core public administration vs agencies, 64; as Crown servants vs institutional members with rights, 230; defensiveness of, 14, 62; free-for-all environment vs age of certainty for, 220; hiring practices, 217–18; historical lack of public support for, 5–6; inward looking, 10 (*see also* inward looking); media on, 5; mission ministers and, 166; neutrality vs partisanship, 37–8, 219, 229; numbers of, 195 (*see also* size/growth of public sector); numbers per MP, 21–2; and policies, vs politicians, 51–2; policy ministers and, 166; policy shaping, 4, 30; self-interest, 103–4, 220, 222, 231; self- vs public interest, 5; as solid workers, 103; speaking truth, 19, 195, 209, 226, 227; standing in society, 223, 230; as "takers," 102–3. *See also* front-line public servants (plumbers); human resource management; minister–public servant relationship; policy specialists (poets); politician–public servant relationship; retired public servants; senior public servants

public service: anonymity of, 59, 205, 229, 259; changes in, 25–6; closed hiring process in, 45; credibility rebuilding, 227; Crown and, 57–8; as deep state, 5; frugality of, 229; functions, 209; future of, 258–9; golden age of, 6, 173; importance of, 209; lack of consensus regarding remedies, 7; organizational culture, 55–6; outsiders in, 50–1; personality of, 57–8; in postwar period, 6–7; public opinion on trust in, 192; during Second World War, 6; self-interest, 17; sheltering of, 4; traditional approach to, 259; trust in, 6–7; as two public services, 12, 18, 234; UK and US compared with Canadian, 44–5; unpopularity of bureaucracies, 4–5; wage cost of, 17. *See also* size/growth of public sector

Public Service 2000, 181
Public Service Alliance of Canada (PSAC), 95; and strategic policy review, 124–5; TBS agreement with, 97–8
Public Service Commission (PSC), 91; as audit agency, 182; deputy ministers and, 39; and direct public dealings, 65; exempt staff and, 52; and merit principle, 227; on pride in service, 139; recruitment of public servants, 217–18

*Public Service Employment Act*, 37, 45–6, 57, 180
*Public Service Modernization Act*, 100
public service/servants (UK): Crossman on, 53; location in London, 44; outsiders in, 45; Thatcher and, 46
public service/servants (US): location in Washington, DC, 44; political appointees in, 44–5; Reagan and, 46
*Public Service Staff Relations Act*, 91
*Public Service Superannuation Act*, 94
Public Works Accommodation Program, 107–8

Question Period: Answer Period vs, 155; ministers and, 154, 160; in UK Parliament, 156

Radwanski, Adam, 78
Ranger, Louis, 176
Rasmussen, Ken, 230
Rathgeber, Brent, 28
rational choice theory, 233, 241, 243
Reaching Home, 80–1
Reagan, Ronald, 46, 47
reallocation of resources, 103, 195–6, 200, 201, 212
Reform Party, 118
regulatory agencies. *See* agencies
Reisman, Simon, 221
remote work, 96–8. *See also* hybrid work arrangements
responsibility: for Afghan vs Hungarian refugee crises, 189; answerability vs, 18; for ArriveCAN app, 137; collective, 59, 169; controversy vs, 252–3; for executive increased numbers, 197; for failures, 5; front-line managers and, 243; for growth in public service, 126; for incompetence, 130; in leadership, 203; for management levels, 126, 208; ministers and, 169; as moving target, 215; and new executive positions, 126; for Phoenix pay system, 196; of prime ministers, 24, 192–3; for service delivery, 202; shared, 178–9; for words/deeds, 190. *See also* accountability
retired public servants: call for reform by, 14; employment opportunities, 200; perspective of, 47–8, 208, 233–4; and private sector management, 85–6
retirement benefits, 143–4
risk aversion, 63, 218, 252, 256
Robertson, Gordon, 173, 181, 213, 220, 249
Rodriguez, Pablo, 157
Roman bureaucracy, 61–2
Roosevelt, Franklin D., New Deal, 6
Rota, Anthony, 249
Roxham Road, 203
Royal Bank of Canada, 98
Royal Canadian Mounted Police (RCMP), 121
Royal Commission on Financial Management and Accountability. *See* Lambert Commission (Royal Commission on Financial Management and Accountability)

Royal Commission on Government Organizations. *See* Glassco Commission (Royal Commission on Government Organizations)
royal commissions: advantages of, 210; on operations, 258; on role, 210
rules and regulations: and behaviour, 229; new public management vs, 64–5; oversight bodies vs, 173; program managers and loss of, 245; and program/service delivery, 229; reporting requirements vs, 11; and spending, 229

salary freeze, 93–4
Samara Centre for Democracy, 24, 28
Savoie, Donald J.: *The Canadian Centre for Management Studies*, 138–40; *Governing from the Centre*, 212; *The Politics of Public Spending in Canada*, 49; *Whatever Happened to the Music Teacher*, 8; *What Is Government Good At?*, 8
Sayre, Wallace, 215
scandals, 119, 202–3; and blame game, 31; debureaucratization and, 31; sponsorship, 119–20, 201–2. *See also* controversies/crises
Second World War: and Crown corporations, 20; and machinery of government, 22
Secretariat of the National Security and Intelligence Committee of Parliamentarians, 26

self-interest: cuts and, 239; failure to deal with, 17; maximization of, 232; policy specialists and, 244; in private vs public sector, 231; public interest vs, 5
senior managers: benefits, 93; and collective bargaining, 93; policy advisory role, 119; program review and, 119. *See also* managers
senior public servants: accountability of, 57, 58; admission of wrong, 61; and blame game, 197; at Canada School of Public Service, 143–4; in Centre for Management Development, 140–1; ethics training, 204; influence over public servants below, 244; and inward looking, 60; and management reform, 85; meetings with ministers, 151–2; NCR location and promotion to, 46; and operations management, 181–2; performance assessment, 185–6; in political arena, 181; public opinion of, 56–7, 207; public opinion of, vs front-line public servants, 243; and public sector management, 56; public trust in, 192; relevance, 244; speaking truth to power, 257; teamwork, 200–1; tenure, 206. *See also* retired public servants
Service Canada: establishment of, 136; passport renewal, 88–90
service delivery. *See* program/service delivery
Shared Services Canada (SSC), 196
Shepherd, Robert P., 118, 216
Siegel, David, 100, 133

Sifton, Clifford, 166
silos: government as collection of, 35; line departments as, 33–4, 42, 50, 61; and policy, 32; in Roman bureaucracy, 62; whole of government approach vs, 35
Simms, Scott, 28
Simpson, Jeffrey, 95
size/growth of government: and accountability, 11; cuts vs, economistic approach and, 239; reduction in, 106
size/growth of public sector, 250; COVID-19 and, 124, 250; efficiency vs, 208; under Harper, 121; media and, 57; as overstaffed, 16, 47, 88, 104; program reviews and hiring increases, 240; public service vested interest in, 225; quality of service and, 193; reduction in, 115; responsibility for, 126; staffing levels in, 47–9; staffing levels in ACOA, 49–50; strategic policy review and, 125
Skelton, O.D., 173
Smith, David E., 184
SNC-Lavalin affair, 202
speaking truth: to one another, 227, 238; in policy, 194–5; by policy specialists, 238; to political masters, 226; to politicians, 19; to politicians vs selves, 123; to power, 194–5, 209, 238, 257; by public servants to themselves, 195
*Speaking Truth to Power* (Wildavsky), ix–x
Special Operating Agencies (SOAs), 45

spending: amounts, 251; on consultants, 193; COVID-19 and, 123–4; defence, 118; efficiency and, 65; efficiency vs growth in, 208; on employer role vs spending oversight function, 70–1; foreign assistance, 118; freezes, 114; growth, and inflation, 106; on outsourced contracts, 65; political parties and growth of, 126; politician–public servant relationship and growth in, 126; prime ministers' decisions regarding, 31, 80; process ministers and, 167; program reviews and increases in, 118–19, 240; provincial governments and levels of, 118; provincial vs federal, 69; public servant frugality with, 229; questions regarding plans, 129; rules and regulations and, 229; under J. Trudeau, 123–4
spending cuts: across-the-board, 112, 114–15, 120, 122–3, 126, 159, 202, 239; adding to expenditure budgets vs, 105–6; blaming for, 106; and blue-collar workers, 126; bolts of lightning and, 196, 256; to capital spending vs operations, 107–8, 126, 239; departments and, 158–9; in departments vs central agencies, 110; failures to deliver, 72; Harper and, 121; and line departments, 106–7; to low-priority programs, 77; minister–deputy minister relationship and, 159; mission ministers and, 164;

politician–public servant relationship and, 126; prime ministers and, 105, 108, 111, 125, 196, 250, 256; program reviews and, 87; program/service delivery and, 66–7; and provincial governments, 107; provincial governments and, 114; to regional/local offices, 126; to research and development, 240; and scandals, 119; status ministers and, 163; "stealth," 118; to transfer payments, 120, 239; to Transport Department, 116; J. Trudeau and, 125; unions and, 66–7, 125, 240

sponsorship scandal, 119–20, 201–2

St Laurent, Louis, 27

Strategic and Service Policy Branch, 137

strategic policy review, 124–5

success(es): as avoidance of controversies, 252; deputy-minister–policy specialist relationship and, 235; failures vs, 5; media and, 51; mission ministers and, 164; PCO clerk's annual reports and, 66, 235; perception of, 185; plumbers/front-line workers and, 191, 192; poets/policy specialists and, 192, 237; spinning of, 197; and visibility, 60. See also failures

surprises. See controversies/crises; missteps/mistakes

Tait, John, 195
Tait Task Force, 7, 72–3, 238

Task Force on Public Service Values and Ethics, 7, 72–3

Tellier, Paul: and Canadian Centre for Management Development, 138; on centralization in PMO, 24–5; and Centre for Management Development, 140; on lack of trust in politician–public servant relationship, 10–11; and management level reduction, 67–8; on post-COVID program/service delivery, 193; on "surprises" for clerk and PM, 31, 249

Thatcher, Margaret, 10, 15–16, 45, 46, 47

Thomas, Paul, 204

Tobin, Brian, 163, 164

*Top of Mind*, 194–5, 209

*Toronto Star*, on budget omnibus bill, 128

Towers, Graham, 173

transparency: and access to information, 62; and accountability impenetrability, 11–12; and inward looking, 18, 55, 83; ministers and, 168; problems associated with, 253; and unwritten code, 83

Transport Department spending cuts, 116

travel: cuts in budget, 103; hybrid working model and, 125; ministers and, 152, 160

Treasury Board: approval, 162; Better Government fund, 210–11; deputy ministers and, 39; strategic policy review, 124–5

Treasury Board Secretariat (TBS): and "699" leave, 95; and Better

Government fund, 211; and Canada School of Public Service, 142, 144, 145–6; challenging programs and spending, 203; and collective bargaining, 65, 95; and compensation levels/ employee benefits, 94; and deliverology, 78; and estimates, 127; executives, 70–1; Finance Department and, 71–2; on firings, 102; on growth of public sector, 124; *Guidelines for Termination or Demotion for Unsatisfactory Performance*, 99–100; and hybrid work arrangements, 173–4; on incompetence, 99; and job eliminations, 106–7; and management level de-layering, 197; and Nielsen Task Force, 110; organizational structure, 70–1; poets staffing, 71; *Policy Framework for People Management*, 99; and private sector, 217; and program reviews, 71–2; PSAC agreement with, 97–8; and return to office post-COVID-19, 96; role/functions, 71, 78, 211; and size of public service, 94; spending oversight, 71; staff numbers, 70–1; and travel budget, 103

truck convoy, 14

Trudeau, Justin: and airport problems, 192–3; and ArriveCAN app, 193–4; and balanced budget, 123; and Bernardo transfer, 219; and CBC, 122; and centralization of government, 253; and centralization of power in PMO, 228; chief of staff, 213; and contracts, 65; and COVID-19 spending, 123; deficit budget, 122, 123–4; and deliverology, 77–9, 181, 182, 251; and efficiency controls, 65; and inflation, 124; minister for "Citizens' Services," 90; and ministers' office staff, 52; ministers on meetings with, 150; and omnibus bills, 127–8; *Open and Accountable Government*, 24, 25–6; on PM-machinery of government relations, 21; and public spending, 65; and Rota affair, 249; and scandals, 202–3; and spending, 123–4, 125, 250; and surplus, 122; task force on service delivery, 90, 251; and threats to family, 191; and work-life balance, 160

Trudeau, Pierre Elliott, 27; at Bonn Economic Summit, 250; and Bonn summit, 106; and cabinet committees, 79; and centralization of power, 213, 214; and centre of government, 23; and Charter of Rights and Freedoms entrenchment, 108; defeat of government, 108; and deputy ministers, 186; and inflation, 106; "Just Society," 6; ministers' contacts with, 150–1; and NEP, 108; and new breed of federal public servants, 23; and Pearson government, 22–3; Pierre Elliott Trudeau Foundation, 203; and PMO, 22–3; and PPBS, 78; and spending, 106, 250

trust: accountability and, 12–13; as bottom line, 7; in government/

public service in postwar period, 6–7
Turnbull, Lori, 128
Turner, John, 27

underemployment, 102
unions: and behaviour, 230; and benefits, 93–4, 223; change and, 71; and collective bargaining, 95; coverage in private vs public sector, 94; and COVID-19 paid leave, 95; and cutbacks, 223; and cuts to science positions, 88; and difficult decisions in human resource management, 104; and dismissal of non-performers, 95; and dual role of government as employer, 93; and inward looking, 55; and non-performers, 95–6, 101; and Phoenix pay system problem, 223; and politicians in human resource issues, 214; prison warden on, 242; private sector unions vs, 217; in public vs private sector, 99; and reshaping of public service, 174; role to gain concessions, 95; and salary freeze, 93–4; and spending cuts, 66–7, 125, 240; and strategic policy review, 124–5; TBS on, 97–8; and unwritten code, 18, 95; and working from home vs office, 96–7. *See also* Public Service Alliance of Canada (PSAC)
unwritten code: about, 83; and behaviour, 103; bureaucracy bashing and, 18, 83; front-line workers/plumbers and, 89–90; and inward looking, 222; management level additions and, 104; media and, 18; PCO clerk's annual reports and, 235; rule removal and, 104; transparency and, 83; unions and, 18, 95
user fees, 115–16, 239

Valcourt, Bernard, 231
values: and accountability, 227–8; and behaviour, 228; champions of, 222; Charter of Public Service, 257; and ethics exercises, 222; fault line and, 72; uncertainty and, 220
Vatican Council, Second, 210
Veilleux, Gérard, 41, 138
visibility: failures and, 60; plumbers and, 191; status ministers and, 162, 163; success and, 60

wage controls, 93
Wallace, Peter, 100
*Wall Street Journal*, "Bankrupt Canada," 111
War Museum, 89–90
Weber, Max, 51, 132, 185, 219, 228, 230–1, 241
WE Charity, 198, 202
welfare state, 22, 173, 234
Wernick, Michael, 212
*Whatever Happened to the Music Teacher* (Savoie), 8
*What Is Government Good At?* (Savoie), 8
Whelan, Eugene, 35, 164
whole of government approach, 21; and accountability, 219–20, 234;

and behaviour, 19; and behavioural theories, 233; deputy ministers and, 187; silos vs, 35

Wildavsky, Aaron, 18; *Speaking Truth to Power*, ix–x

Wilson, James Q., 185, 215; *Bureaucracy*, 73

Wilson-Raybould, Jody, 29

Wise, John, 164

Zelenskyy, Volodymyr, 249